CHANGING PARTY POLICY
IN
BRITAIN

CHANGING PARTY POLICY
IN
BRITAIN
AN INTRODUCTION

Edited by
RICHARD KELLY

BLACKWELL
Publishers

Copyright © Blackwell Publishers Ltd 1999

Editorial matter and organization copyright © Richard Kelly 1999

First published 1999

Blackwell Publishers Ltd
108 Cowley Road
Oxford OX4 1JF
UK

Blackwell Publishers Inc.
350 Main Street
Malden, Massachusetts 02148
USA

British Library Cataloguing in Publication Data

A CIP catalogue record for this book is available from the British Library.

Library of Congress Cataloging-in-Publication Data.
Changing party policy in Britain: an introduction/edited by Richard Kelly.
    p.   cm.
  Includes bibliographical references and index.
   ISBN 0–631–20489–X (alk. paper) 0–631–20490–3 (pbk)
    1. Political parties – Great Britain.   2. Political planning – Great Britain.
  3. Great Britain – Politics and government -- 1945–
I. Kelly, Richard N.
JN1121.C48   1999
324.241'09'049 – dc21

                                                           98–28703
                                                                 CIP

Commissioning Editor: Jill Landeryou
Desk Editor: Fiona Sewell

Typeset in 10½ on 12pt Sabon with Frutiger
by Pure Tech India Ltd, Pondicherry
Printed in Great Britain by
MPG Books Ltd, Bodmin, Cornwall

This book is printed on acid-free paper

Contents

Tables

Contributors

Fergus Carr is Head of the School of Social and Historical Studies and Principal Lecturer in International Politics at the University of Portsmouth. He is co-author of *NATO in the New European Order* (Macmillan, 1996) and editor of *Europe: The Cold Divide* (Macmillan, 1998).

Michael Cunningham is Senior Lecturer in Politics at the University of Wolverhampton, and author of *British Government Policy in Northern Ireland 1969–1989* (Manchester University Press, 1991).

Howard Elcock is Professor of Government at the University of Northumbria and Visiting Lecturer in Political Science at the State University of New York College at Fredonia. He is author of *Local Government: Policy and Management in Local Authorities* (Routledge, 3rd edn, 1994) and *Change and Decay? Public Administration in the 1990s* (Longman, 1991). He is also co-editor of *The Devolution Agenda* (Frank Cass, 1998).

Steven Fielding is Lecturer in Politics and Contemporary History at the University of Salford. He has written widely on Labour Party politics, his most recent publication being *The Labour Party, Socialism and Society Since 1951* (Manchester University Press, 1997).

Ian Forbes is Professor of Politics at the University of Nottingham. He is author of *Marx and the New Individual* (Unwin, 1990) and co-editor of *Politics and Human Nature* (Pinter, 1983) and *Political Theory, International Relations and the Ethics of Intervention* (Macmillan, 1984).

Steven Foster teaches Politics at the Manchester Grammar School. He is author of *Political Parties: Thatcherism Abandoned?* (PAVIC, 1994) and *The Politics of Law and Order Today* (Manchester University Press, 1999).

Robert Garner is Reader in Politics at the University of Leicester. He is author of *Animal Politics and Morality* (Manchester University Press, 1993), *Animal Rights: The Changing Debate* (Macmillan, 1996) and *Environmental Politics* (Prentice Hall, 1996) and co-author of *British Political Parties Today* (Manchester University Press, 2nd edn, 1998).

Richard Kelly teaches Politics at the Manchester Grammar School and the University of Manchester. He is author of *Conservative Party Conferences* (Manchester University Press, 1989), co-author of *British Political Parties Today* (Manchester University Press, 2nd edn, 1998) and co-editor of *Modern British Statesmen 1867–1945* (Manchester University Press, 1997).

Brian Lund is Principal Lecturer in Social Policy at the Manchester Metropolitan University. He is author of *Housing Problems and Housing Policy* (Longman, 1996) and *Towards Integrated Living: Housing Strategies and Community Care* (Policy Press, 1997).

Robert Pyper is Reader in Public Administration at Glasgow Caledonian University. He is author of *The Evolving Civil Service* (Longman, 1991) and *The British Civil Service* (Prentice Hall, 1995), editor of *Aspects of Accountability in the British System of Government* (Tudor, 1996) and co-editor of *Governing the UK in the 1990s* (Macmillan, 1995).

Shamit Saggar is Senior Lecturer in Government at Queen Mary and Westfield College, University of London. He is author of *Race and Public Policy* (Avebury, 1991) and *Race and Politics in Britain* (Harvester Wheatsheaf, 1992) and editor of *Race and British Electoral Politics* (UCL Press, 1998).

Jonathan Tonge is Lecturer in Politics and Contemporary History at the University of Salford. He is co-editor of *Labour's Landslide: The British General Election 1997* (Manchester University Press, 1997).

Preface and Acknowledgements

In recent years, there have been several valuable studies concerning party organization, party doctrine and party members. Yet there has been no single and accessible account of recent and specific policy developments within Britain's governing parties. This is a strange oversight given that specific policies seem to have an increased influence upon modern voting behaviour. In an age of electoral volatility, with voters more inclined to 'shop around' before deciding how to vote, a detailed survey of party policy is therefore required when assessing the parties' performance.

It is not being suggested that specific policy areas have been overlooked by recent publications; the collections of essays assembled by Jones (1994) and Savage et al. (1994) give a useful record of the main developments since 1979. Yet these developments are still to be linked, in a clear and systematic way, to the traditions and character of governing parties in Britain. Conversely, most existing studies of Britain's parties do not include a range of case studies showing how particular policies evolved. It is these two gaps which our book aims to fill.

The editor's introduction, or overview, provides a context for the ten core chapters which follow. It will summarize the functions and importance of political parties in a modern democracy, before surveying the supposed and actual ways in which policy is made within the two main parties. It will pay particular attention to the theories offered by Robert McKenzie's classic work, *British Political Parties*, and the extent to which they have been validated and undermined since 1955.

Each of the core chapters will begin with a brief synopsis, outlining the arguments about to be discussed. Each of the chapters will then be divided into four standard sections: 'The Historical Context: Party Policy 1945–1992'; 'An Unusual Climate: Continuity and Rupture 1992–1997'; 'The 1997 General Election: Campaign and Aftermath'; and 'Conclusion: The Impact of Party Policy'. At the end of each chapter, there will be a 'Chronology of Significant Developments: April 1992 to October 1997', plus a 'Guide to Further Reading'. This standardization, we hope, will allow readers to make swift and effective comparisons, while bringing to the book a clear pattern of analysis.

In the section dealing with the period 1945–1992, authors briskly consider the main parties' approach to their particular policy areas for much of the post-war era, reminding students of the key arguments both between and within those parties and the effect they had upon the wider political landscape. In respect of 1979–1990, the way in which each of the parties coped with the iconoclastic atmosphere of the Thatcher governments will be assessed, along with the pressures this placed upon those responsible for policy formation. That period also provides a useful opportunity for considering the impact of supposedly radical governments in vital policy areas. The extent to which a change of prime minister in 1990 altered Tory policy, and the alternatives offered by Labour, will also be analysed. The policies contained in the 1992 manifestos will be re-examined, highlighting areas of convergence and divergence between the parties and the effect this had upon the parties' electoral performance.

The second section, covering the last Tory government, looks at how the two main parties reacted to the 'aberration' of a fourth successive Tory election victory. Did the surprise election result of 1992, and the somewhat anomolous atmosphere it created, have any significant bearing upon particular policies during those years? Did it make Conservative policy even more ambitious and 'arrogant' than in the previous three periods of government? Was the fine print of opposition parties even more cautious and inhibited? One of the crucial questions to be faced here is the effect of closer European union, following on from the Maastricht Treaty of 1991.

The penultimate section, dealing with the most recent general election and its aftermath, will outline main party positions in the 1997 manifestos, along with any developments which occurred during the election campaign. Consideration will also be given to the influence, if any, of specific manifesto proposals upon the character and outcome of the 1997 campaign. This section will continue by inspecting the parties' response to the last general election, often finishing with an assessment of debates at the 1997 party conferences.

In their conclusions, authors will focus upon questions which have vast implications for the study of British politics. To what extent did party policy in the 1990s develop autonomously and to what degree was it proactive? Did it play a crucial role in shifting the course of state policy, public opinion and the parameters of debate? In tackling these questions, the effect of a globalized economy and European integration is addressed wherever possible, alongside any other factors which limit the options of policy-makers. Did all these factors stifle bold and creative thinking within the parties, or did they finally make the parties more realistic in terms of what they could achieve in office? These questions will be readdressed in the editor's conclusion, which offers a more strategic review of party policy and its importance to modern British politics.

It is hoped that this book will be especially welcomed by students and teachers of government, politics and public administration, whose degree and A-level courses pay more and more attention to policy matters. But we also hope it will provide useful advice to those at the receiving end of these policies, offering some indication of the source, purpose and 'inevitability' of particular ideas. Party activists might also welcome a more detailed exposition of the various policies they have been expected to defend and assail.

This book does assume a reasonable amount of subject knowledge on the part of the reader. Wherever possible, however, we have tried to explain fully terms like 'Clause IV' and 'voter volatility'. Explanations of terms and concepts tend to be offered in the chapters where such explanations are most appropriate, rather than at the earliest opportunity within the whole volume. We have tried to ensure that distracting cross-references are kept to a minimum, so any reader seeking further guidance in these matters should naturally consult the index.

In assembling this study, the editor is grateful to his eleven co-writers for the speed and efficiency with which their chapters were produced. He is also indebted to his colleagues from the politics department of the Manchester Grammar School for their advice and criticism, especially in connection with the structuring of chapters. Our A-level students were kind enough to offer comments on the readability and utility of chapters; for this, the editor offers particular thanks to Toby Greene, Naser Turabi, Robert Cline, Johnny Cohen, Adam Goldstone, David Kay, Daniel Jones, Daniel Maudsley, Bill McCallum, Tom Gilbart and Ben Elton (who assisted greatly in the compilation of the index). The book is dedicated, however, to Zoe Kelly, whose zest for life has always been an inspiration.

R.N.K.
Manchester, December 1997

References

Jones B. (ed.) (1994) *Political Issues in Britain Today*, Manchester, Manchester University Press.

Savage S., Alkinson R. and Robins L. (eds) (1994) *Public Policy in Britain*, Basingstoke, Macmillan.

Party Activity and the Making of Party Policy

An Overview

Richard Kelly

In recent years, political parties have received a bad press. Commentators have drawn attention to the 'failure' of parties to deliver once in government (Marr 1995), their growing 'irrelevance' to a more diverse society (Hall and Jacques 1988), public disenchantment with party politicians (Baggott 1995), declining party membership (Whiteley et al. 1994), and the consequent movement towards a new, 'party-free' style of politics involving pressure groups, referenda and a more powerful, constitution-enforcing judiciary (Ascherson 1994). The granting of operational independence to the Bank of England shortly after the 1997 general election only added to the impression that power and authority were ineluctably slipping away from party politicians.

Yet it is easy to forget that parties remain central to any understanding of British political life. Disraeli observed over a century ago that the essence of Parliament was party, and that without the presence of party activity parliamentary government would be impossible. Far from weakening the validity of this view, the twentieth century has only made it appear too narrow in application: one could easily argue, after all, that party activity has since become vital to almost all aspects of modern British politics. It is undeniable that pressure groups, for example, have usurped some of the parties' traditional functions, especially in relation to popular participation in politics. It is also incontestable that representative democracy (of which parties, as explained below, are the linchpin) has been eroded by the loss of sovereignty to the European Union and the globalization of Britain's economy (Nugent 1994; Marr 1995). The greater willingness to use referenda as a form of government decision making, exemplified in the early months of the Blair government, is likewise difficult to ignore. But these developments require perspective. Any account of modern British politics which ignored them would certainly be defective. Yet any account which ignored political parties would be more than defective: it would be almost surreal.

Before examining their specific policies, it is therefore timely to reconsider the role and importance of political parties in Britain today, with the editor making no secret of his attempt to rescue their tarnished reputation.

The Pursuit of Power

Political parties in Britain have never had an official or constitutional purpose, and the relatively small degree to which they have been funded by the state is symptomatic of the shadowy place they have occupied in the 'dignified' zone of British politics (McConnell 1994). Any attempt to define the role of political parties must therefore proceed with some caution. Yet it can be stated with some confidence that their principal function is to seek office through the attainment of votes. Indeed, this remains the main distinction between parties and pressure groups, whose primary purpose is merely to influence – rather than constitute – the government of the day, while rarely seeking to demonstrate their support at the ballot box.

The extent to which office is a realistic aim naturally varies from party to party; for some, the immediate and perhaps only conceivable aim is to act as a quasi-pressure group, securing enough votes and seats to influence the larger, governing parties (Cunningham 1998). In recent decades, this role has been practised by Plaid Cymru, the Scottish National Party (SNP) and the parties of Northern Ireland; in the case of Plaid Cymru and the SNP, their success in taking electoral support away from the Labour Party in Wales and Scotland seemed to influence Labour's interest in devolution from the late 1960s onwards (see chapter 8). Such influence does not even require the capture of parliamentary seats – merely enough votes to jeopardize seats held by the parties of govern-ment. In this respect, there may even have been limited influence for the National Front in the late 1970s – its support in by-elections arguably stiffening Tory immigration policy (Layton-Henry 1980) – and for the Green Party in the late 1980s, whose 15 per cent vote in the 1989 European elections may have increased the government's interest in environmental policy (see chapter 10).

Yet even for these parties, the long-term aim remains the same: the actual exercise of governmental power, albeit in an altered constitutional environment. The 'territorial' parties listed above may have had little interest in wielding executive power at Westminster, yet all had designs upon office in the devolved assemblies planned by the Blair government. It must also be noted that changes in voting behaviour after 1970 enhanced the potential of smaller parties, as a force both within and upon British governments. The demise of what psephol-ogists termed the 'cube law' (whereby a party's lead in votes would be translated into a bigger lead in seats), and the increased likelihood of hung Parliaments, threaten to give smaller parties a balance of power at Westminster and the sort of pivotal influence enjoyed by 'third' parties in other European democracies (Norris 1997). The Free Democratic Party (FDP), for example, has been a part of the West German and German governments since the 1960s despite an average vote of only 10 per cent, while in Ireland the Labour Party proved an unshakeable part of that country's coalitions between 1992 and 1997, with less than a quarter of the votes at the 1992 general election. In Britain's case, these continental scenarios were demonstrated during the Parliaments of both 1974–1979 and 1992–1997, when the Wilson–Callaghan and Major governments lacked first a substantial and then any majority, and were forced to rely upon pacts with Liberals and nationalists between 1974 and 1979, and alleged deals with Ulster Unionists after 1992 – all of which underlined the importance of parties other than Labour and the Conservatives.

Such parties might have been dismayed by the return of a landslide Labour majority in 1997, fearing the return of hegemonic single-party government and the consequent marginalization of 'third and fourth' parties at Westminster. Solace could be gained, however, from the devolutionary designs of the new government – of signal importance to the SNP in particular – and the continued prospect of a hung Parliament should the vote gap between the two parties, now 13.5 per cent, narrow again in future. Psephologists agree that if a hung Parliament is to be avoided, that gap now needs to be much larger than in the 1950s and 1960s; the sort of votes lead that gave Labour a landslide in 1945 – 7–8 per cent – could only give the Tories a vulnerable majority in 1992 (Leonard 1996). Curtice and Steed (1997, p. 316) argue that for the Tories to win the next general election, they may require a vote lead of up to 11 per cent.

It was supposedly with this in mind that, as premier, Tony Blair retained his belief in the eventual realignment of centre-left politics and a more varied party system, hinted at by his inclusion of Liberal Democrats on a Cabinet subcommittee (dealing with constitutional reform) and his support for proportional representation in European and regional elections. As a result, it was unsafe to declare that the relevance of smaller parties had receded following Labour's return to power.

Advancing Parliamentary Democracy

In carrying out their basic role of pursuing office, parties continue to enhance both the clarity of general elections and the cohesion of parliamentary government. Without parties, voters would be confronted by a bewildering array of candidates, offering a multitude of ideas which had little chance of materializing in government. Parties make general elections seem more cogent by allowing voters not just a choice of representative but a choice of government, nurturing the impression among voters that voting may after all make a difference – an impression likely to have been reinforced by the 1997 election, which led to a wholesale change in government personnel and, according to some commentators, 'a new direction for society... a new style of government... a more classless Britain... an end to xenophobia' (*Observer*, 4 May 1997). In more sober terms, the parties' manifestos certainly enable voters to inspect a number of putative programmes for government and make a potentially rational choice between the policy packages on offer.

The parties' quest for office has, as Disraeli recognized, made an indispensable contribution to the efficacy of parliamentary government. The inherent discipline of parties seeking power has allowed British governments to be formed and, as we saw in 1997, changed with astonishing speed after general elections; only once since 1945 has this process taken more than twenty-four hours after polling ended. In addition, party coherence has normally enabled governments to endure for reasonable periods (shown by the fact that, despite an absence of fixed-term parliaments, Britain has only needed fifteen general elections since 1945), and to pursue policies which a plurality of voters nominally supported at the previous election.

It may be countered that all of this stems not so much from parties *per se* as from Britain's peculiar electoral system, which has usually given a solid overall majority to one party in the House of Commons. In multi-party regimes underpinned by proportional representation, the connection between party and parliamentary efficiency has seemed more oblique. After the Irish general election of 1992, a hung Dáil and inter-party wranglings meant that seven weeks were to elapse before a coalition government could be formed, while the Italian party system has been accompanied by fifty different governments in forty-seven years (Partridge 1995). But the essential point stands: while party systems may be imperfect – and Britain's is arguably one of the least imperfect – such uncertainty and instability would be infinitely worse. In crude terms, effective modern parties impose discipline upon, and restrict the independence of, individual parliamentarians – the *sine qua non* of efficient parliamentary government. The problems of France's Third and Fourth Republics sprang largely from loosely disciplined political parties, with the relative stability of the Fifth Republic after 1958 owing much to the infusion of strong party discipline by followers of Charles de Gaulle (Wright 1986).

Government by party also enhances elections in that voters are able to pinpoint blame or apportion credit for the way the country has recently been run – a mechanism which in 1997 led to the Tories' lowest share of the vote in the twentieth century. Parties, in other words, help ensure that modern British governments stay accountable to the electorate. By remaining disciplined, governing parties stand a good chance of enacting their policy programme and accordingly have only a limited excuse for not doing so. Subsequently, a party in government can be judged on its record at the next general election.

Again, it can be argued that this line of argument comes from the peculiar style of Britain's party system, where one party usually has enough parliamentary seats to carry out its programme without the need for deals with other parties. Continental-style hung parliaments often force the dominant party to dilute its election proposals in the inter-party horse trading which normally follows: the result is that post-election coalitions often obscure accountability in subsequent elections. Furthermore, rising support for third and fourth parties in Britain can mean that anti-government votes are now split, which, under the present electoral system, allows a government of diminishing popularity to remain in office (support for the Thatcher government fell at the 1983 general election, yet its majority more than trebled). Yet even with a more diverse electorate and a more complicated, multi-party system the principle of *faut de mieux* still holds: a government of party politicians is still more easily held to account than a government of disparate independents and is still better equipped to follow policies endorsed by a sizeable body of voters.

The belief that party allows 'strong' government has often provoked the charge that it actually suppresses parliamentary democracy by exalting executive power at the expense of scrutiny from the legislature, making the Commons little more than a 'rubber stamp' for government (Crick 1964). Fashionable in the 1960s, this thesis has since been weakened by the regular defeat and amendment of government policy in Parliament (Norton 1993). Naturally, this has much to do with the absence of solid government majorities in the mid-1970s and mid-1990s, but the frequent setbacks suffered by the second and third Thatcher governments – which were cushioned by landslide majorities after 1983 – also point to a behavioural change among backbenchers on the government side of the House (the defeated Shops Bill of 1986 being just one conspicuous example).

Put simply, MPs are no longer willing, as McKenzie suggested in 1955, to defy their party leaders only when they want to change those leaders. A less partisan electorate has seemingly encouraged MPs to be less partisan in their own attitude towards specific party policy at Westminster (Riddell 1993). Although its majority was much bigger than it had dared hope, the new Labour government might also have cause to accommodate this trend; research carried out by Norton et al. prior to the 1997 general election showed that the new generation of Labour MPs were 'even more willing to break ranks, in more numbers and over a wider range of issues' than their Conservative equivalents (*Sunday Telegraph*, 26 August 1996).

This development is not at odds with the point made earlier about the need to limit MPs' independence, and it does not point to a breakdown in party discipline. What it may involve, despite the new 'codes of conduct' admired by both sets of party leaders after 1997, is a better balance between executive efficiency and parliamentary scrutiny. In any case, party organization is not inimical to a potent legislature and a useful MP. It allows, for instance, an official opposition to emerge at Westminster, able to articulate criticism of the government while acting as an 'alternative government' itself. Deals between party managers, notably whips acting through 'the usual channels', enable Commons debates to cover most of the issues concerning backbench MPs and to make optimum use of time reserved for scrutiny and deliberation. Inter-party arrangements also enable MPs to advance more localized or particular concerns (early day motions and private member's bills being just some of the options available). All this indicates that party ties are the ally rather than enemy of individual MPs trying to make their mark. A Commons which brimmed with eighteenth-century-style independents would undoubtedly be more colourful than the present, party-based arena. But it is unlikely that this would make MPs more influential, either collectively or individually.

It must also be remembered that, in Britain's parliamentary system, it is the parties which act as the legislature's recruiting agents. It is almost impossible to become an MP, and later a minister, without first securing the backing of a political party. In addition, the absence of American-style 'primary' elections means that, in hundreds of 'safe' constituencies (which are still thought to constitute the bulk of parliamentary seats), the selection of a party candidate is normally more important than the election itself: local party members are, in many cases, 'Parliamentary gatekeepers', choosing candidates whose advance to Parliament is then a formality (Norris and Lovenduski 1995). Parties go on to play a huge part in determining the holders of high office in the House of Commons; the prime minister and the leader of the opposition usually owe their positions to having first won leadership contests inside their own parties, while members of a Labour Shadow Cabinet, a deputy Labour prime minister and members of a Labour Cabinet during its first year are also determined by intra-party elections. Furthermore, the Labour leadership contest of 1976, and the Tory contest of 1990, showed how party mechanisms can directly bring about a change of prime minister.

Although it is easy to bemoan a shortage of 'independent' and 'individualistic' MPs in the Commons today, the importance of party to Parliament has clear advantages from a democratic and meritocratic angle. Entry into Parliament as an independent often requires uncommon personal resources, and it is frequently the case that, where the party system is weak, representatives in the legislature become more socially exclusive and dynastic (Duverger 1954; Rose 1976). Britain's parties have therefore ensured that a grocer's daughter, a trapeze artist's son, and the illegitimate son of a crofter's daughter, as well as those from more privileged backgrounds, have reached the apex of political power in this country. Parliament and government have thus been able to draw upon political talent from across the social classes.

Political Participation

To concentrate on the role parties play in Parliament is to risk ignoring one of their key characteristics in democratic states, namely, acting as vehicles for mass involvement in the political system (Hague and Harrop 1987). In Britain, the term 'mass involvement' can be misleading, since it must always be remembered that about 93 per cent of adults are not members of any political party (Parry et al. 1992). Nevertheless, that small proportion who are adds significantly to the number of people engaged in political life. In any liberal democracy, it is scarcely healthy if political activity involves only full-time politicians and state officials and, though each of the two main parties has lost members in recent years, it has still been estimated that they alone contain over 300,000 people with an active interest in British politics (Seyd and Whiteley 1992; Whiteley et al. 1994).

The contribution made by ordinary constituency members to their parties, and therefore to representative democracy, should not be underrated. As mentioned earlier, the selection of parliamentary candidates is one of the parties' most crucial tasks – particularly in those seats which a party is bound to win – and is almost always done locally by local party members. Recent attempts by central party officials to impose candidates have not met with unqualified success. Although Labour's National Executive Committee has since 1989 reserved the right to impose by-election candidates, the merits of this strategy were recently questioned following the party's defeat at an Uxbridge by-election, when the choice of local activists was overruled by national officials – much to the chagrin, it was reported, of many voters (*Daily Telegraph*, 29 July 1997). In the Conservative Party, constituency members have long been jealous of their autonomy in candidate selection, and it was notable that William Hague steered clear of any plan to erode it when he explained his thinking on party reform in July 1997. Unable to impose candidates upon the grass roots, Tory Central Office has even struggled to make its recommendations effective: until he was selected by Stratford-upon-Avon in 1995, ex-minister John Maples was turned down by over thirty local Tory parties, despite glowing reports from national organizers.

The fate of Tim Yeo, Tory MP for Suffolk South and a junior minister until 1994, also reminds us that ordinary party members can halt a politician's career even after he or she has been elected to Parliament. Despite revelations concerning an illegitimate child, Yeo was assured by the prime minister that he could continue in office, but was nevertheless forced to resign after his local party expressed clear disapproval. The lesson was clear: frontbenchers cannot retain their status without the continued support of their constituency party membership.

Yeo was spared the ultimate punishment that constituency members can mete out to MPs, namely, deselection as parliamentary candidate – a move which effectively ends a politician's career. Having lost the confidence of their local party, for either political or non-political reasons, this fate has befallen nearly two dozen MPs since 1979, recent examples being David Young (Labour, Bolton SE, 1994) and Sir George Gardiner (Tory, Reigate, 1996). Conversely, local party members can save an MP's career even when the party establishment would like to end it. The assurance that they would not be deselected encouraged many Eurosceptic Tory MPs to defy – and then forfeit – the party whip at Westminster, allowing them to wage 'guerilla warfare' against Major's government between 1992 and 1996 (Gorman 1994). During the 1997 general election campaign, it was local party activists in Beckenham and Tatton who ensured that Piers Merchant and Neil Hamilton remained official Tory candidates, despite barely concealed protests from national Tory leaders. For all the problems this gave the Tories, there was no sign (at the time of going to press) that their new leader was prepared to strip local members of this prerogative.

Most party members also play an important role in the election of party leaders, which, as explained earlier, has a direct bearing upon who becomes prime minister: to assume national recognition as a 'premier in waiting', Tony Blair first had to be elected in a ballot involving 952,000 actual, and 4 million potential, Labour and trade union members (Kelly 1995a). This also points to the fact that ordinary Labour members would now play a part in any challenge to Tony Blair's position as Labour prime minister – a two-thirds vote in favour of a challenge being needed at the party conference, followed by a ballot again involving all card-carrying members. Indeed, if there is an overwhelming vote for a change of leader among constituency and affiliated members, it is technically possible for a Labour PM to be supplanted against the wishes of most Labour MPs (Kelly 1993). Although Tory leadership elections between 1965 and 1997 were confined to Tory MPs, it was agreed by the party in early 1998 that future one-member-one-vote contests would involve a (OMOV) ballot of party members.

Recent research also suggests that the activity of local party members has a vital influence upon the outcome of elections. Following the 'dealignment' of voters after 1970, general elections are no longer determined solely by national party leaders, fighting national campaigns on national issues through the national media – one simple illustration being the variance of voting patterns from area to area (Leonard 1996). Seyd and colleagues have assembled powerful evidence to show that electoral success now depends more and more upon well-organized, high-profile local parties, able to put their parties' message into a local context. With reference to 1987 and 1992, for example – and taking account of other standard factors – it was shown that Labour did better in those seats where it had an above-average number of activists, while the Tories were more effective at resisting the national swing in seats where they spent more on local campaigns (Seyd and Whiteley 1992; Whiteley et al. 1994). In 1997, the evidence for such trends was less compelling (Curtice and Steed 1997, p. 312). However, the Tories' private pollsters, ICM, did claim a link between the party's vote in individual constituencies and the varying intensity of its constituency campaigns, claiming that 'low contact rate' with voters contributed to the loss of over fifty seats (*Sunday Telegraph*, 5 October 1997).

It should not be forgotten either that ordinary members help keep the parties afloat through various forms of revenue-raising activity (Lemieux 1995). Much has been made of the parties' reliance upon 'institutional' funding from trade unions and large companies (Ewing 1987). Yet this reliance is often overstated. In 1992, for example, Labour raised over £2 million from its constituency members – more than from any trade union – while by 1996 only 45 per cent of Labour's income derived from union donations, compared to 77 per cent in 1987 (*Daily Telegraph*, 14 August 1997). Likewise, three-quarters of overall Tory revenue normally comes from constituency fund-raising and subscriptions (Pinto-Duschinsky 1990). In a democracy where there is still only limited state funding for the parties, members' efforts in this area offer a further assurance that their concerns about what the party stands for will be taken seriously. This leads us to policy.

The Making of Party Policy

McKenzie revisited

The making of party policy refocuses attention upon how parties enhance both elections and parliamentary democracy. Although parties in government have been curbed in recent years by a loss of formal sovereignty to Europe and a loss of economic power to international markets, many still believe that parties have the capacity to effect considerable change in society (see for example Eatwell 1979; Morgan 1990; Jenkins 1987; Kavanagh 1987). Edmund Burke stated two hundred years ago that a state without the means of change also lacked a means of conservation, and it remains the case that a political system's survival requires some facility to change the course of government – particularly if change is deemed necessary by the bulk of voters (as was arguably the case at the 1997 general election). Politicians of both left and right have described and welcomed parties as 'battering rams of change': by first obtaining from the electorate a clear mandate for a set of policies, parties can then use that mandate to overcome institutional and other opposition once in government, thus vindicating the purpose of electoral competition and public accountability (Crossman 1971; Fowler 1991).

The debate about whether parties in office 'make a difference' is complex and long-standing (see conclusion). Yet the Attlee and Thatcher governments, of 1945–1951 and 1979–1990 respectively, do suggest strongly that parties in power can leave a significant mark upon society (Morgan 1990; Young 1989). Indeed, this may help to explain the marginalization of groups offering a non-constitutional route to reform – through violent revolution, military coups or various forms of insurrection (Hunt 1994). Even leftists like Benn, who have criticized recent Labour governments for 'timidity', argue that Labour in power could 'transform' society, if only it showed the same qualities of self-belief and determination it showed after 1945 (Hennessy and Seldon 1987, pp. 307–8).

The way in which party policy is made has lately been the subject of a growing body of academic literature (see for example Minkin 1978, 1993; Ramsden 1980; Shaw 1988, 1994; Kelly 1989a). Yet, until the mid-1950s, it was an area largely ignored by political science. This complacency was to be shattered by the publication of Robert McKenzie's *British Political Parties* in 1955, a study which concerned 'The Distribution of Power Within the Conservative and Labour Parties'. McKenzie's central point was that policy-making in both major parties was carried out in a broadly similar fashion, in that party leaders exercised formidable and unmatched influence – especially when in government. The idea that power over party policy rested overwhelmingly with the party leaders was scarcely novel; indeed, McKenzie conceded that one of his study's principal aims was to validate the 'iron law of oligarchy' outlined by Robert Michels almost half a century earlier. Nevertheless, McKenzie's conclusions were to have a decisive impact upon academic thinking for at least a generation.

McKenzie's treatment of the Conservative Party, however, was itself conservative and offered little in the way of fresh argument, claiming that the party was an 'overt oligarchy', with authority over policy the almost exclusive preserve of the parliamentary leadership (chs 2–3). The party's top-down approach to policy was, according to McKenzie, a clear product of both its top-down, paternalistic ideology (whereby a benevolent elite would attend the needs of a largely deferential society) and its organizational history. The Parliamentary Conservative Party had long preceded the party's extra-parliamentary structure, which was only created after 1867 to help Tory MPs and Tory governments get re-elected following the franchise extension of 1867 (Davies 1995, p. 14). As a result, the National Union of Conservative and Constitutional Associations (set up in 1867 to enfold all voluntary Conservative activity beyond Westminster) was given only an ancillary role – that of an 'electoral handmaiden', or vote-getting machine, for the parliamentary elite. Disraeli, and the other parliamentary architects of the National Union, stressed from the outset that policy would remain the prerogative of the parliamentary leadership (McKenzie 1955, ch. 4). Even the National Union's principal annual gathering – since known as the

Conservative conference – was allowed only an 'advisory' contribution to policy-making, its main task being seen as 'the communication of party policy to the masses' (Kelly 1994, p. 225).

Conservative Central Office, set up in 1870 as the professional or bureaucratic wing of the extra-parliamentary party, was given a similar subservient role: its main organizers (notably its chairman after 1911) were to be appointed and removed by the parliamentary leadership, while none of its assorted organs – like the Conservative Research Department established in 1929 – was to have any independent influence upon policy. McKenzie argued that the survival of these autocratic arrangements was due to the continued acquiescence of most Conservative members, outside as well as inside Parliament. The party, he claimed, had an overriding determination to win elections and took a somewhat militaristic attitude towards the requirements of success. Victory, be it on the field of battle or at the polls, demanded discipline within the ranks and a clear, common policy – ideals which were best determined and secured through strong leadership. The apparently contrary approach of the Labour Party, and the electoral problems it apparently suffered as a result, only strengthened these convictions.

McKenzie, though, sought to prove that Labour's policy-making was not as democratic as many assumed, and that in reality it was as oligarchic as in the Conservative Party – the main difference being that Labour's oligarchy was covert and unofficial (pp. 635–50). Indeed, it was for this controversial claim that McKenzie's study is chiefly remembered, provoking a string of corroborative and conflicting theses.

According to the architects of Labour's 1918 constitution, which had been seen as 'the revered handbook of Party policy and procedure' (G. D. H. Cole 1948, p. 137), the rules of policy-making should reflect Labour's commitment to greater democracy and political participation in society as a whole (Beer 1948). From this idea came a pivotal role for Labour's annual conference – the mass assembly of delegates from the party's constituency branches and affiliated trade unions. The importance of the conference to party policy was made quite clear: it was to be the body from which all power, authority and policy would derive, with 'the work of the party...under the direction and control of the annual conference' (McKenzie 1955, p. 485). Party leader Clement Attlee confirmed that conference was 'the final authority of the party...it lays down the policy of the party and issues instructions which must be carried out...by its representatives in Parliament' (Attlee 1954). The constitution also gave a clear role to conference in the construction of the party manifesto. It was decreed that Labour's parliamentary leadership and National Executive Committee (NEC) would together decide which items of policy from Labour's 'programme' would enter the manifesto, but that the programme could only consist of policies approved by a two-thirds, card-vote majority at the conference.

Conference thus appeared the crucial, democratic link in Labour's policy-making process. Conference delegates would be mandated by their unions or constituency parties to instigate, amend, endorse or reject various policy proposals overseen by an NEC (itself largely elected by conference delegates). Once approved, those policy proposals would have a good chance of guiding the party leadership in Parliament, which, general elections permitting, would then be able to make a lasting difference to public policy and administration. The fact that a Labour leader had to cope with so many alternative sources of power inside the party – conference, NEC, elective Shadow Cabinet and deputy leader, as well as the organizationally pervasive trade unions (which dominated both the votes cast at conference and the funds raised by the party's treasurer) – seemed to make it impossible for a Labour leader to monopolize policy-making in the manner of a Conservative leader.

McKenzie, however, took issue with this 'official' version of power in the Labour Party. For McKenzie, the critical development in Labour history came after 1922, when Labour became first of all the official opposition and then (in 1923) the governing party – a development which the authors of Labour's constitution had only hazily foreseen. Once Labour leaders became either prime minister or prime minister-in-waiting, they were obliged to act in a very different way to that prescribed under official party proceedings. To be effective now, Labour leaders and their frontbench colleagues in Parliament could no longer be governed by rigid and often simplistic demands passed once a year at the conference. They had to be able to act swiftly and flexibly, pre-empting both conference and other extra-parliamentary bodies in the development of policy standpoints; the dynamics of a modern liberal democracy had made such instant policy-making essential to a party's viability.

Yet even in the less 'spontaneous' areas of policy-making, notably the construction and implementation of the manifesto, Labour's parliamentary leaders had acquired powers which made any one of them much more than *primus inter pares*. Although Labour manifestos were supposed to contain only those policies approved by two-thirds of the conference, McKenzie claimed that Labour leaders usually had enough weight to suppress the preferences of the NEC and insist that only the policies with which they felt happy should go into the manifesto. Given the growth of the electronic media, and its tendency to focus upon the party leaders, the NEC would normally appreciate how dangerous it was to fight a campaign with policies which troubled the leadership.

Even if a leader was obliged to carry manifesto policies she or he personally disliked, there was no guarantee that those policies would be implemented should Labour take office. Even Labour's constitution admitted that the party's parliamentarians should give effect to conference policy only 'as far as may be practicable'; and with the constitution failing to indicate which organ of the party should determine 'practicability', this duty inevitably fell to the parliamentary leadership. Linked to this anomaly was the fact that the constitution said nothing about the time and order in which manifesto policies were implemented, allowing the leadership to shelve the policies they disliked – often in favour of their own, newly hatched ideas, prompted by events which were 'unforeseen' at the time the manifesto was framed.

For McKenzie, oligarchic policy-making was both inevitable and desirable. It was inevitable given the vicissitudes and fluidity of modern political life, which were simply incompatible with the creaking, cumbersome mechanisms of party democracy: governmental efficiency was hugely at odds with the effects of meaningful, mass participation in policy-making. It was also inevitable because parties seeking office had to reflect the shifting views of floating voters. According to

McKenzie, these views were by definition more middle-of-the-road than those of party activists. Consequently, a party which 'democratically' adopted the policies of its most active, extra-parliamentary members would only make itself unelectable: party leaders were thus obliged to 'save the party from itself' by ignoring the wishes of those party members who were not personally seeking election to Parliament, reflecting instead the views of the party's MPs – whose views were naturally moderated by the wishes of their constituents.

McKenzie considered such an outcome desirable, not simply because it accorded with his own Downesian or 'consumerist' view of democracy (whereby parties mainly reflect rather than educate public opinion), but because it coincided with his faith in parliamentary government. For those who subscribe to this classic, liberal model of politics, it is vital that, whichever party is in government, ministers are primarily responsible to MPs, with MPs then primarily responsible to their constituents. The delegatory system enshrined in Labour's constitution seemed a direct challenge to the Westminster system, imposing upon Labour leaders and Labour MPs an alternative mandate to the one obtained from the House of Commons and the electorate. To those active in the extra-parliamentary parties, this alternative mandate may well have looked like an extension of democracy. But as McKenzie asserted, the vast majority of voters had no such involvement – so any erosion of parliamentary democracy was an erosion of popular democracy as well.

McKenzie vindicated?

In view of the fact that McKenzie's thesis was most contestable in respect of the Labour Party, it should come as no surprise that, when assessing its validity since 1955, the record of the Labour Party should have received most attention. According to certain ministers who served in them, the conduct of the Wilson and Callaghan Labour governments lent particular credibility to McKenzie's ideas (Crossman 1971; Benn 1980). It was argued by left-wing critics of those governments that Labour Cabinets regularly ignored conference decisions during both the 1960s and the 1970s. The Wilson governments of 1964–1970 were said to have contradicted the wishes of party activists in respect of devaluation of sterling, wage restraint and immigration, while sidestepping the commitment to scrap the Polaris weapons system contained in the 1964 manifesto (Higgins 1984). At one of the conferences during that period, Wilson admitted to delegates that he regarded their decisions as 'warnings but not instructions' – a somewhat eccentric view of conference's constitutional role (Kelly 1989b).

The government of James Callaghan (1976–1979) was alleged to have been even more at odds with party, *qua* conference, opinion. As Kellner later recorded, 'when conference passed resolutions critical of the government, the upshot was 48 hours of embarrassment followed by a continuation of old policies as if nothing had happened' (*Independent*, 26 September 1988). Labour had been elected in 1974 on a manifesto promising a 'fundamental and irreversible' redistribution of wealth, a policy endorsed by subsequent conference resolutions between 1975 and 1978. Yet from 1976 to 1979, the government emphasized the need for strict wage restraint, even after this had been questioned by conference, while agreeing to severe cuts in public spending in return for loans from the International Monetary Fund (IMF) – the terms of which were not discussed with the extra-parliamentary party. Of course, the government was restrained after 1977 by its lack of an overall majority; but the deals which ensured its survival (with the Liberal and nationalist parties) were negotiated unilaterally by the leadership.

The leftward trend of conference decisions in the 1970s culminated in a radical Labour programme by the time of the 1979 general election, although the leadership by then was pursuing 'moderate' and somewhat contradictory policies on which it hoped to seek re-election. This dilemma was apparently resolved by the parliamentary leadership ignoring both the tone of the programme and the wishes of the majority on the NEC, drawing up its own manifesto and presenting it to the NEC *fait accompli*. As Benn later complained, 'most Labour activists fought the 1979 election on a manifesto for which they had little enthusiasm and even less responsibility' (*Guardian*, 16 July 1980).

The constitutional reforms inside the Labour Party between 1980 and 1981 were designed to check these oligarchic tendencies by making the parliamentary leadership more accountable to the extra-parliamentary party – notably through the election of the leader by a new electoral college embracing the whole of the party, replacing the traditional method of a Parliamentary Labour Party (PLP) ballot (Seyd 1987). Between 1980 and 1983, the defection of almost thirty moderate Labour MPs to the Social Democratic Party (SDP), the leftward drift of policy, the Bennite slant of Labour's 1983 manifesto, and the general air of anarchy which pervaded the party all gave the impression that power in the Labour Party had been redistributed from the parliamentary leadership. However, Labour's calamitous defeat at the 1983 general election (gaining a mere 28 per cent of votes) served to underline one of McKenzie's chief justifications for an oligarchic approach to policy-making, namely that only a Westminster elite could be trusted to frame policies attuned to voters' wishes.

After 1983, this was implicitly recognized by the new leader, Neil Kinnock, and his closest Labour associates. Particularly after a second ignominious electoral defeat in 1987, there was a concerted attempt to centralize control over policy and reduce the influence of leftist forces among the constituency parties and the grass roots of certain trade unions (Hughes and Wintour 1990). The policy review of 1987–1989, and subsequent policy documents like 'Meet the Challenge, Make the Change', led to seismic shifts in economic, industrial and defence policy, which made the 'modernization' of the Blair era relatively easy to accomplish. Yet most of these changes were engineered by tightly knit working committees responsible to the leadership, with conference and the bulk of the extra-parliamentary party reduced to observer status (Garner 1990).

This resumption of what Shaw (1988) termed 'social democratic centralism' – power exercised by the few in order to secure 'moderate' policy – could not have occurred without the leadership being supported, at both conference and NEC, by the bulk of trade union leaders, who by then were convinced that radical policy surgery should transcend the trappings of party democracy (Minkin 1993, pp. 395–420). Yet the influence that the unions exercised inside the party's organization, via block votes at conference and to a lesser extent the NEC, was a reminder of McKenzie's claim that union influence usually abetted the leadership's control of policy – enabling the leader to secure 'party' backing for his or her plans simply by dealing with a small number of senior union officials, irrespective of what the bulk of party activists might have wanted. In other words, the mechanics of traditional Labour Party 'democracy' – characterized by the dominance of union block votes – actually made the suppression of democracy easier to achieve, a point demonstrated by successive Labour leaders in the 1950s, 1960s and 1970s and rediscovered by the leadership after 1983 (Shaw 1994).

Ironically, the leader's control over policy was enhanced by the reform of Labour leadership elections in 1981 – a reform which was designed (by Benn's Campaign for Labour Party Democracy) to weaken the leader's autonomy. That leaders were now elected by the whole party, rather than just an exclusive section of it, enabled them to claim a personal mandate for dynamic, domineering leadership, making resistance to the leader's aims that much more difficult to sustain. Furthermore, the cumbersome nature of the electoral college made the deposition of leaders a much less realistic prospect; whereas the challenge to Tory leaders in 1989, 1990 and 1995 took only a couple of weeks, any challenge to Labour leaders (such as Benn's in 1988) could last six months, damaging the challenger's momentum and producing complaints that a challenge only 'distracted' the party (Kelly 1993). Because it is so easily organized, any MPs-only system would have left Kinnock vulnerable after 1987. Instead, the electoral college gave him the security to assert his own policy agenda.

Outwardly, it seems paradoxical that the drive towards a more centralized party, with policy more rigorously controlled by the leader and her or his allies, should have been accompanied by a series of OMOV reforms ostensibly designed to democratize the party. The 1993 conference was especially important in this respect, legitimizing the leader's plans to reform candidate selection, voting procedure at conference and the workings of the electoral college (Kelly 1995a). Yet behind the democratic language lay a belief that, by enfranchising the bulk of ordinary (and rather passive) members, the influence of leftist activists would be diluted, while at the same time reforms inspired by the leader and his clique of advisers would be legitimized (Anderson 1996).

The Blair era has seen a vivid demonstration of this idea. Almost immediately after being elected leader in 1994, Blair instigated a party-wide debate and then vote on the future of Labour's Clause IV, the historic statement of its core beliefs and a perennial *casus belli* within the party. Blair's reform of Clause IV was duly approved, partly because Blair had just received an apparent mandate for change from over 400,000 voters in the 1994 leadership contest. Yet his success was also due to the fact that the party by now was desperate for power at almost any price and recognized that a rejection of Blair's proposals would have been a crippling blow to his – and therefore Labour's – reputation within the country.

Between 1994 and 1997, this rationale allowed Blair – and key allies like Gordon Brown and Peter Mandelson – to impose an almost ruthless discipline upon the party, while steering it towards the 'New Labour' programme they favoured. The draft version of the 1997 election manifesto was, unsurprisingly, put together by the leader and a small number of trusted associates, with virtually no detailed input from established party bodies like the conference or NEC (Jones 1997). Yet it was given democratic legitimacy by a ballot of all party members in the autumn of 1996, which – again unsurprisingly – gave overwhelming endorsement to the leader's policy proposals. All this seemed to represent an historic shift in Labour Party procedure, away from participatory, representative democracy – whereby a few thousand activists, principally via party conferences, discuss in some detail the ongoing development of party policy – towards an alternative, plebiscitary democracy, whereby hundreds of thousands of party members simply approve or reject policy packages assembled by a small number of senior parliamentarians and (often unelected) party officials.

This trend was seen to continue after the 1997 general election. The party document, 'Partnership in Power', outlined plans to downgrade the conference's policy-making role in favour of Labour's National Policy Forum and assorted regional fora (established after 1992), supported by new 'policy commissions' and a 'Joint Policy Committee'. The membership of these bodies would be small so as to allow a more 'measured' style of discussion, which avoided 'adversarial' debate and formalized voting in favour of a more 'informal' quest for consensus. These bodies would also contribute to a 'rolling programme' of policy development over a 'two year cycle', with conference apparently confined to either ratifying or rejecting the finished policy product – a clear sign, to many in the party, that conference is being changed from a serious, deliberative assembly into a 'rally' or celebration of new policies initiated by the leader and his or her advisers (Kelly 1997).

The language of the modern Labour Party, with its stress upon OMOV and its references to a more 'inclusive' and less 'polarized' approach to policy-making, may seem a long way from the procedures described by McKenzie in 1955. Yet the change in style may only conceal a consistency of aim – that aim being the control of policy by a London-based elite. The attainment of such control in the 1990s was accompanied of course by an amazing recovery in Labour's electoral fortunes, thus adding further weight to the Michels–McKenzie 'law' of effective organization.

As McKenzie's treatment of the Conservative Party was less shocking, there has accordingly been less debate about the relevance of his thesis to Tory organization since 1955. Moreover, there has been no lack of corroborative evidence. By 1997, there had still been little structural change within the party; its formal organization remained paternalistic and shorn of the conventional trappings of party democracy. This was especially so in connection with party policy, which remained the acknowledged prerogative of the parliamentary leadership. It was notable that a study of Tory policy-making in 1994 began with the stark sentence 'Nothing becomes Conservative policy without the assent of the leader' (Barnes and Cockett 1994).

The imperious leadership of Margaret Thatcher refuelled the idea that the Tories were a one-man or one-woman band, governed at all times by the leader's own priorities. Naturally, this was an overstatement. Yet it was still significant that the most spectacular Cabinet resignations of the 1979–1990 era (Heseltine 1986, Lawson 1989, Howe 1990) were linked to the alleged absence of collective decision making, policy being said to be determined by the leader and unaccountable advisers like Sir Alan Walters (Ranelagh 1991). Although John Major's governments were supposed to represent a more 'collegiate' style of policy-making, this did not officially extend much beyond Cabinet. Indeed, both the 1992 and 1997 manifestos were put together by a small group of 'A-Team' advisers redolent of the Thatcher era (Hogg and Hill 1995; Jones 1997). Major's description to reporters of the 1992 Tory manifesto – 'It's me, all me' – was taken as a perfect encapsulation of policy-making inside the Tory Party (D. Butler and Kavanagh 1992, p. 107).

During the post-war period, numerous Tory bodies have sought to affect the policy of Tory leaders – the Advisory Committee on Policy, the Conservative Research Department, the Conservative Political Centre, the Policy Steering Committee, various National Union Advisory Committees, plus an assortment of friendly think-tanks like the Centre for Policy Studies and Adam Smith Institute (Charmley 1996). Yet none of these bodies has offered the bulk of Conservative members any established or guaranteed influence, allowing the party to continue evolving policy in the manner of 'a traditional army which relies overmuch on its dashing and daring commanders' (Trend 1987, p. 36). Following the debacle of the 1997 general election, those Conservatives who have long campaigned for a more formalized grass-root input in policy-making were not slow to complain, arguing that the party's poor public image, and its sclerotic constituency organization, had much to do with the limited influence of ordinary members upon the 'red meat' of policy (Charter Movement 1997).

McKenzie refuted?

As will be explained presently, there have been attempts by scholars to refute McKenzie's arguments concerning the Labour Party. Yet it is in connection with the Conservative Party that McKenzie's theory of oligarchy looks most questionable – and not just in relation to subsequent events. A more rigorous examination of Conservative policy-making prior to 1955, such as that undertaken in *Conservative Century*, shows that the picture was much more complicated than McKenzie suggested (Ball 1994; Barnes and Cockett 1994; Kelly 1994). On issues like tariff reform in the early 1900s, trade union reform after 1926, rearmament in the 1930s, industrial policy in the late 1940s and housing in the early 1950s, the leadership's initial policy ideas had to be either dropped or radically amended in the face of pressure from both backbenchers and the extra-parliamentary party.

While McKenzie was right to say that the party put a premium on unity, the history of the party from 1900 to 1955 alone shows that unity was not obtained simply by leaders issuing diktats which were meekly obeyed by the rest of the party – until it decided upon a change of leader. More often than not, unity was only attained after the leader had reconciled competing interests and ideas within the party. Balfour, for example, may have claimed to prefer the advice of his valet to that of the party conference – but it should be remembered that he proved one of the most inept Tory leaders this century, presiding over a calamitous split in 1905 and three election defeats. After Churchill capitulated to backbench and conference pressure in 1947 (over post-war industrial policy), R. A. Butler surprised few Party members by saying that 'the days had gone by…when policy was brought down from Mount Sinai as tablets of stone, with the faithful often blinded by what they saw' (R. A. Butler 1971, p. 137). In short, the lack of formal democracy inside the Conservative Party has not prevented the leadership's wishes being circumvented: what many scholars have overlooked is that this has been done through informal, *ad hoc* pressure rather than precise, organizational procedures.

This point is particularly important when assessing more recent events. Although the period after 1979 witnessed no major, organizational change, the party has still been subjected to crucial attitudinal changes among both back-benchers and activists – changes which have had no small impact upon the course of Tory policy (Kelly 1995b). Deference towards the leadership, always exaggerated by outsiders, has virtually disappeared in many sections of the party, blowing apart any lingering idea that loyalty and solidarity are (as Lord Kilmuir insisted in the 1950s) 'the Tories' secret weapon' (Kelly 1995c).

To understand this, it is necessary to recall socio-economic and political developments. The embourgeoisement of society – both the cause and effect of the Tories' electoral success after 1979 – bred a new confidence within Tory ranks. Instead of seeing themselves as representing an embattled and minority middle class, as they had done for most of the century, Conservatives became more inclined to see themselves as the new *vox populi*, with a sure feel for the new, average voter. There was thus even less of a tendency to accept that the leadership 'knew best' when it came to policy, and much more of a tendency to assert specific ideas of their own – and to be impatient when the leadership appeared not to listen. The party's phenomenally long spell in office after 1979 also led to a sense of invincibility among many party members – a feeling that, however fractiously the Tories behaved, Labour 'must lose'. With their hegemony assured, it now seemed as if dissent and robust debate were luxuries that could be afforded.

At Westminster, it was already clear by the mid-1980s that Tory MPs were no longer ready to follow the leader until they wanted to change that leader; instead a growing body was now prepared to question the leader's judgement on specific policy issues without necessarily wanting a *coup d'état*. The Thatcher governments discovered this on a range of issues, notably the reform of local government finance, Sunday trading and the funding of higher education (Norton 1987). The effects of these rebellions were often cushioned by the government's large majority. Once that disappeared in 1992, those rebellions became no less frequent and their impact more serious. Henceforth, Tory policy had to be constructed with an even greater sensitivity to backbench opinion, sending out a rather damaging impression of weak, vacillating leadership (Young 1994; Riddell 1994).

This was demonstrated within weeks of the 1992 election when sixty-nine Tory MPs signed an early day motion calling for a 'fresh start' to the government's dealings over Europe, a portent of the immense difficulty Major was to have steering the Maastricht legislation through Parliament. The 'fresh start' motion was also significant in that twenty-five of its signatories had only been elected to Parliament in 1992, stirring fears that the new generation of Tory MPs were 'Thatcher's children', whose iconoclastic and individualistic views made them hostile to all forms of collective discipline (Baker and Fountain 1996).

The division over Europe among Tory MPs was to manifest itself in the government's ambiguous policy on the European single currency. Put simply, the government's majority was so slender that it could not afford to rebut, clearly and consistently, those with strong Eurosceptical views. Thus, having had the whip withdrawn in 1994 (following their abstention on a European Finance Bill), eight Eurosceptic MPs were still able to leave some mark upon government policy. As the *Daily Telegraph* (9 January 1995) noted:

> It appears there can be no compromise between their aims and Mr Major's ambition to place Britain at the heart of Europe. Yet they have taken a stance which strikes a deep chord in middle England and, with current Parliamentary arithmetic, are in a position to exert much influence.

Such influence had in fact been shown only weeks before the *Telegraph*'s piece, when the 'sceptic eight' helped defeat the government's proposals for VAT on fuel. This served as a reminder that not only European policy needed to be recast as a result of dissent among Conservative MPs – other clear examples being the rationalization of the coal industry in October 1992, the privatization of railways in May 1993 and the privatization of the Post Office in 1994 (for other examples see Kelly 1995c).

As indicated earlier, it was not just dissent at Westminster which made Tory policy embrace wider sections of Tory opinion. After 1979, it became increasingly obvious that the Tory conference was not, after all, a mere festival of worship for the leader (Kelly 1996). Dissent from the floor at the 1987 conference had led to a major revision of the government's poll tax policy, forcing it to be implemented at one fell swoop rather than phased in as Ridley and Thatcher had originally planned. Indeed, in their comprehensive account of the poll tax, Butler et al. admit that the influence of Tory conferences 'appears at every turn...as driving forces behind the evolution of the policy' (1994, pp. 249–50). Two years later, it was again strongly expressed opinions at the conference which led to the Conservatives fielding official parliamentary candidates in Northern Ireland – an 'integrationist' measure clearly at odds with the government's devolutionary-cum-consociational policy for Northern Ireland (Cunningham and Kelly 1995).

The conference's influence upon policy is easily overlooked because it normally occurs in oblique fashion. Margaret Thatcher, for example, conceded that the conference regularly affected the actions of her government, for the simple reason that she 'trusted its instincts', which, in any case, usually coincided with her own (Kelly 1988). She was therefore inclined to 'sound out' conference either to clarify her own thinking or to stiffen her resolve in later Cabinet battles – a particularly important factor between 1979 and 1982. It must also be remembered that any criticism of existing policy is seldom reflected in either the wording of motions or the eventual voting. With conference having no formal, constitutional role in policy-making (akin to that it has in the Labour Party), such paraphernalia have never been deemed that important. Instead, conference goers have registered their views through the medium of free-range debate – often taking scant notice of the motion supposedly under discussion – with those on the platform trusted to sense and then cater for any clear views which emerge; the poll tax change of 1987, for example, had nothing to do with the rather bland motion on local government which started the conference debate.

Finally, it would be wrong to examine the policy influence of Tory conferences without reference to the party's 'conference system' – the network of regional and sectional Tory conferences which precedes, and culminates in, the main October gathering. These less publicized conferences, such as those of the Scottish, Welsh, Young and Women Conservatives, naturally provide further opportunities for ordinary party members to suggest and scrutinize policy. During the 1980s, some of these suggestions bore a strong similarity to eventual government policy – most notably the reform of married women's taxation, an issue sparked by the Conservative Women's Organization and their special, 'highflyer' conferences of 1985–1986 (Kelly 1989a, pp. 123–7).

As a result, these preliminary conferences act as an early-warning system for party leaders and their senior colleagues in Parliament, allowing them to revise and initiate policy – often in time for the main October conference. At that conference, new proposals can be unveiled to an impressed audience of activists, thus avoiding any damaging dissent which might otherwise have surfaced at that media-soaked event. Between 1979 and 1996, commentators were right to point out that ministers' speeches were nearly always greeted by tumultuous applause, yet they were wrong to think that this applause sprung from naivety, deference or sycophancy on the part of activists: more often than not, their enthusiasm came from a relief that their concerns, expressed earlier in the Tories' 'conference season', had at last been accommodated by the leadership.

This aspect of Tory conferences was demonstrated, with important effect, during the second Major government. In 1993, preliminary Tory conferences had expressed much concern about the 'declining moral climate' of society, and it was largely in response to this that Major's flagging government unveiled its Back to Basics crusade at the main conference later that year (Durham 1995). Commentators at that conference noted that the initiative was warmly received; yet it was applause for being receptive rather than inventive. Undeterred by the fate of Back to Basics, the preliminary conferences of 1994 and 1995 were much detained by public disorder and the 'need' for more prison sentences. This placed the Tory leadership in a difficult position, as most of the objective evidence which emerged at this time – from various penal experts and Home Office studies – showed that custodial sentencing had only a limited effect upon actual and putative offenders (Foster 1999). However, Major and his senior colleagues were by this stage aware that a restive membership could easily produce a fractious conference, which, with the party's public standing already low, they were anxious to avoid. As a result, Michael Howard unashamedly played to the gallery at both the 1994 and 1995 conferences, promising more prison sentences and more prisons – a policy which, while dismaying nearly all government advisers, underlined the influence which Tory conferences can wield upon Tory governments.

Although the Tories' conference system has not been widely recognized outside the Tory Party, it has not gone unnoticed, it seems, in the higher ranks of the Labour Party. The style of the new policy fora mentioned earlier, and the approach to party-wide policy-making described in 'Partnership in Power', have strong echoes of Tory practice: the proposed 'rolling programmes' and 'policy cycles', with the results ratified at the annual Labour conference, replicate much of the Tory conference system. Labour's new distaste for 'divisive' ballots and 'simplistic' motions likewise recalls the style of debate historically favoured at Tory conferences.

There is a huge irony in all this, for having been derided for so long as less important than Labour's, Tory conferences are now being recognized as the true model of an 'efficient' party assembly, better equipped to marry grass-root participation in policy to the demands of government. Yet an even greater irony is that, at a time when traditional-style Tory conferences are being emulated by Labour, they are being spurned by the Tories themselves, whose recent autumn conferences recall those of Labour twenty years ago. Speakers from the floor no longer seem so content with the old, subtle processes and, egged on by maverick MPs and former leaders, are acting like delegates to a 1970s Labour conference. All this conspires to make McKenzie's observations look amazingly dated.

In relation to the Labour Party, it needs to be remembered that McKenzie's rejection of party democracy did not go unchallenged. In the 1970s, Minkin's detailed account of *The Labour Party Conference* restated its importance, noting how Labour leaders went to extraordinary lengths to secure conference backing via 'agenda manipulation' and the 'arm twisting' of union leaders (Minkin 1978, pp. 300–18).

In his second edition of *British Political Parties*, McKenzie supported his original claims by pointing to the way in which Labour leader Hugh Gaitskell dismissed the decision of the 1960 conference to support independent nuclear disarmament: 'What sort of people do you think we [the leadership] are?', Gaitskell had asked in his response to conference. 'Do you honestly think we can accept a decision like this?' (McKenzie 1955, second edition 1963, pp. 611–18). Yet, for Minkin, the real point lay in the huge effort Gaitskell then made to have the decision reversed at the conference of 1961 – a sure sign that its participants mattered to policy formation. Like the leaders of the Conservative Party, Gaitskell recognized that a party leader cannot be successful unless the party unites behind the policies she or he expounds to the electorate: this often requires a lot of work at party conferences, converting or accommodating members' wishes.

Minkin accepted McKenzie's claim that most Labour policies were initiated by the leadership, but added that most of these initiatives did take account of established or expected conference opinion; the conference was thus 'a unique forum of mood and opinion inside the party', which duly 'circumscribed the position of the Parliamentary leadership' (Minkin 1978, p. 317). Interestingly, this view coincided with much of the present author's verdict on how Tory conferences 'worked' – that is, how they accorded policy influence to ordinary party members. In essence, both conferences have provided parliamentary leaders with a framework within which they can formulate detailed policy, but with an eye to party unity. Historically, it would appear that the Tories' 'conference system' has accomplished this more effectively than Labour's annual conference – as the authors of 'Partnership in Power' seem to acknowledge.

It was suggested earlier that recent organizational reforms inside the Labour Party strengthen the leadership *vis-à-vis* the membership, OMOV having only provided a democratic gloss for the steady centralization of power since 1983. So far, these changes have been a brilliant success for the leadership, transforming Labour into a formidable, election-winning machine without much serious reaction inside the party. Yet the strategy is not without its dangers. As Seyd and Whiteley revealed, Labour members are neither devoid of strong opinions nor naturally passive about the way the party conducts itself; nor are they instinctively submissive to the wishes of the leader (Seyd and Whiteley 1992, chs 6, 7). The potential for dissent within the party is therefore obvious; it has simply been contained in recent years by a thirst for power. Now that power has been achieved, it will be interesting to see how long the leadership can rely upon the membership's acquiescence over policy, especially as so much of the Blair agenda seems to clash with traditional Labour beliefs.

If intra-party dissent were to resurface, the OMOV culture which Blair has fostered in recent years could make the management of dissent much harder than in the 1960s and 1970s. As mentioned earlier, union block votes – about which Labour's modernizers have been so dismissive – did allow leaders to contain party friction through deals with small groups of union officials. OMOV ballots are much more difficult to predict and their participants much harder to 'pocket'. If Labour's wider membership becomes less docile, and starts to advance conflicting policies, then it is unclear how 'New Labour' will cope. Even allowing for the 'non-adversarial' arrangements prescribed in 'Partnership in Power', the outcome could still prove messy and embarrassing for the leadership.

Party Activity and Party Policy: A Growing Importance

As indicated in the opening paragraph of this chapter, the diversification (or 'dealignment') of society has put parties on the defensive. It has been widely suggested that the new, multifarious range of pressure groups is more able to reflect the new, multifarious range of interests in society, a superiority strengthened by the main parties' association with 'outmoded' class interests. With voters now more particularistic in outlook, it is suggested they are less attracted to the package deals offered by parties, and are drawn instead to the more specific attractions of narrowly focused, decentralized pressure groups (Baggott 1995).

It could be argued, however, that these same social trends only increase the importance of political parties in modern Britain, highlighting one of their perennial functions in a democracy. As McKay (1993, p. 82) noted in respect of American politics:

Even in the most divided society, some conciliation between competing and conflicting interests must occur if government is to operate efficiently. Political parties help this conciliation process by providing united platforms for the articulation of diverse interests.

The fragmentation of interests in Britain, and the emergence of a more Americanized, classless society, underline McKay's point about the utility of political parties. It is easy for the new breed of classless, individualistic citizens to pursue particular interests, while dismissing the broader view (and resulting policy trade-offs) embodied by political parties. Yet, at some point, those interests still have to be adjusted in the face of competing demands. This is the task that still falls to parties in government, and is one which has become more challenging and urgent given the exponential growth of society's interests. Even outside government, parties still have a crucial role to play in this respect; for it is through the development and projection of its policies that a party reminds the public, and sometimes its own members, that particular concerns must ultimately be looked at in the general context of society.

The dealignment of voters since 1970 has left the parties with much less habitual support at elections (Denver 1994, ch. 2). For that reason alone, specific party policies have become more important, both to the makers of policy and to the voters themselves. Yet if the parties are to embrace a wide enough electorate to win power – and then use it efficiently – those specific policies must somehow aggregate the demands of a complex liberal democracy, while also taking account of external pressures such as those imposed by the European Union and global market forces. The significance, and difficulty, of modern party policy cannot be overstated: that is the reasoning behind the ten chapters which follow.

References

Anderson P. (1996) 'Blair's Plebiscite', *New Statesman and Society*, 5 April.

Ascherson N. (1994) 'Fuzzy Democracy', *New Statesman and Society*, 11 March.

Attlee C. R. (1954) *As It Happened*, London, Macmillan.

Baggott R. (1995) *Pressure Groups Today*, Manchester, Manchester University Press.

Baker D. and Fountain I. (1996) 'Eton Gent or Essex Man? The Conservative Parliamentary Elite' in Ludlam S. and Smith M. J. (eds) *Contemporary British Conservatism*, London, Macmillan.

Ball S. (1994) 'The National and Regional Party Structure' in Seldon A. and Ball S. (eds) *Conservative Century*, Oxford, Oxford University Press.

Barnes J. and Cockett R. (1994) 'The Making of Party Policy' in Seldon A. and Ball S. (eds) *Conservative Century*, Oxford, Oxford University Press.

Beer M. (1948) *A History of British Socialism*, London, Heinemann, pp. 102–7.

Benn T. (1980) *Arguments for Democracy*, London, Cape.

Butler D. and Kavanagh D. (1992) *The British General Election of 1992*, London, Macmillan.

Butler D., Adonis A. and Travers T. (1994) *Failure in British Government: The Politics of the Poll Tax*, Oxford, Oxford University Press.

Butler R. A. (1971) *The Art of the Possible*, London, Hamish Hamilton.

Charmley J. (1996) *A History of Conservative Party Politics 1900–1996*, London, Macmillan.

Charter Movement (1997) *Charter News*, October.

Cole G. D. H. (1948) *A History of the Labour Party from 1914*, London, Routledge and Kegan Paul.

Crick B. (1964) *The Reform of Parliament*, London, Weidenfeld and Nicolson.

Crossman R. H. S. (1971) *Inside View*, London, Cape.

Cunningham M. (1998) 'The Parties of Wales, Scotland and Northern Ireland' in Garner R. and Kelly R. *British Political Parties Today*, Manchester, Manchester University Press.

Cunningham M. and Kelly R. (1995) 'Standing for Ulster', *Politics Review*, 5, 2.

Curtice J. and Steed M. (1997) 'The Results Analysed' in Butter D. and Kavanagh D. *The British General Election of 1997*, Basingstoke, Macmillan.

Davies A. J. (1995) *We, the Nation*, London, Little, Brown.

Denver D. (1994) *Elections and Voting Behaviour*, Hemel Hempstead, Harvester Wheatsheaf.

Durham M. (1995) 'Renewing Conservatism', *Talking Politics*, 8, 1.

Duverger M. (1954) *Political Parties*, London, Methuen.

Eatwell R. (1979) *The 1945–1951 Labour Governments*, London, Batsford.

Ewing K. (1987) *The Funding of Political Parties in Britain*, Cambridge, Cambridge University Press.

Foster S. (1999) *The Politics of Law and Order Today*, Manchester, Manchester University Press.

Fowler N. (1991) *Ministers Decide*, London, Chapmans.

Garner R. (1990) 'Labour and the Policy Review', *Talking Politics*, 3, 1.

Gorman T. (1994) *The Bastards*, London, Pan.

Hague R. and Harrop M. (1987) *Comparative Government and Politics*, London, Macmillan.

Hall S. and Jacques M. (1988) *New Times*, London, Lawrence and Wishart.

Hennessy P. and Seldon A. (1987) *Ruling Performance*, Oxford, Blackwell.

Higgins S. (1984) *The Benn Inheritance*, London, Weidenfeld and Nicolson.

Hogg S. and Hill J. (1995) *Too Close to Call*, London, Little, Brown.

Hughes C. and Wintour P. (1990) *Labour Rebuilt*, London, Fourth Estate.

Hunt S. (1994) 'The Fringe Parties' in Robins L., Blackmore H. and Pyper R. (eds) *Britain's Changing Party System*, London, Leicester University Press.

Jenkins P. (1987) *Mrs Thatcher's Revolution*, London, Cape.

Jones N. (1997) *Campaign 1997*, London, Indigo.

Kavanagh D. (1987) *Thatcherism and British Politics*, Oxford, Oxford University Press.

Kelly R. (1988) 'Party Tricks', *Spectator*, 8 October.

Kelly R. (1989a) *Conservative Party Conferences*, Manchester, Manchester University Press.

Kelly R. (1989b) 'Party Conferences: Do They Matter?', *Talking Politics*, 2, 1.

Kelly R. (1993) 'Choosing Labour Leaders', *Politics Review*, 3, 1.

Kelly R. (1994) 'The Party Conferences' in Seldon A. and Ball S. (eds) *Conservative Century*, Oxford, Oxford University Press.

Kelly R. (1995a) 'Labour's Leadership Contest and Internal Organisation', *Politics Review*, 4, 3.

Kelly R. (1995b) 'Power in the Tory Party', *Politics Review*, 4, 4.

Kelly R. (1995c) 'The Left, the Right and the Whipless', *Talking Politics*, 8, 1.

Kelly R. (1996) 'The Power of the Tory Conference', *Spectator*, 5 October 1996.

Kelly R. (1997) 'The Tory Way is the Better Way', *Political Quarterly*, 68, 3.

Layton-Henry Z. (1980) 'Immigration' in Layton-Henry Z. (ed.) *Conservative Party Politics*, London, Macmillan.

Lemieux S. (1995) 'The Future Funding of Political Parties', *Talking Politics*, 7, 3.

Leonard D. (1996) *Elections in Britain Today*, London, Macmillan.

Marr A. (1995) *Ruling Britannia*, London, Penguin.

McConnell A. (1994) 'Should Parties be Funded by the State?' in Robins L., Blackmore H. and Pyper R. (eds) *Britain's Changing Party System*, London, Leicester University Press.

McKay D. (1993) *American Politics and Society*, Oxford, Oxford University Press.

McKenzie R. T. (1955) *British Political Parties*, London, Heinemann.

Minkin L. (1978) *The Labour Party Conference*, Manchester, Manchester University Press.

Minkin L. (1993) *The Contentious Alliance*, Edinburgh, Edinburgh University Press.

Morgan K. O. (1990) 'The Labour Party's Record in Office', *Contemporary Record*, 3, 4.

Norris P. (1997) *Electoral Change since 1945*, Oxford, Blackwell.

Norris P. and Lovenduski J. (1995) *Political Recruitment*, Cambridge, Cambridge University Press.

Norton P. (1987) *Parliament in Perspective*, Hull, Hull University Press.

Norton P. (1993) *Does Parliament Matter?*, Hemel Hempstead, Harvester Wheatsheaf.

Nugent N. (1994) *The Government and Politics of the European Union*, London, Macmillan.

Parry G., Moyser G. and Day N. (1992) *Political Participation and Democracy in Britain*, Cambridge, Cambridge University Press.

Partridge H. (1995) 'Italy: An Unusual Democracy', *Politics Review*, 5, 2.

Pinto-Duschinsky M. (1990) 'The Funding of Political Parties Since 1945' in Seldon A. (ed.) *UK Political Parties since 1945*, Hemel Hempstead, Harvester Wheatsheaf.

Ramsden J. (1980) *The Making of Conservative Party Policy*, London, Longman.

Ranelagh J. (1991) *Thatcher's People*, London, Fontana.

Riddell P. (1993) *Honest Opportunism*, London, Hamish Hamilton.

Riddell P. (1994) 'Major and Parliament' in Kavanagh D. and Seldon A. (eds) *The Major Effect*, London, Macmillan.

Rose R. (1976) *The Problem of Party Government*, London, Pelican.

Seyd P. (1987) *The Rise and Fall of the Labour Left*, Basingstoke, Macmillan.

Seyd P. and Whiteley P. (1992) *Labour's Grass Roots*, Oxford, Clarendon Press.

Shaw E. (1988) *Discipline and Discord in the Labour Party*, Manchester, Manchester University Press.

Shaw E. (1994) *The Labour Party Since 1979*, London, Routledge.

Trend M. (1987) 'The Tories' Battle Plans', *Spectator*, 28 February.

Whiteley P., Seyd P. and Richardson J. (1994) *True Blues*, Oxford, Oxford University Press.

Wright V. (1986) *The Government and Politics of France*, London, Hutchinson.

Young H. (1989) *One of Us*, London, Macmillan.

Young H. (1994) 'The Prime Minister' in Kavanagh D. and Seldon A. (eds) *The Major Effect*, London, Macmillan.

1 | Economic and Industrial Policy

Steven Fielding and Jonathan Tonge

Synopsis

This chapter concentrates on how the parties viewed the best way to structure the relationship between government, market and trade unions in order to maximize economic growth. Since 1945 there have been two distinct macro-economic approaches, one associated with the 1945–1951 Labour governments, the other with the Thatcher administrations of the 1980s. Whilst different, both sets of policies were responses to changing perceptions of what was economically and electorally possible. Thus, this chapter emphasizes the extent to which economic policy-making was not an autonomous activity.

The Historical Context: Party Policy 1945–1992

For much of the post-war period, party debates about economic policy were overshadowed by arguments which had been established in the 1930s. In particular, the memory of the interwar recession and the unemployment which followed made policy options largely based on the market politically incredible for nearly a generation. It took the end of the long post-war boom in the 1970s, something which generally discredited the reputation of government economic intervention, to change this situation.

Britain entered World War II with a Conservative-dominated government whose macro-economic policy was informed by *laissez-faire*. Accordingly, government confined itself to keeping finances in balance and maintaining taxes as low as possible. If this meant the jobless rose to three million, as they did in 1932–1933, then so be it. Mass unemployment was a temporary consequence of the free market which, if left alone, would right itself. Consequently, government ignored appeals, often from trade unions, for tax increases to pay for job creation schemes. It thought such palliatives would only damage prospects for recovery. In any case, ministers saw the unions as a potential hazard: if they drove workers' wages too high, they would reduce profits, the driving force behind growth (Thorpe 1992, pp. 70–85).

During the later 1930s, the Labour party developed an alternative to *laissez-faire*; this included taking selected industries into state ownership and, influenced by John Maynard Keynes, using fiscal and monetary measures to manage demand. Labour believed this combination of direct and indirect intervention would increase growth and reduce unemployment. The war caused many Britons to look on Labour's proposals with favour. This was because, after the fall of France, the coalition government was forced to increase the role of the state substantially, to the benefit of all. Government assumed responsibility for vital industries and raised taxes to unprecedented levels: by 1944 unemployment stood at 54,000. The Conservative majority in cabinet accepted the abandonment of *laissez-faire*, but only as a temporary wartime expedient. Even so, under pressure from Labour members, the Cabinet endorsed the 1944 White Paper on Employment Policy. This contained the assurance that government now accepted as one of its 'primary aims' the maintenance of a 'high and stable level of employment' (Jefferys 1991).

Labour's 1945 general election victory ensured that government's wartime economic role was not reduced with the peace. The party's manifesto had argued that only state action could prevent the return of mass unemployment. Accordingly, Clement Attlee's administration extended the state's role in three ways. First, it nationalized 20 per cent of the economy, embracing natural monopolies, such as gas and electricity, and incompetently managed industries, like coal and rail. Labour expected state ownership to increase the efficiency of such concerns. Second, Labour used interest rates and government's ability to tax and spend to manage demand. Keynesian theory stipulated that government could boost sluggish demand and avoid a rise in unemployment by cutting interest rates and taxes whilst increasing spending. By raising interest and tax levels at the same time as cutting government spending, ministers believed they could, if necessary, also prevent demand outrunning domestic capacity and so minimize inflation and a balance of payments crisis. Finally, Labour attempted to improve productivity in private manufacturing and established a number of bodies to allow ministers and representatives from both sides of industry to discuss the matter. This attempt to influence the micro-economy failed: neither employers nor unions appreciated government 'meddling'. Exporters were especially complacent about increasing competitiveness as the war had reduced most of their rivals to rubble.

Popular support for Labour's policies forced the Conservative party to revise its attitude to *laissez-faire*, albeit reluctantly. By the time Winston Churchill returned to power in 1951, Conservatives adhered to the Keynesian macroeconomic approach and accepted the permanence of the nationalized sector. Historians have described this high level of agreement over economic policy as the 'consensus' (Kavanagh and Morris 1994). Yet both parties contained dissidents. Many active Labour members wanted to nationalize more industries so the state would dominate the economy, while within Conservative ranks were those wanting to return all nationalized industries to private hands. Even so, such views were marginalized as Britain in the 1950s enjoyed unprecedented growth and full employment: in such circumstances there seemed little reason to overturn the existing direction of policy.

By the early 1960s, however, it was becoming clear that Britain's economic performance lagged behind that of its newly reconstructed competitors. The Conservative government, led by Harold Macmillan, established the National Economic Development Council (NEDC) in 1962 to encourage employers and union leaders to increase efficiency. However, the NEDC was no more than a talking shop, lacking powers to implement decisions. Macmillan also applied to enter the Common Market, hoping that free access to Europe would stimulate activity. French opposition frustrated his ambition. The 1964–1970 Labour governments, led by Harold Wilson, were even more concerned to improve economic performance. With this in mind, Wilson created the Department of Economic Affairs (DEA), which published a National Plan in 1965. None the less, the DEA's lack of statutory powers meant it soon became irrelevant. Wilson also attempted to join the Common Market but, like the Conservatives, was rebuffed by the French.

During the 1960s both parties became preoccupied with the trade union 'problem' as, according to popular analysis, the unions reduced productivity and so limited growth. Full employment meant labour was in short supply, so unions could confidently push for wage rises. These fuelled inflation, which made exports less competitive; strikes in pursuit of wage increases also disrupted production. From 1945, various governments had attempted to construct voluntary agreements with unions to limit their demands, but with little long-term success. Hence, in 1969, Wilson proposed outlawing certain types of industrial action. Opposing interference in their affairs, the unions frustrated his move by mobilizing opinion within the Labour Party. After winning the 1970 general election, Edward Heath's Conservative government introduced a more draconian Industrial Relations Act, which also met stiff resistance.

By the early 1970s the bipartisan consensus over economic policy was criticized with increasing vehemence within both parties. Circumstances were changing: the long post-war world boom, the basis for much of Britain's well-being, had come to an end. In addition, massive oil price rises hit industry, and competition from overseas was intensifying. Nationalized industries had become a byword for inefficiency, whilst Keynesian demand management failed to prevent rises in both unemployment and inflation.

Wanting a new direction, the Labour left called for a massive extension of nationalization. This was the basis of the Alternative Economic Strategy (AES), which assumed Britain could isolate itself from harmful international developments. The 1974–1979 Labour governments, led by Wilson and, after 1976, James Callaghan, recognized the world economy could not be ignored: they rejected the AES. Instead, the leadership reassessed the merits of demand management, but was unable to take decisive action due to opposition within the party. Labour in power became preoccupied with reducing inflation, which reached 25 per cent in 1975. This it tried to do through a series of agreements with the unions. In return for wage restraint, Labour made various concessions, such as repealing Heath's Industrial Relations Act. Inflation did fall. To many people, however, the unions seemed to dictate terms to government: by 1978, 82 per cent of those polled thought they had too much power. As if to confirm this view, the unions cut loose in 1978–1979 and led a wave of strikes known as the 'winter of discontent'. This ended Callaghan's hopes of winning the 1979 general election.

With Labour divided over macro-economic policy, the initiative lay with Margaret Thatcher, elected Conservative leader in 1975 as the standard bearer of the right. Under her leadership, the Conservatives embraced monetarism, which stipulated that macro-economic policy should be based upon rigid control of the supply of money in the economy. Monetarists claimed that inflation was caused by an increase in the supply of money beyond gains in production. Too much money chased too few goods, increasing the price of those goods.

Conservative macro-economic policy had as its primary goal the curbing of inflation – not maintaining full employment. Thus, in line with monetarist doctrine, government aimed to reduce the broad measure of money supply known as M3, which was based upon notes and coins in circulation, plus bank deposits. The Conservatives attempted to do this through high interest rates, curtailing borrowing, reducing the public sector borrowing requirement and allowing floating exchange rates. Whilst technically novel, however, in many ways monetarism simply confirmed the established prejudices of the Conservative right against state intervention and the unions.

Winning three general elections in a row (those of 1979, 1983 and 1987) gave Thatcher the chance to destroy the old consensus and establish one of her own: she was also helped by considerable North Sea Oil revenues. The main thrust of government policy during the 1980s was twofold. First was withdrawing the state from the economy; specifically, refusing to help failing businesses and privatizing nationalized industries (see table 1.1). Second was reforming the labour market, principally by legislating to weaken the unions, and so promoting a more 'flexible' labour force, not one allegedly entrenched behind various workplace restrictive practices (see table 1.2).

By increasing interest rates and reducing government spending, Thatcher in her first years of power exacerbated the impact of the recession. This, together with her failure to control the price of sterling – which rose as a result of its new status as an oil currency – made exports, already uncompetitive, too expensive. Arguing that her policy would weed out only weak businesses, Thatcher also destroyed what might have otherwise been viable concerns. Unemployment trebled in 1979–1981, reaching 13.3 per cent of the total workforce, whilst gross domestic product (GDP) fell by 2.5 per cent, largely the result of a collapse of the country's export-based manufacturing capacity, which slumped by 25 per cent. As a result, the prime minister came under intense pressure to intervene to save jobs. Recalling the lessons of Heath's 1970–1974 government, she rejected such calls. Elected in 1970, similarly pledged to reduce state intervention, Heath made a U-turn within a year to save various major companies from going to the wall. In 1971 he even felt it necessary to nationalize Rolls-Royce. Despite abandoning his original policy, Heath's efforts made little impression on the economy and the Conservatives lost power in 1974 (Coopey and Woodward 1997). In contrast, Thatcher stuck to her guns and sacked any Cabinet critics.

Table 1.1 *Main sales of nationalized industries 1979–1996*

Year(s)	Industry / company	Amount raised (£billion)
1984–1995	British Telecom	14.2
1990–1996	Electricity companies	13.1
1979–1988	British Petroleum	8.1
1986–1992	British Gas	5.3
1989–1992	Regional water companies	3.4
1988–1990	British Steel	2.4
1987–1988	British Airports Authority	1.2
1982–1986	Britoil	1.1
1987–1989	Rolls Royce	1.0
1981	Cable and Wireless	1.0
1984–1985	Trustee Savings Bank	1.0

Source: HM Government 1996; Jones 1997; Lee 1994

Table 1.2 *Significant trade union legislation 1979–1993*

Act	Main effects
Employment Act 1980	New closed shops restricted; public funding for secret strike ballots; no legal immunity for secondary strike action
Employment Act 1982	Existing closed shops restricted; political strikes prohibited
Trade Union Act 1984	Secret ballots required for strikes; secret ballots needed for political levy
Employment Act 1988	Secret ballots required for election of union officials; dismissal of workers for not being union members illegal; union disciplining of members who decline to join strikes illegal
Employment Act 1990	Secondary strike action illegal; closed shop abolished
Trade Union Act 1992	Internal union elections more frequent
Trade Union Act 1993	Unions to give employer notice of strike ballot; further restriction of union ability to discipline members

Source: Roberts 1996; Farnham and Lupton 1994; Coxall and Robins 1994

One reason for Thatcher's success was that popular attitudes had changed since the early 1970s. Many voters were now convinced that a temporary period of mass unemployment was required to help the economy become more efficient. Under the Conservatives, however, mass unemployment proved endemic. Reaching 3.2 million in 1982, the jobless figures only briefly dipped below 2 million – 8 per cent of the workforce – in the late 1980s (see table 1.3). The suspicion was that this suited Thatcher. Unemployment undermined worker resistance to labour market reform and minimized wage-driven inflation. The defeat of the 1984–1985 miners' strike symbolized how much weaker the unions had become.

Table 1.3   *Unemployment under Thatcher 1979–1989*

Year	Unemployment (% of workforce)
1979	5.0
1980	6.4
1981	9.9
1982	11.7
1983	12.2
1984	11.8
1985	11.4
1986	11.4
1987	10.3
1988	8.2
1989	7.1

Source: OECD

By the late 1980s, the economy appeared to be performing well: some commentators stated that Thatcher had reversed its long-term decline. Many in work also did well under the Conservatives. Due to cuts in direct tax, disposable incomes increased, although subsequent rises in indirect taxation meant the overall tax burden remained largely unchanged. In addition, shares in privatized companies were sold at preferential rates to millions of small investors, who made quick profits. Yet the overall Thatcher effect was often overstated: growth remained in line with long-established trends whilst many improvements in productivity were due to the contraction of the labour force rather than higher investment. At the time of her third election triumph in 1987, industrial output was lower than that of 1979. Moreover, Thatcher's ambition to reduce public expenditure as a percentage of GDP was frustrated by mass unemployment: in 1980 it stood at 43.2 per cent; by 1995 it was 42.5 per cent (Marsh and Rhodes 1992).

After becoming Conservative leader in 1990, John Major was confronted with the question of whether to consolidate or continue the Thatcher 'revolution'. Whilst his rhetoric sometimes sounded distinct, economically Major was at one with his predecessor. The principle difference was one of context: Major faced a global recession, deepened in Britain by the late 1980s consumer boom engineered by chancellor Nigel Lawson. These difficulties were compounded by membership of the exchange rate mechanism (ERM). Britain had finally entered the European Economic Community (EEC) in 1973; since that point, there had been increasing pressure from within the community to standardize practices to reduce barriers to free trade. Created in 1979, the ERM was an outgrowth of this, the object being to reduce variation in currency values, something which could harm trade between members. Britain joined the ERM in 1990 whilst Thatcher was still prime minister.

The ERM represented the first step towards a single European currency. Members of the European Union (EU), as the EEC was now termed, fixed national exchange rates in relation to a weighted average of European currencies. Whilst linked to each other, currencies could increase or decrease their value – but only by a maximum of 6 per cent. The narrowness of this banding would cause Major terrible problems after the 1992 election. In joining the ERM, some Conservatives believed they had secured increased competition and low inflation. Within the rules of the ERM, the 'soft option' of currency devaluation was replaced by tighter controls upon prices and costs. The value of sterling would be preserved if necessary by high interest rates, which would also cure inflation. In contrast, devaluation risked higher import costs, leading to price rises.

Not all Conservatives were happy over entry to the ERM. In the late 1980s, Lawson had shadowed the Deutschmark as a precursor to entry. Thatcher and her economic adviser Alan Walters were sceptical over the value of ERM membership, the delay in entry contributing to Lawson's resignation in October 1989. Norman Lamont, chancellor from 1990 to 1993, was – in private – also unconvinced. The constraints imposed by the ERM, including tight controls upon public expenditure in addition to currency regulation, ensured that Britain's recession in the early 1990s was deepened and prolonged.

Labour strategists saw no need to change tack with the advent of Major: the party had undergone a significant modification of policy since the 1987 general election. Labour had fought the 1983 election on the AES and, as a result (many thought), suffered a critical loss of support. The new leader, Neil Kinnock, strived to moderate policy to win back votes: internal opposition meant Labour had to lose another election to give his argument sufficient force. The resulting policy review – conducted between 1988 and 1991 – underpinned Labour's subsequent approach to the economy.

The review marked Labour's move from direct state intervention and put a large question mark against demand management. It accepted the market was 'essential' to efficiency (Labour Party 1989, p. 10). Whilst the state retained a role, its function was 'not to replace the market but to ensure that markets work *properly*' (Labour Party 1992, p. 11). Government was to confine itself to creating a framework to foster investment and competitiveness through creating a skilled workforce and building an adequate infrastructure. The review also confirmed that privatized industries would not be renationalized. Instead, Labour promised to subject them to more controls, beefing up the powers of those regulatory bodies established by the Conservatives but widely seen as too weak. Similarly, Labour did not propose to reverse Conservative union legislation, although it did undertake to guarantee certain individual rights at work.

Some saw the review as an attempt to win votes by adopting Conservative policies. Thatcher had, after all, shown that many voters disliked paying high rates of direct tax, saw the unions in negative terms and believed the state to be inefficient. If Labour were to win power again, it needed the support of such people. Yet there was another stimulus. Nationalization and demand management had failed to promote growth and efficiency. Moreover, John Smith, the shadow chancellor, argued that the power of global capitalism had grown since the 1970s. Thus, if a future Labour government followed the Keynesian path it would not improve growth; instead, the international markets would cause the currency to collapse. Consequently, Labour had to embrace the new macro-economic orthodoxy, which had the pursuit of low inflation as the primary goal, or fail to achieve anything.

Whilst Conservative success in the 1992 general election was unexpected, it should not have been. Despite a deep recession, the party was still seen as most competent to run the economy, whilst labour was popularly associated with unnecessarily high taxation. The latter perception was encouraged by Conservative propaganda, which warned of Kinnock's 'tax bombshell' should he win power. This 'bombshell' exploded when Smith announced Labour intended to raise the top rate of tax from 40 to 50 pence and increase the national insurance contributions of top earners to fund improvements in pensions and child benefit. Smith claimed this would detrimentally effect only 20 per cent of tax payers. However, he was unable to persuade voters of this, a failure which helped lose his party the election (Butler and Kavanagh 1992).

An Unusual Climate: Continuity and Rupture 1992–1997

Despite winning his own mandate, Major stayed true to the macro-economic priorities established by his predecessor: his governments remained committed to low inflation, cutting taxes, reducing spending, privatization and labour market reform.

Unfortunately for Major, Thatcher had privatized the most profitable concerns. Moreover, whilst few called for the return of state ownership, by the 1990s privatization no longer seemed a panacea. Consumers complained of price rises and poor service, whilst 'fat cat' directors were pilloried in the press. Major still sought to sell off what he could. This was a reflection of the prime minister's own dedication to reducing the state but also, in the light of the recession, his desperate need to raise funds. None of his privatizations generated public excitement; in fact, most were unpopular. Thus, although he sold British Coal to private investors, after the 1984–1985 miners' strike it was of little significance: in 1979 it had employed 235,000; by 1996 this number had fallen to 17,500. The troubled sale of British Rail was described by even one Conservative MP as a 'privatization too far'. When plans were announced to privatize the Post Office – which had always been run by the state – such was the outcry that Major withdrew them.

Trade union reform was also much less popular under Major. During the 1980s the unions had suffered a massive decline in influence: between 1979 and 1996 membership fell from 13.3 to 7.3 million; from covering just over half the labour force, unions by the mid-1990s accounted for only one-third. Working days lost through strikes were, in the 1980s, half those of the 1970s. Thus, most voters no longer saw unions as a significant cause of Britain's economic troubles. Despite this, after 1992, the government introduced one further Act (see table 1.2 above). One new reason for this continued enthusiasm was purely political. Knowing many voters in 1992 saw Labour as dominated by the unions, the Conservatives hoped further legislation would embarrass their rivals. If the Labour leadership opposed these measures, it would confirm voter suspicions; if it accepted them, they might arouse union dissent within the party's ranks.

Another aspect of labour market reform – training policy – marked a departure from previous practice and indicated the new significance of microeconomic policy. Whilst a 'skills revolution' had been promised by the Conservatives in the late 1980s, not much had been done. By the early 1990s, however, the belief that British workers were uniquely underskilled had become widespread; so had the idea that a serious skills shortage was imminent and that this would deeply impair economic performance. Thus, training was now viewed by both Labour and the Conservatives as vital. Major appreciated the need to take the initiative on this matter; he also saw a further opportunity to reduce the role of government. For all her rhetoric, Thatcher had mitigated unemployment with limited but still state-funded job creation schemes coordinated by the Manpower Service Commission (Tonge 1997). After 1992, however, Major ensured that responsibility for improving workforce skills was ceded to training and enterprise councils dominated by the private sector.

Further privatization and labour market reform paled into insignificance compared to the consequences of sterling's exit from the ERM. Sterling had entered the ERM worth 2.95 Deutschmarks, a value seen by many as unsustainable. Thus, within weeks of Major's re-election, sterling was subject to pressure from international currency dealers, who did not believe it could remain at that level. This became a self-fulfilling prophecy. When such speculators sold their sterling holdings, the currency soon hit the bottom of its ERM banding. This forced Lamont to spend as much as $38 billion buying back sterling so that it did not fall below the permissible level. He also increased interest rates, at one point twice in a day, to make sterling more attractive to investors (Stephens 1996). Despite these measures, in September 1992 Lamont was forced to devalue and so leave the ERM. In attempting to avoid this outcome, government funds had been badly depleted, whilst high interest rates undermined the country's economic recovery.

Being forced out of the ERM damaged the Conservatives politically, as the public ceased to see them as more competent to manage the economy than Labour. Moreover, in order to make good the now huge deficit in finances, Lamont raised taxes in his March 1993 budget. Thus, having warned of a Labour tax 'bombshell' in 1992, the Conservatives detonated their own in 1993, further reducing their credibility. Even Lamont's dismissal failed to change popular perceptions. Ironically, leaving the ERM gave Lamont's successor, Kenneth Clarke, greater discretion to quicken recovery from the recession: it also made exports cheaper (Wickham-Jones 1997).

That Labour benefited from the political consequences of the ERM debacle was incongruous, as the party had supported entry. Had Kinnock won the election, Labour would undoubtedly have found itself in a similar position to the Conservatives'. None the less, Kinnock had not won, something many in the leadership blamed on the party's tax plans. Thus, after Smith became leader, his successor as shadow chancellor, Gordon Brown, quietly buried the 1992 proposals.

With Smith's death in 1994 and the election of Tony Blair, Labour experienced what appeared to be a further shift in economic policy. Yet, although Blair described his party as 'New Labour', his approach had been anticipated by the policy review. Defeat in 1992 simply meant that Labour moved further away from the state and towards the market. Undoubtedly, Blair was much more clear in following the logic of the review's implications and had no problem in publicly praising the market. None the less, the main novelty in New Labour's approach to the economy was in presentation more than policy.

This was exemplified in October 1994 when, wanting to emphasize that Labour had changed, Blair successfully called for Clause IV of the party's constitution to be revised. First drafted in 1918, this clause committed the party to extend the 'common ownership of the means of production, distribution and exchange'. Many considered these words meant Labour was pledged to extending state economic ownership. Yet, in practice, this was never the case: even the nationalizations of the 1940s were undertaken for pragmatic reasons. Whilst rarely having any impact on policy, the clause, none the less, associated Labour with what was by the 1980s a generally unpopular economic approach. Blair's own Clause 4 promised the party would foster a 'dynamic economy', partly based on the 'enterprise of the market'. This had already been established in the policy review: the problem was that few voters believed it. What Blair did was shout from the rooftops that Labour had moved from state intervention, so that even the most obtuse voter appreciated the fact. Similarly, in May 1995 Blair delivered the annual Mais lecture, in which he fully committed Labour to macroeconomic orthodoxy (Blair 1996, pp. 75–97). Smith had done this whilst shadow chancellor, but had not made sufficient impact: Blair made sure he did not make the same mistake.

Both Blair and Brown considered that if Labour were to win power it had to convince voters that it was 'safe' on tax. After debating whether it was possible to raise the top rate of tax, they erred on the side of caution. Thus, in January 1997 Brown promised that Labour would neither increase the basic rate of direct tax, increase its top limit nor raise VAT during its term in office. He also pledged to follow Conservative spending plans for his first two years in power (Jones 1997, pp. 73–111).

The 1997 General Election: Campaign and Aftermath

The 1997 general election campaign revealed little new about either of the two parties' economic policies. Labour had taken advantage of Major's reluctance to call an early election by publishing a draft manifesto in the summer of 1996; as noted above, details of the party's tax and spending commitments had also been spelt out in the new year (Fielding 1997). Although confirming that Labour and the Conservatives agreed about macro-economic policy, the campaign re-emphasized the extent to which they differed elsewhere.

The Conservatives entered the campaign with the slogan 'Britain is Booming. Don't Let Labour Blow It.' According to various criteria, the economy was performing well: the GDP had increased by 3 per cent during the previous twelve months; exports to the EU were at an all-time high; incomes were rising at twice the rate of prices; and the number of those seeking work and claiming benefit was at its lowest point in six years. Yet exit from the ERM, and the tax rises which followed, meant the Conservatives gained little credit for this (Cowley 1997). Thus it was Labour which, by 1997, was popularly regarded as the party most able to manage the economy.

Desperate to improve their position, Conservative MPs had called on Clarke to cut direct taxes. However, the chancellor realized that any large reductions immediately prior to an election would be thought cynical. In any case, millions continued to be in receipt of unemployment and welfare benefits – the price of Conservative labour flexibility. This meant there was little scope to cut taxes, as government borrowing remained at over £30 billion. Thus, in his November 1996 budget, Clarke only reduced the basic rate by 1p – and that by imposing spending limits on government departments many thought unsustainable.

In the campaign itself, the Conservatives largely reiterated themes first developed by Thatcher twenty years before: thus, voters were reminded of the merits of low tax, limited government and weak unions. The party made much of contentious evidence which suggested that, by pursuing this trinity, Britain had become the enterprise centre of Europe. Labour was said to threaten this competitive advantage because of its 'instinctive' preference for higher taxes and big government as well as its close links to the unions (Conservative Party 1997). In contrast, Labour confirmed its acceptance of the need for market competitiveness but criticized the Conservative vision of labour flexibility as too narrow. This, the party argued, had created an insecure, low-skilled and badly paid workforce which was itself an impediment to growth. Whilst Labour also advocated a flexible labour force, and so confirmed it would not repeal even the most recent union legislation, it stated that flexibility was not enough: what was required was 'flexibility plus'. This meant government had to promote a better-educated and skilled workforce, encourage investment in both infrastructure and research, and legislate on measures such as the minimum wage to ensure 'fair' treatment at work. These policies would all promote a more efficient market (Labour Party 1997).

The Conservative assertion that, despite appearances, Labour under Blair remained a high-taxation party tied to state intervention strained credibility. None the less, Conservatives questioned Brown's commitment to following the Major government's spending plans, as these proceeded from the assumption that £1.5 billion would be raised by a further round of privatization. Their question was: would Labour also privatize to fill this gap or, instead, raise taxes? Brown confirmed that, if necessary, he would privatize; Labour no longer had a principled attachment to the public sector. Indeed, Labour's pragmatism was a central theme of the party's campaign: unlike 'Old Labour', the party was now ready to accept the market, if efficacious. Labour speakers asserted that the Conservatives were now the dogmatists tied, for ideological reasons only, to market solutions to economic problems. This approach pleased many disillusioned 1992 Conservative voters. However, it increased tensions in Labour's own ranks. Many members had reluctantly accepted that Labour would not renationalize industries sold off since 1979: that their leaders might actually pursue their own privatization programme seemed incredible.

The Conservatives also did their best to discredit Blair's claim that Labour was now the 'entrepreneur's champion'. They attacked the long-standing proposal that, under Labour, workers would be able legally to force employers to recognize their representation by a trade union if a majority of employees voted for it. As they continued to believe unions were an enemy of the market, Conservative speakers argued that as this measure would increase union membership, it would harm efficiency. In fact, the party promised to weaken unions further through legislation under which they could be sued for instigating strikes in essential services which caused 'excessive' disruption. The Conservatives also criticized Labour's commitment to introducing a minimum wage, because they believed it would reduce the number of jobs for low-paid workers. Blair countered by stating that, even with Labour's reforms, Britain would still have the most restrictive union laws of any western country.

That a flexible workforce gave Britain a competitive advantage over the rest of Europe was a central Conservative argument against the Social Chapter of the Maastricht Treaty. Major believed his opt-out, secured in 1991, had been crucial to Britain's subsequent recovery from recession. That Labour proposed to set this opt-out aside was presented as another reason why a Blair government would endanger competitiveness. Yet, as the Social Chapter's main provisions merely involved establishing workers' councils in larger firms and awarding – unpaid – extended parental leave, this claim convinced few. British-based employers with factories in mainland Europe saw no reason to fear the chapter. Moreover, Labour pledged to resist any further moves to increase regulation emanating from the EU.

Whilst united against the Social Chapter, Conservatives were badly split over another EU issue: economic and monetary union (EMU). The party's official line was that it would 'wait and see' whether to join the European single currency after it had been formed in 1999. This was designed to minimize dividing the likes of Clarke, who favoured entry, from many of his colleagues, who did not. Opponents of EMU argued that, once in the system, the value of sterling would be determined by German bankers, who would thereby control Britain's destiny. Proponents argued that the value of sterling was already influenced by speculators – they had forced Britain's exit from the ERM. Moreover, EMU promised currency stability within the EU, which would promote trade and encourage growth. Such differences went deep, so deep in fact that 190 Conservative candidates contravened party policy by announcing their opposition to participation under any circumstances.

Whilst the Labour leadership appeared more positive about the single currency, it had also adopted a 'wait and see' policy. Moreover, appreciating the unpopularity of the issue amongst voters, Blair, like Major, was also committed to a referendum before entry. One reason for this was that some Labour MPs opposed entry: they were concerned that, as membership entailed reducing government deficit to 3 per cent of GDP, the state would no longer be able to mitigate the impact of a recession. Even so, Labour's dissidents disavowed public demonstrations of opposition because they did not want to endanger their party's election chances.

Due to these internal differences, the ERM – despite its decisive significance for the future management of the domestic economy – was not a major matter of inter-party debate. Another factor was that both leaderships tacitly recognized that, once the single currency was established successfully, Britain could not afford to remain too long outside it.

The sheer scale of the Conservatives' eventual rout meant that no one policy could be blamed for their loss of power. Certainly, Major's replacement as leader, William Hague, gave no early indication that he intended to overhaul economic policy as part of his 'Fresh Start'. This impression was confirmed by the subsequent annual Conservative conference, where debate focused on social matters rather than economic affairs. There was one important exception: hoping to end the damage caused by the issue, Hague promised not to join the single currency within the next ten years. Whilst this did not especially please the likes of Clarke, by now on his party's backbenches, in the wake of the election. Conservative Euro-enthusiasts did not make much of a public fuss. In any case, many thought Hague was not conceding much: given Labour's huge majority, few Conservatives expected him to be prime minister until after 2007, if ever.

Labour in power followed policies mapped out by Blair before the election: it charted what he termed a 'third way' between market freedom and state intervention. This was exemplified by the July 1997 budget's mix of liberalization and interventionism.

Brown's first measure as chancellor, announced within days of Labour's victory, was to give the Bank of England 'operational responsibility' to set interest rates. This reduced government influence to an extent even Thatcher had not countenanced and was described by Blair as 'the biggest decision in economic policy making since the war'. Brown's object was to facilitate long-term economic stability, which Labour deemed vital to growth: interest rates influenced inflation and economic activity in general. Hitherto, all chancellors had set rates; in so doing, they had taken political factors into account. For example, prior to the election, Clarke had been criticized for not raising interest rates to reduce consumer demand because it would have been electorally unpopular. Brown, therefore, claimed that giving responsibility to the bank meant rates would become 'free of political manipulation'. Thus, the measure was intended to encourage potential investors to put their money into the British economy. None the less, Brown retained the ability to set the annual inflation target: the bank's freedom was thereby constrained. However, many Labour members despaired that their government had abandoned such an important means of influencing economic activity. Others welcomed the move as a step towards a fully independent central bank, something most successful economies possessed.

In the most obvious demonstration of continuity with the Major government, it was confirmed that, in order to keep to Conservative spending limits, Labour would proceed with the privatization of the Benefits Agency medical service and the Department of Social Security's property estate. It was similarly revealed that consideration was being given to selling a majority share in the London tube to the private sector. Labour also announced that it would revive the Private Finance Initiative (PFI), started under Lamont. The PFI's object was to use private capital to fund state projects. Thus the private sector could build a hospital on the understanding that it would then be leased to the state. Labour saw this as central to its ambition to build more schools and hospitals without raising taxes.

Labour's commitment to the free market was especially clear with regard to the EU. Whilst the new government signed the Social Chapter, Blair told fellow European socialists: 'We must be competitive and, to be competitive, knowledge, skills, technology and enterprise are the keys, not rigidity, unnecessary regulation and old-styled intervention' (*Guardian*, 6 June 1997). Consequently, at the June EU summit, Blair opposed the newly elected French socialist government's attempt to reduce the number of the unemployed in the EU through increasing labour market regulation. Yet, while superficially similar, Labour's notion of labour flexibility was distinct from that of the Conservatives. Under Blair, policy was to 'empower' workers, to give them sufficient opportunities to accumulate the necessary skills to increase their employability and so prosper in the global market. This was why education was the government's first priority.

Labour's 1997 manifesto had confirmed that no privatized industry would be taken back into state hands, even the most recent case of rail. This had much dismayed many union leaders and others in the party. Once in office, however, Labour ministers urged the agencies appointed to regulate privatized concerns to use their powers more enthusiastically. Some believed there was a case for legislation to increase regulation of the utilities to protect consumers and the environment further. John Prescott, in charge of transport, also called for legislation to increase the supervision of the rail network, so he could stop its fragmentation and foster a more efficient, integrated public transport system. Moreover, at Labour's 1997 conference, there was talk that if any troubled rail franchisees became bankrupt, Prescott would allow the publicly owned British Rail to tender for their leases, along with other private companies.

The Brown budget's most significant direct intervention in the economy was his 'welfare-to-work' package, funded by a £5.2b 'windfall' tax levied on privatized companies. This tax was popular with an electorate which resented 'fat cat' directors and chief executives who had prospered as a result of leaving the public sector. The key element was the provision of subsidized jobs and training or education to 250,000 18–24-year-olds who had been without work for six months or more. The levy was also to finance employment subsidies for some older people unemployed for over two years; in addition it was to underwrite childcare and training for single parents seeking work. The object of this package was to enable individuals to obtain skills and experience to equip them better for the job market. Whilst the Conservatives had come to appreciate the need for a better-trained workforce, they strongly criticized this measure, in particular the fact that it was funded by an increase in tax.

'Welfare to work' was a short-term measure to improve the situation of specific groups. Labour's long-term economic ambition, which would make such interventions unnecessary, was to increase investment in manufacturing so it would become more competitive. This had been the aim of all post-war Labour governments, but none had been able to encourage sufficiently higher levels of investment. To facilitate these, Brown abolished the advance tax credit on dividends; this removed an important financial advantage which accrued to shareholders. Brown's object was to encourage companies to retain more of their profits as investment rather than using them as dividends paid to shareholders.

According to Brown, Labour's economic objects in the late 1990s were the same as Attlee's in the 1940s: 'high and stable levels of employment'. There were, however, new constraints on policy, including public hostility to tax and the power of the global markets, which meant Labour had to adopt more 'modern' – that is, more market-based – means to achieve the same goals. Thus, at Labour's 1997 conference, the new chancellor promised 'employment opportunities for all' by the twenty-first century. Others thought Brown's 'modern' means would prevent the party from achieving its traditional end. Many Labour members and others remained sceptical and considered that far more state intervention, financed by higher tax, was required. In contrast, Conservatives objected that Labour's policies involved too much government meddling in the country's economic affairs. Only time will tell whether Labour in power can confound such critics.

Conclusion: The Impact of Party Policy

Post-war economic policy-making has been largely determined by the prevailing orthodoxy of the day, which, in turn, followed contemporary developments in world capitalism. In the decades following 1945, economic orthodoxy was influenced by the belief that government could beneficially manipulate market activity; latterly it has been coloured by the conviction that, if the market is to prosper, it has to be left alone. The former doctrine appeared credible after World War II because 1930s *laissez-faire* was thought to have failed whilst state intervention had saved Britain from military defeat. The world boom which followed 1945 created the circumstances for success. The stock of those advocating *laissez-faire* rose in the 1970s as a result of the apparent inability of both direct and indirect state intervention to deal with the onset of an international recession.

Parties were never, however, ciphers for the economic orthodoxy of the day: ideology and the character of electoral support also played a role. To simplify, Labour was predisposed to see the state as superior, whilst the Conservatives thought big government imperilled freedom. Labour's close links with the unions encouraged it to view unemployment as anathema; the Conservatives, a more middle-class party, saw inflation as the main enemy. Yet if a party were persuaded that its prejudices compromised electoral success, they could, eventually, be reassessed. After 1945 the Conservative leadership accepted state intervention in time to win the 1951 election. Whilst in the 1980s Labour was reluctant to embrace the market, this had, none the less, occurred by 1997.

In addition, party policy has made a difference. By simply holding office a party can give the impression that, as Thatcher once said, 'there is no alternative' to its policies. This influence could sometimes be felt decades later. During World War II, the Conservatives distanced themselves from unqualified *laissez-faire*. None the less, if Labour had not been elected in 1945, the nationalization of key industries – which lasted until the 1980s – would probably not have occurred. Similarly, in 1976 Labour prime minister Callaghan questioned the utility of demand management. However, it was the Conservative victory of 1979 which decisively shifted government policy in the direction of the market. By holding office until 1997 the Conservatives privatized, reformed the labour market, and reduced direct taxation to an extent beyond the imagining of even the most stalwart of 1970s Thatcherites.

Whilst in the 1990s economic policy proceeds from the belief that government should do much less than once thought, there have been constant constraints on policy. The international economy has always exerted a powerful influence over domestic affairs. It is, in fact, arguable that demand management made a marginal contribution to Britain's economic growth: the main factor was the world boom. The value of sterling has always been of crucial consequence, as it dictates the price of imports and exports. Yet governments have never been able to determine its international rate fully: Major's was but the third administration since 1945 to be forced to devalue the currency due to speculation.

Such pressures are now greater than ever. Insulation from currency speculation dramatically diminished after the abolition of exchange controls in the early 1980s. Moreover, international competition is significantly keener than it once was. In 1963 Wilson warned that, if productivity did not improve, Britain would be surpassed by the likes of Germany and Japan. Britain having long been overtaken by those two economies, during the 1980s the 'Asian Tigers' roared over the horizon.

Since 1973 Europe has figured ever larger as an influence on policy-making. Labour and Conservatives supported Britain's entry into the EEC, hoping it would stimulate domestic growth. The pursuit of a single European market with no barriers to trade has meant that various indigenous economic practices have become subject to standardization by Brussels. Whilst the Conservatives resisted common regulation of the labour market, even they joined the ERM. The proposed single currency will do much more than simply reduce variations in currency values. However, it is debatable, given the state of the international currency markets, whether government's ability to influence the value of sterling will be much reduced if Britain joins. In or out of the single currency, Britain's economic sovereignty is already greatly compromised.

By the early 1990s both Labour and the Conservatives accepted the need for macro-economic stability based on low inflation in conjunction with 'prudent' government spending and taxation. They hope that this steadiness – rather than direct state intervention and demand management – will produce sustainable growth. Once policy-makers had aspired to manage the economy; now both parties recoil from such a grand objective, considering that, in the light of present orthodoxy, improving supply in the micro-economy is where government can do most good.

In particular, attention now rests on the nature of the domestic labour market. Whilst not subject to globalization, the labour market can be directly influenced by government action in a variety of ways. Moreover, the state of the labour market is also seen as crucial to Britain's future success within the international economy. Conservative policy since 1979 has focused on taking government out of the labour market, in order to reduce regulation of employment conditions and deny unions the capacity to challenge employers' authority. The result has been an increase in unemployment and the proliferation of low-paid,

Table 1.4   *Economic growth under Labour and Conservative governments 1952–1989*

Period	Party in power	Average growth in GDP per year (%)
1952–1964	Conservative	2.98
1965–1970	Labour	2.65
1971–1974	Conservative	2.60
1975–1979	Labour	2.02
1980–1989	Conservative	2.27
1952–1989		2.57

Source: Johnson 1991

unprotected, part-time work. The Conservatives hoped thereby to create a pool of 'flexible' workers which would attract foreign investors. Under Blair at least, Labour came to see this flexibility as a virtue, but not in itself. The party won power in May 1997 pledged to invest billions in training, education and workplace experience. This is to ensure the workforce becomes skilled as well as flexible and so able to command higher wages and enjoy better security – to the benefit of the economy as a whole.

The focus of contemporary economic policy within both parties is more modest than hitherto. None the less, it may be that, having lowered their sights, policy makers might, actually, achieve something of worth. It is salutary to note that, whether under a regime of demand management or *laissez-faire* (see table 1.4), Britain's trend rate of growth has remained much the same – and significantly lower than that of its major competitors.

Chronology of Significant Developments: April 1992 to October 1997

September 1992	Britain forced to leave the ERM
March 1993	Chancellor Norman Lamont increases taxes in wake of ERM exit
May 1993	Lamont replaced as chancellor by Kenneth Clarke
October 1994	Tony Blair calls for the revision of Labour's Clause IV
May 1995	In his Mais lecture, Blair fully commits Labour to macroeconomic orthodoxy
November 1996	Clarke reduces the basic rate of tax by 1p to 23p
January 1997	Gordon Brown, Labour's shadow chancellor, promises not to raise direct tax and to adhere to Conservative spending limits
April 1997	During the election campaign, both parties confirm they will hold a referendum before entering the European single currency

May 1997	New Labour government grants Bank of England the power to set interest rates
June 1997	Labour ends Britain's opt-out from the European Social Chapter
July 1997	Chancellor Gordon Brown presents Labour's first budget for almost two decades: he introduces a 'welfare-to-work' scheme financed by a windfall tax

References

Blair, T. 1996, *New Britain*, London: Fourth Estate.

Butler, D. and Kavanagh, D. 1992, *The British General Election of 1992*, London: Macmillan.

Conservative Party 1997, 'You Can Only Be Sure with the Conservatives', London: Conservative Central Office.

Coopey, R. and Woodward, N. 1997, *Britain in the 1970s*, London: UCL Press.

Cowley, P. 1997, 'The Conservative Party: decline and fall' in Geddes, A. and Tonge, J. (eds), *Labour's Landslide*, Manchester: Manchester University Press.

Coxall, B. and Robins, L. 1994, *Contemporary British Politics*, London: Macmillan.

Farnham, D. and Lupton, C. 1994, 'Employment relations and training policy' in Savage, S., Atkinson, R. and Robbins, L. (eds), *Public Policy in Britain*, London: St Martins.

Fielding, S. 1997, 'Labour's path to power' in Geddes, A. and Tonge, J. (eds), *Labour's Landslide*, Manchester: Manchester University Press.

HM Government 1996, *Public Expenditure Statistical Analysis*, London: HMSO.

Jefferys, K. 1991, *The Churchill Coalition and Wartime Politics, 1940–45*, Manchester: Manchester University Press.

Johnson, C. 1991, *The Economy Under Mrs Thatcher, 1979–1990*, Harmondsworth: Penguin.

Jones, B. (ed.) 1997, *Politics UK*, Hemel Hempstead: Prentice Hall.

Jones, N. 1997, *Campaign 1997*, London: Indigo.

Kavanagh, D. and Morris, P. 1994, *Consensus Politics from Attlee to Thatcher*, Oxford: Blackwell.

Labour Party 1989, 'Meet the Challenge, Make the Change', London: Labour Party.

Labour Party 1992, 'It's Time to Get Britain Working Again'.

Labour Party 1997, *New Labour: Because Britain Deserves Better*, London: Labour Party.

Lee, G. 1994, 'Privatisation' in Jones, B. (ed.), *Political Issues in Britain Today*, Manchester: Manchester University Press.

Marsh, D. and Rhodes, R. 1992, 'The implementation gap: explaining policy change and continuity' in Marsh, D. and Rhodes, R. (eds) *Implementing Thatcherite Policies*, Buckingham: Open University Press.

Roberts, D. (ed.) 1996, *British Politics in Focus*, Ormskirk: Causeway.

Stephens, P. 1996, *Politics and the Pound*, London: Macmillan.

Thorpe, A. 1992, *Britain in the 1930s*, Oxford: Blackwell.

Tonge, J. 1997, 'Britain' in Compston, H. (ed.), *The New Politics of Unemployment*, London: Routledge.

Wickham-Jones, M. 1997, 'The management of the economy' in Geddes, A. and Tonge, J. (eds), *Labour's Landslide*, Manchester: Manchester University Press.

Guide to Further Reading

For a solid survey of the British economy, see S. Pollard, *The Development of the British Economy, 1914–1990* (London: Edward Arnold, 1992, 4th edn). A good analysis of Labour's changing attitude to the economy is provided by N. Thompson, *Political Economy and the Labour Party* (London: UCL Press, 1996). A stimulating account of Thatcher's 'revolution' in Conservative policy is found in A. Gamble, *The Free Economy and the Strong State* (London: Macmillan, 1988). For information about the Major era, see W. Bonefeld, A. Brown and P. Bunham, *A Major Crisis?* (Aldershot: Dartmouth, 1995).

2 | Europe and Foreign Affairs

Fergus Carr

Synopsis

This chapter examines party policy with regard to Europe and foreign affairs. The analysis concentrates upon Europe as relations with the European Union (EU) and the question of European integration have come to dominate the recent political agenda. The issue of Europe will, however, be addressed within the wider context of British foreign policy.

The Historical Context: Party Policy 1945–1992

Elite consensus 1945–1960

Winston Churchill saw British foreign policy in global terms, having three 'circles' or spheres of interest: Europe; the British Empire and Commonwealth; and the Atlantic relationship. As George has observed, 'this doctrine, with perhaps some variation in the relative weight placed on the various elements, became part of the British post-war consensus on policy' (1991, p. 34). Although the notion of consensus has been subject to critique (see Butler 1993), if it is defined as 'a broad area of agreement between the leaderships of both main parties when they are in office' (Seldon 1994, p. 513) then consensus rather than discontinuity does mark the development of British foreign policy.

Bevin, the post-war Labour foreign secretary, sought the strongest possible Anglo-American cooperation in order to retain a world role for Britain and to secure Washington's support for British foreign policy in general. The establishment of the North Atlantic Treaty Organization (NATO) in 1949 was a triumph for Bevin and cemented the Atlantic orientation of policy for successive British governments. The United States looked to Britain to play a leading role in the European Recovery Programme and in the establishment of an integrated economic community in Western Europe. Bevin resisted Washington's integrationist agenda and sought to promote a model of inter-state consultation and cooperation in the Western Union and Council of Europe. The Labour government rejected participation in the Schuman Plan of 1950, which led to the creation of the European Coal and Steel Community (ECSC) consisting of France, West Germany, Italy and the Benelux countries.

In 1951 Winston Churchill returned to office. The European policies of the new Conservative government were identical to those of its Labour predecessor. Eden, as foreign secretary, followed Bevin in his distrust of supranationalism and support for transatlantic policies. The British government resisted participation in the ill-fated European Defence Community and rejected inclusion in the 'relaunch' of Europe which followed the Messina Conference of 1955. Britain proposed free trade rather than the customs union favoured by the Six, and intergovernmentalism rather than supranationalism. The result was that the Six created the European Economic Community (EEC) in 1957 and Britain went on to found the rival European Free Trade Association (EFTA) in 1959.

Conversion to Europe 1960–1975?

In July 1961 Harold Macmillan announced his government's decision to open negotiations with the Six to ascertain terms to join the EEC. This historic decision marked a reappraisal of policy begun late in 1959, but it would be an oversimplification to suggest that full membership was immediately sought (see Camps 1965, p. 313). Macmillan noted, 'somehow or other a bridge must be built, to prevent the widening of the economic and trading gap and undue discrimination' (1972, p. 315). The difficulty was that the Six looked for British acceptance of the Treaty of Rome as a basis for inclusion and not a form of associate status. At the same time President Kennedy made clear his preference for British membership. Indeed Washington's backing for the Six 'annoyed the British and added to the feeling that the "special relationship" was in danger of being supplanted by a "special relationship" between the Six and the United States' (Camps 1965, p. 283). It can be argued as a consequence that Macmillan was not radically altering course in applying for membership but seeking a 'new political and economic base which would underpin Britain's existing world role: that base would be Europe' (Greenwood 1992, p. 79).

In the post-Suez era Britain was slowly adjusting to the conditions of Washington's support, the limits of Commonwealth political cohesion and the success of the Six. At the 1962 Labour Party conference, Gaitskell was to condemn the Conservative application as ending a 'thousand years of history'. The Labour leader claimed only to oppose entry on the terms and not on principle, but warned that federation meant an end to 'Britain as an independent nation state' and 'must wreck the Commonwealth' (Williams 1979, pp. 734–5). While Gaitskell could therefore be seen to be in line with the post-war consensus, his stance must also be seen in the context of a party divided by the issues of nationalization and unilateral disarmament, and 'not for the last time, rejection of membership of the EC became a useful unifying issue around which the Party could unite across its left–right divisions' (George and Haythorne 1996, p. 113).

In 1966 Harold Wilson announced his Labour government would make an application to ascertain the terms for membership of the European Community (EC). In an election speech Wilson had maintained the Gaitskellite conditions for British membership but confirmed he would enter if the terms were correct (see Sked and Cook 1993, p. 235). Wilson's conversion appears encouraged by a number of political and economic factors (see J. W. Young 1993, p. 108; Kitzinger 1973, p. 280). Wilson secured the backing of the Labour Party conference and the majority of the Parliamentary Labour Party (PLP). None the less a significant majority of Labour MPs opposed membership, but de Gaulle averted further divisions by vetoing Wilson's application just as he had done Macmillan's.

In the 1970 general election all three major parties pledged membership of the EC if the terms were right. Heath's new Conservative government negotiated entry and placed the case before Parliament (see George 1990, pp. 42–70). A minority of Conservative MPs campaigned against their government, including Enoch Powell and John Biffen. It was calculated that somewhere between thirty-three and sixty-two Conservative members were opposed and about seventy doubtful (Kitzinger 1973, pp. 169–83). The Labour Party in opposition was deeply divided. The Shadow Cabinet was divided six in favour, seven against and three undeclared. The PLP was divided 100 for entry, 131 opposed and 40 uncommitted (Pimlott 1993, p. 584). Wilson's concern was the party and his leadership: he duly opposed entry on the 'Tory terms' and pledged renegotiation.

The Labour government of 1974 duly renegotiated the terms of Britain's entry but still faced major internal party divisions. The renegotiated terms were voted on in the Cabinet in March 1975, with sixteen in favour and seven opposed. The PLP was divided, with 138 supporting the leadership's endorsement of the terms, 145 opposed and 32 abstaining (Sked and Cook 1993, p. 304). The government, with Conservative support, carried the day, but the special Labour Party conference rejected membership by two to one. Wilson turned to a referendum in June, a 'skilful mechanism which enabled the Labour Cabinet to continue in being despite the widest possible gulf between its members on such a key issue' (Morgan 1992, p. 367).

The Thatcher era: 1979–1990

Margaret Thatcher's policy towards the EC was negative in character and uncompromising. The central issue of the first Thatcher government was the cost of British membership. She demanded 'Britain's own money back', and in the 'battle of budgets' confirmed the image of Britain as the reluctant European. Thatcher matched strident defence of national interests in the EC with renewal of the special relationship with the United States. The Falklands War in 1982 underlined the prime minister's commitment to national values and sovereignty.

The Labour Party in opposition moved leftwards and in the 1983 general election Labour pledged withdrawal from the community, cancellation of the Trident nuclear submarine programme, non-deployment of Cruise missiles, and greater public spending. The Conservatives pledged to remain in the EC, sustain nuclear deterrence and further privatization. Labour won 28 per cent of the vote, its worst share since the 1920s, losing support to both the Conservatives and the new Liberal Social Democratic Party (SDP) alliance.

From 1984 the key European issues were associated with institutional reform. Thatcher favoured attainment of the 'genuine Common Market envisaged in the original treaty, a force for free trade not protectionism' (Thatcher 1993, p. 548). The problem for the British leader was that whilst other member states wished to complete the internal market, the majority also sought means to enhance economic and political union. In December 1985 the Luxembourg Summit agreed to several reforms and amended the treaty by the Single European Act (SEA). It set the deadline of the end of 1992 to complete the single market, limited the requirement for unanimity in the Council of Ministers to new policy proposals, and granted a limited increase in powers for the European Parliament.

The impetus to new levels of European integration were taken up at the EC Hanover Council in 1988, which established the Delors Committee to explore the stages towards European monetary union (EMU). Delors reported in April 1989, envisaging a three-stage transition to monetary union and a transfer of decision-making power to the community. In May 1989 the commission published a draft of a Charter of Fundamental Social Rights. The tone of British reaction to the new integrationist agenda was set by Thatcher's Bruges speech of September 1988. The prime minister declared that Britain's 'destiny is in Europe, as part of the Community', but qualified this: 'that is not to say that it lies only in Europe'. Thatcher believed 'willing and active cooperation between independent sovereign states is the best way to build a successful European Community. To try to suppress nationhood and concentrate power at the centre of a European conglomerate would be highly damaging and would jeopardize the objectives we seek to achieve.' She further argued that 'we have not successfully rolled back the frontiers of the State in Britain only to see them reimposed at a European level, with a European super-state exercising a new dominance from Brussels' (see Salmon and Nicoll 1997, pp. 210–11). The Social Chapter was dubbed a 'socialist charter': 'we emphatically do not need new regulations which raise the cost of employment'. These convictions set Britain apart from the Franco-German alignment that took Europe forward.

At the Madrid European Council in June 1989 British isolation was only prevented by pressure from the chancellor, Nigel Lawson, and the foreign secretary, Geoffrey Howe. However, in July 1989 Howe was sacked as foreign secretary, and in October 1989 Lawson resigned because of the prime minister's continuing resistance to joining the exchange rate mechanism (ERM). Strains within the Tory leadership had clearly emerged but need to be set against a deteriorating economy and the introduction of the controversial poll tax. Yet the final straw for the prime minister would be Europe, as Thatcher again sought to stand against the European tide.

At the Strasbourg summit in December 1989 the European Council agreed to hold an intergovernmental conference (IGC) on EMU, and the Dublin Summit in April 1990 established a second conference on political union. Thatcher's response was to reject vigorously the Delors concept 'of a federal Europe in which the European Parliament would be the Community's House of Representatives, the Commission – its Executive, and the Council of Ministers – its

Senate. "No, No, No" I said' (Thatcher 1993, p. 833). Sir Geoffrey Howe resigned as leader of the House, attacking Thatcher's position and style. Howe's resignation prompted a leadership ballot, with Michael Heseltine challenging the prime minister over both the poll tax and Europe. Hugo Young states that it was Thatcher's 'stance on Europe and the future shape of the Community that had been not only the pretext but also, it seemed, the profound and ultimate cause of the party's removing its support from her' (H. Young 1991, p. xiv).

The prelude to the storm: 1990–1992

John Major's leadership marked a change of style but not necessarily of substance in Conservative European policy. The prime minister declared Britain should be at 'the very heart of Europe' (*Guardian*, 12 March 1991) but sought to limit the integrationist agenda of the IGC. The Treaty on European Union negotiated at Maastricht in December 1991 and formally signed on 7 February 1992 was presented as a triumph for John Major. 'Opt-outs' were secured for Britain from key stages of EMU and the Social Chapter. The treaty did not commit its signatories to a federal goal and an intergovernmental basis of unanimity was retained for common foreign and security policy (CFSP). The impending general election of April 1992 had a salutary effect on the Conservative party, inducing unity rather than division. The Labour Party, now committed to Europe (see George and Rosamond 1992), whilst critical of the omission of the Social Chapter, did little to challenge Major's position. The political storm was instead to follow the election, with the ratification of the Maastricht Treaty.

An Unusual Climate: Continuity and Rupture 1992–1997

The new European order

Thatcher's legacy to her successor was of orthodoxy in defence and foreign policy. Defence policy was wedded to nuclear deterrence, the 'special relationship' and NATO. European policy was conditioned by concern for Atlanticism, sovereignty and autonomy. The east–west tensions of the 'new Cold War' sustained such policies and the Gulf War of 1990–1991 was an opportunity to reassert a strategic role of global significance. The rapid transition in international order that followed the collapse of communism in Europe and the demise of the Soviet Union challenged, however, the 'givens' of British foreign policy. The new order afforded opportunities, promptly recognized in Paris and Bonn, for the EU to establish itself not just as the hub of the European economy but as a genuine international actor in security and foreign policy. The Maastricht Treaty declared that CFSP 'shall include all questions related to the security of the European Union, including the framing of a common defence policy, which might in time lead to a common defence' (Article J.4.1). The EU looked to the Western European Union (WEU), the European alliance whose original form had preceded NATO, to 'elaborate and implement discussions and actions of the

Union which have defence implications' (Article J.4.2). Britain, sensitive to any erosion of NATO's role in Europe, resisted proposals to integrate the WEU into the EU. Instead the WEU was to be both the defence component of the EU and a means to strengthen the European 'pillar' of NATO. This pivotal role was accepted by both the WEU and NATO, with the latter agreeing in 1994 to make its resources available to the WEU for operations in pursuit of CFSP. In the run-up to the 1996 IGC, advocates of reform, however, including the commission and some key member states, refocused on EU–WEU relations and the process of CFSP decision making, challenging the British position once again.

Ratification of the Maastricht Treaty

The Conservative electoral victory in 1992 granted the new government an overall majority of twenty-one. The figure was to be of considerable significance to the ratification of the Maastricht Treaty. A combination of rebel Tory MPs and opposition party support for inclusion of the opt-outs left the government vulnerable and weak. The Conservative leadership struggled through a parliamentary siege of amendments and uncertain votes which were to damage its credibility and authority. The Social Chapter became a key issue, as Labour's bid to secure its inclusion was seen by the Tory Eurosceptics as a means to scupper the bill. An unholy alliance of rebel votes and Labour threatened the government with a bill it could not accept. The government's response, which was effectively to stall, raised questions as to the rights of parliamentary debate, the legal requirements of treaty ratification and the limits of crown prerogative (see Baker et al. 1994). The climax of the war of attrition came on 22 July 1993, when the government's motion on the Social Chapter was defeated by eight votes. Twenty Tory MPs had defied their leadership and forced John Major to call a vote of confidence the following day. The vote was won 339 to 299 (one Tory abstention), but only after the 'most serious parliamentary defeat suffered by a Conservative Government in the twentieth century' (Baker et al. 1994, p. 57).

The process of ratification was affected by both domestic and European politics. The first and second readings of the Maastricht Bill were passed in May 1992, but parliamentary scrutiny was suspended when the Danish referendum rejected the treaty in June. The Danish vote encouraged eighty-four Conservative MPs to support a motion calling on Major to make a 'fresh start'. The Eurosceptic cause was strengthened by the financial crisis of 'Black Wednesday' (16 September 1992), when Britain was forced to suspend its membership of the ERM. The Conservative Party conference revealed deep divisions over Maastricht. Douglas Hurd warned the party not to tear themselves apart over Europe (see *The Times*, 7 October 1992). Labour was not free from dissent either; Bryan Gould resigned from the Shadow Cabinet to oppose the bill, and sixty-six Labour MPs refused to follow the party line on the third reading – voting against the government instead of abstaining. Labour could, however, only benefit from Tory divisions and sought to sustain the government's problems and not create their own.

EC summits in Lisbon and Birmingham agreed to resume the ratification process despite the Danish position. In November 1992 Major sought approval for a paving motion to resume passage of the Maastricht bill. The motion was opposed by Labour, who claimed it was not integral to the treaty itself, but supported by the Liberal Democrats, who claimed it was. The government won by just three votes. Thirty-two of its MPs had rebelled, giving clear warning of the task ahead. Following the Edinburgh summit of December 1992, which granted concessions to secure Danish support, demands grew for a British referendum. A cross-party rally in Trafalgar Square campaigned for a referendum and included figures such as Bill Cash, Teddy Taylor, Teresa Gorman, Tony Benn and Peter Shore. Thatcher led the referendum campaign in the Lords. The government wavered before accepting an amendment which, with Labour's official opposition, was defeated in both Houses. When the Danes accepted the Maastricht Treaty in a second referendum in May 1993, the rebels had lost their tacit support and stood alone. The government, however, was no stronger and could not assume a majority. The third reading was successful, despite forty-six Tory rebels, but this still left two votes to be taken on 22 July. These were Labour's amendment to prevent ratification without the Social Chapter, and the government's to note its opt-out policy. Labour failed by one vote but the government lost too, forcing the vote of confidence.

The Tory Eurosceptics

The full scale of dissent within the parliamentary Conservative Party over Maastricht is unclear. In terms of voting, the 'Fresh Start' motion attracted eighty-four Tory MPs, while thirty-two rebelled on the paving motion and twenty on the critical Social Chapter motion. The 'die-hard' rebels were sustained by good organization, finance and the support of powerful figures in the Conservative Party (see Gorman 1993; Ludlam 1996). The available evidence, however, suggests a wider basis of concern if not rebellion amongst the Conservative parliamentary party. It is helpful to recognize that Conservative MPs, just like their Labour counterparts, are far from cohesive in their dissent or support over European matters. Ludlam (1996) has divided the opponents of Maastricht into different categories; veteran anti-marketeers, constitutionalists opposed to further loss of legislative sovereignty from Westminster, and neo-liberal Thatcherites concerned at the loss of independent monetary policy. The classification of Conservative divisions has exercised a number of commentators (see Norton 1992; Ashford 1992; Garry 1995) and revealed not only gradations of opinion but correlation to other policy divisions – economic, social, etc. Baker, Gamble and Ludlam have suggested that the key issues for understanding these divisions are national sovereignty/interdependence and extended government/limited government, replacing the simple 'wet/dry' division (Baker et al. 1993, p. 425). Indeed it can be argued that by the 1990s 'Europe' had become the key polarizing divide in the Conservative Party. Research conducted in 1994 revealed the scale of concern amongst Tory MPs with issues of 'Euro-governance'. Whilst a majority of MPs believed the advantages of EC membership outweighed the disadvantages, two-thirds did not think sovereignty could be pooled, and over half concerned wished for an Act of Parliament to establish the supremacy of Parliament over EU legislation (Baker et al. 1995). Whilst there was broad support for Major's vision of Europe (see Major 1993) there was also a more 'sceptical parliamentary Conservative Party than visible behaviour at Westminster would suggest' (Baker et al. 1995, p. 221).

EMU and Conservative divisions

The ratification of the Maastricht treaty did not end Conservative divisions over Europe. The Maastricht commitment to EMU and the timetable to a single currency became, despite the British opt-out, a focal point for Euroscepticism. The sceptics wanted to retain sterling and feared a loss of sovereignty over the domestic economy. The official government position was to defer a decision on the single currency until the political and economic circumstances were clear, but in the interim to stay in the negotiations. This policy position was challenged in the Cabinet and on the backbenches. In the Cabinet Michael Portillo, Michael Howard, Peter Lilley and John Redwood were to oppose participation, while Kenneth Clarke and Michael Heseltine supported the official line. In May 1994 Portillo broke ranks and voiced his opposition to a single currency on television (see Stephens 1997, p. 312). Clarke openly disputed Portillo's views, arguing that it 'is quite possible to have monetary union without political union' (K. Clarke, 1995, p. 6).

The European Communities Finance Bill in November 1994, which increased member states' contributions, triggered opposition amongst Tory backbenchers. Major made the bill an issue of confidence and won with Ulster Unionist support. Eight Tory MPs, however, abstained and lost the whip as a consequence (another joined them). The rebels demanded entry to the single currency be ruled out before they would return to the party line. The perilous state of the government's majority was amply demonstrated in March 1995 when a Labour motion criticizing Conservative European policy was only just defeated (319–314). Norman Lamont, the former chancellor, sided with Labour, as did the Ulster Unionists, now facing the Anglo-Irish framework document. The outcome was settled by the rebels with five abstaining but four voting with the government. In April the whip was restored to the rebels without conditions.

Pressure on Major built from the opposition, from within the Cabinet and from the backbenches. The prime minister's adoption of a more sceptical tone on Europe pleased but did not appease the Tory Eurosceptics. On 22 June 1995 John Major called on his critics to 'put up or shut up' (*The Times*, 23 June 1995) and instigated a leadership election. The prime minister duly defeated his challenger, the former Welsh Secretary John Redwood, by 218 votes to 89 (22 Tory MPs abstained or spoilt their ballots). While this measure resolved the leadership issue until the next general election, it did little to heal Conservative divisions. At the same time the EU agenda moved forward; the Madrid summit in December set March 1996 as the commencement for the IGC on institutional reform and January 1999 as the target date for EMU.

The EU timetable generated new pressures inside the Conservative Party. In July 1996 David Heathcoat-Amory resigned as paymaster general because the government was failing to stop the 'relentless drive to political union'. Dissent within the Conservative Party and pressure from without brought the issue of a referendum to the fore. In June 1996 Bill Cash, with the support of seventy-four Tory MPs, called for a referendum on Britain's place in Europe. Sir James Goldsmith's new Referendum Party pledged to force a plebiscite on Europe and stand against any MP who did not support the cause. In the Cabinet a referendum became an increasingly attractive option for managing the party through the single currency issue. Major had indicated a referendum 'could be necessary, [and] it could be desirable' (*The Times*, 2 March 1995) if a future government decided to join the single currency or major constitutional change emerged from the IGC. By the spring of 1996 the issue was more urgent and, despite Clarke's misgivings (see Stephens 1997, pp. 339–44), the Cabinet agreed that, if the government decided to join a single currency during the course of the next Parliament, that decision would be subject to confirmation in a referendum.

The management of European policy was then made more difficult by a number of issues that affected both public and party opinion. The 'beef crisis' and European ban on British beef exports added fuel to the sceptics' fire, while controversies surrounding the European Court, fishing and agricultural interests gave Europe a poor press. EMU remained, however, the single most divisive issue for the Conservative Party. The single currency debate was reopened with a vengeance in November 1996. It was sparked by the imminent meeting of European finance ministers to prepare implementation plans for EMU and the circulation of confidential documents which appeared to compromise Britain's opt-out. The documents, from the European Monetary Institute (EMI) and the Treasury, indicated that even if Britain did not join the single currency its budgetary plans would be under close scrutiny from Brussels. Terms and conditions of the proposed measures to facilitate economic cohesion for EMU also caused concern. The Treasury Report suggested the 'current proposals will not be acceptable to Parliament' (*Sunday Times*, 24 November 1996).

The revolt escalated when MPs were refused a debate on the floor of the House and scrutiny was confined to a standing committee. By the time Clarke addressed the Commons and reassured members that the opt-out remained secure, the damage had been done. Indeed the issue would not go away and Conservative ministers and MPs continued to revisit official policy. Pressure mounted for a rejection of EMU membership in the lifetime of the next parliament. The chancellor allegedly threatened his resignation and warned that other middle-rank and junior ministers would follow him if official policy was revised (see *The Times*, 6 December 1996). Despite 10 Downing Street issuing statements in favour of Clarke, press coverage of ministerial divisions was sustained (see *Independent on Sunday*, 8 December 1996). Malcolm Rifkind's warning that the single currency would lead to a 'crucial, permanent and significant' loss of national control (*The Times*, 10 February 1997), and his subsequent announcement that the government was not neutral on monetary union but 'on balance hostile' (*The Times*, 20 February 1997), openly displayed the scale of difference between foreign secretary and chancellor. With a general election just weeks away the Conservative Party remained critically divided over Europe, which would clearly affect its credibility as a party fit to form the next government.

The 1997 General Election: Campaign and Aftermath

The campaign and Europe

The 1997 general election campaign highlighted the issues of sleaze and Europe, both to the detriment of the Conservative Party. While Labour had an established lead in the polls, the Conservatives were considered divided by the majority of people and consequently not a credible party of government (Harrop 1997, p. 314). The issue of Europe emphasized Conservative disunity and absence of a coherent strategy.

The Conservative leadership adopted a sceptical tone towards Europe from the start of the year and sought to link this stance with the image of firm protection of British interests at the IGC. Major attacked the Social Chapter and overregulation as a key cause of unemployment and lack of business competitiveness (see *The Times*, 4 April 1997). He further hardened his position over the single currency, stating he 'would not like to be the Chancellor of the Exchequer who went to the dispatch box and said, "well, I no longer have control over interest rates"' (*The Times*, 27 January 1997). The Cabinet further issued statements that it was unlikely that Britain would enter the single currency in 1999 or that EU convergence would permit a launch on that date (see *The Times*, 24 January 1997). Major also challenged Franco-German policies for 'flexibility' or a 'multi-speed' Europe. He argued that all member countries should retain a veto, in order to stop small groups of states approving deeper integration at the expense of others. Rifkind stressed that Britain's vision of Europe was a 'Partnership of Nations' and warned that greater centralisation of power, at the expense of national institutions, undermines rather than strengthens the Union. The foreign secretary threatened to block the IGC if qualified majority voting (QMV) were extended to CFSP and immigration. The Conservative government also declared its opposition to Franco-German proposals to incorporate the WEU into the EU as its defence arm.

The Tory Party offensive was nullified, however, by both its own membership and the Labour Party. Clarke maintained the single currency debate in the party, suggesting Britain could be among the first wave of countries joining during the next parliament (*Financial Times*, 29 January 1997). Stephen Dorrell was reported to have added to the disarray, by issuing a statement accepting that participation had not been ruled out in 1999 after saying it had (*The Times*, 4 March 1997). Opposition to the single currency came from over 150 Tory backbenchers who announced they would oppose it in their election addresses. Major claimed policy had not changed but accepted that Conservative candidates could express personal preferences, and then offered a free vote on the single currency in the next Parliament if he were re-elected (*The Times*, 18 April 1997). Clarke simply stated such candidates were 'wrong'.

Conservative attempts to portray Tony Blair as inexperienced and weak included his depiction as a ventriloquist's dummy on the knee of Chancellor Helmut Kohl. Labour's response was to stress its defence of British interests,

Blair's patriotism and a sceptical tone on integration. On the single currency Gordon Brown warned that there were 'real obstacles facing Britain and other countries that are increasingly difficult to overcome by 1999. Getting it right is more important that getting it quickly. We will apply strict British economic tests in the British economic interest' (*The Times*, 21 February 1997). By April Tony Blair had adopted a more sceptical tone: 'Let me be absolutely clear: if the issue of Britain joining a single currency in the next Parliament arises – and I stress the "if", just as our Manifesto will stress the "if" – then the final say will be with you, the British people, in a referendum' (*The Guardian*, 2 April 1997).

In the pre-election skirmishing, Labour policy positions concurred with the Conservatives' on many key European issues. Blair, for example, announced he would use the veto to prevent small groups moving ahead with deeper integration; both Blair and Major threatened the Amsterdam Treaty if British fishing were not protected from 'quota hopping'; and both sought to maintain border protection and NATO's primacy. As Riddell put it, 'the real contrast is less one of policy than of attitude' (*The Times*, 26 March 1997).

Both Conservative and Labour manifestos pledged a referendum on the single currency. The Conservative manifesto retained the 'wait and see' line:

> It is in our national interest to take part in the negotiations. Not to do so would be an abdication of responsibility. A single currency would affect us whether we are in or out. We need to participate in discussions in order to ensure the rules are not fixed against our interests. The national interest is not served by exercising our option – one way or the other – before we have to. (Conservative Party 1997, p. 47)

The Labour manifesto like its Conservative counterpart stated the need for genuine convergence of economies before participation; however:

> to exclude British membership of EMU for ever would be to destroy any influence we have over a process which will affect us whether we are in or out. We must therefore play a full part in the debate to influence it in Britain's interests. (Labour Party 1997, p. 38)

Significant divergences concerned Labour's endorsement of the Social Chapter and Tory rejection of social regulation. The Conservative approach to the forthcoming Amsterdam summit was that it was a 'moment of truth', that the 'European Union itself should do less, but do it better' and that 'we will not accept other changes to the Treaty that would further centralise decision-making, reduce national sovereignty or remove our right to permanent opt outs' (Conservative Party 1997, pp. 45–6). Labour was to stress a 'fresh start in Europe, with the credibility to achieve reform', to 'stay in, but in a leading role', and to oppose 'a European federal superstate' (Labour Party 1997, p. 37).

It can be argued that the differences of nuance, emphasis and implied direction in the manifestos probably meant more to the parties themselves than to the electorate. What was important about the European issue in the campaign was what it said about the parties, about their ability to follow a coherent strategy.

Labour in office

The new Labour government commenced office with clear signals of continuity with the past. The transatlantic alliance was reaffirmed with President Clinton's visit and address to the Cabinet. Clinton's depiction of a 'unique partnership' (*The Times*, 30 May 1997) was matched by Labour's public concern that the European 'agenda' should not jeopardize NATO. Robin Cook, the foreign secretary, also sought to present change in foreign policy; he proclaimed a new era in Britain's relations with Europe. He said the new government 'would draw a line under the sterile, negative and fruitless confrontation which was the policy of the previous Government' (*The Times*, 8 May 1997).

The Labour government was swiftly drawn into negotiations at Amsterdam to revise the Maastricht Treaty. The issues for Britain at the talks were: the relationship of the WEU to the EU; border controls; the creation of jobs; fish quotas; and the Social Chapter. The prime minister, Tony Blair, was to claim success for Britain at Amsterdam. The treaty did not integrate the WEU into the EU but left it as a 'possibility' should the European Council so decide. CFSP was amended under article J.7 to include the progressive framing of a common defence policy, but the national veto was retained by the requirement for unanimity under article J.13. A protocol to the treaty granted the United Kingdom border control, a Chapter on Employment recognized job creation, and agreement was claimed with the commission on Britain's quotas for fishing. While question marks remained against the precise relationship of the national veto to QMV on flexibility, Blair had little difficulty in ignoring the call of the new Tory leader, William Hague, for a referendum on the treaty (see *Financial Times*, 28 June 1997).

In July, Cook launched his strategy for putting human rights at the centre of British foreign policy. Amongst the measures adopted were new criteria for licences for arms exports in order to try to prevent usage for internal repression (see *FCO Daily Bulletin*, 28 July 1997). Annual reporting on sales was also presented as an answer to the implications of the Scott enquiry on arms to Iraq. The foreign secretary dispelled doubts about his commitment to the policy when in September he blocked two arms contracts to Indonesia. The emphasis on values in foreign policy was further underlined in his Labour Party conference speech, which addressed the issues of the environment, banning landmines and the promotion of human rights.

The Labour conference endorsed a party and leadership riding at the top of the polls. While at the fringe Austin Mitchell and Lord Shore warned against Euro-enthusiasm, the main body of the conference did little to concern Blair's leadership. Calls for Trident to be scrapped were defeated by 56 percent to 44 percent. On Europe, Blair maintained the new emphasis on engagement, arguing that 'we cannot shape Europe unless we matter in Europe' (*The Times*, 1 October 1997). In contrast William Hague opened the Conservative Party conference with low personal poll ratings and the spectre of European divisions haunting proceedings. Europe was an important issue for both the rank and file, who expressed their anger at disloyalty in the parliamentary party, and the leadership, who sought a settled line on the single currency. On the eve of the conference, the reported Shadow Cabinet line was clearly sceptical, ruling out membership of the single currency for a decade but granting Tory MPs a free vote to avoid a rebellion (*Observer*, 12 October 1997). The decision had been taken in the absence of three pro-European members, Stephen Dorrell, Sir George Young and David Curry, whose return prompted the adoption of a new line – membership would not be 'for the foreseeable future'. Hague denied divisions but had clearly had to compromise by leaving the timetable open to interpretation. His view of Europe was indicated in a speech that declared that 'there is a limit to European integration. And I might say, in my opinion, we are near that limit now' (*The Times*, 11 October 1997). Hague's scepticism was underlined in his unreserved apology to the country for the 'great mistake' of entry to the ERM and its clear association with the single currency decision. The Conservative leader's admission, however, that 'there will always be some serious differences in any serious party' (*The Times*, 11 October 1997) pointed to a future in which party policy on Europe would remain a matter of contention.

Conclusion: The Impact of Party Policy

Whilst the linkage of domestic political structures to foreign policy-making has been well established (see Frankel 1975; Macridis 1976; Farrands 1988; M. Clarke 1992), the role of political parties in relation to foreign affairs is less well defined. The foreign policy process is traditionally seen as executive-dominated, elitist and centralized. As Clarke has observed, 'more than any other policy area, foreign policy is identified as that which must be conducted by the executive; it is concerned with the exercise of sovereignty in relations with the outside world' (M. Clarke 1988, p. 72). Vital found that 'in law, no less than in fact, the conduct of Britain's foreign affairs is the peculiar concern and undivided responsibility of the Executive – a Crown prerogative' (Vital 1968, p. 47). For some this is also a matter of preference that 'politics should stop at the water's edge', to insulate foreign policy from the disruptions of domestic political strife (see Waltz 1968, p. 63). The consequences are the subordinate role of Parliament and political parties in the foreign policy process. In Barber's terms, the 'sectoral process', confined to those within the executive and those outside who have 'special interests and knowledge of the issues under review', deals with the vast bulk of foreign policy-making (Barber 1976, pp. 117–19). In contrast the 'general process', including 'the formal office holders, the departments of government, groups and political parties, the public and the mass media', is seen as only being capable of handling a small number of issues (Barber 1976, pp. 119–21). Barber suggests that the issues dealt with by the 'general process' are those which are especially important or especially controversial, and in defining those categories draws attention to the critical role of the media (Barber 1976, p. 121). As we have seen, the issue of Europe in British politics has assumed precisely such an important and controversial status, thereby involving political parties in the policy process.

A critical function of political parties is the legitimacy they can bestow upon political decisions, which has 'evolved from the direct expression of social group interests (integration) to the structuring and implementation of mass public opinion (responsibility)' (Hix 1995, p. 530). Political parties are therefore distinctive by virtue of the linkage they provide between citizens and policy-makers; as Lawson puts it, 'their raison d'être is to create a substantive connection between rulers and ruled' (1980, p. 3). The issue of European integration brings political parties into the foreign policy process and raises questions about the legitimacy of decisions. Membership of the EU has blurred the boundaries of what hitherto could be considered foreign and domestic policy. Europe brings foreign policy into the domestic realm, and parties seek to influence public and government on what cannot be presented by the executive as a solely externalized policy agenda. Executives need to carry Parliament on a range of policy issues from monetary affairs to social policy, defence and security. All of this provides opportunities for party intervention. Europe is, however, at the same time a potential threat to parties which are 'essentially a national and local phenomenon', and some are hostile to Europe 'precisely because they consider it undermining of the national political culture which gave rise to them and their values' (Gaffney 1996, p. 2). It is therefore not surprising that concepts such as sovereignty and autonomy become integral to the response of British political parties to Europe as they attempt to influence public opinion. It is also not surprising that the legitimacy of decisions emanating from Brussels are challenged by sections, if not the whole, of domestic political parties.

The analysis of the relationship of British political parties, government policy and European integration needs to acknowledge the dynamics of the policy process. Integration is neither a linear process nor isolated from the domestic reaction of member states and their publics (see Taylor 1997). Parties are at the interface of the process of public reaction and the executive. When sections of the party of government challenge the executive's management of European integration, they therefore challenge the legitimacy of the policy process and the authority of its leadership. Electoral credibility is called into question by the process, which, as we have seen, is particularly difficult to manage for a party with a small majority. The executive's capacity to negotiate at the European level becomes more strained as decisions have to be mediated through a divided or factionalized party. Party management has at times appeared more important for both Conservative and Labour than the external agenda. Parties therefore do affect state policy, but as the experience of the Major government illustrated, their influence, even at its strongest, may be best seen as a negative power. The European agenda is still running, however, and promises a rich vein of issues for British political parties.

Chronology of Significant Developments: April 1992 to October 1997

June 1992	Danish referendum rejects Maastricht
September 1992	'Black Wednesday'
November 1992	Paving motion passed by three votes
May 1993	Second Danish referendum accepts Maastricht

July 1993	Government defeated 324–316 on Social Chapter; government wins confidence vote 339–299
November 1994	Government wins European Communities Finance Bill vote; eight Tory MPs lose the whip
March 1995	Government defeats Labour motion on its European policy 319–314
July 1995	Major defeats Redwood in Tory leadership election
November 1996	EMI and Treasury reports on single currency fuel debate in Commons
May 1997	General election
June 1997	Amsterdam Summit
October 1997	Conservatives say no to abolishing the pound 'for the foreseeable future'

References

Ashford, N. 1992 'The Political Parties' in George, S. (ed.) *Britain and the European Community: The Politics of Semi-Detachment*, Oxford: Clarendon Press.

Baker, D., Gamble, A. and Ludlam, S. 1993 '1846...1906...1996? Conservative Splits and European Integration', *Political Quarterly* 64, 420–34.

Baker, D., Gamble, A. and Ludlam, S. 1994 'The Parliamentary Siege of Maastricht 1993: Conservative Division and British Ratification', *Parliamentary Affairs* 47(1), 1, 37–60.

Baker, D., Fountain, I., Gamble, A. and Ludlam, S. 1995 'Backbench Conservative Attitudes to European Integration', *Political Quarterly* 66, 221–33.

Barber, J. 1976 *Who Makes British Foreign Policy?*, Milton Keynes: Open University.

Butler, A. 1993 'The End of Post-War Consensus: Reflections on the Scholarly uses of Political Rhetoric', *Political Quarterly* 64, 435–46.

Camps, M. 1965 *Britain and the European Community 1955–1963*, London: Oxford University Press.

Clarke, K. 1995 'Chancellor's Speech to European Movement Gala Dinner', http:wwwhm-treasury.gov.uk/pub/html/press.

Clarke, M. 1988 'The Policy-Making Process', in *British Foreign Policy: Tradition, Change and Transformation*, Smith, M., Smith, S. and White, B. (eds), London: Unwin Hyman.

Clarke, M. 1992 *British External Policy-Making in the 1990s*, Basingstoke: Macmillan.

Conservative Party 1997 'You can only be sure with the Conservatives', London: Conservative Party.

Farrands, C. 1988 'State, Society, Culture and British Foreign Policy', in *British Foreign Policy: Tradition, Change and Transformation*, Smith, M., Smith, S. and White, B. (eds), London: Unwin Hyman.

Frankel, J. 1975 *British Foreign Policy 1945–1973*, London: Oxford University Press.

Gaffney, J. 1996 *Political Parties and the European Union*, London: Routledge.

Garry, J. 1995 'The British Conservative Party: Divisions over European Policy', *West European Politics* 18(4), 170–89.

George, S. 1990 *An Awkward Partner: Britain in the European Community*, Oxford: Oxford University Press.

George, S. 1991 *Britain and European Integration since 1945*, Oxford: Blackwell.

George, S. and Haythorne, D. 1996 'The British Labour Party', in *Political Parties and the European Union*, Gaffney, J. (ed.), London: Routledge.

George, S. and Rosamond, B. 1992 'The European Community', in *The Changing Labour Party*, Smith, M. and Spear, J. (eds), London: Routledge.

Gorman, T. 1993 *The Bastards*, London: Pan.

Greenwood, S. 1992 *Britain and European Integration*, Oxford: Blackwell.

Harrop, M. 1997 'The Pendulum Swings: The British Election of 1997', *Government and Opposition* 32(3), 305–19.

Hix, S. 1995 'Parties at the European Level and the Legitimacy of EU Socio-Economic Policy', *Journal of Common Market Studies* 33(4), 527–54.

Kitzinger, U. 1973 *Diplomacy and Persuasion*, London: Thames and Hudson.

Labour Party 1997 'New Labour: because Britain deserves better', London: Labour Party.

Lawson, K. 1980 *Political Parties and Linkage*, New Haven CT: Yale University Press.

Ludlam, S. 1996 'The Spectre Haunting Conservatism: Europe and Backbench Rebellion', in *Contemporary British Conservatism*, Ludlam, S. and Smith, M. (eds), London: Macmillan.

Macmillan, H. 1972 *Pointing the Way 1959–1961*, London: Macmillan.

Macridis, R. 1976 *Foreign Policy in World Politics*, Englewood Cliffs NJ: Prentice Hall.

Major, J. 1993 'Raise Your Eyes, There is a Land Beyond', *The Economist*, 25 September.

Morgan, K. 1992 *The People's Peace*, Oxford: Oxford University Press.

Norton, P. 1992 'The Conservative Party from Thatcher to Major', in *Britain at the Polls 1992*, King, A., Crewe, I., Denver, D. Newton, K., Norton, P., Sanders, D. and Seyd, P. Chatham: Chatham House.

Pimlott, B. 1993 *Harold Wilson*, London: HarperCollins.

Salmon, T. and Nicoll, W. 1997 *Building European Union*, Manchester: Manchester University Press.

Seldon, A. 1994 'Consensus: A Debate too Long?', *Parliamentary Affairs* 47(4), 501–14.

Sked, A. and Cook, C. 1993 *Post-War Britain*, Harmondsworth: Penguin.

Stephens, P. 1997 *Politics and the Pound*, London: Macmillan.

Taylor, P. 1997 'Prospects for the European Union', in *New Challenges to the European Union: Policies and Policy Making*, Stavridis, S., Mossialos, E., Morgan, R. and Machin, H. (eds), Aldershot, Dartmouth.

Thatcher, M. 1993 *The Downing Street Years*, London: HarperCollins.

Vital, D. 1968 *The Making of British Foreign Policy*, London: George Allen and Unwin.

Waltz, K. 1968 *Foreign Policy and Democratic Politics*, London, Longman.

Williams, P. 1979 *Hugh Gaitskell*, London: Jonathan Cape.

Young, H. 1991 *One of Us*, London: Macmillan.

Young, J. W. 1993 'Britain and the EEC, 1956–73: An Overview', in *From Reconstruction to Integration: Britain and Europe since 1945*, Brivati, B. and Jones, H. (eds), London: Leicester University Press.

Guide to Further Reading

S. George's *An Awkward Partner: Britain in the European Community* (Oxford: Oxford University Press, 1990) provides a good account of Britain's relations with Europe. For a study of the Conservatives, the economy and Europe, see P. Stephens, *Politics and the Pound* (London: Macmillan, 1997). A clear depiction of the European project is provided by R. McAllister's *From EC to EU: An Historical and Political Survey* (London: Routledge, 1997).

3 | Health, Education and Social Security

Brian Lund

Synopsis

New Labour's social policies have absorbed many elements of the Conservative approach developed by the Thatcher and Major governments. The 'old' consensus on welfare provision was based on demand management for full employment plus state social service expenditure as a route to national efficiency and social harmony. This has been replaced by a new accord with an emphasis on expenditure restraint, obligations rather than rights, 'customer' care, private–public partnerships and performance standards. The stability of this new consensus will depend on the success of New Labour – constrained in the long term by the criteria for membership of European monetary union – in delivering low unemployment and high-quality social services without increasing personal taxation.

The Historical Context: Party Policy 1945–1992

1945–1976: the consensus years?

Some commentators have divided the post-war history of the welfare state into two phases. The 'classic' era, lasting from 1944 to 1976, was 'dominated by the assumption, shared by all political parties, that the state alone could guarantee "full" employment, a minimum income for all and the universal provision of other services (such as health care and education) to the highest possible standard' (Lowe 1993, p. 357). This welfare 'consensus' was followed by a time of friction, the ascendancy of the ideology of the New Right, and the subsequent reconstruction of the welfare state.

The use of the term 'consensus' to depict the period 1944 to 1976 has been contested (Pimlott 1989; Glennerster 1995; Marlow 1997) but, viewed against the panorama of ideas and events in the nineteenth and twentieth centuries, the notion looks true. Many influential Conservatives may have expressed profound doubts about state welfare in private but they held their tongues in public (Cockett 1995, pp. 60–1). Disagreements emerged about the scope of social provision, and the onward march of the welfare state was not as linear as some authors have claimed. However, the public discord focused mainly on the cost of welfare rather than on the twin beliefs – dominant in the nineteenth century and revived in the mid-1970s – that state welfare was a threat to liberty and created more problems than it solved.

The consensus was based on the theoretical harmony between economic growth and public expenditure achieved by John Maynard Keynes in his *General Theory of Unemployment and Money* (1936), and was underpinned by the idea of investment in 'human capital'. Demand management would help to secure 'a high and stable level of employment' (Department of Employment 1944), and the allocation of resources to education, social security and health care would enhance individual welfare *and* boost national efficiency, bringing gains to all citizens. Thus educational reform would release the 'hidden talent' of the nation, and social security would maintain the physical efficiency of the working population. Free medical treatment, according to Beveridge and Bevan, would reduce the cost of health care because people in need of medical attention, unrestrained by the worry of deterrent charges, would obtain early treatment. The idea that welfare promoted economic efficiency was supported by the notion of 'universal' services as a route to a form of equality. If every person was entitled to welfare services on equal terms then equality of status would be enhanced; all would be equal as citizens.

The Conservatives and social policy 1951–1964

Willetts (1992) refers to a wet/dry cycle in post-war Conservative social policy. There was a dry cycle between 1951 and 1957 when the welfare state was contained. Expenditure on housing increased in the period 1951–1954, but insurance benefits only just kept pace with inflation (Dilnot et al. 1984, p. 20), means-tested national assistance payments lost value in relationship to average earnings (Atkinson 1969, p. 20), expenditure on health care (especially capital expenditure) was restrained (Webster 1996, p. 6), and the expansion of education was barely sufficient to accommodate the additional children born in 1945/6 as they progressed through the system. Expenditure on 'social services' as a proportion of gross domestic product (GDP) declined by 0.2 per cent between 1951 and 1955.

In the late 1950s, under the influence of the 'middle way' espoused by Harold Macmillan, the welfare state began to expand. This expansion was not without opposition; Peter Thorneycroft, the chancellor of the Exchequer, and his Treasury team resigned in January 1958 following Macmillan's refusal to accept cuts in public expenditure (Timmins 1996, p. 178).

Labour and social policy 1964–1970

Labour's commitment to state welfare strengthened in its opposition years. In the influential *The Future of Socialism*, Tony Crosland (1956) argued that the success of state economic management had made public ownership irrelevant to the achievement of socialist objectives. Inequality could be reduced by developing the social welfare system if the necessary finance came from progressive taxation and the divisive impact of means testing was eliminated. This 'revisionist' view of socialism shaped the social policies of Harold Wilson's governments. Crosland, when minister for education, issued Circular 10/65 requesting local education authorities to submit plans for comprehensive education, and the proportion of children in comprehensive schools increased from about 10 per cent in 1966 to over 30 per cent in 1970. Between 1963 and 1968 spending on education increased by 6.9 per cent, health by 6.0 per cent, social security by 6.6 per cent and housing by 9.6 per cent. None the less, the strategy of 'universalism' provoked disagreements within the party; the decision to increase family allowances, clawing back the expenditure through the tax system by reducing child tax allowances, was bitterly opposed by the chancellor, James Callaghan (Deacon and Bradshaw 1983, p. 69).

Stop/go/stop: social policy in the 1970s

During the late 1960s the Conservative Party's social policy entered a dry cycle, but Edward Heath's flirtation with a more *laissez-faire* approach to the economy was brief and was never applied to education and health care. When unemployment reached 4 per cent in 1972, demand was injected into the economy by spending on welfare services. Efficiency in the delivery of services was promoted by the creation of administrative structures thought necessary for rational planning.

The Labour government (1974–1979) introduced some egalitarian legislation in its first two years of office as part of its 'social contract' with the unions (Castle 1993, p. 462). In 1975 the family allowance was replaced by child benefit. This was paid to the mother in respect of all children, and child tax allowances (which benefited those families with the highest incomes) were phased out. In 1976 local authorities were required to submit plans for a comprehensive system and, by 1979, 80 per cent of children attended such schools. The 1975 Social Security Act made national insurance contributions fully earnings-related up to a ceiling, and the Social Security (Pensions Act) 1975 introduced a state earnings-related pension scheme (SERPS) based on the individual's twenty best years of contribution. The 1975 Social Security Benefits Act provided a non-contributory invalidity pension for disabled non-insured men and women under retirement age. These measures, together with the decision to increase the basic state pension in line with earnings, had an egalitarian impact and helped to direct income towards women with children.

The increase in the welfare spending that had followed Heath's policy 'U-turn' continued but, in 1976, the Keynesian cord linking public expenditure to economic growth was severed. The injection of demand into the economy through public expenditure had produced high inflation, low growth and rising unemployment – 'stagflation' as it was called. In 1976 attention began to focus on the relationship between the specifics of social policy and economic growth. In a speech at Ruskin College the prime minister, Callaghan, commented that 'there is no virtue in producing socially well-adjusted members of society who are unemployed because they do not have the skills'. Callaghan's statements on education reflected his adoption of a popular thesis on the causes of Britain's economic problem – there were too few producers of 'marketed' goods (Bacon and Eltis 1976).

Following the economic crisis of 1976 and the visit from the International Monetary Fund (IMF), social policy expenditure stabilized in real terms and reduced as a proportion of GDP. Public expenditure on education declined from 6.4 per cent of GDP in 1975/6 to 5.1 in 1979/80, and National Health Service (NHS) expenditure fell from 4.9 to 4.4 per cent of GDP over the same period (Hills 1990, pp. 38, 94). These cuts were met with bitter opposition from the rank and file of the Labour Party, and set the climate for a move to the left in the party in the early 1980s.

Callaghan's policy contained traces of an approach to social and economic policy cultivated by what came to be called the 'New Right'. The New Right asserted that:

- public expenditure 'crowded out' the private sector by absorbing human resources and, if additional expenditure was financed by higher public borrowing, then the demand for credit raised interest rates and made private investment more expensive;
- public services were monopolies – without competition they *must* be inefficient;
- state expenditure interfered with individual liberty by taking resources from individuals and supplying services that individuals might not want.

Sir Keith Joseph and Margaret Thatcher injected elements of New Right thinking into Conservative welfare ideology, but its impact was tempered by the strong voice of 'One Nation Conservatism' in the party. The 1979 manifesto did not include proposals for fundamental reform of state welfare; it promised to cut income tax at all levels by a move towards indirect taxation and to contain public expenditure by eliminating waste and inefficiency.

Holding the line: Conservative policy in the 1980s

Whatever else Thatcher and her successor, John Major, did they did not curb the state's call on the tax-payer.

Jenkins 1995, p. 10

Despite the prominence given to the welfare state as a causal factor in Britain's economic and moral decline, Thatcher only tinkered with the system in her first two governments. The value of basic state insurance benefits was maintained in line with inflation but not average earnings; earnings-related sickness and unemployment benefits were curtailed; capital expenditure on housing was reduced; and central government subsidies to local housing authorities were cut. However, these economies were insufficient to compensate for the additional spending generated by higher unemployment, the growth in the number of lone parents, and the health and social security requirements of an ageing population. Public expenditure on social welfare was 23.9 per cent of GDP in 1986/7 compared to 23.2 per cent in 1977/8 (Hills 1990, annexe). The Social Security Act 1986 introduced greater selectivity into the social security system, restricted entitlements under SERPS, and encouraged the purchase of 'personal' pensions. None the less, fundamental reform of the social welfare system, other than granting a right to buy at a substantial discount to 'social' housing tenants, was left to Thatcher's third term.

Bringing the market to the state

In her memoirs Thatcher declared that the Conservative Party manifesto of 1987 'went to the heart of my convictions' (Thatcher 1995, p. 572). Its flagship was the community charge, better known as the poll tax, which was designed to reduce pressure on public expenditure. 'Everyone will be aware of the costs as well as the benefits of local services', the 1987 manifesto stated (Conservative Party 1987, p. 63), and 'this should encourage people to take a greater interest in the policies of their local council and in getting value for money'. The manifesto also contained radical proposals for the reform of state welfare.

The right of the Conservative Party had been interested in education vouchers for many years but even Joseph, when secretary of state for education, was unable to overcome the objections to vouchers advanced by civil servants. His successor, Kenneth Baker, declared that he 'wanted to achieve the results of a voucher scheme, namely real choice for parents and schools that responded to that choice by improving themselves' (Baker 1993, p. 212). The 1988 Education Reform Act introduced a national curriculum and local management of schools. Each school received an income based on a per capita sum for every child registered. Enrolment was 'open' (but related to the number of children accommodated in 1979) and the opportunity for schools to opt out of local education authority control into direct funding by the central government (grant-maintained status), following a ballot of parents, was offered.

Nicholas Ridley, secretary of state for the environment, expounded the rationale of his housing reforms in '*My Style of Government*' (1991). He was 'determined to weaken the almost incestuous relationship between some councils and their tenants' and he saw the solution as 'being able to provide housing benefit on a sufficiently generous scale to enable all tenants to be in a position to pay their rents, and at the same time to bring rents up towards market levels' (Ridley 1991, p. 88).

Radical reform of the health care system was not included in the 1987 manifesto; but suddenly, in January 1988, a review of the NHS was announced. The outcomes of this review were contained in the National Health Service and Community Care Act 1990, which established the framework for an 'internal market' involving a purchaser/provider division in the NHS, with 'Health Commissioners' and general practitioner (GP) fundholders purchasing services from trusts and private suppliers.

The Major effect

John Major's election as prime minister seemed to indicate a return to 'middle way' conservatism. Major stated that the welfare state was 'an integral part of the British instinct', and that he wanted to create 'a classless society' (quoted in Timmins 1996, p. 480). Part of the value of child benefit, which had declined in the Thatcher era, was restored and spending on education and the NHS was increased. Education spending rose from 4.8 per cent of GDP in 1989/90 to 5.3 per cent in 1992/3, health care and personal social service expenditure from 5.7 per cent to 6.8 per cent, and social security from 10.7 per cent to 13.2 per cent – with unemployment expenditure doubling from £4.5 billion in 1989/90 to £9 billion in 1992/3 (Fleming and Oppenheimer 1996). The community charge was replaced by the lower and more progressive council tax, with the lost local revenue being replaced by higher central government grants to local government (financed by an increase in value added tax).

The Citizen's Charter, launched in July 1991, was Major's distinctive contribution to the delivery of 'internal' markets. It attempted to set standards that public services would be expected to deliver – 'to teach the nanny manners' (Lord McAlpine, *Sunday Times*, 13 May 1992). However, its mixture of private finance, contracts, market testing and privatization – thought necessary to deliver the required performance – 'tended to reinforce the impact of the market approach to public services' (Timmins 1996, p. 493).

The 1992 Conservative Party manifesto continued the emphasis on improving the quality of public services by exposing providers to competition. John Major's foreword stated 'I do not believe the answer to every problem is simply for government to dig deeper in your pocket. I believe it often lies in changing the way government works; in making it respond to you' (Conservative Party 1992, n.p.). The Labour Party's opposition to the purchaser/provider division focused on health care. Its argument that 'internal' markets were a prelude to dismantling the NHS made an impact on the electorate and prompted the Conservative Party to state in its 1992 manifesto that it was 'totally committed to the National Health Service' (Conservative Party 1992, p. 27), a pledge that was constantly reinforced throughout the 1990s.

An Unusual Climate: Continuity and Rupture 1992–1997

The Conservatives and public expenditure

The image of the Conservatives as the low-tax party was the cornerstone of their 1992 election victory, but the budget deficit, forecast at £28 billion before that general election, reached £50.2 billion in 1993/4 (Wilcox 1996, p. 88). Immediate reductions in public expenditure proved difficult to achieve. The NHS reforms were expensive to implement, and public suspicion that the service was 'not safe in Conservative hands' (Willetts 1992, p. 137) needed to be soothed by cash. The changes in the educational system had removed local government from its dominant position as a distributor of resources, leaving central government more exposed to the unpopularity associated with spending cuts. The 1988 Housing Act had set up an open-ended commitment to use housing benefit to cushion the move to market rents, with the result that expenditure on housing benefit soared from £4,049 million in 1988/9 to £10,440 million in 1993/4.

The budget deficit was bridged by big tax increases, which caused discontent on the right of the party. When John Redwood challenged Major for the leadership in June 1995, he declared that 'the Conservative Party is a tax cutting party or it is nothing' (quoted in Jeffrey 1995, p. 12), but his proposal to save £5 billion – by the dubious expedient of promoting members of the Cabinet who cut expenditure – served only to demonstrate the difficulties of a 'quick fix' to public expenditure.

Cutting public expenditure demands a long-term strategy. In 1993 Michael Portillo, then chief secretary to the Treasury, announced a fundamental review of public expenditure, which would examine programmes 'where better targeting can be achieved, or from which the public sector can withdraw altogether' (Hansard, 8 February 1993, col. 683). A number of initiatives – started in 1993 and linked to a 'back to basics' policy – began to have an impact.

Foster (1994, p. 81) maintains that 'the debate on the growth of Britain's underclass is absolutely central to the revival of ideological tension within the Conservative Party'. Charles Murray's thesis (Murray 1990) that the welfare programmes of the United States and Britain had spawned an underclass – 'married to the state', with attitudinal failings and a tendency to reproduce itself – was reflected in Major's notion of 'back to basics'.

Major's version of the association between welfare and dependency was restrained and expressed in broad terms. In 1993 he told the Conservative Party conference that 'it is time to return to core values, time to get back to basics... to accepting responsibility for yourself and your family... and not shuffling it off on other people and the state'. No such restraint was exercised by other members of the cabinet. Peter Lilley, secretary of state for social security, announced that he had a 'little list, who [*sic*] never would be missed, of ladies who get pregnant just to jump the housing list', and Redwood, having visited an estate in Wales that housed a high proportion of single-parent families, declared that single parenthood was 'one of the biggest social problems of our day' (quoted in CPAG 1993, p. 5).

The rhetoric of 'back to basics' foundered in a flurry of sex scandals involving Conservative MPs. However, the right of the Conservative Party continued to develop the notion that state welfare had produced a dependency culture and that this culture was associated with both a crisis in the family and an increase in crime. In her second volume of memoirs, Thatcher included a chapter with the title 'Virtue's Rewards' that was based firmly in the ideas of Charles Murray (Thatcher 1995, pp. 538–64). The approach was reflected in the domains of social policy controlled by Cabinet members closely associated with Thatcher. Jobseeker's Allowance, introduced by Lilley and Portillo in October 1996, replaced both unemployment benefit and income support for unemployed people. It was intended to be 'a means of support while an unemployed person looks for work, not an income for a lifestyle divorced from work' (Department of Employment/Department of Social Security 1994, p. 10). Eligibility for unemployment benefit, without a test of means, was reduced to six months, and the payment of Jobseeker's Allowance became conditional on compliance with the instructions of an employment service adviser. The introduction of Jobseeker's Allowance provided the opportunity for experiments in 'workfare', whereby people who had been unemployed for a long period were required to work in special schemes as a condition of benefit.

The cost of invalidity benefit had increased from £4 billion in 1984/5 to over £8 billion in 1994/5 because the number of claimants doubled. In 1995 invalidity benefit was replaced by an incapacity benefit with stricter eligibility criteria and a lower level of payment. Spending on housing benefit was also curtailed, by restricting benefit entitlement to average rents in an area and by allowing single people under 25 to claim housing benefit only on the cost of shared accommodation. However, the largest single reduction in expenditure came in the housing capital programme – reduced from £3,812 million in 1993/4 to £2,451 million in 1995/6 (Wilcox 1996, p. 15).

Quasi-markets

In the early 1990s the term 'quasi-market' was applied to the reforms in education, health care and housing introduced in the late 1980s. It was justified by the argument that providers of welfare services competed for the business offered by publicly financed purchasers. Major, as steward of Thatcher's reforms, made no significant changes to the operations of these quasi-markets, although the 1993 Education Act made opting out easier and established national agencies to supervise opted-out schools.

The Labour Party

The experience of the 1987 general election led the Labour Party to cost its 1992 manifesto proposals carefully and to set out the sources of revenue to finance the programme. Labour's most expensive pledges were of increases in child benefit and retirement pensions and of an immediate 'recovery programme' costing £1.1 billion. These would be financed by the abolition of the ceiling on national insurance contributions and the introduction of a 50 per cent tax rate on earnings above £36,375.

Whatever may have been the causes of Labour's defeat in 1992, many of the party's policy gurus thought that the tax consequences of its expenditure commitments were of paramount importance. The opinion surveys indicating that the public was prepared to pay higher taxes for better services seemed as deceptive as the polls that had predicted a Labour victory. Timmins (1996, p. 491) captures the mood:

> Despite Kinnock's red rose transformation of the party; despite a recession in the Tory heartlands; despite John Smith's bank managerial probity over his fiscal and economic plans – despite all this it appeared the electorate would not back what, by Labour's past standards, was an extremely mild version of tax, spend and

redistribute... If Labour could not deliver at least some redistribution, what could it deliver? Suddenly, all taboos went. Something close to panic set in.

John Smith, the new Labour leader, reacted by setting up a Commission on Social Justice. Its report, *Social Justice: Strategies for National Renewal* (1994), published after the death of Smith, set the bearings of Labour's social policy. Although many of its detailed recommendations were to be neglected by 'New' Labour, the importance of the report rests in its rejection of 'Levellers' Britain' with 'its strategy for social justice based primarily on redistributing wealth and incomes, rather than trying to increase opportunities and compete in world markets'. The commission endorsed the 'High Road of Investors' Britain' with a mission to:

- 'transform the welfare state from a safety net in times of trouble to a springboard for economic opportunity. Paid work for a fair wage is the most secure and sustainable way out of poverty';
- 'radically improve access to education and training, and invest in the talent of all our people';
- 'promote real choices across the life-cycle in the balance of employment, family, education, leisure and retirement'. (Commission on Social Justice 1994, pp. 20–1)

'New' Labour

The election of Tony Blair as its leader heralded a fundamental change in the ethos of the Labour Party. Blair gave prominence to the 'liberal socialism' tradition in the development of the labour movement and declared that an ideological refoundation of the party took place when, in 1995, Clause IV was revised and 'the party clearly said that we are in politics to pursue certain values, not to implement an economic dogma' (Blair 1995, p. 15). The influence of the ethical dimension of 'liberal socialism' was soon reflected in social policy. Blair announced that 'the Left has undervalued the notion of responsibility and duty, and it is time to understand how central it is to ourselves' (Blair 1996, p. 42). These 'warm words' were converted gradually into specific policies. A windfall tax on the profits of the privatized public utilities would finance the creation of 250,000 openings for work, education and training, but these opportunities would be matched by corresponding obligations on young people to take up these places. Home/school contracts would be introduced and single parents would be offered advice by a proactive Employment Service to develop a plan to find work. However, many of Labour's policies did not fit neatly into a 'rights implies obligations' paradigm. 'Old' Labour pledges such as minimum wage legislation and the phasing out of the 'assisted places' scheme were retained but given a new twist by being linked specifically to cost reductions and opportunities for new spending. Minimum wage legislation, so it was argued, would reduce public expenditure by placing some of the cost of social security on the employer, and the abolition of the assisted places scheme would free resources to reduce class sizes in state schools.

The 1997 General Election: Campaign and Aftermath

The Conservative Party

In late 1995 the Conservatives were 24 per cent behind Labour in the opinion polls, and Major had no alternative but to continue in office until the end of his term in the hope that a 'feel good' factor, generated by the improving economy and income tax cuts, would improve the fortunes of his party. The looming election dominated the political scene throughout 1996.

The 1996 November budget tried to strike a balance between reducing government borrowing, cutting income tax, and improving those public services of most concern to the electorate. The chancellor reduced the standard rate of income tax by 1p (to add to the 1p cut made in April), the 20 per cent band was extended, and personal tax allowances were increased in real terms. To project a reduction in the public sector borrowing requirement (PSBR) in 1997/8 and future years – thereby conforming to the criteria for joining a single European currency – indirect taxes on alcohol and tobacco were increased, entitlement to housing benefit was restricted, and single-parent benefit and the lone-parent premium (paid with Income Support) were frozen as a first step to abolition. State capital expenditure was projected to fall by £4.1 billion, with some of the shortfall met by private finance; a reflection, perhaps, of the way that capital expenditure, financed by state borrowing, counts as part of the PSBR. It was assumed that a clamp-down on tax avoidance would raise £6.7 billion over three years, that NHS expenditure would increase in real terms, and that spending on education would rise by £830 million (4.4 per cent) in 1997/8 (a figure strongly disputed by local government). However, the projections of expenditure on health and education in 1998/9 and future years made very limited provision for growth.

New social policy initiatives were in tune with Major's stewardship of the Thatcherite agenda. A pilot scheme of nursery vouchers was started in four authorities, and in early 1997 all parents of 4-year-olds received their nursery vouchers. Vouchers were designed to introduce greater competition in pre-school educational provision, but the outcome was the opposite of what had been intended. Headteachers in state schools indicated that if a child attended the nursery class of the local school then this would assist entry to the mainstream school at the age of 5. The result was that many voluntary sector playgroups were forced to close. The opposition parties condemned nursery vouchers as bureaucratic and wasteful.

An education bill was introduced to Parliament that extended delegated school budgets to cover 95 per cent of local authority expenditure and allowed central inspection of local education authorities. No doubt encouraged by the decision of Tony Blair and Harriet Harman to send their children to 'selective' schools, the bill contained proposals to assist the creation of more grammar schools. In addition, all grant-maintained schools could select up to 50 per cent of pupils by general ability, and local education authority (LEA) schools were to be permitted to select up to 20 per cent of pupils by ability or aptitude.

These 'selective' elements of the bill were lost when the general election was called.

Two new measures were announced by the Conservatives immediately before the dissolution of Parliament. If re-elected they promised to enable a non-earning partner to transfer her or his used tax allowance to the earning partner – but only if the couple were married. The cost of the scheme was estimated at £1.2 billion. A rebate on national insurance contributions would be given to young people to be invested in a personal pension scheme, with the state guaranteeing a minimum pension equivalent to the existing basic state pension.

The Labour Party

'New' Labour's election strategy was dominated by the attempt to modify its image as the party of 'tax and spend'. This was accomplished by the issue of a draft manifesto in July 1996 that was endorsed by a vote of party members and ratified by the 1996 annual conference. Traditionally Labour had approached taxation as a method of redistributing income, but, in the draft manifesto, taxation was seen as a method of raising resources, with tax proposals 'hypothecated' to specific spending proposals.

The process of obtaining party endorsement of the draft manifesto encountered only two difficulties. A proposal to abolish child benefit for 16–18-year-olds, and to concentrate the available resources on encouraging the children of poorer parents to stay on at school, was quietly dropped when it encountered opposition in the party and was condemned by the Conservatives as a tax increase. At the 1996 conference Barbara Castle led a movement to commit Labour to restoring the link between pensions and earnings, a commitment made in the 1992 manifesto. After some turbulence, a compromise was reached whereby the leadership promised to set up a review of pensions policy.

Free of the prospect of another party conference before the general election, the Labour leadership began to 'refine' New Labour's policies. Labour's commitment to ending selection in schools was modified; existing grammar schools would remain unless parents petitioned the government to end selection at 11. In January 1996 Gordon Brown announced that there would be no change in the 23p basic rate of tax or the 40p top rate for the lifetime of the next Parliament, and that the public spending totals set by the Conservatives would be retained for two years. This announcement was another attempt to slay the tax/spend dragon and neatly escaped the 'trap' set by Kenneth Clarke in his November budget. If a shadow spending minister wanted to change the proposals set out by Clarke (by, for example, retaining one-parent benefit), then he or she would have to find the resources from elsewhere in the budget earmarked for his or her future department.

The Liberal Democrats

In 1992 the Liberal Democrats had promised to increase the standard rate of income tax by 1p to finance additional educational expenditure. This policy was retained and became the centrepiece of the Liberal Democrat's election strategy.

Paddy Ashdown accused the Labour and Conservative parties of 'synchronized swimming' on social policy. What made the Liberal Democrats distinctive, he maintained, was their rejection of the 'terrible fatalism that seems to grip politicians' and their willingness to ask people to pay more for education (Ashdown 1997, p. 7).

The election campaign

The 'social policy' contents of the party manifestos are summarized in table 3.1. During the formal campaign Labour's principal 'spin-doctor', Peter Mandelson, moved the agenda from issue to issue on an almost daily basis, allowing no single issue to dominate events. For a short period Europe was prominent, and the Conservatives tried to link the high social spending of France and Germany to high unemployment and Labour's greater enthusiasm for European integration. Labour's accusation that the Conservatives' new proposals to enable young people to build up a personal pension would mean the end of the basic state pension had an impact towards the end of the campaign, and, although Labour promised to adopt the Conservatives' spending targets for two years, the impression was given that the NHS and state education would be safer in Labour's hands.

New Britain

Brown's budget, announced to Parliament on 2 July, set the framework for the implementation of Labour's manifesto. Details of the windfall tax and the linked 'welfare-to-work' programme were given, and some of the projected surplus from the windfall tax was earmarked to support a programme of capital investment in schools. Resources were also allocated to encourage single parents to find work, with up to £100 per week of expenditure on childcare to be disregarded in calculating the Family Credit of a single parent with two or more children of school age. However, although not announced in the budget statement, the cuts in allowances for single parents proposed by the Conservatives in 1996 were confirmed.

The 'surprises' in the chancellor's package were an extra £1 billion for education and £1.2 billion for health care in 1998/9, which contradicted Labour's election promise to adopt the Conservative spending plans for two years. If these additional resources had not been committed, then both health care and education would have encountered major problems in 1998/9. The Conservatives had planned only a 1.2 per cent real increase in health care spending and the provision for education was £600 million short of a standstill budget, after allowing for a modest teacher pay settlement. Officially the resources for this additional spending came from the Contingency Fund, but Brown's budget raised £5 billion in extra revenue by the abolition of tax credits to pension funds.

Education secretary David Blunkett's White Paper, *Excellence in Schools* (Department of Education and Employment 1997), set out Labour's policies on education. It confirmed Labour's manifesto commitments and signalled an enhanced role for local government in monitoring standards and improving

Table 3.1 *Election manifestos 1997*

Feature	Conservative	Labour	Liberal Democrat
Title	'You can only be sure with the Conservatives'	'New Labour: because Britain deserves better'	'Make the difference'
Taxation	Over the next parliament, our aim will be to achieve our target of a 20p basic rate of income tax, while maintaining a maximum tax rate of no more than 40p. We will give priority to future reductions in personal taxation that help families looking after dependent children or relatives by allowing one partner's unused personal allowance to be transferred to a working spouse where they have these responsibilities.	New Labour is not about high taxes on ordinary families. It is about social justice and a fair deal. To encourage work and reward effort, we are pledged not to raise the basic or top rates of income tax throughout the next Parliament. Our long-term objective is a lower starting rate of income tax of ten pence in the pound. We will introduce a budget within two months after the election to begin the task of equipping the British economy and reforming the welfare state to get young people back to work. This welfare-to-work programme will be funded by a windfall levy on the excess profits of the privatised utilities.	We will raise the basic rate of income tax by one penny in the pound – from 23p to 24p – to help finance our £2 bn per year programme of education investment. We will increase the amount of income which people can receive before they start to pay income tax by £200 per year to £4,245. This tax cut will be paid for by introducing a new rate of tax of 50%, payable on taxable income of over £100,000 per year. We will put 5p on a packet of cigarettes and use the money to restore free eye and dental checks for all and freeze prescription charges.
Social security	No Conservative government will sign up to the Social Chapter or introduce a national minimum wage. At present, Project Work is helping 100,000 people who have been unemployed for more than two years in	There should be a statutory level beneath which pay should not fall – with the minimum wage decided not on the basis of a rigid formula but according to the economic circumstances at the time….	We will encourage a flexible labour market, while protecting the low paid with a regionally variable, minimum hourly rate. We will restore access to benefits for 16 and 17 year-olds. In the longer term,

cities around Britain.... we will extend the programme to cover the long-term unemployed nationwide.

At the start of the next parliament we will set out proposals to enable all young people entering the workforce with a personal pension fund paid for through a rebate on their national insurance contributions. This would give them a pension significantly higher than they would currently receive from the state.

We will give 250,000 under-25s opportunities for work, education and training. Four options will be on offer, each involving day-release education or training leading to a qualification.... Rights and responsibilities must go hand in hand, without a fifth option of life on full benefit.

We will encourage employers to take on those who have suffered unemployment for more than two years with a £75-a-week tax rebate paid for six months, financed by the windfall levy.

The basic state pension will be retained as the foundation of pension provision. It will be increased at least in line with prices. We will examine means of delivering more automatic help to the poorest pensioners – one million of whom do not even receive the Income Support which is their present entitlement ... Too many people in work, particularly those on low and modest incomes and with changing patterns of employment, cannot join good-value second schemes. Labour will create a new framework – stakeholder pensions – to meet this need.

we aim to scrap the lower rate of income support for those under 25.

We will establish a self-financing Benefit Transfer Programme allowing those who have been unemployed for a year or more to turn their unemployment benefits into an incentive for employers to recruit and train them.

We will replace Income Support and Family Credit with a simpler, more efficient Low Income Benefit that increases the financial incentives for people going back to work.

We will create an additional top-up pension for pensioners with incomes below the Income Support level. This will be indexed to earnings and tapered as outside income increases. The basic state pension will remain indexed to prices.

We will replace the State Earnings Related Scheme (SERPS) with a scheme under which all employees have personal or occupational pensions.

We will abolish standing charges for water.

Family

But we now have the opportunity to achieve a massive expansion in wealth and ownership so that more families can

We will uphold family life as the most secure means of bringing up our children. Families are the core of our

We will repeal the Child Support Act and abolish the Child Support Agency. Where there are disputes between the

Feature	Conservative	Labour	Liberal Democrat
	enjoy the self-respect and independence that comes with being self-sufficient from the state.

The family is the most important institution in our lives. It offers security and stability in a fast-changing world. But the family is undermined if governments take decisions which families ought to take for themselves. Self-reliance underpins freedom and choice. | society. They should teach right from wrong. They should be our first defence against anti-social behaviour. The breakdown of family life damages the fabric of our society.

... While recognising the need for flexibility in implementation and for certain exemptions, we support the right of employees not to work more than 48 hours per week; to an annual holiday entitlement and to limited unpaid parental leave. These measures will provide a valuable underpinning to family life.

We are committed to retain universal Child Benefit where it is universal today – from birth to age 16 – and to uprate it at least in line with inflation. | parents, these should be settled by the courts, not by an inflexible formula.

We will introduce a statutory right to parental leave and develop Maternity Benefit into a new, flexible parental benefit to be shared between partners.

We will, over time, extend tax relief on workplace nurseries and other forms of day nursery care.

We will make pensions fairer to women by working to replace the contributory system with pension rights based on citizenship and residence in the UK.

We will introduce a Partial Capacity Benefit ... to assist those in work who cannot fully support themselves. |
| Education | First, we will set national targets for school performance that reflect our objective of ensuring Britain is in the top league of international standards across the whole spectrum of education.

Second, we will require every school to plan how to improve its performance, and to set targets which relate to similar schools and national standards.

Third, we will give all parents full information on the performance of their child's school. | Labour will never force the abolition of a good school whether in the private or the state sector. Any changes in the admission policies of grammar schools will be decided by local parents.

All Local Education Authorities (LEAs) must demonstrate that every school is improving. For those failing schools unable to improve, ministers will order a 'fresh start' – close the school and start afresh on the same site. Where good schools and bad schools | Our first priority is to: Give children the best start in life by providing high quality early years education to every 3 and 4 year old whose parents want it ... This will be the first call on our £2 billion annual programme of extra investment in education.

We will:

Increase funding for books and equipment in schools. In the first year we will double spending on books and equipment. Reduce primary school class |

Fourth, to underwrite our pledge, we will ensure action is taken to bring any under-performing school up to the mark.

We propose to assess every child at five.

We will require local authorities to delegate more of the schools' budgets to the schools themselves. We will give them more freedom over the employment of their staff and over admissions. And, where they want it, we will allow them to take over ownership of their assets, so they can make best use of resources.

We aim to help one in five schools become specialist schools.

We will allow all schools to select some of their pupils.

We will help schools to become grammar schools in every major town where parents want that choice.

coexist side by side we will authorise LEAs to allow one school to take over the other to set the underperforming school on a new path.

We will use the money saved by scrapping nursery vouchers to guarantee nursery places for four year-olds … We will set targets for universal provision for three-year-olds whose parents want it.

Every school needs baseline assessment of pupils when they enter the school, and a year on year target for improvement.

We will reduce class sizes for five, six and seven year-olds to 30 or under, by phasing out the assisted places scheme, the cost of which is set to rise to £180 million per year.

There will be education action zones to attack low standards by recruiting the best teachers and head teachers to under-achieving schools …

We will increase the powers and responsibilities of parents. There will be more parent governors and, for the first time, parent representatives on LEAs.

LEA performance will be inspected by Ofsted and the Audit Commission.

sizes so that within 5 years no child between 5 and 11 will need to be in a class of more than 30. Tackle the backlog of repairs. Support children with special needs,

We will devolve as many powers as possible to schools and give them more control over their budgets. We will bring grant-maintained schools and City Technology Colleges into this new framework and scrap the Funding Agency for Schools.

We will scrap the bureaucratic voucher scheme … and ensure a variety of provision from a wide range of public, private and voluntary providers.

We will phase out the Assisted Places Scheme and use the money saved to enable LEAs, if they wish, to enter local partnership schemes.

Health

We will continue, year by year, to increase the real resources committed

We will raise spending on the NHS in real terms every year and put the

We will place an immediate 6-month halt on the finance driven closure of beds and

Feature	Conservative	Labour	Liberal Democrat
	to the NHS, so NHS spending will continue to share in a growing economy. We shall implement the new Primary Care Act which will enable all family doctors to provide a broader range of patient services within their surgeries. This will include 'super surgeries' and practice-based cottage hospitals that can offer faster and more local treatment. We will not close any long-stay mental hospitals unless it can be shown that adequate care services exist in the community.	money towards patient care. And a greater proportion of every pound spent will go on patient care not bureaucracy. There can be no return to top-down management, but Labour will end the Conservatives' internal market in healthcare. Labour will cut costs by removing the bureaucratic processes of the internal market. The savings achieved will go on direct care for patients. As a start, the first £100 million saved will treat an extra 100,000 patients. GPs and nurses will take the lead in combining together locally to plan local health services more efficiently for all the patients in their area.	wards, and set up an independent audit of needs and facilities. We want all GPs to have the benefits of flexibility and access to services currently enjoyed by fundholders. Those who choose to manage their own affairs will be able to do so on their own or as part of a consortium. Those who do not will be able to leave management to the local health authority. We will invest at least an extra £540 million every year... This will be paid for by closing the loophole that allows employers to avoid paying National Insurance contributions on certain benefits in kind and by putting 5p on the price of a packet of 20 cigarettes. We will make prevention a priority. We will immediately abolish charges for eye and dental check-ups and freeze prescription charges. We will ban tobacco advertising. We will create an independent and powerful Food Commission..... We will build on current pilot schemes to bring together Health Authorities and Social Services Departments within the framework of elected local authorities.

Source: Conservative Party 1997; Labour Party 1997; Liberal Democrats 1997

school performance. Rather than use 'opting out' and competition to improve the quality of education, Labour chose to concentrate on setting and monitoring standards: each school would be required to set targets, monitored by the local authority, which would be required to draw up an education development plan. These would be vetted by the Department of Education's Standards and Effectiveness Unit.

Conclusion: The Impact of Party Policy

New Labour, New Britain

In some respects Mrs Thatcher had more effect on the Labour party than she may have done on the Conservative party.

Kavanagh, 1994, p. 11

Following the defeat of 1979 the Labour Party turned inwards and to the left. In the early 1980s there were at least three 'lefts' in Labour's ranks. The 'hardliners' of the Militant organization attempted to promote class conflict, whereas the 'new urban left', prominent in inner London and a few provincial cities, advocated citizen participation in local service delivery and positive action to promote the interests of oppressed minorities. The 'classic' left, disappointed at the reductions in public expenditure in the late 1970s, pushed for improved public services financed by redistributive taxation, and demanded a vigorous defence of trade union rights. Tony Benn, although unsuccessful in his bid for the leadership, managed to unite the various left-wing factions, but the 1983 manifesto – described as 'the longest suicide note in history' – heralded a crushing defeat. Labour obtained 27.6 per cent of the vote, only 2.4 per cent more than the Liberal/Social Democrat Party (SDP) Alliance.

Under the leadership of Neil Kinnock the party moved steadily to the right, but was unexpectedly defeated in 1992. Had John Smith lived then it is possible that Labour would have adhered to its 1992 policies. Led by a man with *gravitas* and faced by a government wounded by the events of 'Black Wednesday' and split over Europe, Labour might have won a comfortable majority in the 1997 election. However, the 'modernizers' in the party were convinced that further reform was necessary and, following the election of Blair as leader, change took place at a frantic pace. The modernizers' case on markets, taxation, public expenditure and public services was set out by Peter Mandelson and Roger Liddle in *The Blair Revolution: Can New Labour Deliver?* (1996). They asserted that New Labour welcomed 'the rigour of competitive markets as the most efficient means of anticipating and supplying consumers' wants, offering choice and stimulating innovation', but that 'left to themselves, markets tend to reinforce inequalities and may entrench privilege. Only in these circumstances should markets be regulated.' The real issue, they said, was not high taxation versus low tax 'but fair rather than unfair tax', and 'Labour's aim should be to change the pattern of public spending, not jump to the conclusion that nothing can be done without a large overall increase' (Mandelson and Liddle 1996, pp. 22–3). On public services they declared that New Labour should aim to:

- uphold the goal of a welfare state which is universal in its reach but no longer uniform in what it offers;
- guarantee access for all to a decent minimum quality of life and fair life chances, while permitting greater individual freedom of choice;
- marry public and private finance and provision, rather then seek to drive them apart;
- promote individual responsibility, not dependency;
- ensure effective provision of services that offer people a hand-up, not just cash payments that give them a hand-out. (Mandelson and Liddle 1996, p. 143)

Frank Field's *How to Pay for the Future* (1996a) developed the theme. 'Welfare', he said, 'reflects the pivotal role which self-interest plays within our motivations' and 'the growing autonomy of voters – wishing to do "their own thing" determined on the basis of free association – will be the touchstone of the new welfare' (Field 1996a, pp. 2–4). He put forward a scheme for 'stakeholder' pensions, involving compulsory contributions into regulated private pension schemes and the phasing out of SERPs (Field 1996b).

Field also cultivated the notion of 'hand-ups' rather than 'hand-outs', and rejected the view that welfare should be given as a right and free of stigma, with the argument that:

> One of welfare's roles is to reward and to punish. The distribution of welfare is one of the great teaching forces open to advanced societies. As Christian morality becomes unsustainable without being recharged in each generation by waves of new Christian believers, so societies must seek different ways of affirming right and wrong conduct. Welfare has such a role . . . But this, of course, does not explain why I believe character is being revived in the debate on restructuring welfare. I have nothing to add here because I do not believe character, as I have defined it, should ever have been eclipsed. (Field 1996a, p. 111)

Blair appointed Field as minister for social security and welfare reform, with a brief 'to think the unthinkable' on social security, and Geoff Mulgan, from the think-tank Demos, was appointed as a senior policy adviser. Mulgan reached the conclusion that the fundamental problem of welfare was the 'socially excluded', about 8 per cent of the population, 'who stay poor: who leave school with no qualifications after a school life of inattention, truancy and disruption; who live in areas where nearly 50 per cent of all crimes are committed; who provide most of the single-parent families, the drug addicts – the chronic losers' (Lloyd 1997, p. 14). The answer was the discipline of work.

In the 1997 general election campaign the Conservatives had been caught between attacking 'New' Labour and claiming that 'New' Labour was really 'old' Labour in disguise. On occasion they asserted that, if Labour was elected, the grip of the unions and the left would be reasserted. Many Labour party activists may have harboured similar thoughts, but the leadership calculated that the euphoria of election victory would continue into the conference season. The government acted quickly to entrench policies likely to generate opposition from inside the party. Cuts in benefits for single parents were confirmed, it was announced that benefit entitlement would be reduced to zero as a penalty for refusing work or training, and a quick decision was made on the recommendations of the Dearing report on higher education; students, except those with parents on limited incomes, would pay fees, but these would be added to maintenance loans and repaid after graduation. However, there was a significant adjustment in the leadership's approach to pensions. Frank Field had wanted SERPS to be phased out, but the terms of reference of the task force set up to review pensions policy specifically included its retention. This may have been the outcome of technical difficulties encountered in converting Field's ideas into specific proposals, but the move can also be interpreted as an attempt to minimize party discontent on a matter that had generated unrest at the 1996 conference.

The pensions issue reflects a tension in the party on welfare reform that has the potential to become a major source of internal conflict. 'New' Labour's rejection of taxation and welfare systems specifically designed to redistribute income runs against the grain of party tradition, and the 'tough love' of workfare may prove unacceptable to the membership unless sufficient permanent and reasonably paid jobs can be created. Roy Hattersley – once regarded as on the right of the party – expressed the views of many Labour activists when he said:

> Providing the disadvantaged with more chances is a cruel deception if they are not given the material ability to take them...No one who has lived through the past twenty years can honestly believe that the tax system cannot be used to make substantial changes in the pattern of income distribution. Margaret Thatcher was the most redistributive prime minister in British history. She took from the poor and gave it to the rich. (Hattersley 1997)

In a speech to the Fabian Society in early August 1997 Peter Mandelson announced that a Cabinet unit would be established, chaired by the prime minister, to tackle the problem of social exclusion. Roy Hattersley welcomed the creation of the unit but condemned Mandelson's speech as a series of generalities 'with more public relations than policy' (*Guardian*, 16 August 1997). The influence of the 'classic' left in the Labour Party was demonstrated by the failure of Peter Mandelson to be elected to the National Executive.

The proposals contained in the consultative document 'Partnership in Power' (Labour Party National Executive 1997) were directed at smothering these potential frictions by reducing the influence of the annual conference in the policy-making process. Labour's traditional internal decision-making structure – based on constituencies, trade unions and affiliated organizations submitting resolutions to annual conference – was to be replaced by a complex dispersal of policy deliberations and decision making. Objectors to the proposals argued that the 'sharp' ends of the process – 'the initial formulation of resolutions at local level, and the theatrical hammering out of grand conglomerated positions at conference' (Taylor and Bentley 1997) – would be blunted. The drawing up of reports for debate at party conference by a new Joint Policy Committee would be dominated by the chair of the committee, the prime minister (Livingstone 1997). Despite resolutions from ninety constituency parties objecting to the proposals, they were approved by conference.

The Conservative Party

Labour's rights–obligations link echoed Major's 'back to basics' philosophy and led to accusations that Labour had stolen the Conservatives' clothes. If so, then the fit was better, for the Tory claim to the moral high ground had become fragile. They had been in power for eighteen years but their own rhetoric suggested the standards in schools were declining, social security fraud was rife, and a dangerous 'underclass' had emerged. Moreover, the 'sleaze' associated with certain Conservative MPs could be interpreted as the moral rot spreading from the top downwards.

Labour's usurpation of the Tory approach to social policy has created problems for the Conservatives because New Labour has found fresh language to package the idea that welfare encourages dependency. Most electors now identify welfare reform, workfare, family values, the drive to improve standards in schools and a reduction in state bureaucracy as Labour issues. In his first two years of opposition the leader of the Conservative Party, William Hague, will concentrate on reforming the party machine, but, when policy positions have to be developed, he will face a dilemma unless Labour's policies fail or are modified by the left. If he moves to the right of Labour then he risks being pushed to the ideological fringes; but a Conservative Party with more redistributive policies than Labour – although advocated by some 'One Nation Tories' (Gilmour 1997) – seems strange. Perhaps the old left/right division will become less relevant and the Conservatives will adopt a more tolerant, libertarian stance, maintaining that individuals must be free from state interference but, in return, must bear the consequences of their behaviour (Duncan and Hobson 1995). Portillo's speech to a fringe meeting at the 1997 Conservative Party conference signalled such an approach. He appeared to distance himself from Thatcherite condemnation of 'deviant' lifestyles and asked Conservatives 'to deal with the world as it is now' in their 'attitude to the personal relationships that people choose to enter'. He noted that 'For good or ill, many people nowadays do not marry and yet head stable families with children', but 'the important thing is that people recognise the responsibility they have when they conceive children' (*Guardian*, 10 October 1997). Such a stance would enable the Conservatives to depict Blair as promoting an authoritarian, 'nanny' state. The approach received some support from Hague, who called for a more tolerant, compassionate conservatism. Compassion, of course, does not necessarily mean redistribution of income to alleviate poverty.

Social welfare services can now be divided into two sectors. State health care and education are part of the 'universal' sector, used by the 'middle England' voter so important to New Labour's electoral success. Improving these services without increasing personal taxation will be an important element in achieving the second term that New Labour craves. Blair has protected his right flank by ensuring that part of the blame for underachievement in schools is directed towards inefficient local authorities, bad teachers and a minority of neglectful parents, but his left flank remains exposed to the Liberal Democrats and 'classic'

Labour Party activists, as was demonstrated in November 1997 when forty-seven Labour Members of Parliament, with the support of their constituency parties, either abstained or voted against the legislation that reduced benefits to single parents.

Social security, 'social' housing and the personal social services (indeed anything with 'social' in its title) form part of the 'residual' welfare state increasingly used only by the 30 per cent of the population described by Hutton (1995) as 'absolutely disadvantaged'. When speaking of this sector Labour's post-war language of 'redistribution', 'justice', and 'equality' has been replaced by that of 'obligations', 'duties' and 'zero tolerance'. This language echoes the Conservative rhetoric of 'back to basics' but is delivered with a salvationist fervour. Marquand (1996) has outlined the rationale of this approach. He makes a distinction between hedonists and moralists, active and passive, to give a four-fold classification 'in place of the simple dichotomy of individualism and collectivism'. Marquand finds a tradition of 'active collectivism' in the Labour Party that valued collective provision 'as underpinnings of personal and cultural growth, of engagement in the common life of society and so of self-development and self-fulfilment' (Marquand 1996, p. 21). According to Marquand, passive collectivist hedonism is to be found in the work of Tony Crosland and is characterized by welfare provision as an instrument 'for maximising morally neutral satisfaction'.

Marquand clearly finds 'passive hedonism' repugnant, believing that, under its influence, 'the notions that rights should be balanced by duties, that activity was better than dependence and that the point of collective provision was to foster self-reliance and civic activism came to be seen as patronising or elitist or (horror of horrors) judgemental' (Marquand 1996, p. 23). He goes on to say:

> hedonistic collectivism contains a built-in flaw. By definition, the redistribution it demands makes some people better off and others worse off. Also by definition, it can offer no convincing moral argument for doing so. If rights are not balanced by duties, why should the rich make sacrifices for the poor? If collective provision is not a means to moral improvement, why should those who are not in need of it pay taxes to pay for it? If the public domain is not a place of engagement, governed by a service ethic, what is to prevent it from becoming a battleground for predatory vested interests? Hedonistic collectivists could not answer these questions. (Marquand 1996, p. 24)

New Labour has a mission. The socially excluded are to be returned to the flock and, to assist their return, state benefits will be restrained – conveniently releasing resources for the 'universal' sector. To succeed, the mission requires the generation of work – not just any work, but work with reasonable pay and prospects. If such jobs are not created then the 'socially excluded' will remain outsiders and, even with firm management of Labour's annual conference, Labour's 'Hattersley tendency' will be difficult to contain.

Chronology of Significant Developments: April 1992 to October 1997

September 1992	'Black Wednesday' – withdrawal from the exchange rate mechanism (ERM)
April 1993	Council Tax replaces Community Charge (poll tax)
October 1993	John Major's 'back to basics' speech
1993	Education Act sets up a new funding agency for 'opted out' schools
1995	Trial nursery voucher scheme established
1995	Incapacity Benefit replaces Sickness and Invalidity Benefits
October 1996	Jobseeker's Allowance replaces Unemployment Benefit and Income Support
November 1996	Last budget of Conservative Government – income tax cuts and severe restraint of public expenditure from 1998
June–August 1997	Series of policy reviews established by New Labour, including a pensions and the tax and benefits system.
July 1997	First New Labour budget; White Paper *Excellence in Schools* published
October 1997	Tony Blair's speech to Labour Party conference places emphasis on the work ethic, flexible labour markets, giving, duty and family life; William Hague's speech to Conservative Party conference highlights self- reliance, compassion, tolerance and the traditional family

References

Ashdown, P. 1997 'Introduction' in 'Make the difference', London: Liberal Democrats.

Atkinson, A. B. 1969 *Poverty in Britain and the Reform of Social Security*, Cambridge: Cambridge University Press.

Bacon, R. W. and Eltis, W. A. 1976 *Britain's Economic Problem: Too Few Producers*, London; Macmillan.

Baker, K. 1993 *The Turbulent Years: My Life in Politics*, London: Faber and Faber.

Blair, T. 1995 '*Speech at a Fabian Society commemoration of the fiftieth anniversary of the 1945 general election*', 5 July 1995, reproduced in *New Britain: My Vision of a Young Country*, London: Fourth Estate.

Blair, T. 1996 *New Britain: My Vision of a Young Country*, London: Fourth Estate.

Castle, B. 1993 *Fighting All the Way*, London: Macmillan.

Cockett, R. 1995 *Thinking the Unthinkable*, London: Fontana.

Commission on Social Justice 1994 *Social Justice: Strategies for National Renewal*, London: Vintage.

Conservative Party 1987 'The next moves forward', London: Conservative Party.

Conservative Party 1992, 'The best future for Britain', London: Conservative Party.

Conservative Party 1997 'You can only be sure with the Conservatives', London: Conservative Party.

CPAG (Child Poverty Action Group) 1993 'Main events', *Poverty*, 86 (Winter), p. 5.

Crosland, C. A. R. 1956 *The Future of Socialism*, London: Jonathan Cape.

Deacon, A. and Bradshaw, J. 1983 *Reserved for the Poor*, London: Blackwell/Martin Robertson.

Department of Education and Employment 1997 *Excellence in Schools*, cm 3681, London: HMSO.

Department of Employment 1944 *Employment Policy*, Cmnd 6527, London: HMSO.

Department of Employment/Department of Social Security 1994 *Jobseeker's Allowance*, London: HMSO.

Dilnot, A.W., Kay, J. A. and Morris, C. N. 1984 *The Reform of Social Security*, Oxford: Oxford University Press.

Duncan, A. and Hobson, D. 1995 *Saturn's Children: How the State Devours Liberty, Prosperity and Virtue*, London: Sinclair-Stevenson.

Field, F. 1996a *How to Pay for the Future: Building a Stakeholders' Welfare*, London: Institute of Community Studies.

Field, F. 1996b *Stakeholder Welfare*, London: IEA Health and Welfare Unit.

Fleming, J. and Oppenheimer, P. 1996 'Are government spending and taxes too high (or too low)?', *National Institute Review*, July, pp. 58–76.

Foster, S. 1994 *Political Parties: Thatcherism Abandoned*, Sheffield: Sheffield Hallam University.

Gilmour, I. A. 1997 'A party heading for the rocks', *Guardian*, 4 October.

Glennester, H. 1995 *British Social Policy since 1945*, Oxford: Blackwell.

Hattersley, R. 1997 'Why Labour is wrong about income tax', *Guardian*, 6 August.

Hills, J. (ed.) 1990 *The State of Welfare: The Welfare State in Britain since 1974*, Oxford: Oxford University Press.

Hutton, W. 1995 *The State We're In*, London: Jonathan Cape.

Jeffrey, B. 1995 *John Redwood and Popular Conservatism*, London: Tecla Editions.

Jenkins, S. 1995 *Accountable to None*, London: Hamish Hamilton.

Kavanagh, D. 1994 'A Major agenda' in *The Major Effect*, Kavanagh, D. and Seldon, A. (eds), London: Papermac.

Keynes, J. M. 1936 *General Theory of Unemployment and Money*, London: Macmillan.

Labour Party 1997 'New Labour: because Britain deserves better', London: Labour Party.

Labour Party National Executive 1997 'Partnership in Power', London: Labour Party National Executive.

Liberal Democrats 1997 'Make the difference', London: Liberal Democrats.

Livingstone, K. 1997 'An unequal kind of partnership', *New Statesman*, 29 August.

Lloyd, J. 1997 'A plan to abolish the underclass', *New Statesman*, 29 August.

Lowe, R. 1993 *The Welfare State in Britain since 1945*, London: Macmillan.

Mandelson, P. and Liddle, R. 1996 *The Blair Revolution: Can New Labour Deliver?* London: Faber and Faber.

Marlow, J. 1997 'Metaphor, intertextuality, and the political consensus', *Politics*, 17 (2), pp. 127–34.

Marquand, D. 1996 'Moralists and hedonists' in *The Ideas that Shaped Post-War Britain*, Marquand, D. and Seldon, A. (eds), London: Fontana.

Murray, C. 1990 *The Emerging British Underclass*, London: IEA Health and Welfare Unit.

Pimlott, B. 1989 'Is post war consensus a myth?', *Contemporary Record*, 2 (6), pp. 12–14.

Ridley, N. 1991 *'My Style of Government': The Thatcher Years*, London: Hutchinson.

Taylor, J. and Bentley, T. 1997 'Tony's new model revolution', *New Statesman*, 25 July.
Thatcher, M. 1995 *The Path to Power*, London: HarperCollins.
Timmins, N. 1996 *The Five Giants: A Biography of the Welfare State*, London: Fontana.
Webster, C. 1996 *The Health Services since the war. Vol. 2*, London: HMSO.
Wilcox, S. 1996 *Housing Finance Review 1996/7*, York: Joseph Rowntree Foundation.
Willetts, D. 1992 *Modern Conservatism*, London: Penguin.

Guide to Further Reading

The Five Giants: A Biography of the Welfare State (London: Fontana, 1996) by Nicholas Timmins gives a full account of the politics of the development of state welfare since 1945. Details of the Conservative approach can be found in *Modern Conservatism* (London: Penguin, 1992) by David Willetts. The impact of 'Thatcherism' and John Major's term of office are discussed by Simon Jenkins in *Accountable to None* (London: Hamish Hamilton, 1995).

The 'old' Labour perspective on state welfare is analysed in Howard Glennerster's *British Social Policy since 1945* (Oxford: Blackwell, 1995). A comprehensive account of 'New' Labour's social policies has yet to be written, but Frank Field's *How to Pay for the Future: Building a Stakeholders' Welfare* (London: Institute of Community Studies, 1996), and *The Blair Revolution: Can New Labour Deliver?* (London: Faber and Faber, 1996) by Peter Mandelson and Roger Liddle, offer signposts to the future.

4 | Law, Order and Civil Liberties

Steven Foster

Synopsis

This chapter begins with an exploration of party policy as it emerged from the twilight of the bipartisan consensus in the late 1970s. The impact of Thatcherism and Bennism are both examined, as is the response of the parties to the very different political climate of the late 1980s. Thereafter the chapter's focus shifts to the extraordinary intensification of policy-making after 1992, highlighting how and where the two main parties converged, together with the ongoing interplay between rupture and continuity which makes this such a bewildering yet fascinating period. The chapter then moves on to a descriptive analysis of the 1997 manifestos, concluding with an appraisal of the rather uneven impact of party policy.

The Historical Context: Party Policy 1945–1992

Bipartisan consensus: law and order policy 1945–1970

Party policy for the first quarter century after 1945 was largely based on the belief that, if left in the hands of its elites, the criminal justice system would check the tide of criminality without threatening the historic liberties of the British citizen. Such optimism was in part the product of how that system, particularly the police, emerged from the rigorous of wartime. In addition, evidence was accumulating that liberal progressive thinking in sentencing and penal affairs was beginning to bear fruit. Liberal progressives claimed that sparing use of custodial sentencing maximized the penal system's potential to rehabilitate offenders. Then as now it was feared that such apparent generosity would simply encourage criminals to offend. However, the absence of a significant increase in crime rates, at least until the middle of the 1950s, suggested that a cost-effective way of controlling criminality had been found.

Unsurprisingly, reality was not always in accord with such heady optimism (Bottoms and Stevenson 1992, p. 10). However, this was insufficient to disturb the tranquillity of the main parties. This was so even when party members expressed their own disquiet. In a letter dated 27 August 1958 Lord Butler, then the Conservative home secretary, noted that 'Later in the autumn I am to answer 28 bloodthirsty resolutions at the Conservative conference... it is with the greatest difficulty that we have chosen at least one out of the 28 which is at least moderate' (quoted in Bottoms and Stevenson 1992, p. 11). A consensus existed that sensible, executive adjustments, after full consultation with the Home Office mandarins, would suffice to ward off crisis. In such circumstances, the opposition was almost obliged not to make political capital when things went awry. An excellent example of this was Labour's 1964 manifesto, which 'after thirteen years of continuous Conservative government... said nothing about law and order, or the government's record' (Downes and Morgan 1997, p. 90). Indeed, it was not until 1966 that the two main parties found something tangible over which to disagree.

The consensus threatened? Conservative policy-making 1970–1983

It is beyond the scope of this chapter to examine those developments which finally shattered the optimism of the immediate post-war years. The first party to respond was the Conservatives, whose 1970 election manifesto remains a watershed in post-war law and order politics. Critically, it broke with tradition by drawing attention to the governing party's record in office, a strategy repeated in the two elections of 1974. Though conceived in slightly different circumstances all three manifestos possessed this central theme: that a refusal or inability to tackle order-defiance directly encourages criminality *per se*. In this way Labour was presented as the cause of its own difficulties. The support given to militant trade unionism by certain members of the Shadow Cabinet, most notably of the National Union of Mineworkers (NUM) during its 1972 strike, together with the decision of Harold Wilson's February 1974 administration not to prosecute the rebel Clay Cross councillors, were cited as evidence of Labour's irresponsibility and general unfitness to rule.

In this way Edward Health laid the basis for Margaret Thatcher's more sustained assault on Labour's record in 1979, law and order being one of the Conservatives' five priority policy areas. The manifesto promise to restore respect for both the rule of law and established authority hinted strongly at an expansion in the power of law enforcement agencies. Yet some commentators have subsequently placed a question mark over whether or not the Conservative manifesto departed dramatically from the consensus in terms of policy (Kettle 1983, p. 219). The Conservatives made four main pledges. Three of these concentrate on sentencing and penal affairs: a free vote on the return of the death penalty for murder; the restoration of the courts' power to sentence young offenders for a period of under three years; and a tougher regime at detention centres, capable of delivering a 'short, sharp shock'. However, in both scope and impact they appear to have been limited measures, especially when compared to Conservative policy in the age of Michael Howard. The vote on capital punishment (taken on 19 July 1979) was lost by the surprising majority of 119. Nor did the subsequent Criminal Justice Act (CJA) 1982 really challenge the principle that custodial sentencing should be used as sparingly as possible, especially in juvenile cases (Downes and Morgan 1997, p. 113). The fact that Labour voted for this piece of legislation is further evidence of this. Similarly, the much-vaunted 'short, sharp shock' regimes were quietly phased out after the pilot projects proved unsuccessful.

In policing the manifesto was equally moderate. Its main commitment was to honour in full the Edmund–Davies committee's recommendations on police pay, a policy only marginally at odds with Labour's. This apparent reticence can be excused, since all parties were awaiting the recommendations of the Royal Commission on Criminal Procedure (RCCP). The commission had been set up in the aftermath of the notorious Confait Affair, which had resulted in the wrongful conviction of three young men for arson and murder in 1972. The commission's brief was to enquire into the desirable balance between police power and individual liberty. When its findings were finally published in January 1981, the Conservatives responded by pressing for the codification of police powers minus many of the safeguards on which the RCCP had insisted. However, the significance of this is blunted by the following points. Primarily, Conservative policy was doing little other than following the lead given by the police, something which radical criminologists insist was common practice for all governing parties throughout the post-war period (Gilroy and Sim 1987, pp. 78–9). This theme is taken up by Kettle (1983, p. 221), who argues that in the run-up to the 1979 election Labour introduced legislation which would have significantly increased police powers and, in the event of victory, paved the way for a similarly authoritarian response to the RCCP.

Without questioning the Conservatives' commitment to a more overtly authoritarian agenda, the above does suggest that Conservative policy was moving with rather against the bipartisan consensus. Subsequently, when placed under more intensive scrutiny Conservative policy became much more moderate. During the report stage of the Police and Criminal Evidence (PACE) Bill (and much to the police's chagrin) the Conservatives tabled 170 amendments before the bill fell with the dissolution of Parliament in 1983. When Parliament recommenced its scrutiny of PACE, the new home secretary, Leon Brittan, disappointed the police staff associations further by bringing the bill into line with the findings of the Scarman report on the 1981 Brixton riots. Even in its amended form PACE remained a controversial measure, though not necessarily because it broke with the hidden, authoritarian underbelly of the bipartisan consensus.

The Consensus destroyed: Labour's response

Doubts over the radicalism of the 1979 Conservative manifesto and subsequent record in office make Labour's response far more central to a possible eclipse of the consensus. In their extensive study of party manifestos Downes and Morgan (1997, pp. 91–3) argue that Labour's policy developed but slowly: from indignation that law and order should have been exploited for partisan purposes (1970), through complete silence (1974), and on to an ill-judged attempt to convince the electorate that criminality and order-defiance were beyond the control of liberal democratic government (1979). Only after 1979 did the trajectory of Labour policy assume a different direction.

The interplay of three factors – Benn's theory of political renewal, the rise of a new left and the subsequent history of policing – was instrumental in this process. Paradoxically, yet in keeping with recent developments inside the Conservative Party, they ensured that policy developed in accordance with the views of Labour's metropolitan activist base and the interests it represented. This is why the electorate was offered such a clear choice of rival policies in 1983. Bennism insisted that Labour's future lay in embracing the daily struggles of the masses. In turn this would provide the basis for their eventual mobilization, not around the broken promises of social democratic paternalism but in the prospect of a direct transfer of power to working-class organizations. It was a renewal strategy self-evidently inspired by workplace struggle. However, the new generation of radical Labour activists soon applied it to law and order. It is at this point that the second and third factors merge. The urban left identified new constituencies, those which suffered most at the hands of the 'fire-brigade' style of policing designed to maintain public order. The urban rioting which occurred in 1980 and again in 1981, followed by a series of violent incidents on picket lines, convinced them that under Thatcher this method was being used to crush the dissent her economic policies had generated (Brake and Hale 1992, p. 2). Convinced of the inadequacy of parliamentary opposition under such circumstances (Seyd 1987, p. 34) and confident in their leadership of the larger metropolitan authorities, the urban left was determined to resist. It was a strategy which was to have profound consequences for Labour's law and order policy-making.

In keeping with radical criminology, the 1983 manifesto completely downgraded crime as an issue of importance. Like most social ills identified by Labour it could not be tackled directly. Only the elimination of mass unemployment offered a permanent solution. Instead, after making the historic noises about the need to keep petty criminals out of prison and make conditions more tolerable inside, policing emerges as the party's principal policy area. Certain policies – an alternative to the Police Complaints Board (PCB), for example – were in keeping with the views of the RCCP and were in turn accepted by the Conservatives. Others, by contrast, were not. The PACE Bill, despite Conservative concessions, was to be scrapped and in its place new statutory limitations on police powers drawn up. The new spirit was also extended to police accountability. Fully elected police authorities with the power to direct police policy were to be established throughout Britain, a policy which owed a large debt to the new MP for Blackburn, Jack Straw. There is no way of knowing whether or not these measures would have curbed police discretion or enhanced accountability. The Greater London Council's (GLC's) own model police authority for example, was to have been much more powerful (Oliver 1987, p. 188). The measures did, however, highlight Labour's determination to confront the steady drift towards authoritarianism, which, under the Conservatives, was in danger of becoming a flood. Yet a huge problem loomed before the authors of Labour's alternative policy on law and order. Like the rest of the manifesto, it merely served as a signpost to Labour's worst ever post-war electoral performance. Soon Labour would join the Conservatives in believing that the best thing to say about law and order was very little indeed.

In the shadow of Leeds Castle: Conservative policy 1983–1992

Conservative policy-making after 1983 reflects the party's steady disengagement from law and order politics. There are a number of reasons for this. First, the issue lost much of its saliency during this period. In neither the 1987 nor the 1992 election did law and order figure as a significant issue (Denver 1994, p. 92). Coupled with the Lawson boom, this helped to ease the pressure on Conservative policy-makers to match the rhetoric of early Thatcherism with similarly hardline policies. Second, it was during this period that the Conservatives were forced to come to terms with the failure of law enforcement agencies to tackle rising crime rates (Morgan and Newburn 1997, pp. 2–3). Compounding this was the growing penal crisis: the prison population was rising but to little positive effect. Hence the importance of a third factor. Neo-conservative thinking which had underpinned the 1979 manifesto was soon to be displaced by its rival concept: neo-liberalism.

The former was the product of a cultural reaction amongst Conservative politicians (led in Britain by J. Enoch Powell) to what they saw as the wanton abandonment of key governing principles by the British state. By contrast, the latter was much more the product of 'globalisation', defined as 'a process of hollowing out as peripheral functions are shedded [*sic*] to focus upon the core competencies of the state that enhance its competitive position' (Leishman et al. 1996, p. 10). Neo-liberalism was just as much a part of Thatcherism as neo-conservatism. At first, Thatcher intervened to ensure that their contrasting priorities did not lead to confrontation, largely by attempting to 'ring-fence' law and order from any process of 'hollowing out'. However, for reasons which will become more apparent below, this became an increasingly unattainable prospect. Hence, by the time John Major assumed the leadership of the party, the imposition of new public management (NPM) techniques, as opposed to the need to re-establish automatic respect for traditional authority, had become the driving force behind his party's policy-making. Cash limits, target setting and performance indicators – to say nothing of deregulation and privatization – were eventually to transform Conservative policy-making. Though their full impact was not to be experienced until after 1992, they first emerged during the late 1980s under the pragmatic stewardship of Douglas Hurd.

The 1983 manifesto theme, that the public should also play a part in the fight against crime, had become far more prominent by 1987, to a point where certain overlaps existed between the Conservatives and the Callaghan government of the previous decade. Inevitably, this demanded a more systematic reappraisal of party policy. The key event in the process was the seminal meeting at Leeds Castle, Kent, on 28 September 1987, attended by the then Conservative home secretary, Douglas Hurd, and his chief Home Office advisers led by David Faulkner, a Home Office authority on sentencing. The meeting was a marriage of two influences: neo-liberalism and the Home Office's long-standing concern to structure sentencing practice in order to alleviate the crisis in Britain's prisons. Faulkner's views can be crudely summarized in the formula 'Prison is an expensive way of making bad people worse.' His perspective, based on years of empirical research, was to receive further endorsement when the Woolf report into the 1990 Strangeways Prison riot was published early in 1991.

The main offspring of this meeting was the 1990 White Paper *Crime, Justice and Protecting the Public*. The Criminal Justice Bill which followed was duly focused on the most awkward of offenders: persistent, non-violent, and the main cause of overcrowding in jails. In future, sentencers were to be discouraged from using the custodial option for this type of offender, largely by being prevented from taking into account the number of offences committed and the number of previous convictions. Led by Lord Chief Justice Taylor, the judiciary expressed its disapproval of any measure undermining its discretion. David Waddington, Hurd's successor, was rather more concerned about its impact on Conservative unity. However, the apparent lack of interest in law and order at this time persuaded Waddington to retain the broad thrust of the proposals. Subsequently, the minister of state, John Patten, worked furiously to construct a body of support for the bill – soon to become the CJA 1991 – amongst Conservative MPs; a classic example of party policy following where the Home Office led.

The growing influence of neo-liberalism also impacted upon policing policy, though by no means as dramatically. The highly centralized structure of the new Crown Prosecution Service (CPS), which began work on 1 January 1986, is indirect evidence of this. The RCCP had intended the CPS to be a federal body and hence more responsive to the views of local constabularies. Treasury influences, however, ensured the opposite occurred. By the 1990s, the CPS had fallen easy prey to the imposition of cash limits. Not even the reforms made to PACE were to have such damaging effects upon police morale as the record number of discontinued cases which followed (Rose 1996, pp. 124–5, 135). By then, however, the chill winds of financial restraint were being experienced more directly. Following the Financial Management Initiative (the embodiment of NPM), the Home Office issued its famous Circular 114/1983, which imposed private sector management techniques on chief officers for the first time. This was followed five years later by Circular 106/1988, which made requests for additional staff dependent upon a demonstration that existing staff were being fully exploited. Amongst other things this led to a slowing in the growth of police establishments. Despite earlier Conservative boasts to the contrary (Taylor 1987, p. 301), the number of police officers in England and Wales grew by a total of 9.27 per cent in the 1980s. This compares to corresponding figures of 28.21 and 25.08 per cent for the 1960s and 1970s respectively.

In 1979 the Conservative manifesto implied government had to take the fight to the criminal and, moreover, to find the necessary resources even when trimming budgets elsewhere. Though law and order budgets were treated more sensitively than most, all of the policies discussed above point to the surreptitious but inexorable abandonment of this commitment (Savage and Charman 1996, pp. 41–2). The one exception to this process of disillusion and disengagement was public order law, which simultaneously offered a clear policy continum with the unrestrained neo-conservatism of the 1970s. Within weeks of the

Tories' 1979 election victory, a Green Paper was published which eventually led to the Public Order Act (POA) 1986. The Act was the greatest statutory assault on public protest in five decades. First, the law on public order offences was both extended and deepened (ss. 4–5). In addition, ss. 11–13 granted to police officers new powers to control processions, whilst for the first time s. 14 extended these to assemblies. This last section was aimed deliberately at picketing, and highlights Conservative determination to target the law at specific groups. Exactly the same point can be made for s. 39, which created a new offence of criminal trespass. This was inserted in response to the annual Peace Convoy's progress through the West Country (Ewing and Gearty 1990, p. 127). Together with evidence that resources were being diverted into public order policing, such a comprehensive range of measures encouraged speculation that, though the prime minister's interest in law and order had waned, the effects of this were confined to the rather mundane business of crime prevention (Morris 1994, p. 304).

A safer party

The Conservatives' desire for more pragmatic policy-making was mirrored in the attitude of the Labour Party, though not always for the same reasons. For Neil Kinnock, Thatcherism spelt such a threat to the interests of Labour's key constituencies that anything which preserved that threat had to be challenged. It was shortly to become apparent that his chief target was Labour's own 1983 manifesto. However, as Kinnock attempted to bring his party round to his perspective, two questions dogged his efforts: when would political circumstances permit such a reappraisal and from where would be find any alternatives?

These problems were particularly acute in the case of law and order. Embarrassing outbreaks of order-defiance intensified in the first four years of Kinnock's leadership and made a rapprochement with the police – Kinnock's main objective at this time (Reiner 1992, p. 264) – extremely difficult to translate into policy terms. A stalemate ensued. Party policy was still influenced by the urban left, even though it had lost control of the policy-making process. Labour's law and order policies for the 1987 general election were constructed on this contradiction. Anodyne crime prevention strategies were Labour's only detailed policy commitment, largely because they were the least likely to offend. On policing, the core of the 1983 manifesto, it was largely silent. Only in the aftermath of Labour's third successive defeat was Kinnock finally able to establish a comprehensive review of policy. In 1990 a White Paper, *A Safer Britain*, finally revealed the fruit of the leadership's intellectual travails.

Despite the many changes it brought, *A Safer Britain*, together with the relevant sections of the 1992 manifesto, highlights the ongoing stand-off between left-wing activists and the party leadership. The former's influence is countered but not obliterated, especially in respect of Labour's theory of crime: 'Thatcherite economic and social policies have created the conditions which undermine community safety' (Labour Party 1990, p. 5). However, it is not until attention shifts to public order and civil liberties that one finds another echo of the radicalism of 1983. Sentencing policy remained in line with Labour's unchanging commitment to limiting the use of custody, which in any case had just been reaffirmed as the central theme of Conservative thinking. Precisely the same point applies to penal affairs. Again like the Conservatives, though far less grudgingly, Labour accepted the perspective of the doyen of the liberal establishment, Lord Woolf, whose report into the Strangeways Prison riot Labour was also pledged to implement. In policing and unlike the Conservatives, Labour was committed to the reform of PACE – though not its repeal – and fully elected police authorities. However, in contrast to its position in the 1983 manifesto, Labour was extremely vague as to how a new PACE would look and anxious to demonstrate that fully elected authorities would in no way threaten the operational autonomy of chief constables. Such ambiguity serves only to confirm the impression that an assault on the authoritarian state was the last item on the Labour leadership's agenda (Reiner 1992, p. 265).

As implied above, the one aspect of Labour policy which retains a clear link with 1983 and, even more significantly, established clear blue water between Labour and the Conservatives was public order and civil liberties. Evidence for this lies in Labour's parliamentary voting record. Its opposition to PACE has already been mentioned. Further, from 1983 Labour consistently opposed the annual renewal of the Prevention of Terrorism Act (PTA). Finally, in 1986 Labour voted against the POA. It is, however, worth remembering that the party's commitment to civil liberties was of very recent standing. Significantly, and serving perhaps as a pointer to the future, neither repeal nor amendment of the PTA and POA appeared in the 1992 manifesto.

Conservative and Labour policy compared

Like 1987's, the 1992 campaign was a lacklustre affair (Downes and Morgan 1997, p. 99). Despite Labour's slightly more aggressive stance in the run-up to the election, the party leadership appears to have taken the decision not to campaign on the law and order issue, a decision which was in keeping with Conservative strategy. The pattern of policy development since 1987 also precluded the possibility of radical eve-of-poll initiatives. Crucial differences did continue to separate the parties. Their contrasting views on the causes of crime, Labour's ongoing concern with policing, and the very different voting records on anti-terrorist and public order legislation must all be acknowledged. This is particularly so if we are to make sense of the very different pattern of policy-making which took place after 1992. However, the overwhelming impression of the 1992 election is one of convergence. Accord had been re-established on that most important of criminological issues: the value of prison. More importantly, and reminiscent of the pattern of events before 1970, neither party wished to politicize law and order. This is insufficient perhaps for one to conclude that a bipartisan consensus had been reconstructed, but a long march from 1983 all the same.

An Unusual Climate: Continuity and Rupture 1992–1997

The central feature of this period is the fact that both main parties abandoned the caution which had marked their attitude to law and order in the election campaign. One factor was the emergence of law and order as the fastest-rising political issue of the period. By November 1995 it was the fourth most salient issue, registering a 177 per cent increase in importance since 1990 (*The Times*, 28 November 1995). A second factor, however, was much more significant. For the first time since the breakdown of the bipartisan consensus, the Conservatives were forced to fight for occupancy of their own policy terrain. Relations between the two parties were thus turned upside down, leading to an extraordinary brinkmanship in which policy-making became more akin to a grotesque game of poker.

Law, order and Conservative politics

These factors generated an unprecedented surge towards authoritarianism, a tendency encouraged by internal developments within the Conservative Party. Electoral considerations identified law and order as an issue likely to expose the continued existence of 'Old' Labour. At some point, or so this argument went, an intensifying authoritarian agenda would force Tony Blair and later Straw into an embarrassing abandonment of their hard line, or risk a damaging internal split. In addition, a neo-conservative stance on law and order would soon prove essential in restoring unity to the governing party. Paradoxically, thanks to the controversy growing over the CJA 1991, the issue was itself a source of dissent (Rozenburg 1994, pp. 295–9). However, the restoration of internal unity over law and order (Kenneth Clarke effectively suspended the key sections of the Act in spring 1993) soon metamorphosed law and order into a device to restore internal unity. Though Major was unable to offer meaningful concessions on the future of the welfare state and European integration, law and order presented no such problems.

This tendency became even more pressing given the growing determination of the 'bloodthirsty' annual conference to influence debate. In 1993, 244 hardline resolutions on law and order were submitted to the conference organisers. Over the following four years the home secretary's speech was consistently used to announce new policy initiatives, thereby maximizing their unifying impact. Howard, who became home secretary on 27 May 1993, excelled in playing his conference audience to perfection. Yet to use conference in this way obliged him to feed it with precisely the policies it wanted (Foster 1995). As he discovered to his cost in 1994 when he retreated over a compulsory identity card (ID) scheme, the conference's choice of dishes may have been limited but it knew what it liked.

The Howard reforms

Under Howard's direction, sentencing and penal affairs saw the most dramatic changes in law and order policy-making since 1945. Not only did he storm the ramparts of Leeds Castle; in doing so he inflicted a far greater defeat on progressive forces than Thatcher had ever achieved or possibly intended. It was in his now famous '27 points' speech to the annual conference on 6 October 1993 that Howard gave the clearest indication of his thinking. This speech is best remembered for his insistence that prison had a unique ability to incapacitate offenders which far outweighed its failings elsewhere. Two years later, once again in a policy package designed for and presented to the annual conference, Howard announced his alternative to the CJA 1991, an Act he had neutered in July 1993. The key innovations were twofold, though both revived the theme of reduced judicial discretion, which also figured in Hurd's more pragmatic approach. First, minimum sentences were to be introduced for persistent burglary and drug dealing. Second, the principle of mandatory life sentencing was extended for a second conviction for any one of a category of violent crimes other than murder, where it already applied. This is the so-called 'two strikes and you're out' principle, heavily influenced by trends within the United States.

Via the White Paper, *Protecting the Public*, published on 3 April 1996, the conference proposals led directly to the Crime (Sentences) Bill, unveiled in the Commons on 25 October the same year. However, the absence of a commanding government majority, and unprecedented opposition in the House of Lords, thwarted Howard's plans. A limited form of judicial discretion was included in the final draft, but this was not before he had locked Labour into a new consensus. Repeat offending, even when it did not involve crimes of violence, now sufficed to merit a custodial sentence.

This initiative constitutes the most significant rupture in criminal justice politics since 1945. Unabashed, Howard continued his offensive in respect of prison regimes. His predecessors had committed themselves reluctantly to the main findings of the liberalizing Woolf report in the White Paper *Custody, Care and Justice*, published in September 1991. By contrast, Howard placed an emphasis on more punitive measures and a corresponding increase in the powers of prison officers: mandatory drug testing, the shackling of prisoners during hospital visits, and the return of the 'short, sharp shock' concept for young offenders. Ironically, however, the single greatest factor in the deterioration in prison conditions was not the result of new policy. Though the wholesale privatization of prisons was eventually rejected in May 1995, Howard used the lower running costs of private prisons to justify the ongoing search for economies within the state sector. The 13 per cent savings demanded of the Prison Service by the 1995 budget had devastating consequences for the service, the more so because of the need to finance the additional security measures demanded by the Learmont report. General Learmont had been requested by Howard to report into the breakout at Parkhurst Prison in January 1995. His findings, published the following October, were a damning indictment of the Prison Service Agency. Howard's immediate response was to sack the agency's chief executive, Derek Lewis. However, anxious that this might not prove enough to appease his own supporters, Howard also declared his intention to prioritize spending on security above all else. The gap which separated Howard from Woolf thus became a chasm, something which exacerbates the sense of discontinuity with the 1980s. Yet if this is so, it is a rupture aggravated by continuity elsewhere. The gap between the rival priorities of neo-conservatism and neo-liberalism – a contradiction of Thatcherism – was being closed, but only at the expense of those who worked within or who were otherwise dependent on the Prison Service.

The same tension is also apparent, though not as manifestly so, in Conservative policy on policing (Leishman et al. 1996, pp. 17–20). A dualism not dissimilar to that in penal policy developed under Howard, whereby the continued pursuit of economies was married to compensatory increases in police power. As we have seen, the left would argue that the latter was merely the continuance of deeper post-war trends. However, the growth in statutory police power during the 1990s was striking. None of the Thatcher administrations contemplated measures as wide-ranging or as controversial. Early evidence of Howard's commitment to increasing police power came with the decision to abolish the suspect's unconditional right to remain silent. Though he was subsequently forced to tone down his original proposal, this ancient right was abolished by ss. 34–9 of the controversial Criminal Justice and Public Order Act (CJPOA). A wide-ranging piece of legislation, the Act also increased police powers to obtain and retain body samples (ss. 54–9) and to stop and search members of the public in specially designated areas (s. 60). The latter was particularly significant because it enabled the police to act on their suspicions alone, a principle seemingly at odds with the logic of PACE.

Another burst of legislation occurred two years later. The Criminal Investigations and Procedure Act (CIPA) 1996 went some way to meeting police objections to the low conviction rate. On 2 April in the same year, a new Prevention of Terrorism (Additional Powers) Act was passed through the Commons in under six hours. This built upon reforms already made in 1994, largely by extending further the use of blanket stop-and-search powers untrammelled by the need for reasonable suspicion. The passage of the Act also illuminates the deployment of this issue in an attempt to force Labour back towards the civil liberties lobby. Howard gave Straw little or no warning of his intentions. Yet he still demanded Straw's cooperation on a guillotine motion forcing the bill through just before the Easter recess, knowing this would provoke Labour backbenchers into a row with the leadership. Howard's final piece of legislation was the Police Act 1997, introduced ostensibly to bring police surveillance powers into line with those held by MI5. Like the Crime (Sentences) Act this was subject to Lords amendments which countered Howard's original plans. Peers rejected the clause allowing chief officers to authorize the use their own forces made of the powers granted. Yet, once again, Howard succeeded in drawing the Labour leadership into a consensus on this issue. Later this was to undermine the Lords' determination to impose some form of external check.

Elsewhere, however, the pro-police policy-making reached its limits, once again highlighting the continuity with the Hurd era, at the same time taking Conservative policy further away from the 1979 manifesto. Responding to accusations of inefficient management, in May 1992 Clarke had set up the Inquiry into Police Responsibilities and Rewards, chaired by Sir Patrick Sheehy. It is true that when, on 23 October 1993, Howard passed judgement on Sheehy's recommendations he protected junior ranks from sweeping change. It should not be overlooked, however, that the core principles of fixed-term contracts and performance-related pay are now established, if only for the more senior ranks. Further, late in 1993 Howard permitted the Home Office Review of Police Core and Ancillary Tasks (the Posen Inquiry) to identify the police's 'core' tasks, the implication being that those falling outside this definition would be vulnerable to civilianization. Finally, it must also be remembered that it was Howard who supervised the passage of the Police and Magistrates Courts Act 1994, together with the Police Act 1996, both of which significantly strengthened the power of the home secretary to shape the priorities and practices of the forty-three constabularies in England and Wales. Future Conservative home secretaries who wish to do so will at the very least possess the statutory power to implement Sheehy's agenda.

Once again, therefore, the one area of Conservative policy representing unbroken continuity, stretching back through the 1980s to Heath and Thatcher, was public order law. This was developed further in part V of Howard's CJPOA. Even more so than in 1986, the Conservatives targeted the Act at specific groups. Preventive police powers were created to suppress New Age Travellers (ss. 61–2 and 77–80), raves (ss. 63–6 and to a lesser extent ss. 70–1), animal welfare and road protesters (ss. 68–9) and, finally, squatters (ss. 72–6). These measures were particularly interesting since they seemed to allow the police to intervene in events taking place on private property with the owners' consent, a development at odds with broader Conservative thinking. However, as we shall see below, these were desperate times for the Conservative Party and, of course, desperate times have historically called for desperate public order legislation.

Jack and Tony: partners against crime

More so than in the case of the Conservatives, rupture was the dominant feature of Labour policy after 1992. It began with the appointment of Tony Blair as shadow home secretary immediately after Labour's election defeat. In a way which mirrored the strategic thinking of Major and Howard, Blair also used law and order to realize other, overtly political objectives. Precisely because few voters expected much from Labour, it was the ideal issue for demonstrating a break with both its own past and those client groups which appeared to dominate party counsels. Eventually this led Labour towards a distinctly authoritarian and populist stance, completely at odds with the party's post-war history. Yet, at first, Blair was keen to complement this with strongly pragmatic policies. It was the Conservatives who were dubbed ideologically motivated and consequently incapable of finding practical solutions to pressing problems. This was made clear in one of Blair's final speeches as shadow home secretary. Speaking to the Police Foundation on 14 June 1994, Blair spoke of his determination to avoid 'the false choice between punishment and prevention'; whether a policy was likely to work was to be the only criterion (*Guardian*, 15 June 1994).

Labour's first policy statement after its election defeat, 'Partners Against Crime', was published on 13 September 1994. In isolation, it was not the most radical of documents. Yet seen in context 'Partners Against Crime' went some way towards creating the new paradigm for policy-making which was to be Blair's main legacy. The document made clear the party's new-found determination to distinguish between the criminal act and the offender's background. Blair had of course already introduced this concept via both the famous soundbite 'tough on crime, tough on the causes of crime' and his speech to the 1993 party conference (*Guardian*, 1 October 1993). In addition, 'Partners Against Crime' also established the eradication of criminality as the party's principal law and order priority, with a willingness to consider tough judicial responses: 'There can be no excuse for committing a crime and those who do so should be brought to justice' (Labour Party 1994, p. 13). One of the failings of *A Safer Britain* was that it gave the impression of wanting to restrict custodial sentencing for its own sake. Instead, 'Partners Against Crime' argued that its opposition to prison was practical rather than ideological. With only one in 750 crimes resulting in a custodial sentence, Labour reasoned, it was senseless to focus scarce resources on the penal system.

This was intelligent, politically aware policy-making, aimed at exploiting public concern over the persistent failure of the Conservatives to tackle the crime problem. It did not, however, constitute a radical programme for reform. It was his successor Jack Straw who inherited Blair's strategic thinking, 'fleshed it out [and] equipped it with the apparatus of policy' (McKie 1997). Under his stewardship Labour's policy-making developed in the most unanticipated directions: Straw intended nothing less than the colonization of Conservative social authoritarianism. The first of his many initiatives was in low-visibility public disorder, an area of policy which has always invited a populist response. In their drive to promote custodial sentencing Straw was convinced that the Conservatives had overlooked the growing tide of anti-social behaviour. On 19 June 1995 a consultation document, 'A Quiet Life – Tough Action on Criminal Neighbours', was published. Its main proposal was a new power for the courts – the community safety order – breach of which could lead to a custodial sentence of up to seven years. Anti-social behaviour was thus criminalized, and it was the courts, rather than welfare agencies, who had ultimate responsibility to enforce a remedy. Six weeks later, in a speech to a Lewisham audience on 4 September, Straw uncovered a second threat to the social fabric: the hordes of 'beggars, winos and addicts' allegedly disturbing the tranquillity of town centres up and down the land. In the ensuing debate Straw also declared his sympathy for 'zero tolerance' policing, then being pioneered in New York. The third element of Labour's policy on public order was announced on 2 June, when Straw spoke up for the principle of curfews on children under the age of 10. At first, the party seemed unsure about the desirable extent of such a measure. Later, after its general election victory, its attitude was to harden.

These interventions bear obvious comparison with Thatcher's policies as leader of the opposition, epitomized in Straw's comment that 'It is disorder which leads to crime and the threat of disorder which leads to crime' (Travis 1995). The left were outraged (*New Statesman and Society* leader, 15 September 1995). One of the most salient of the resulting critiques suggested that Labour had acquired the mantle of social authoritarianism precisely because it no longer intended to use fiscal policy to alleviate the impact of the free market. In the 1960s and 1970s it could afford to be both liberal and pragmatic over crime, since it remained hopeful that welfare economics would counter the threat of mass alienation within the urban poor. By 1996, knowing that mass alienation had indeed taken root, and yet being unwilling to eradicate it, Labour could only offer 'the pain of free market capitalism but with state financed counselling to soften the blow'. The alternative to this 'depoliticisation of economics' was simply to say nothing (Elliott 1996). Far from returning to the disengagement of the Kinnock era, Straw remained unapologetic, insisting that his policies would none the less benefit Labour's traditional constituency: the poorest and most vulnerable, who suffered most from low-visibility public disorder. Those who condemned him were contemptuously dismissed: 'Let them try living on an estate with some criminal gangs living on the same street, and feel the sense of powerlessness it produces' (quoted in McKie 1997).

A separate consequence of the above was to draw Labour even closer to the police staff associations. The exceptionally warm reception Blair had had from the Police Federation's annual conference in May 1993 was reciprocated when, in his speech to the Police Foundation, Blair confirmed Labour's opposition to the Sheehy report and Posen Inquiry. Later still, on 5 February 1996, Labour launched its own campaign against low conviction rates, no doubt delighting police officers with a thinly veiled attack on the CPS, reform of which became one of Labour's five law and order priorities. Interest in declining conviction rates led Labour to support the CIPA, despite its controversial sections on the disclosure of evidence.

The above invites the accusation of opportunism. However, when we move to the issue of police powers and public order law, the accusation is more serious: the abandonment of the principled stance to have emerged from the 1980s. Blair himself had set a precedent when, on 14 April 1994, he insisted on an abstention rather than outright opposition on the third reading of the Criminal Justice and Public Order Bill. However, given his views on public order and 'zero tolerance' policing, Straw almost invited the Conservatives to test further Labour's resolve, to say nothing of his control of Labour backbenchers. Consequently, it was during his tenure that the war of attrition launched by Howard reached peak intensity.

Straw's disregard for the role inherited from Roy Hattersley (protector in chief of individual liberty) had become clear via Straw's support for the new Security Services Act 1996, which enhanced the role of MI5 in crime fighting. The watershed, however, occurred later, over prevention of terrorism legislation and the 1997 Police Bill. On 14 March 1996 Labour abandoned its policy on the PTA by abstaining on the vote for its annual renewal. Twenty-five MPs rebelled. Exactly two weeks later Straw compounded this felony in the eyes of these critics by pledging Labour's cooperation over the guillotine motion which was to secure the passage of the Prevention of Terrorism (Additional Powers) Act. This was put to the vote on 2 April, whereupon thirty Labour rebels joined the Liberal Democrats in the 'No' lobby. Leading commentators were quick to point to the dangers of Straw's stance. In particular it was argued that New Labour could never again credibly challenge the request of law enforcement agencies for emergency powers (Young 1996). Kettle (1996) supports this by relating Straw's actions to his earlier decision on the annual renewal of the PTA. 'When Labour had cringed once, they were committed to a policy of cringe. There was no way without humiliation that they could oppose Howard's . . . new bill.' More importantly, he went on to draw a comparison with the Labour Party of Wilson and James Callaghan: 'Offered the warm embrace of the governing class, Labour fell into it. The same old Labour which has found itself weak in the presence of duty so often before.' Labour's policy had ruptured, yet in contrast to Straw's initiatives on crime, it had merely returned to the status quo ante.

Once again, though, Straw remained wedded to his defensive strategy. The final test was the passage of the Police Act. Here, he stood accused of taking the spirit of cooperation a stage further by actively hampering the efforts of MPs to introduce liberalizing amendments (Young 1997a). As with the Crime (Sentences) Act, it took that despised institution, the House of Lords, to remind the Labour Party of the importance of legal and political accountability – truly, a remarkable finale to a remarkable era.

The 1997 General Election: Campaign and Aftermath

Its continued prominence in opinion polls, together with the time invested in policy-making, guaranteed law and order a high profile throughout the campaign. Unsurprisingly, Labour made the Conservatives' record in office a key election theme, and the Labour leadership was not overly concerned about the populist tone it often struck. Straw's comments to residents of a crime-ridden Kent housing estate, that 'Our pensioners are prisoners in their own homes ...Surely the prisoners should be those who commit the crimes, not those who are the victims of crime?' (*Guardian*, 26 April 1997), would not have been out of place at the annual Conservative conference. It is testimony to Labour's discipline, or perhaps to the centralized nature of its campaigning, that such a speech, unthinkable in 1983, raised scarcely a murmur in 1997. Evidence reaffirming the idea of a convergence between the two main parties is thus easy to uncover. Whilst distinct differences remain, a remarkable overlap now marks their manifestos.

The Labour and Conservative manifestos reappraised

Labour's pledges were grouped into eight sections, five of which – the fast-track scheme for juvenile offenders, imposition of the community safety order, appointment of a 'drugs tsar', decentralization of the CPS, and a statutory obligation on local authorities to develop crime prevention partnerships – were its priorities (Labour Party 1997, pp. 319–20). In this way Labour retained both its key policy commitment from 1992 and a connection with the welfare progressives. The purpose of a fast-track system for persistent juvenile offenders is of course to keep them out of jail.

It is the additions and omissions, however, which bring out the extent of the rupture in Labour policy. Labour has picked up on traditionally Conservative concerns (juvenile delinquency, the link between crime and disorder and the low conviction rate) and outflanked them with its own high-profile policy innovations. This has come at a price, though one which its leadership seems quite willing to pay. One aspect of this is the much lower profile, when compared to 1992, given to the principle of non-custodial sentencing. Labour's belated and rather reluctant opposition to the Crime (Sentences) Act is important here.

Likewise, reform of PACE and the 1964 Police Act, both of which appeared as late as 1992, are missing. Much more importantly, although Labour retained its commitment to a Bill of Rights for the UK, one wonders how this can be reconciled to Labour's positions on the CJPOA, the PTAs and the Police Act 1997. The manifesto's silence on this point is likely to echo throughout Labour's period in office (Young 1997a).

The relevant section of the Conservative manifesto is entitled 'A Safe and Civil Society' and is divided into a number of subsections ranging from safer communities to tackling drug abuse (Conservative Party 1997, pp. 348–51). Aside from some very specific commitments over closed-circuit television (CCTV) and a voluntary ID scheme, the main policy absent from Labour's manifesto is reform of the Crime (Sentences) Act. The Conservatives hope to remove those amendments forced on them by the House of Lords. It is, however, symptomatic of the Conservatives' post-1992 difficulties that much of the remainder appears as little more than a defensive parry. This is the most striking feature to emerge from a comparison of the two documents. The imposition of time-reduction targets on youth courts, 'child crime teams', the Parental Control Order, and encouragement for chief constables to develop 'local schemes to...improve public order' (p. 349) all bear more than a passing resemblance to the rival manifesto. In their defence the Conservatives can argue that some of these policies evolved from their own initiatives. This has some merit in respect of persistent juvenile offenders. However, even here one has to question whether initial interest was prompted by a reaction to an earlier Labour proposal. Only in their persistent opposition to local authority coordination of crime prevention programmes, and in their refusal to consider a major reform of the CPS, can the Conservatives genuinely claim to have been untouched by Labour's influence.

A principled opposition?

It would be quite wrong to assume that because of the obsessive reactions of its two rivals the Liberal Democrats ignore growing public anxiety over crime. For example, on 27 February a policy document detailing plans for combating criminality were published. The theme also figures strongly in the 'Crime and Policing' section of their manifesto (Liberal Democratic Party 1997, pp. 369–70). At the same time key differences emerge which suggest that, here at last, the Liberal Democrats possess policies which make them distinctive. This is especially the case in sentencing, where the party restates its belief in the the CJA 1991 in a way quite lacking in the Labour manifesto. Likewise, the Liberal Democrats are much more explicit in their determination to divert resources towards crime prevention programmes.

A second area of divergence is the Liberal Democrats' focus on the community, as opposed to the criminal justice system, as the principal forum for tackling crime. Labour would of course point out that many of its policies are structured around the need to strengthen the community. If so, this is not always reflected in its manifesto, which has acquired a more overtly statist complexion. The importance of the community even extends to certain aspects of Liberal Democrat policy on policing. The commitment to find the resources for an extra

3,000 officers is qualified by the insistence that they are all assigned foot-patrol duties.

It is in the more general area of police management and powers that the third and most significant difference appears. Though there is no pledge to introduce sweeping reforms of the 1964 Police Act, the Liberal Democrats at least acknowledge the link between effective crime prevention and public confidence in accountability procedures. The pledge to monitor the use of stop-and-search powers, especially in relation to ethnic minorities, is particularly refreshing. So, too, is the recognition that a huge democratic deficit has opened up in the area of European police cooperation. Again, it would be inappropriate to overstate these differences. They are enough, however, for the Liberal Democrats to emerge as the one party interested in broadening the law and order policy agenda.

A crime and disorder bill

In the Queen's Speech, Labour honoured its main election pledge by promising to lay before Parliament a Crime and Disorder Bill. Before the new home secretary had the chance to elaborate on what it might include, another pledge was also redeemed. On 11 June 1997, a second Firearms (Amendment) Act passed through the Commons, effectively outlawing the private ownership of handguns. Details of the Crime and Disorder Bill were released during September and October. On 25 September Labour clarified its plans for combating juvenile crime. Three weeks later, on 15 October, those working in the youth court system were given a foretaste of the brave new world that awaited them. Neither announcement heralded a major departure from the manifesto, yet both provide a deeper insight into Labour's thinking. The package of measures aimed at juvenile crime undoubtedly contained many welfare-oriented measures. At the same time, and in keeping with the Community Safety Order, a strongly punitive element is equally present. It is now confirmed that parents who fail to meet the conditions of a parenting order will eventually face a custodial sentence. To be a persistently bad parent is thus to commit a criminal offence. In similar vein, Labour's plans for the youth court system end the monopoly on locking up children under 15 enjoyed by social services departments. In the case of so-called 'spree offenders' (the hard core of persistent child criminals), youth courts will also possess powers of detention. Labour admitted that the principal victims of this policy would be 15–16-year-olds currently residing in adult prisons. Secure accommodation created for them is now likely to be reserved for the spree offenders, highlighting the limits to the welfarist element in Labour's plans for criminal justice.

These restatements confirm two of the greatest changes in Labour policy: a partial embrace of custodial sentencing and the pivotal role given to the courts in the fight against crime and order-defiance. Likewise, one can expect the profile of police officers on Britain's streets to continue to rise. This emerged in the course of the debate on curfews. Labour had not been particularly explicit about them in its manifesto. Yet the statement of 25 September confirmed plans granting officers power to impose a 'blanket' curfew on all children under the age of 10 if so requested by local residents. Immediately, however, the Scottish Office indicated that it would be happy to see the measure extended to all children, right up to the age of majority. This announcement was prompted by the decision of Strathclyde police to place Britain's first blanket dawn-to-dusk curfew on all children in an entire town, Hamilton in Lanarkshire. Understandably, the proposal led to a heated debate between senior officers and the Scottish Council for Civil Liberties. That the Scottish ministers' default position was to support the police can only fuel speculation that Labour's social authoritarianism has some way to travel yet before it loses momentum.

To defend themselves the Labour leadership can point to a number of countervailing measures which suggest that it has not broken completely with its concern for civil liberties. Even one of its most stringent critics has welcomed Labour's review of immigration and asylum seeking (Young 1997b). Yet the curfew debate raises the distinct possibility that Labour policy, once again, has become a prisoner of the most powerful criminal justice elites. Young (1997b) notes that the Code of Practice drawn up by Straw in respect of the police's new surveillance powers creates a loophole of such magnitude that the Lords' amendment establishing some form of independent authorization loses much of its impact. Perhaps New Labour really is a contradiction in terms, after all?

Conclusion: The Impact of Party Policy

The most striking feature of party policy in the 1990s is the manner in which it moved from the margins to the centre of party political debate. Its impact on the outcome of the 1997 general election therefore should not be underestimated. Law and order was in so many respects the ideal canvas on which New Labour could advertise itself. Equally, the Conservatives' counter-attack pushed Labour much further towards authoritarianism than many of its MPs wanted. The previous section noted how Labour's future policy-making will continue to bear the stamp of Conservative influences.

Yet despite the innovation shown by both parties, one cannot help but sense the fundamentally reactive nature of their responses. Perhaps it is because law and order touches upon the individual and collective neuroses of British citizens that policy-making is so sensitive to scandal and so vulnerable to the sort of populist opportunism seen since 1992. It is to their credit that both Labour and the Conservatives remained aloof from this for as long as they did. However, once Heath and Thatcher released this particular genie from the bottle, it has proved very difficult to contain. The only concerted effort made by a party to be proactive was after the 1987 general election, when the Conservatives attempted to draw up a definitive policy-cum-philosophy on sentencing. Even then, however, the initiative came not from the party but from the Home Office.

Yet the sad truth about populist responses remains: they simply perpetuate the mythology which pervades law and order policy-making. This is the belief that it is possible for liberal democratic government to check crime and disorder through the authoritarian option of containment and confinement. By advertising such wares before an ever more desperate electorate, parties tend simply to raise unrealistic expectations from which later they invariably wish to retreat. This is not to say that party initiatives fail to have an impact beyond the electoral arena. To cite but one example, the decision to encourage a greater use of prison, especially for juveniles, can have a desperate impact upon thousands of lives. As Noel Smith (1997) notes with brutal candour, 'To anyone who has spent time in a British prison, it is easy to understand how men facing the bleak prospect of time behind the walls of HMP [Her Majesty's prison] might choose to try anything that might smash the drab routine of their lives and give them a kind of release.' However, on the issue of greatest concern to both the public and many within the criminal justice system – curbing criminality whilst maintaining individual liberty – party policy has had singularly little impact. Perhaps this explains the 'wave effect' seen in the 1980s and 1990s. Following a period of intense policy-making, both main parties looked to downgrade public expectations largely by refusing to engage in political debate. Pragmatic management of resources – or laying a claim to this particular skill – rather than policy innovation became the order of the day. In this respect, it will be fascinating to see whether or not there is a similar retreat in the course of the current Parliament. Only one aspect of law and order politics seems to have survived the rigours of populism and pragmatism, engagement and retreat: the power of Britain's criminal justice elites, and their role in regulating the lives of Britain's citizens, continue to expand. Party policy has not always been the prime mover behind this. It may not have escaped the reader's attention, however, that rarely has it ever done anything to reverse it.

Chronology of Significant Developments: April 1992 to October 1997

October 1992	Controversial and ill-fated Criminal Justice Act 1991 comes into force
February 1993	Murder of James Bulger generates unparalleled public anxiety over criminal behaviour, signalling beginning of the end of the Hurd–Faulkner era
May 1993	Michael Howard becomes home secretary
October 1993	Howard makes '27 points' speech to Conservative conference
December 1993	Criminal Justice and Public Order Bill published in tandem with Police and Magistrates Courts Bill
September 1994	Labour's policy document 'Partners Against Crime' launched
June 1995	Jack Straw announces plans to tackle low-visibility public disorder, opening new era in Labour's policy-making
September 1995	Straw makes 'beggars, winos and addicts' speech in Lewisham

October 1995	Howard declares intention to introduce minimum sentencing, whilst extending applicability of automatic life sentences
February 1996	Shadow Cabinet approves Straw's decision to drop Labour's opposition to annual renewal of the PTA
March 1996	Straw agrees to Howard's request for cooperation on proposed guillotine motion to ensure passage of the Prevention of Terrorism (Additional Powers) Act
April 1996	Conservatives' White Paper on criminal justice, *Protecting the Public*, published
October 1996	Crime (Sentences) Bill unveiled in Commons
November 1996	Police Bill published
March 1997	Straw unveils 'six point plan' for juvenile crime and disorder – the following day Conservatives publish a Green Paper on same subject

References

Bottoms A. and Stevenson S. (1992) 'What Went Wrong? Criminal Justice Policy in England and Wales 1945–1970' in Downes D. (ed.), *Unravelling Criminal Justice* (Basingstoke, Macmillan).

Brake M. and Hale C. (1992) *Public Order and Private Lives* (London, Routledge and Kegan Paul).

Conservative Party (1997) 'Conservative Party Manifesto' in Austin T. (ed.), *The Times Guide to the House of Commons May 1997* (London: Times Books).

Denver D. (1994) *Elections and Voting Behaviour in Britain* (Hemel Hempstead, Harvester Wheatsheaf).

Downes D. and Morgan R. (1997) 'Dumping the "Hostages to Fortune"' in Maguire M., Morgan R. and Reiner R., *Oxford Handbook of Criminology* (Oxford, Oxford University Press).

Elliott L. (1996) 'Labour's Mean Streets', *Guardian*, 4 June.

Ewing K. and Gearty C. (1990) *Freedom Under Thatcher* (Oxford, Oxford University Press).

Foster S. (1995) 'The Trials of the Home Secretary', *Parliamentary Brief*, December.

Gilroy P. and Sim J. (1987) 'Law, Order and the State of the Left' in Scraton P. (ed.), *Law, Order and the Authoritarian State* (Milton Keynes, Open University Press).

Kettle M. (1983) 'The Drift to Law and Order' in Hall S. and Jacques M. (eds), *The Politics of Thatcherism* (London, Lawrence and Wishart).

Kettle M. (1996) 'Cowardice in the Face of the Ruling Class', *Guardian*, 3 April.

Labour Party (1990) *A Safer Britain* (London, Labour Party).

Labour Party (1994) 'Partners Against Crime' (London, Labour Party).

Labour Party (1997) 'Labour Party Manifesto' in Austin T. (ed.), *The Times Guide to the House of Commons May 1997* (London: Times Books).

Leishman F., Cope S. and Stane P. (1996) 'Reinventing and Restructuring: Towards a New Policing Order' in Leishman F., Loveday B. and Savage S. (eds), *Core Issues in Policing* (London, Longman).

Liberal Democratic Party (1997) 'Liberal Democratic Party Manifesto' in Austin T. (ed.), *The Times Guide to the House of Commons May 1997* (London: Times Books).

McKie D. (1997) 'Puritan Jack Plods the Police Beat,' *Guardian*, 26 April.

Morgan R. and Newburn T. (1997) *The Future of Policing* (Oxford, Oxford University Press).

Morris T. (1994) 'Law and Order' in Kavanagh D. and Seldon A. (eds), *The Major Effect* (Basingstoke, Macmillan).

Oliver I. (1987) *Police, Government and Accountability* (Basingstoke, Macmillan).

Reiner R. (1992) *The Politics of the Police* (Hemel Hempstead, Harvester Wheatsheaf).

Rose D. (1996) *In the Name of the Law* (London, Jonathan Cape).

Rozenburg J. (1994) *The Search for Justice* (London, Hodder and Stoughton).

Savage S. and Charman S. (1996) 'Managing Change' in Leishman F., Loveday B. and Savage S. (eds), *Core Issues in Policing* (London, Longman).

Seyd P. (1987) *The Rise and Fall of the Labour Left* (Basingstoke, Macmillan).

Smith N. (1997) 'Enter the Dragon', *Guardian*, 24 September.

Taylor I. (1987) 'Law and Order, Moral Order' in Miliband R., Saville J. and Pantich L., *The Socialist Register 1987* (London, Merlin).

Travis A. (1995) 'Straw Defiant on Begging', *Guardian*, 9 September.

Young H. (1996) 'Blair Sacrifices Liberty in Search of Power', *Guardian*, 29 February.

Young H. (1997a) 'Wake Up and Defend Our Basic Freedoms', *Guardian*, 4 March.

Young H. (1997b) 'Police March over Straw Barricade', *Guardian*, 14 October.

Guide to Further Reading

An excellent introduction to the historical background of law and order policy is T. Morris, *Crime and Criminal Justice since 1945* (Oxford, Blackwell 1989), whilst D. Rose's more polemical *In the Name of the Law* (London, Jonathan Cape 1996) provides vital material on the contemporary crisis within the criminal justice system. Party manifestos and their immediate political context are analysed at length by D. Downes and R. Morgan, 'Dumping the "Hostages to Fortune", in the latest edition of the *Oxford Handbook of Criminology* (Oxford, Oxford University Press 1997). Elsewhere, J. Rozenburg, *The Search for Justice* (London, Hodder and Stoughton 1994), provides detailed insight into the debate within the Conservative Party over the Criminal Justice Act 1991, whilst R. Reiner's *The Politics of the Police* (Hemel Hempstead, Harvester Wheatsheaf 1992) is ideal for the changing contours of police policy in the 1980s. The evolution of Conservative policy on police powers and public order is dissected with some animosity by K. Ewing and C. Gearty, *Freedom Under Thatcher* (Oxford, Oxford University Press 1990). Finally, S. Foster, *The Politics of Law and Order Today* (Manchester, Manchester University Press 1999), covers the current debates within criminal justice from an overtly political perspective.

5 | Immigration and Racial Equality

Shamit Saggar

Synopsis

The broad sweep of British party policy in the field of racial equality reveals three essential characteristics in relation to the period up to 1997. The first has been the overwhelming degree to which these policy concerns have been intertwined with the parties' anxieties over immigration policy. Second, there has been a strong reactive element running through party-based debates over policy, which, with a few notable exceptions, has ensured that there has been a relative absence of reasoned policy development. The exception to this was the attempt to forge a fresh racial integration policy framework under Labour in the 1960s. Finally, in the latter part of this period it is hard to overlook the strong influence of electoral considerations in shaping party policy questions.

The Historical Context: Party Policy 1945–1992

Policy dualism: race relations and immigration in the 1950s

The turning point in early post-war racial politics came with the eruption of racial violence in 1958. Over the August Bank Holiday, so-called race riots took place in Notting Hill and Nottingham, resulting in a major escalation of the saliency of the immigration question (Pilkington 1988). In this revised context, the immigration hardliners on the Conservative backbenches were presented with a new and decisive opportunity to press home the case for a policy change. Their attempts placed the Conservative administration on the wrong foot and succeeded in throwing up a cross-party consensus to 'do something', but, crucially, failed to bring about a substantive change of policy. This failure is doubly surprising since the political context of foreign policy and empire had altered fundamentally by 1958. For one thing the debacle of Suez in 1956 had created a more pragmatic perspective on the value of the empire and Commonwealth. In essence, it was now permissible to raise the following calculus: if the hostile reaction of India and others following Suez showed that the Commonwealth was of little use to Britain at a time of crisis, why, then, should Britain seek to give special preference to the Commonwealth in its immigration policy? This quickly became a powerful rhetorical argument swilling around the grass roots of the Conservative Party. The neo-realism that it purported to advance also found an element of support in Labour's grass roots.

That said, an important rival interpretation has sought to argue that the move to introduce statutory controls was, *de facto*, first established in 1958. The riots had highlighted the government's reluctance to adopt explicit policy, placing leading Conservative politicians on the defensive. General public scepticism towards uncontrolled immigration and concerted pressure from party activists combined at this time (Dean 1992). Messina (1989) reports that the 1959 election soaked up some of this pressure. This was not so much because race and immigration were major issues in the election campaign as because the party's immigration hawks received a strong boost. Tougher, anti-immigration Conservative candidates did especially well in 1959, especially in the Midlands, he notes.

The upshot of this spell was that the philosophy beneath the *laissez-faire* policy lay in ruins by 1959 (Cmnd 7695). The notion of abandoning free entry no longer attracted strong principled criticism within Conservative ranks (Smith 1991). Freeman (1979), Katznelson (1973) and others have claimed that Conservative policy now shifted to the questions of how and when to bring in controls. Meanwhile, having conceded important ground on immigration, the party's liberal wing had been active in trying to fashion a new outlook towards other, related aspects of foreign policy. In a major illustration of this change, the drive towards decolonization was given a fresh lease of life by a party that had until recently claimed to symbolize empire. Thus Harold Macmillan announced to the South African Parliament in early 1960: 'The wind of change is blowing through this continent, and whether we like it or not, this is . . . a political fact' (Childs 1986, p. 111).

The statutory controls in fact took much longer to emerge than many had envisaged after the 1958 riots. Eventually, a fresh bill was published to introduce a tiered entry system in 1961 and given royal assent in 1962. The legislation was reasonably modest in its scope, serving to create a queuing system based on voucher categories for would-be immigrants. Yet its adoption was grounded in a political assumption that held that the Act would put the whole immigration issue into touch. It was also hybrid in its pedigree, containing both the outlook of racial arguments from the party's grass roots and the reasoned assessment of pragmatists who sought to retain the link between the new controls and labour market needs. In any case, the real importance of the 1962 Act was that it was a partisan, non-consensual measure (Spencer 1997). Any attempt to present its principle as bipartisan was stillborn. Labour's opposition, though ambivalent at local level, was wholehearted. Three overlapping reasons have been put forward for Labour's adversarial stance. First, the party rallied round the claim that the Act had knowingly undermined Commonwealth unity, a point for which it received some limited support from other Commonwealth governments. Second, continuing its preoccupation with principle, the party argued that the legislation breached the spirit of socialist internationalism; this argument was inevitably aimed at, and well received by, the more ideologically motivated activist wing of the party. Finally, the distinctive leadership of Hugh Gaitskell was an important factor on the issue, not least because of the sharp turnaround on policy following the elevation of his successor, Harold Wilson, in 1963 (Saggar 1992).

A proactive liberal policy framework

Labour's start in office was associated with a number of policy changes as well as an element of policy continuity. The most striking changes stemmed from the fact it entered office in 1964 with a clear-cut commitment to outlaw overt racial discrimination. What it had in mind was far from obvious, though most observers believed that a policy of targeting discrimination in the public sphere lay at the heart of this commitment (Rose 1969). The origins of this commitment were in fact complex and multi-faceted in Labour's own ranks. A prime source of the policy had come from a band of idealistically minded MPs and activists who had supported the backbench efforts of Fenner Brockway in the 1950s to introduce an anti-discrimination bill (Hindell 1965). Although his efforts had come to nothing, this campaign had left its mark among Labour's left, who believed that it was important to counter the anti-immigrant rhetoric of Tory backbenchers such as Norman Pannell and Cyril Osborne (Saggar 1992, p. 101). However, alongside the idealists existed others in the Labour Party who took a more judicious approach to the policy pledge. This group, pragmatists at heart and linked to the party's trade union sponsors, felt that Labour needed to be cautious in fleshing out its policy. One particular worry they had was that an inadequately framed law that covered the workplace might have the effect of, first, curbing the implied leeway of existing white trade unionists, and, second, unintentionally stirring up racial competition and ill-feeling in the labour market (Miles and Phizacklea 1984). The upshot was that Labour's fresh start to race relations policy was underscored by a strong need to balance these rather contrasting forces.

Notwithstanding this constraint, Labour's new home secretary, Sir Frank Soskice, started the ball rolling and began preparations for a comprehensive review of available policy models and options. In doing so, he gave backing to the notion that the party's policy stance had to be guided by something stronger than reactive *ad hoc*-ism. Having secured a first Race Relations Act on the statute book by mid-1965, the party could reasonably claim to have made progress towards this initial goal. Furthermore, the arrival of his successor, Roy Jenkins, at the Home Office in late 1965 ushered in an expected second phase in which policy would be built upon and, it was hoped, expanded (Saggar 1996). A second Act therefore became the objective of liberals both in government and in opposition.

Much has been made by scholars of Labour's policy initiative at this time (Holmes 1988). However, it is as well to remember that a counter-perspective can be offered to suggest that the policy in fact owed more to continuing the legacy inherited from the Conservatives. For instance, it would be a mistake to think that racial integration policy was born after the change of government. The 1962 Commonwealth Immigrants Act had also established a loose, embryonic framework for integration policy discussion. This involved a series of specialist expert working parties to examine key areas of public policy such as housing, education, policing, and so on. The 1965 Race Relations Act merely converted much of this machinery into the National Committee for Commonwealth Immigrants (NCCI) to 'coordinate on a national basis efforts towards the integration of Commonwealth immigrants into the community' (Messina 1989, p. 37). The Conservatives' priority in 1962 had been to introduce a statutory system of controls but at the same time to begin work on the question of easing domestic racial tensions. Labour, in this sense, merely added and contributed to existing priorities.

Moreover, the counter-thesis has greater validity when it is recalled that one of Labour's first acts upon entering government was to declare the end of its policy of opposing the 1962 Act. This turnaround is commonly explained by two factors. First, the new party leader, Wilson, was determined to demonstrate his leadership direction at an early stage to both party and country. A blatant reversal of policy on immigration therefore amounted to a convenient instrument for his agenda (Deakin 1972). Second, the party's leadership were plainly shocked to witness the extent to which anti-immigrant popular sentiment could be harnessed to hurt the party (McKenzie and Silver 1968). The defeat of Patrick Gordon-Walker, the foreign secretary designate, in the 1964 general election in Smethwick graphically illustrated the need for caution. Therefore, in backing the existing policy of annual renewal of the 1962 controls, Labour signalled its desire to establish a cross-party consensus on immigration.

Race and consensus politics

The question of consensus is important in explaining developments from the mid-1960s to the mid-1970s. Ultimately the real significance of the liberal policy reforms of this era lies not so much in their content as in the cross-party tacit agreements that were pursued on race relations and immigration policy (Banton 1985). The notion of a *quid pro quo* helps us to understand the pattern of policy direction. Throughout this period, it is clear that the two major parties agreed to two interrelated propositions. First, it was accepted that extensions of liberal race relations reforms could only be built on the back of a tough regime of immigration controls. No party therefore sought to question the rationale for controls and their gradual tightening over this period. Moreover, a glance at survey data from this period reveals that the main parties were justified in fearing an electoral backlash by appearing to be weak on immigration: between 1964 and 1970, an average 74 per cent of the electorate believed that 'too many immigrants had been let into the country' (Butler and Stokes 1974, p. 461). This amounted to nothing less than a one-way bet as far as party strategy towards immigration policy was concerned. Second, building on this dictum, it was understood that both major parties would avoid competing for support in the whole area of immigration and race relations. For this reason, it is apparent that

Conservative frontbenchers persistently refrained from attacking Labour as either weak on immigration or the friend of immigrants and ethnic minorities (Layton-Henry 1992).

In this context we can account for the powerful reverberations in the Conservative Party following Enoch Powell's notorious 1968 intervention. His speech not only defied party discipline within Tory ranks, a powerful transgression in itself, but was also viewed as a calculated bid to shatter the inter-party consensus (Rich 1986). Powell was quickly disciplined, but his actions had placed the consensus on an unsettled footing (Schoen 1977). Furthermore, whilst the Conservative leadership stuck to the agreement and steered clear of making electoral capital out of the row, it is clear that the impact of Powell was to reinforce a latent suspicion in the minds of the electorate. This held that the Tories were essentially the party of anti-immigration policy and that a cosy agreement with Labour entered into by Edward Heath prevented it from claiming this 'natural' territory. In any case, evidence has been gathered to show that the Conservatives benefited from the fallout of the Powell episode in the 1970 election (Miller 1980; Studlar 1978). The consensus broadly persisted through the following Conservative administration.

Maintenance of consensus had its price, however. Messina (1989, 1997) has stressed that cross-party efforts to keep race off the agenda of party competition merely ended up encouraging extremist polarization both within the parties and beyond. By the early 1970s it was clear that a strong wave of public support could be marshalled by the extreme right National Front, much of which was the result of single-issue protest. The Front's electoral appeal peaked in 1974 and it remained a powerful force throughout the decade. Meanwhile, the left of the Labour Party had begun to lose faith in the Labour administration of 1974–1979 and were keen to sponsor the development of new protest action involving disaffected and alienated groups. Finally, the Tory right had begun to rebuild and restructure the party in a root-and-branch fashion after the election of Margaret Thatcher as leader in 1975. One interpretation, therefore, of the era of consensus over race and immigration might be that the wonder lay in the fact that it had lasted as long as it did (Saggar 1996).

Racial politics and electoral calculus after 1974

With the demise of consensus politics, the major parties turned to new agendas and priorities. On the Labour side, this entailed the politics of risk and even crisis management as the party discovered that, once in office, the issue of immigration ranked near the top of the pile of those on which it had lost the initiative. At the same time, however, the party maintained the edifice of the liberal policy framework, and by 1975–1976 was ready to build on this. The third and final Race Relations Act was enacted in 1976 and served to extend substantially the provision of law. In particular, progressive politicians in Labour's ranks, led once again by Roy Jenkins at the Home Office, were successful in incorporating the doctrine of indirect discrimination into the coverage of the new law. Its major significance lay in the adoption of the principle of indirect discrimination, whereby public policy efforts could be geared to examining and rectifying policy outcomes without the need to show deliberate intent to exclude ethnic minorities. This principle amounted to a huge advance for the party's leftist activists and its growing number of ethnic minority activists, though it had the effect of alienating many Tory potential supporters. In the event, a Tory frontbench instruction to support the bill's second reading was defied by the rebellion of a number of backbenchers.

More importantly though, the difficulty for Labour lay in the fact that, outside Westminster, hardly any public opinion could be found to support the new Act. Indeed, at a time when Labour was preoccupied with integration and discrimination questions, the vast bulk of public opinion was captured by vociferous and sustained opposition to further immigration (Crewe and Sarlvik 1980). Finally, the 1976 Malawi crisis, involving another Asian refugee influx, further underlined the drift that had set in.

It was into this void that the political strategy of the Conservative renewal was put. A simplistic electoral calculus underpinned the Conservative departure from consensus. This strategy viewed the ten or fifteen years prior to 1975 as an aberration and departure from the logic of rational party competition. On a range of issues – trade union rights, social welfare, law and order – the Conservatives became convinced that a large gap had opened up between popular opinion and their own position. Immigration represented a further and compelling illustration of this breach (Saggar 1998). The party thus elected to follow the thread of this analysis to its logical conclusion. Arguably, immigration policy amounted to one of the easier policy domains in which the party began to reposition itself to the right. Two notable commitments were made, first to halt any new waves of fresh immigration by introducing a comprehensive new nationality law, and second to introduce a register of dependents in order to gauge the extent of additional secondary immigration that remained in the pipeline. Both initiatives were immediately lauded by the popular press and struck a chord in public opinion. Furthermore, leading party figures were given the go-ahead to adopt a new, abrasive rhetoric in communicating the policy position. Senior Tories such as William Whitelaw, shadow home secretary and a reputed champion of 'one nation' Tory principles, were placed to endorse the new hardline position. This pattern was epitomized by the party leader, who in early 1978 described and identified with white fears of 'an alien culture' that might 'swamp' the British (Layton-Henry 1992). Polling evidence recorded the electoral popularity of this stance, thereby reaffirming the position of the Tory hardliners who saw racial politics as a rich harvest from which to draw sustenance (NOP 1978).

The triumph of 'one nation' moderation 1979–1990

At first glance, it might seem puzzling to describe the 1980s as an era in which racial politics and party politics shifted in the direction of moderation. After all, this was a period in which strong Thatcherite leadership and rhetoric served to move the party to the hardline right. The Thatcher agenda had begun by moving in this direction whilst in opposition, and thereafter used elected office to deliver identifiable policy outcomes in the same spirit. In the area of trade union reform, for instance, party policy in the 1980s drove the government to a series of laws that fleshed out many of their earlier pledges. However, there are important exceptions to this general pattern, and the field of race and immigration seems to amount to a subtle de-escalation of the priorities of the 1970s.

Several factors drove this turnaround. To begin with, by 1981 the Conservatives were able to point to the adoption of the Nationality Act as tangible proof of their commitments in action. A quantification of potential dependents still waiting to enter Britain had also been made. Furthermore, the first signs of a slow-down in the rate of New Commonwealth primary immigration were already apparent some time before the new government took office (Saggar 1992). These factors had the impact of allowing the Conservatives to claim that the immigration question had been tackled with diligence and urgency. However, they also had the effect of slowly removing the saliency of the immigration issue itself. In electoral terms, by 1983, despite the doom-laden predictions of radical critics of the Tory strategy, the immigration issue had more or less fallen off the edge of the agenda of mainstream politics (Crewe 1983).

Moreover, the party had entered office boasting of something of an uncompromising position towards race relations. An implied suggestion was that Conservative government would usher in a new era, in which greater attention would be paid to the need to integrate newcomers by seeking changes in their patterns of behaviour and expectations (Behrens and Edmonds 1981). The cultural practices of immigrants, so the rhetoric ran, would be subject to examination to see if these contained or implied any disintegrative tendencies. Rhetorically at least, the party's hardliners promised a discernible reordering of priorities. An early test of this challenge was the fate of the Commission for Racial Equality, the government's official race relations quango. Despite a fierce campaign by hardliners to extinguish this body, principally for symbolic reasons, liberals within the administration were able to form a successful coalition to retain it and, in the longer run, give it fresh leeway to develop its own initiatives. This outcome amounted to a major victory for the party's moderate wing (Messina 1989).

However, the biggest influence upon the Conservatives' emerging policy were events themselves. For instance, in spring 1980 the first of a series of urban riots broke out in several British cities; the following year urban disorder escalated yet further with significant problems in Brixton in south London and in Toxteth on Merseyside. A further wave of riots in 1985 in Tottenham (north London), Handsworth (Birmingham) and, again, Brixton continued this pattern of crisis management. A gut response from many Tory politicians was to condemn these events as serious examples of lawlessness and, in the eyes of some hardliners, as acts merely of personal wickedness (Benyon 1984).

However, at a higher level, it is important to note that the problem was swiftly handled within a more sober policy framework. Michael Heseltine emerged from this discussion as an environment secretary with newly expanded scope and powers. Dubbed the new minister for Merseyside, Heseltine led a heavyweight task force comprising business leaders, Whitehall mandarins, local government officials and others, whose purpose was to examine radical options to tackle underlying economic decay in Liverpool and other comparable cities.

Additionally, the Conservative government's independent inquiry into the disorders, presided over by Lord Scarman, a senior law lord, provided another powerful counter-argument to the hardline right (Scarman 1981). It concluded that any viable analysis of the cause of the disorders and resultant policy recommendations could not overlook the issues of (1) inappropriate and insensitive policing methods, (2) the strength of street-level black perceptions of police harassment, and (3) the impact of racial discrimination in jobs, housing and so on. Scarman's contribution was to neutralize the weight of right-wing rhetoric that sought to reduce the entire issue to one of the guilt of black youth. Instead, he effectively championed a loosely based coalition, headed by senior Tory ministers such as Heseltine, Sir George Young, Whitelaw and others, that preferred to engage with the problems of racial exclusion, urban decline and criminal justice (Parkinson and Duffy 1984). Again, the right was forced onto the back foot.

The Thatcher years are characterized by this kind of delicate balance between the party's right and left wings over the politics of race. Meanwhile, liberal, one nation-style Tories assumed an ever more proactive stance in trying to build bridges to ethnic minorities. Indeed, by the mid-1980s it had become common to see influential right-wingers lending their weight to this task. Norman Tebbit, Lord Young and Leon Brittan, among others, all became associated with the new spirit of dialogue (Saggar 1998). The eclipse of the immigration issue in electoral terms certainly aided this agenda as Tory strategists focused on affluent, middle-class ethnic minorities – East African Asians in particular – who held an ever-smaller direct stake in immigration policy. These Central Office-led efforts tended to yield few dividends, however. Electoral data reveals that, despite successive handsome election victories, the Conservatives achieved no meaningful breakthrough in attracting black and Asian voters. The party's share of the ethnic minority hovered between 10 and 18 per cent at this time (Saggar 1997b). At the level of the party's rank and file, ethnic minority members continued to be rare (Whiteley et al. 1994). Furthermore, the attitudes of existing white members tended to remain as hostile as ever towards immigration and immigrant rights (Messina 1997).

The 1980s also saw the emergence of a new right-wing critique of race couched in the politics of culture and nationhood (Levitas 1986). A core element of this critique focused on the trajectory of multicultural education programmes pursued at local level. In a controversial case, a Bradford headteacher, Ray Honeyford, came into conflict with his local education authority (LEA) masters following his public criticism of these policy programmes. Honeyford was transformed into a folk hero of the right, who believed at a more general level that such policy both was being pursued as an article of doctrine and had the result of stoking up disintegrative tendencies. Organizations such as the Parental Campaign for Choice in Education (PACE), headed by Baroness Cox, entered the fray, arguing that multiculturalism had become a dangerous ideological force in its own right. PACE was joined by a number of right-wing groups, many informally organized on the fringes of the Conservative Party, such as the Monday Club, the Salisbury Group, the London Swinton Circle, the Social Affairs Unit, the Libertarian Alliance and others (Gordon and Klug 1986). Their wider agenda now shifted a range of pseudo-rational arguments concerning black criminality, immigrant reproduction patterns, and black social values and morality. In policy terms, New Right campaigners worked diligently by focusing on the education sphere in particular. A major victory was eventually achieved through the 1988 Education Reform Act, which isolated Christianity as the primary element of state religious instruction. Gamble (1988) has written of Thatcherism as a powerful fusion of two ideological traditions: economic libertarian thought alongside social authoritarianism. Using this template it is possible to account for the rising influence of New Right arguments at this time, based on an interest in forms of social behaviour attributed to different ethnic groups.

Radical black politics

For Labour the 1980s spelt an era of permanent opposition, and this in turn had a number of key implications for its approach to race and immigration issues. To begin with, it is fairly easy to show the link between disillusionment with the experience of Labour in office on one hand and the rise of a radical politics of exclusion on the other (Saggar 1991). This process had its beginnings as far back as 1975 with the establishment of the Labour Party Race Action Group (LPRAG). This was effectively an internal lobby group for black and ethnic minorities within Labour's ranks, and soon became identified with the younger cohort of left-wingers in the party. By 1979 it had developed a powerful critique of the recent history of the Labour Party (LPRAG 1979). It was broadly accepted that the 'failure to deliver' thesis carried weight and could not be dismissed. Solutions to this deficit, it contended, might include liberalization of the party's future stance on immigration and serious backing for equal opportunities policy (NEC 1980).

Black party activists therefore instigated their campaigns on the basis of a certain degree of self-criticism by the party hierarchy. By the early 1980s sufficient momentum had been built to allow the emergence of the Black Sections Movement. The activists pushed forward with three demands. First, they sought greater priority to be given to black and ethnic minority interests in policy-making, thus developing the notion of a distinctive race agenda in British politics (Saggar 1997c). Second, they pressed for an opening up of participation opportunities for black people in the party generally (e.g. candidate selection) and in party policy-making structures specifically (e.g. the idea of formal black sections affiliated to local constituency parties – Shukra 1997). Third, they targeted black representation and placed great emphasis on the need to gain a black presence at Westminster. In practice, the latter two goals tended to prevail and disporportionate press comment was attached to the absence of black Labour MPs (Roberts 1984).

The radical race critique and campaign were closely intertwined with the rise of the party's left wing at this time (Seyd and Whiteley 1992). First, one area of particular growth was in local government, where many radical municipal socialist administrations attached priority to the themes of radical and gender equality (Lansley et al. 1989). Following the 1987 election defeat, a wholesale exercise was launched to reposition the policies of the party by abandoning traditional left-wing territory (Smith and Spear 1992). Black Sections activists were not exempt from this drive and were forced to seek an accommodation with the party leadership or risk direct conflict. Second, much of the passion of the radical critique evaporated once the parliamentary beachhead had been gained. Four prominent Black Sections activists entered the Commons in June 1987, most of whom began to distance themselves from an insistence on party constitutional change to permit black-only sections. The withdrawal of support by some of these figures had the effect of leaving other activists relatively isolated, and additionally served notice to the party leadership that an embarrassing showdown could be avoided (Sewell 1993). Third, by the end of the decade influential voices in the party began to question the intellectual premise of the radical race agenda thesis. Figures such as Roy Hattersley, a controversial and unpopular politician in the eyes of the left and Black Sections activists, tackled the argument head on. In 1989 the party finally declared that a discrete racial section was ruled out in constitutional terms. A new Black Socialist Society took its place, presented as a compromise between both sides, but in reality amounting to a clear ideological defeat for radical black activists (Shukra 1990).

An Unusual Climate: Continuity and Rupture 1992–1997

Racial equality issues have in recent times adopted something of a lower profile in party politics. The largest factor driving this lesser saliency, as previously noted, has been the substantial decline in the related question of immigration. By the early 1990s British party politics could no longer be described as openly racially charged, as had been the case in the 1960s and 1970s. However, beneath this, there had emerged a new, subtler concern with racial and ethnic themes. The 1992–1997 Parliament demonstrated the importance of these themes and in particular focused attention on an old, continuing question: to what extent, and in what sense, was race a factor that could be used by the Conservatives to mobilize electoral support against the Labour Party? The journalistic shorthand for this question was widely known as the 'race card' debate and had been circulating, on and off, around British party competition since the days of Smethwick. In this five-year period renewed attention was given to this debate, which, in turn, tended to overshadow many of the major parties' ongoing interests and activities in racial and ethnic politics. The electoral courting of ethnic minority voters was a case in point. Another impact was seen in the development of a growing politics of European integration, itself involving an element of hostility towards an implied relaxation of British border controls. In this section we shall examine developments in the thinking behind campaigns to attract, or hold on to, ethnic minority electoral support (a debate that chiefly involved the Conservative Party). We shall also discuss the importance of controversies over ethnicity and representation (a debate that was centred in Labour circles at this time).

Courting ethnic minority votes

Successive Conservative election victories from 1979 onwards had failed to shape the fundamental electoral alignment of ethnic minorities. Survey research pointed to overwhelming Labour backing; traditional divisions of social class, education, residency and generation were generally not associated with significant variations in party support (Norris 1997, pp. 137–9). 'Race trumping class, and much else' had consequently emerged as a slogan that summarized this picture. Furthermore, scholars had devoted extended space to trying to unlock this puzzle (Messina 1989; Studlar and Layton-Henry 1990; Saggar 1998). Conservative strategists had grown accustomed to this bleak picture, though some recalled the great flurry of interest first shown in the so-called 'ethnic vote' after 1974 (Saggar 1997b). At that time interest from the right was driven by a form of Downsian logic: minority voters, it was believed, potentially held the key to victory in close-fought election campaigns, and sidelining their interest probably made no long-term sense. By the 1990s an element of this argument remained alive in elite party circles but was weakened by the fact that a decade's efforts had yielded few, if any, dividends (table 5.1).

Conservative attempts to poach Labour's ethnic minority supporters therefore took on a new face in the 1992 election and in the run-up to the 1997 contest. Three differences from previous initiatives stood out. First, Tory strategy tried to make a virtue out of the background of the party leader, John Major. As he was the first post-Thatcher leader, pressure quickly mounted for Major to distinguish his own personal agenda from the Thatcher years. Thus, from 1991 onwards Central Office launched an attempt to portray Major as a politician who, perhaps for generational reasons alone, was described as emotionally comfortable in a multiracial, multicultural society. The background of his predecessors, from both main parties, at the helm of the ship of state were contrasted with Major's formative years in politics. For instance, great play was made of Major's spell in local politics, when on Lambeth Council he led a purge of right-wingers who were attempting to drum up anti-immigrant support. Major was therefore presented as a rare force prepared to stand up to the forces of the Powellite whirlwind that was then sweeping through his party. In contemporary terms, strategists took care not to confuse this self-image with any suggestion that a Major-led party was in any way weak on immigration policy. However, what it did mean, they believed, was that he held no hidden prejudices in his approach to race relations. One seasoned journalist, Peter Kellner (1991), wrote that this feature of Major's leadership was likely to be reflected in a fresh political drive to 'overhaul British political morality'. Promoting harmonious race relations was therefore viewed by Major supporters as a ready practical measure within a larger moral agenda. The longer-term fate of that agenda seemed rather less

Table 5.1 *Levels of Labour and Conservative support among ethnic minorities at general elections 1974–1992 (per cent)*

Party	1974[a]	1979	1983[b]	1987	1992[b]
Labour	81	86	83	72	81
Conservative	9	8	7	18	10

[a] October 1974 general election
[b] Recalculated average of Asian and Afro-Caribbean support levels
Source: adapted from: CRC 1975; CRE 1980, 1984; Harris Research Centre 1987; Ali and Percival 1993

impressive by the mid-1990s. In any case, Major chose to give his personal backing to several new policy and promotional initiatives, including organizations such as Business in the Community, tackling inner-city regeneration, and ethnic minority training and mentoring projects. In 1993, his personal change of emphasis was perhaps weakened following the replacement of Kenneth Clarke, a notable one nation liberal on race relations, with Michael Howard at the Home Office.

Whatever is said of the Major personal touch, there is little doubt that by the mid-1990s, when he faced threats to his leadership, these earlier priorities had come to haunt him. A constant criticism within the party ranks, from all factions at times, was that Major suffered from an inability to see bold policy changes through. Racial politics were far from exempt in this regard. For example, critics on the liberal wing of the party noted with horror the case of John Taylor, a high-profile black parliamentary candidate who was effectively abandoned by Central Office in the face of grass-roots racist opposition to his candidacy (Rich 1997). Future waves of minority candidates and their white allies in the party learnt a brutal lesson from this case. Major nevertheless persisted in giving a liberal lead within the party, and to a large extent was able to neutralize the heavy guns of the anti-immigration lobby in the run-up to the 1997 election (Saggar 1997d).

Second, Tory strategy began to experiment with class-based appeals to Asian voters. Previously, the bulk of Tory campaigns for the 'ethnic vote' had been framed by a form of cultural argument. This held that a subliminal bond existed between the core values of traditional Conservatism on one hand and the British Asian community on the other. Examples that were cited by proponents of this thesis included a belief in traditional educational methods, personal thrift, respect for law and order, and maintenance of familial and social deference. On this kind of argument the party had placed its appeal to Asian voters in particular, who, it was claimed, were the natural allies of the Conservative Party. By the mid-1990s potentially serious loopholes were identifiable in political rhetoric of this variety. For one thing, the Labour Party under its new leader, Tony Blair, had made great strides towards claiming similar bourgeois ideological territory as its own. Additionally, it was suspected that middle-class Asian voters might well have been flattered by such appeals but not necessarily moved by them.

Conservative thinking therefore moved towards the claim that certain essentialist class interests and identities were at stake in choosing between the Tories and a centrist-minded Labour Party. Thus, the class profile of Asians in general, and ethnic Indians (the most numerous sub-group) in particular, was thought to be at the core of any future ethnic campaign. This new element tended to operate alongside the traditional cultural pitch and ultimately was eclipsed by Tory rhetoric that had grown fond of viewing Asians in ethnic-specific terms. The upshot was a recipe for muddle, with senior Tory politicians often unclear and uncertain over which approach to adopt. However, in at least trying to deploy a simple class-centred appeal, this strategy owed much to the wider debate that took place within Tory ranks as to how to counter the attractiveness of New Labour. Ironically, the priorities of ethnic campaign politics came as close as they

Table 5.2   *Voting intentions among Asians and blacks 1996–1997 (per cent)*

Party	Asian[a]	Black[b]
Conservative	25	8
Labour	70	86
Lib. Dem.	4	4
Other	1	1
(Undecided/refused/not voting	22	21)

[a] Of those naming a party (689)
[b] All except those certain not to vote (703)
Source: MORI 1996, 1997

have ever been to shadowing, if not integrating with, the mainstream electoral calculus of a major political party (table 5.2).

Third, Conservative bids to court ethnic minority voters began for the first time to acknowledge, very tentatively at first, that the party's own self-image might present obstacles. For instance, it was tacitly accepted under the tenure of Chris Patten as party chairman that the underrepresentation of ethnic minorities as party members and activists was a serious long-term impediment to the party's prospects of winning ethnic minority support. A similar claim was advanced in relation to local and parliamentary election candidates. It had been conventional in the party to claim that these deficiencies were an undersupply problem, with few ethnic minorities coming forward to take part (Geddes 1993). The revised orthodoxy now began to assess whether, and if so to what degree, the party presented itself as an attractive vehicle for political participation and ambition. A survey by Whiteley, Seyd and Richardson (1994) revealed that at most 1 per cent of party members were of ethnic minority origin; given the party's haemorrhaging in membership since then, it is likely that the true figure after the 1997 electoral rout is much lower. This study also highlighted continuing, strong anti-immigrant sentiment in the party's rank and file. Fully 70 per cent of party members surveyed in 1992 reported that the party should espouse a policy to 'encourage the repatriation of immigrants'. One commentator, Messina (1997), notes, somewhat depressingly, that this level of backing for a hardline anti-immigrant posture has scarcely changed from the picture found in earlier surveys in the 1970s and 1980s.

In normal operating circumstances, the party's liberals had usually turned to the One Nation Forum (established in 1986), the internal bridge organization, to try to promote ethnic minority involvement. The forum had followed on from the experience of the Anglo-Asian and Anglo-West Indian Societies, but had conspicuously failed to achieve any notable breakthroughs. The problem once more was one of self-contradiction serving to put off potential recruits. Typically, a handful of successful branches that had been fostered at local level found themselves undermined by white activists in mainstream local associations who refused to be dislodged from their hardline position. Solomos and Back's (1995) study of Birmingham showed this tension at play, effectively reducing the morale and reputation of the forum with every turn of the ratchet.

Ethnic entryism and Labour's dilemmas

Whilst Tories arguably muddled and meddled with wooing ethnic minorities, the scene in Labour Party politics was far from calm at this time. Labour's problems during the 1990s stemmed from the question of what form ethnic minority representation should take in the party. Earlier in the 1980s this kind of dilemma had been played out in relation to the constitutional position of autonomous black and ethnic minority bodies, and had culminated in the stand-off over black sections. An allied theme within this debate had been the thorny question of candidate selection.

The party by now faced two interrelated criticisms. The first was that it needed to be more proactive in increasing the numbers of ethnic minorities gaining selection in winnable parliamentary seats. The spirit of this criticism sought to compare the radical advancement of female candidate opportunities (which had followed from the policy of all-women shortlists) with the much slower progress experienced by ethnic minority hopefuls. The second was that the philosophy behind a long-term campaign to raise opportunities was designed to make the party more accessible and accountable to ethnic minority voters who had backed Labour with such loyalty. The suggestion that Labour had historically exploited its ethnic minority supporters surfaced again. Moves to challenge discrimination at the level of candidate selection were thus part of this wider agenda.

As if these tensions were not serious enough, the progress of black and Asian would-be candidates in the 1990s was dogged by a new and even more vexed set of controversies. Attention switched to the probity of individual selection races and membership drives at constituency level. Ten years previously, the arrival of the first crop of ethnic minority Labour MPs had caused a swelling of expectations among minority activists within the party. Worries over specific difficulties surrounding individual nominations were placed on the back burner. The new intake, it was argued, would begin the process of equalizing, and hopefully calming, the relationship between minority supporters and the Labour Party. A decade on, it was increasingly apparent that this earlier hope had been naive and simplistic. The chief illustration of this reality was the fraught nomination processes of a number of constituency parties involving ethnic minority candidates. These rows tended to grow more acrimonious in cases involving Labour-held seats or among Tory marginals where Labour's hopes were high. The common thread running through these constituency rows was the allegation that black and Asian members had deliberately set out to hijack local parties in order to push through favoured ethnic minority nominations. This kind of allegation had been first witnessed in the constituency of Ealing Southall in west London, where, between 1985 and 1989, huge local pressure had built up to dislodge the incumbent white Labour MP. The adoption of an Asian replacement who went on to hold the seat in 1992 only served to establish a powerful precedent for further such deselection campaigns. As expected, after 1992 similar developments began taking place in Labour strongholds characterized by long-serving white MPs. In addition, specific allegations of corruption, ballot-rigging and even intimidation of party members characterized many of these disputes. Selection contests in Glasgow Govan, Manchester Gorton and Birmingham Sparkbrook and Small Heath stood out as examples of especially heated controversy.

A degree of caution is called for in interpreting these controversies and trying to put them into some historic and institutional context. To begin with, as commentators have pointed out, the Labour Party has had a long track record of comparable arguments over the role of ethnicity and ethnic ties in shaping representation (Geddes forthcoming). In the 1920s and 1930s Irish Labour Party activists faced a constant complaint that their loyalties were divided between the party on one hand and the Irish Republic – and even Rome – on the other (Fielding 1993). Later, during the 1950s and 1960s, it was the turn of Jewish party members, who, it was alleged, harboured loyalties to the state of Israel (which many of course did) and sympathies with Jews in other parties (which many did not), and that this, curiously, undermined the legitimacy of their role in party affairs. By the 1990s, it was Asians (and often specific sub-groups, such as Mirpuri Pakistanis in several northern mill towns), with ties of ethnicity and kinship, that became the new focus of the older complaint.

Furthermore, the old complaints over ethnic-based membership drives tended to be rather ill-considered by the mid-1990s. The party had launched a major effort to recruit fresh members to the long-term re-election cause and, in this context, it was many of the half-forgotten urban constituency parties that had been most active. One observer, Pinto-Duschinsky (1997), has suggested that the party in fact had much to be grateful for, in managing to attract new members in inner urban areas where it had traditionally found it difficult to tap fresh support. Moreover, a decided shift within the party towards individual member democracy at this time meant that ordinary new members were often attracted to the party on the basis of having some say in decisions such as candidate selection. If as a consequence new Asian recruits sought to promote the chances of fellow Asian candidates, it seemed churlish for party elites to object given that the party had committed itself to a new spirit of grass-roots influence. Elsewhere, specific allegations of wrongdoing plainly inflicted damage on individual candidates as well as the party's image more broadly. In the case of Glasgow Govan, in 1997 an outcry ensued following allegations of bribery by the Asian nominee, Mohammed Sarwar, leading to an embarrassing post-election party inquiry (table 5.3).

Table 5.3 *Ethnic minority candidates and elected MPs from three main parties 1987–1997*

Party	Candidates			MPs		
	1987	1992	1997	1987	1992	1997
Labour	14	9	14	4	5	9
Conservative	6	8	11	0	1	0
Lib Dem[a]	8	6	19	0	0	0

[a] The 1987 figures refer to the performance of the Liberal-Social Democratic Party (SDP) Alliance
Source: Butler and Kavanagh 1987, 1992, 1997

Whatever the final legacy of these persistent rows, it was fair to say that, by the mid-1990s, Labour faced a set of awkward dilemmas in relation to race and immigration. First, it remained committed to, and therefore vulnerable on, the notion that ethnic minority voters amounted to a natural Labour-voting constituency. The charge that the party would, *ceteris paribus*, overlook the promotion of ethnic minority interests and representatives was one that plainly hurt the party hierarchy. Second, by strengthening the 'ethnicity-counts' perspective, it was still possible for the party strategists to claim that Asian votes in particular could be delivered on the say of a small handful of Asian elites. Community politics in that sense amounted to a less than flattering image of an outdated party leadership striving hard to meet expectations of patronage and other spoils. Third, the party sensed itself to be in two minds about the need to defend, even promote, cultural and ethnic diversity. A pollster-driven leadership recognized the huge potential for negative, anti-Labour voting if the party sought to subscribe too closely to such values, often popular among its activists. Any thought of a relaxation of immigration controls was summarily ruled out, therefore. However, at one and the same time, a new inclusionist rhetoric had began to characterize the party's broad national appeal to the electorate. This held that a trade-off had to be reached between fostering common identities and values for national cohesion and simultaneously accepting, even sponsoring, the notion that diverse, non-uniform identity might serve as a source of long-term strength. The policy implications of such dilemmas became significant and pressing following Labour's electoral triumph in 1997.

The 1997 General Election: Campaign and Aftermath

By the time of the 1997 general election, the major political parties had grown accustomed to the sensitive management of race and immigration issues. To be sure, the parties had over thirty years of experience on this front, experience which had broadly indicated that a fusion of strong external controls and liberal integration measures had served both parties in government reasonably well. Beyond this, neither party sought to add any new or innovative approach to racial equality, though the Tory right continued be influenced by libertarian and neo-conservative thought on the subject. Labour for its part had successfully neutralized the voice of racial equality radicals in its own ranks, and thus entered the 1997 contest with no discernible lobby that sought to emulate a US-style affirmative action approach to policy. The Liberal Democrats, out of the running to determine policy as usual, remained wedded to two core principals: first, the idea that wholesale electoral reform would in itself transform candidacy opportunities for ethnic minorities, and second, a rather dated and isolationist belief in unspecified relaxation of immigration controls.

The upshot of these forces was that racial equality and immigration were essentially on the back burner of electoral politics and public policy, a position that the major parties preferred to maintain. Beyond these pressures within the parties, however, two major concerns overshadowed debates over racial and ethnic politics. The first was a replay of familiar arguments over the race card, and the second was a growing association between political hostility to European integration and hardline immigration rhetoric.

Replaying or revising race card politics?

As already mentioned, the long run-up to the 1997 election was characterized by quite exceptional coverage given to the argument that a deeply unpopular, incumbent Tory government would inevitably turn to anti-immigration sentiment to bolster its thin electoral prospects. The bulk of these worries centred on controversies over the government's asylum and refugee policies. Legislation that had been introduced in 1993 by the Conservatives was quickly branded as insufficient or an overreaction by the government's supporters and critics alike. By 1995, plans within the Conservative administration were well advanced to bring in a follow-up new bill that would both substantially impede the rights of those potentially claiming asylum and also weaken the access of individual cases to public funds. The significance of the bill was that it was opposed by Labour with a heavy heart. Labour's front bench, in other words, recognized that these proposals might have the effect of outmanoeuvring Labour by making it look like an immigration-friendly party. The *Daily Telegraph* announced in 1995 that 'Proposals for immigration curbs... are an attempt to woo back Tory supporters attracted by the more moderate policies espoused by Tony Blair.' A little later, Labour itself confirmed its sense of exposure by unsuccessfully making a plea to hive off discussion of the entire bill to a rarely used *ad hoc* committee of the House of Commons (Riddle 1995).

Momentum of this sort persisted right up to the election itself. It had been fuelled principally not so much by any presumed motive on the part of the Conservative Party as by the Labour Party's early declaration that it did not intend to concede easy votes on the back of the immigration issue. Labour's shadow home secretary, Jack Straw, declared 'We should not allow so much as a cigarette card to come between the Labour Party and the Tory Government over immigration' (quoted in Saggar 1997a, p. 703). In many respects, the race card had come full circle, with both parties, but Labour especially, basing their strategic outlooks on the need not to be outbid on immigration. This stampede to the supposed safe territory of the right was reminiscent of the picture that had prevailed in the 1960s. On this occasion, however, there was little suggestion that a bipartisan consensus existed, or ought to be established, effectively to sideline the whole issue.

Instead, the race card thesis prevailed in the thoughts of many independent observers as well as among Labour strategists. The claim turned out to be fairly hollow when measured against the content and nature of the eventual election campaign. This unexpected outcome has been interpreted either as the failure to fulfil the logic of the 1992–1997 Parliament's concern with asylum, or, alternatively, as the result of exaggerated prophecies that the Conservative government would exploit the issue for electoral gain. Between these diverse assessments there are three main factors which account for the nullification of the thesis in 1997.

First, the influence of the Major leadership, cited previously, cannot be easily dismissed. Returning to earlier profiles of Major as a notable liberal on race relations, it was clear that there was resistance at the highest levels to any campaign explicitly centred on immigration policy. Major's earlier collaboration with Patten had taught him that electoral victory and exploiting the immigration issue were not necessarily synonymous. Second, any pro-campaign to win votes on the immigration issue was unlikely to deliver the scale of support that would have been required by a Tory administration suffering heavy unpopularity. The principal reason for this was that the immigration issue had largely ceased to be salient in British electoral politics and had effectively been off the agenda of party competition for more than a decade (Crewe 1983). An attempt to treat the issue in terms of its high-profile divisive impact, last witnessed in the late 1970s, would have amounted to a courageous though flawed tactic. Third, in harnessing the issue, much depended on the timing and style of its communication. In 1992 the party had successfully made reference to the issue in passing, by suggesting that it belonged to a secondary but important agenda of competence issues that prevented Labour from 'being fit to govern'. The primary agenda of competence was made up largely of tax-and-spend issues and had created a major obstacle to Labour's prospects. By 1997 similar ploys to question the opposition's competence for office lay at the core of the Tory strategy. However, by alluding explicitly to immigration it was likely that the Tory strategy might prove to be counter-productive. Immigration, in other words, was an issue that ordinarily served the Conservatives well, but only so long as it could be deployed in secondary, not primary, agenda terms. The 1997 election provided no such opportunity.

The growing influence of 'Europhobia'

Whilst the race card was (to mix metaphors) something of a barkless dog in 1997, it is striking to note that virtually the only Conservative intervention on immigration in the campaign came from a right-wing backbencher most noted for his views on Europe. The specific case of Nicholas Budgen's speech, in which he lamented the 'substantial social problems immigration had brought', perhaps mattered less than the general audience to which this type of political message was aimed. Budgen had spent much of 1992–1997 at the head of a group of Tory parliamentary rebels who had persistently challenged the Major leadership over Europe. Many within this fairly stable group were also known first for their right-wing credentials, second for their espousal of a social authoritarian perspective on areas such as law and order and family policy, and third for their hostile attitude towards immigration. The cumulative effect of their various activities was to entrench in the Conservative Party a large segment of opinion that is commonly known as Europhobic. It is worth noting here that Budgen was Enoch Powell's protégé and had represented the same West Midlands seat. Indeed, Powell's only contribution to the 1997 campaign was to issue a statement endorsing Budgen's remarks and emphasizing anti-immigration and anti-European positions.

The link with the Powellites is important. It had been Powell's supporters who, in the 1960s and 1970s, had been the first to accept the mantle of 'Little Englanders'. This faction within Tory ranks had originally gone on the offensive against the party leadership but had within a short time widened their dispute with the Heath-led party to the question of European Community membership. Reluctant Europeans they were not, as much of their critique hung on an essentialist belief in the strength of separate island development, which they believed was both Britain's heritage and destiny. This world view also rejected the logic of security or trade interdependence, not merely with Europe but also in relation to Britain's traditional relationship with the United States. Much of their assumption centred on a particularistic reading of the roles of English culture and values in shaping a national identity and sense of belonging. In this context, the notion of significant immigration, particularly from the Commonwealth, was viewed with deep suspicion and resentment. Budgen and his fellow Europhobes represented a contemporary link with that earlier critique. Cultural and economic independence remained high on the agenda in the modern setting of the 1990s, as did a firm belief in decisive state authority to shape, even regulate, social behaviour. A forthright opposition to immigration, coupled with a sceptical view of the prospects of integration policy towards those immigrants already settled in Britain, therefore amounted to a natural and predictable position for this faction to adopt.

In the longer run, the influence of anti-Europeanism is unlikely to wane in the William Hague-led Conservative Party. An anti-European faction exists and occasionally thrives not only for reasons of ideological belief, but also in large measure due to the social character of the defeated Tory Party. The party's age profile has risen considerably as younger, less committed members have fallen away, leaving older and less European-minded loyalists. For generational reasons, many of those who remain would have witnessed the cultural and social transformations that were associated with immigration from the 1950s to the 1970s. Instinctively opposed to the original influx, many have remained doubtful about liberal race relations efforts in the years since. Under Hague, the party faces the task of opening up its ranks and its machinery, recruiting fresh blood to its membership, and modernizing its appeal to groups such as women, ethnic minorities, the young, and single parents. On all these fronts, it faces a significant challenge, and progress is likely to be slow and patchy. The continuing presence, often predominance, of the European issue will mean that the Old Guard – if it can be dubbed as such – will continue to hold a major flag around which to rally. Earlier signs of moving the party in a more liberal direction on racial equality and immigration, an allied concern of the Europhiles, are therefore unlikely to be fulfilled.

Conclusion: The Impact of Party Policy

Britain's two major political parties have experienced four important phases in their relationship to, and development of, racial equality policy and immigration policy. To begin with, at the start of the post-war period both parties grappled with the labour market and other economic aspects of early immigration from Commonwealth sources. This era lasted from the early post-war years through to the late 1950s, at which time immigration and the great 'Race Question' rapidly rose up the political agenda. The initial phase is therefore often described as a pre-political age, when discussion and debate over policy gathered momentum within the closed ranks of government and party elites but, crucially, did not resonate in party political discourse more generally. Race and immigration, we should remind ourselves, in essence were not political issues in Britain at this time. The important underlying theme of these years was the ongoing tension between responses to immigration in economic terms and in social ones. The latter dimension ultimately prevailed, and by the beginning of the following decade it was common practice for party policy debates to view the matter entirely as one of managing the social consequences of largely unplanned immigration.

The second phase stretches from the early 1960s to the mid-1970s and is often thought of as a golden age of consensus. As we have seen, this period was defined by the cross-party agreement to treat immigration as a non-issue. Parties, therefore, in effect prevented themselves and one another from following the logic of rational party competition. Adoption and espousal of immigration policies explicitly reflective of public opinion were not ruled out at this time; however, it was tacitly understood that this could only take place against a backdrop in which both major parties shifted rightwards in a loosely synchronized manner. The purpose of the consensus was not merely to dampen the political dimension of immigration but also to allow the introduction of a basic institutional framework for integration policy. Racial harmony thus became a central policy objective of both parties and was embodied in the enactment of important legislation in 1965, 1968 and 1976.

This phase came to a dramatic close shortly after the passage of the third Race Relations Act in 1976. Consensus was broken at the start of a new and ultimately short-lived third period, in which the Conservative Party embraced a populist ticket on immigration. Right-wingers hostile to immigration took control of the party's policy and repositioned the party to fit more closely with the heavily skewed distribution of public opinion. With a head of steam developing, in mass public sentiment against immigration, it was not difficult for the Thatcherites to achieve their desired objective. A strongly party political approach by the Tories was met in turn by a growing radicalization of race equality debates within the Labour Party. Black autonomy demands and the Black Sections Movement grew out of this development and had come to dominate many aspects of the party's urban organization and appeal by the mid-1980s. For this reason, it is perhaps more appropriate to think of this third phase as the age of radicalism and non-consensual tendencies in both parties. Oddly enough, despite these centrifugal pressures, race and immigration issues fell down the political agenda as quickly as they had arisen. The result was that radical factions had been organized and marshalled in both parties on race, but by the mid-1980s these developments were far removed from the mainstream political landscape, in which such concerns mattered less than ever.

Finally, a fourth phase spans the decade prior to the 1997 general election, in which racial questions have generally been relegated to second-order concerns by both major parties, though specific aspects of the issue continue to cause reverberations within party policy-making circles. For Labour, a position of complacency had caused worry among critics, who have emphasized what they perceive as the grossly unbalanced relationship between Labour's policy priorities and its persistently high support among ethnic minorities. Rows over entryism and illegitimate ethnic loyalties have periodically bubbled to the surface, illustrating just how fraught and distrustful this relationship has become in recent times. In the Conservative Party steady efforts to boost ethnic minority participation have invariably been sidelined by party heavyweights such as Lord Tebbit. By introducing the language of 'loyalty tests', there is little doubt that the party has deterred whatever modest backing and goodwill it had among ethnic minorities.

This current phase, however, is one in which both parties' policies have stressed the appropriateness of tackling equality matters through mainstream policy frameworks and instruments. The effects of social and economic policy in addressing various forms of inequality and inequity have tended to grow in importance for both parties. In the run-up to the 1997 contest this theme became a major area of concern for both parties, but in particular formed a central tenet of Labour's preoccupation with social exclusion. Therefore, the politics of racial equality policy, as a result of the 1997 election's decisive outcome, has been not so much marginalized as reinvented and reconfigured into a much broader public policy agenda.

Chronology of Significant Developments: April 1992 to October 1997

April 1992	John Taylor, Conservative candidate in Cheltenham, loses safe seat; six ethnic minority MPs elected including first Conservative since 1900 (Nirj Deva in Brentford and Isleworth)
June 1992	Winston Churchill MP makes speech criticizing Conservative immigration policy and black British identity
October 1992	British National Party local council by-election victory in Millwall, Tower Hamlets
October 1993	Asylum Act
November 1995	*The Times* outlines possibility of 'race card' behind Tory immigration and asylum policies; Tony Blair attempts to stage debate over Asylum Bill in special *ad hoc* House of Commons committee – he fails but is seen to be trying to tackle his party's perceived weakness on the immigration issue
May 1996	Fresh legislation to cope with shortcoming of 1993 Asylum Act
January 1997	Launch of fresh Conservative high-profile campaign to woo ethnic minority supporters in general election
April 1997	Nicholas Budgen MP (Conservative) makes only high-profile anti-immigration speech in 1997 general election campaign

May 1997	Record number of main party ethnic minority parliamentary candidates (forty-four), of whom nine successfully elected (all Labour) – defeat of only Tory incumbent (Deva); first ethnic minority ministerial appointment (Boateng, minister of state at Health)
August 1997	New Conservative Party Leader, William Hague, makes an appearance at Notting Hill carnival
September 1997	Hague launches party modernization project – includes clear objective to raise ethnic minority participation in party affairs and candidate selection
October 1997	Prime Minister Blair makes speech to Labour Party conference emphasizing racial inclusion and opportunities for ethnic minorities; Lord Tebbit makes speech at Conservative Party conference attacking multiculturalism as a recipe for another Yugoslav-style disaster

References

Ali A. and Percival G. (1993), *Race and Representation: Ethnic Minorities and the 1992 Elections*, London: CRE.

Banton M. (1985), *Promoting Racial Harmony*, Cambridge: Cambridge University Press.

Behrens R. and Edmonds J. (1981), 'Kittens, kippers and kipper boxes: Conservative populists and race relations', *Political Quarterly*, 52.

Benyon J. (ed.) (1984) *Scarman and After*, London: Pergamon.

Butler D. and Kavanagh D. (1987) *The British General Election of 1987*, Basingstoke: Macmillan.

Butler D. and Kavanagh D. (1992) *The British General Election of 1992*, Basingstoke: Macmillan.

Butler D. and Kavanagh D. (1997) *The British General Election of 1997*, Basingstoke: Macmillan.

Butler D. and Stokes D. (1974), *Political Change in Britain*, London: Macmillan.

Childs D. (1986), *Britain since 1945*, London: Routledge.

Cmnd 7695, *Report of the Royal Commission on Population*, London: HMSO.

CRC (Community Relations Commission) (1975) *Participation of Ethnic Minorities in the General Election of October 1974*, London: CRC.

CRE (Commission for Racial Equality) (1980), *Votes and Policies*, London: CRE.

CRE (Commission for Racial Equality) (1984), *Ethnic Minorities and the 1983 General Election*, London: CRE.

Crewe I. (1983), 'The disturbing truth behind Labour's rout', *Guardian*, 13 June.

Crewe I. and Sarlvik B. (1980), 'Popular attitudes and electoral strategy', in Layton-Henry Z. (ed.), *Conservative Party Politics*, London: Macmillan.

Deakin N. (1972), 'The immigration issue in British politics', unpublished PhD thesis, University of Sussex.

Dean D. W. (1992), 'Conservative governments and the restriction of Commonwealth immigration in the 1950s: the problems of constraint', *Historical Journal*, 35.1.

Fielding S. (1993), *Class and Ethnicity: Irish Catholics in England 1880–1939*, Buckingham: Open University Press.

Freeman G. (1979), *Immigrant Labour and Racial Conflict in Industrial Societies*, Princeton NJ: Princeton University Press.

Gamble A. (1988), *The Free Economy and the Strong State: The Politics of Thatcherism*, London: Macmillan.

Geddes A. (1993), 'Asian and Afro-Caribbean representation in elected local government in England and Wales', *New Community*, 20.1.

Geddes A. (forthcoming), 'Labour and ethnic entryism', *New Community*.

Gordon P. and Klug F. (1986), *New Right, New Racism*, London: Searchlight Publications.

Harris Research Centre (1987), 'Political attitudes among ethnic minorities', unpublished data set JN98746.

Hindell K. (1965), 'The genesis of the Race Relations Bill', *Political Quarterly*, 36.

Holmes C. (1988), *John Bull's Island*, London: Routledge.

Katznelson I. (1973), *Black Men, White Cities*, London: Oxford University Press/Institute of Race Relations.

Kellner P. (1991), 'Major overhaul of British morality', *Independent*, 1 November.

Lansley S., Goss S. and Wolmar, C. (1989), *Councils in Conflict: The Rise and Fall of the Municipal Left*, London: Macmillan.

Layton-Henry Z. (1992), *The Politics of Immigration*, Oxford: Blackwell.

Levitas R. (ed.) (1986), *The Ideology of the New Right*, Cambridge: Polity Press.

LPRAG (Labour Party Race Action Group) (1979), *Don't Take Black Votes for Granted*, London: LPRAG.

McKenzie R. and Silver A. (1968), *Angels in Marble: Working Class Conservatives in Urban England*, London: Heinemann.

Messina A. (1989), *Race and Party Competition in Britain*, Oxford: Clarendon Press.

Messina A. (1997), 'Ethnic minorities and the British party system in the 1990s and beyond', in Saggar S. (ed.), *Race and British Electoral Politics*, London: UCL Press.

Miles R. and Phizacklea A. (1984), *White Man's Country*, London: Pluto Press.

Miller W. (1980), 'What was the profit in following the crowd?', *British Journal of Political Science*, 10.1.

MORI (Market and Opinion Research Institute) (1996), 'Asian voting: preliminary results', unpublished briefing notes, February.

MORI (Market and Opinion Research Institute) (1997), 'Black Britain', *British Public Opinion*, July.

NEC (National Executive Committee) (1980), *Labour and the Black Electorate*, London: Labour Party.

NOP (National Opinion Polls) (1978), 'Immigration and race relations', *Political, Social and Economic Review*, 14.

Norris P. (1997), *Electoral Change since 1945*, Oxford: Blackwell.

Parkinson M. and Duffy J. (1984), 'Government's response to inner-city riots', *Parliamentary Affairs*, 29.4.

Pilkington E. (1988), *Beyond the Mother Country: West Indians and Notting Hill White Riots*, London: I. B. Taurus.

Pinto-Duschinsky M. (1997), 'The Conservative Party after 1997', unpublished paper presented to the EPOP (Elections, Parties and Opinion Polls) conference on the 1997 general election, University of Essex, September 1997.

Rich P. (1986), 'Conservative ideology and race in modern British politics', in Layton-Henry Z. and Rich R. (eds), *Race, Government and Politics in Britain*, London: Macmillan.

Rich P. (1997), 'Ethnic politics and the post-Thatcher Conservative Party', in Saggar S. (ed.), *Race and British Electoral Politics*, London: UCL Press.

Riddle P. (1995), 'A speech to test Labour: the election starts here', *The Times*, 16 November.

Roberts H. (1984), *Black Sections and the Labour Party*, London: Ernest Bevin Society.

Rose E. J. B. (1969), *Colour and Citizenship*, London: Oxford University Press/Institute of Race Relations.

Saggar S. (1991), 'The changing agenda of race issues in local government: the case of a London borough', *Political Studies*, 39.

Saggar S. (1992), *Race and Politics in Britain*, Hemel Hempstead: Harvester Wheatsheaf.

Saggar S. (1996), 'Immigration and economics: the politics of race and immigration in the post-war period', in Fawcett H. and Lowe R. (eds), *The Road from 1945*, London: Macmillan.

Saggar S. (1997a), 'Racial politics and the 1997 general election', *Parliamentary Affairs*, post-election special issue, autumn.

Saggar S. (1997b), 'The dog that did not bark: race and immigration issues in the 1997 general election', in Geddes A. and Tonge J. (eds), *Labour's Landslide*, Manchester: Manchester University Press.

Saggar S. (1997c), 'Analysing race and elections: some conceptual uncertainties', in Saggar S. (ed.), *Race and British Electoral Politics*, London: UCL Press.

Saggar S. (1997d), 'Pipeline politics', *India Today*, 31 March.

Saggar S. (1998), 'A late, though not lost, opportunity: British South Asian electors and the Conservative Party', *Political Quarterly*.

Scarman, Lord (1981), *The Brixton Disorders, 10–12 April 1981: Report of an Inquiry*, Cmnd 8427, London: HMSO.

Schoen D. (1977), *Enoch Powell and the Powellites*, London: Macmillan.

Sewell T. (1993), *Black Tribunes: Black Political Participation in Britain*, London: Lawrence and Wishart.

Seyd P. and Whiteley P. (1992), *Labour's Grassroots: The Politics of Party Membership*, Oxford: Clarendon Press.

Shukra K. (1990), 'Black sections in the Labour Party', in Gouldbourne H. (ed.), *Black Politics in Britain*, Aldershot, Avebury.

Shukra K. (1997), 'New Labour, old debates', in Saggar S. (ed.), *Race and British Electoral Politics*, London: UCL Press.

Smith M. M. (1991), 'Windrushers and orbiters: towards an understanding of the official mind and colonial immigration to Britain, 1945–51', *Immigrants and Minorities*, 10.3.

Smith M. and Spear J. (eds) (1992), *The Changing Labour Party*, London: Routledge.

Solomos J. and Back L. (1995), *Race, Politics and Social Change*, London: Routledge.

Spencer I. (1997), *British Immigration Policy since 1939*, London: Routledge.

Studlar D. (1978), 'Policy voting in Britain: the coloured immigration issue in the 1964, 1966 and 1970 general elections', *American Political Science Review*, 11.1–2.

Studlar D. and Layton-Henry Z. (1990), 'Non-white minority access to the political agenda in Britain', *Policy Studies Review*, 9.2.

Whiteley P., Seyd P. and Richardson J. (1994), *True Blues*, Oxford: Clarendon Press.

Guide to Further Reading

A detailed topic-by-topic bibliographical essay can be read in the 'Guide to further reading' in S. Saggar, *Race and Politics in Britain* (Hemel Hempstead:

Harvester Wheatsheaf, 1992). Additionally, the author is the editor of a recent state-of-the-art volume that provides comprehensive coverage of race and electoral themes: S. Saggar (ed.), *Race and British Electoral Politics* (London: UCL Press, 1998).

Besides many of the book-length and/or research monographs that have appeared on the broad subject of race, immigration and British politics and society, it is important to remember that scientific journals continue to be a source of detailed, high-quality analysis. On certain topics in particular, it is striking just how many excellent analytical pieces have been published by the first three of the journals listed below. For general coverage of various racial and ethnic themes, the reader is directed to *New Community, Ethnic and Racial Studies* and *International Migration Review*. The last of these has always held a wide interest in many countries other than Britain, and it is helpful therefore to be able to draw on its coverage given to direct comparisons with Britain. The first title has, since 1992, made a much more robust effort to include articles with a European focus. Other journals worthy of attention in this field include *Patterns of Prejudice, Immigrants and Minorities, Race and Class, Critical Social Policy*, and the *British Journal of Sociology*.

Elsewhere, scientific journals have devoted limited though usually good-quality attention to race and ethnicity in relation to specific political science themes. Among them, *Political Studies* has included several useful papers on aspects of political philosophy, *Policy and Politics* has tackled important urban politics debates over participation and political power, and the *British Journal of Political Science* has published a number of useful articles on electoral politics, drawing heavily on examples from the United States.

Finally, readers keen to locate a journal committed to news-item-led coverage of 'race politics' are directed to *Race and Immigration*, renamed in 1993 the *Runnymede Bulletin*. Published by the Runnymede Trust, this monthly title has provided an additional outlet for lively, though occasionally superficial, debates, especially in relation to the politics of identity and audits of public policy effectiveness.

6 | Sex Equality

Ian Forbes

Girl presence, not girl power.

Wainwright 1997

Synopsis

Political parties are slow to respond to demands for sex equality, and generally adopt cautious policies. Campaigns by women have changed the political agenda, so that the public and parties alike now accept that sex equality policies are necessary and desirable. Post-war developments in these policies reveal that the parties are easily distinguishable from each other. Foundational ideological perspectives are reproduced in relation to women: the Conservatives defend the traditional family and rely on merit to produce just if unequal outcomes; the Labour Party is more inclined to argue from the principle of equality and may even support policies intended to produce equality of outcome; while the Liberal Democrats promote equality of opportunity so long as individual liberty is not transgressed.

The achievements of government up until 1979 are contrasted with the cold climate for equality policy under Margaret Thatcher and John Major. Offsetting factors, such as the impact of Europe and the emergence of municipal feminism, are discussed briefly. The period from 1992 to 1997 is shown to be crucial for bringing about a dramatic change in the representation of women in Parliament, and for the development of a range of policy objectives that would feed directly into the new Labour government. The chapter concludes with some reflections on the effect that government has on the ability of a party to affect policy and on the possible impact that the new intake of women and the connections with the women's movement may have on the success, implementation and further development of sex equality policy.

With thanks for the assistance of Victoria Leach, and for the improving suggestions of Alison Edgley, Richard Kelly and Joan Orme.

The Historical Context: Party Policy 1945–1992

Sex equality policy will always be found in that shifting terrain between two variables: what women want and what is politically achievable given the structures, processes and norms governing the range of their choices, opportunities and freedoms. Both variables have undergone significant change since 1945. Women's wants have developed and broadened, their expression sharpening rather than changing. The fight for political and economic enfranchisement, for social justice and a safe public existence, continues, while claims to new cultural freedoms and equalities arise. Political possibilities have also changed, within the relatively rigid parameters of a society that has a constitutional monarchy atop a Parliament elected with a crude first-past-the-post voting system, an advanced industrial economic structure replete with a competitive market system, and the liberal rule of law. Despite the demands for social and cultural change, these parameters remain, reinforcing, in one form or another, the western conception of the family and a public/private divide. In all, there is a set of traditions, practices and assumptions as well as cleavages of class, gender and colour that impact upon all women in Britain, just as the development of women's consciousness and expansion of women's roles presents new challenges. In this setting, political parties struggle to develop sex equality policies that are relevant, effective and attractive, and properly based within a much more fluid and varied political value base.

The core political demand of women has remained constant – the simply stated but consequentially radical claim for genuine equality. Women have challenged the social and political structure and the assumptions upon which it rests, and pressed for changes within that structure, especially at the systemic level. There is also some evidence to suggest that women are at the forefront of a general value shift that stresses environmental concerns and an attachment to autonomy within the affective bounds of a supportive community (see Wilkinson 1994). Nevertheless, the differences between women – by virtue of age, education and employment – are associated with a variety of value orientations and contrasting levels of commitment. As a result, there is still no single and unifying 'women's agenda' that has any systematic electoral force.

There is, however, a changed climate in terms of political culture and the acceptance of a set of values relating to sex equality. The political parties have responded – albeit differently – to the conflicts over value and meanings and to the political demands that have arisen out of women's political activity and developments in British political culture. Their responses, however, are best described as episodic, only occasionally resolute and almost never proactive. The explanation for this must include an appreciation of the limitations that arise from the structural nature of British politics, whereby women are routinely excluded from elite positions and where the voting system offers little reward for women organizing politically.

Moreover, women's campaigns for sex equality are complex. For many but not all women, change to the structure is seen as the primary requirement, while there is also considerable disagreement about both the most appropriate arena in which to introduce change and the methods to be employed. Younger women benefit from earlier campaigns by women but are less likely to identify with feminism, the women's movement and party political activity (Wilkinson 1994, pp. 40, 45). Also, the agenda for change is wide-ranging, including equal opportunities (pay and conditions at work), social issues (the family, childcare and housing), cultural issues (violence and images of women), and personal politics (abortion and sexuality). Within these dimensions of political structure, political space and political action, parties find plenty of room to manoeuvre.

An historical overview helps us to see that the equality policies of the political parties reflect their differing ideological proclivities. It is also the case that all the major parties are divided internally on policy lines. The pro-feminist sections of each party have to conduct similar campaigns to achieve their major objectives. These are to get sex equality on the agenda and to increase the representation of women in the key positions in the party hierarchy (particularly as members of Parliament, of government or of Shadow Cabinets). Once sex equality is on the agenda, arguments turn on the nature of women-friendly policy, the goals to be achieved and the means of implementation.

The end of World War II had diverse effects on women's rights and independence. Women remained a key part of the workforce, but increasingly on a part-time basis, as they were expected to maintain their role and duties as home-makers and childcarers. Thus women were regarded in quite functional terms. While one royal commission studying the low birth rate blamed 'feminism', the three women on another royal commission – this time on equal pay – were forced to submit a minority report in support of the very principle of equal pay. Agitation for sex equality policy in the late 1940s and the early 1950s focused on equal pay and the universalist programmes designed to bring social justice to the mass of the population. While heralded as significant pieces of egalitarian legislation, the welfare and benefit reforms of the period made official the designation of woman as wife and mother, and man as breadwinner and head of household. Moreover, the focus on the public realm meant that the 'informal' provision of welfare in the family was not part of the equation (Lewis 1992, p. 36), even though, as Wilson claimed, the creation of paid social work was a recognition of just this type of work (1980, p. 188).

The scale of economic and social policies and the lack of an integrated gender analysis inevitably led to changes that were detrimental to women, coinciding with changes that would lay some of the foundations for progress for women. Educational reforms, for example, put into place a major prerequisite for greater equality of opportunity for women – education for all regardless of class, sex or ethnic origin. At the same time, Churchill ruled out equal pay for women teachers, a situation that was not rectified until the Burnham Report of 1952. The Education Act of 1944, introduced by the Conservative R. A. Butler, represented the nature and extent of the developing consensus over government policy in an increasingly secular and egalitarian age. In essence, the commitment to state provision of education signified a starting-gate approach to equality of opportunity. That approach was developed and integrated into the larger policy consensus. Starting-gate equality was something to which even the Hayekian right in the Conservative Party – a group that was soon to include the young

Margaret Hilda Roberts, later Thatcher – could not object (Charmley 1996, p. 137). The Conservative Party did not move beyond this simplistic view of equal opportunities, so it not surprising that the government of the 1950s and early 1960s left no great mark on sex equality policy.

In policy terms, the first post-war Labour government was not innovative, preferring to pursue large-scale solutions and employing a planning methodology, even though the party conference of 1947 voted four to one in favour of equal pay. The closest that government got to a gender analysis was the reiteration of functional stereotypes for both women and men. Changes continued in the Labour Party itself, however, with the setting up of the Women's Advisory Committee in 1951. The history of sex equality policy would have been very different had not the Labour Party defined itself and its tasks in government in terms of dealing with inequality, particularly poverty. Their central question has been about the best way to eradicate poverty within a strong and viable economy, leading to many internal party battles over the definition of the task and the means to implement it. In the face of a strong historical commitment to the orthodoxy of a quasi-Marxist restructuring of the commanding heights, one faction tried to lead the party towards an interventionary and corporate engagement with a mixed economy. This revisionist faction has been led by a succession of men in the party – Hugh Gaitskell, Harold Wilson, Tony Benn, Neil Kinnock and Tony Blair. These fights for control of the party have tended to dominate, creating the context within which all Labour Party policies are best understood. Sex equality policy is no exception.

With this background, it is perhaps surprising to find any commitment at all to sex equality. However, the battles in the Labour Party have involved regular expressions of key values, within which there can be found the basis for government action. Gaitskell, for example, in a Labour Party report to conference in 1959, talked less about class conflict and more about 'concern for the disadvantaged and the oppressed' and 'a belief in social justice' (see Jones 1996, p. 46). This indicated a turn to specific statements, leading to detailed policies to advance general egalitarian ends, rather than a reliance on universalist principles demanding a total politics of (class) revolution (albeit through the ballot box and government). In 1974, Tony Crosland took the argument further. Equality was crucial to the Labour vision and responsibility, but this meant 'more than a meritocratic society of equal opportunities' (Jones 1996, p. 98). A wider *social* equality was intended, with a 'greater clarity about egalitarian priorities' (Jones 1996, p. 98). This emphasis on the nature, extent and importance of equality and an egalitarian approach sets the Labour Party apart in British politics. In practical terms, it means that there is a significant overlap between the aims and objectives of the party, with its historical focus on employment issues, and a considerable part of the women's movement, which was burgeoning throughout this period. It reveals how constructive links between the Labour Party's and women's concerns over equality could be formed, and why women would choose to be active within the Labour Party.

The argument over revision and orthodoxy in the Labour Party impacted on sex equality policy in a very straightforward way. Put briefly, if the orthodox approach was right, then all efforts should be turned to restructuring the economy, after which the gender-neutral benefits of equality would automatically and freely flow to all. Mass support was required for just one conception of equality. If the revisionist approach was preferred, however, then the political strategy was very different. It involved dealing with specific political problems in different segments of the economy and society. Piecemeal reform invites partial solutions, a heightened activism of special-interest groups, and a plurality of political interpretations of equality. Whatever the battles in the party, the outcome when in government was a great deal closer to the revisionist approach. This was crucial for women. The revisionist account allowed a space for single-issue political groups (like women), was receptive to the voices calling for specific criticisms of aspects of the mixed economy, such as low pay and discrimination at the workplace, and invited ameliorative legislation. Such changes were worthwhile, and would not merely strengthen the capitalist market economy and delay its destruction. Acknowledging the legitimate interests of women, allowing them to develop their political voice within the party, and introducing new policies created a loyalty to the party as a genuine route for bringing about change.

Evidence that women were seeking to exert influence in favour of piecemeal reform comes from the manifesto for employment rights produced by the Working Women's Charter as early as 1964. The Labour Party manifesto of 1964 committed itself to equal pay for equal work and in 1966 the Labour government set up a tripartite study group on the subject. The following year saw the National Executive Committee (NEC) set up a study group on sex discrimination, and Labour MP Joyce Butler introduced the first private member's bill to outlaw discrimination against women. Further pressure was applied by the Ford strike by women in 1968–1969, and by the activities of the Equal Pay Campaign Committee (Lovenduski and Randall 1993, pp. 180–1). By 1969, both parties were publishing reports on women's equality – 'Towards Equality for Women' from Labour and 'Fair Share for Fair Sex' from the Conservatives – and opposing sex discrimination in their manifestos. The formation of an all-party equal rights group confirmed the salience of this issue.

The first sex equality legislation to reach the statute books was the Equal Pay Act, introduced in 1970 by Barbara Castle, minister for employment in the Labour government. It represented the culmination of a campaign for equal pay that had stretched back to the 1940s (Lewis 1992, p. 40). There have been no discernible negative outcomes for the employment rates and market for either women or men, but there are disagreements about the effectiveness of the policy for women (Lewis 1992, p. 81). The second piece of legislation was preceded by reports and commitments from both parties. A Labour Party study group produced 'Discrimination against Women' for discussion in 1972. A year later the Conservatives announced their intention to legislate on sex equality with their consultative document 'Equal Opportunities for Women', in which they reiterated the case for a meritocratic society based on procedural equality of treatment. The legislative process proper began with the White Paper *Equality for Women* in 1974, the year that the European Economic Community gave priority to sex equality in the First Social Action Programme. The Sex Discrimination Act 1975 was piloted through the House of Commons by Labour's home secretary

Roy Jenkins, who deliberately modelled its provisions on US experience. It introduced into law the concepts of direct and indirect discrimination and made provision for an education, advisory and enforcement agency, the Equal Opportunities Commission (EOC), which commenced operations in 1976. These laws were innovative in the British context. As Meehan (1985, p. 4) has pointed out, they guaranteed a new form of equality to a specified group in society, identifiable by sex and marital status. This legislation manifested the preference within the Labour government for a revisionist approach to Britain's problems.

While 'the equality legislation of the 1970s...was enacted with the active support and direct engagement of organized women' (Lovenduski and Randall 1993, pp. 182–3), the creation of the EOC signalled a temporary halt to the inclusion of feminists in policy-making. The EOC, in its first years, adopted a timid approach, preferring persuasion rather than a rigorous application of the law and its powers. This new change agency effectively sent out the message that little was to change, and excluded the women's movement from the policy and implementation process. The end of the Labour government in 1979 signalled the end of the post-war consensus on employment, welfare and social policy. Sex equality policy, like every other policy, was about to be conducted within a very different climate.

Margaret Thatcher and the new symbolic order

The election of Margaret Thatcher as leader of the Conservative Party and Her Majesty's official opposition in 1975 represented a major personal and political triumph. The Conservative Party claimed:

> Nothing could have helped the cause of women more. The advance of women has been slow; age-old customs and attitudes have had to be changed. But when a woman has been chosen as a potential Prime Minister, difficulties and arguments over putting women into positions of authority in other fields look petty. (Conservative Party 1975, p. 1)

Her election was emblematic of the social changes overtaking Britain's political elite and exemplified the increasing representation of the professional rather than the 'well-born', the city rather than the country, and the younger over the older in the Conservative Party. The sense of satisfaction among many women over her achievement was enormously strengthened by her election as the first woman prime minister in Britain. It can be seen as one of the post-war turning points in the political culture of Britain. Thatcher's election was consistent with long-term developments in the value base and social perceptions of late twentieth-century Britain. In the country as a whole, Thatcher was easily accepted as a capable and effective leader. In defying stereotypical assumptions, she lent an incalculable credibility to the idea that the Conservative Party was a modern party, attuned to the wishes of the people, offering relevant solutions to long-standing problems.

In regard to sex equality, however, Thatcher was worse than her male predecessors. Having reached the highest office, she pulled the ladder up after her, ensuring that throughout her eleven years in charge no other woman (apart from Baroness Young, leader in the House of Lords) sat at the Cabinet table. There were some at minister of state level, but none was sponsored or promoted further. Thatcher dismissed sex equality from a feminist standpoint in favour of a rugged individualism, whereby talent and effort would receive their reward in a well-organized society with a minimal state. She remained a role model high above a glass ceiling of her own construction. She often expressed conservative social views, and felt that the proper place for women with children was in the home. Her government presided over an economic recession, a severe blow to the existing sex equality policies that relied upon continued growth to raise standards for women without threatening male privilege.

However, women's political efforts seemed to increase rather than stop or slow. This occurred principally at local authority level, spearheaded by women in Labour authorities. It is a remarkable testimony to the energy, drive and ingenuity of women that the equality battles were not abandoned but simply moved to new and more fertile ground. The 1980s stand as one of the most successful periods of activism, as the women's movement expanded and new phenomena, like municipal feminism and the equal opportunities movement, developed (see Gladwin 1996). Once again, it was the Labour Party's concern with equality as a principle and a political practice that enabled women to act (often against the wishes of Labour men, and against the backdrop of an uncertainty about the place of equality in Labour politics: Hodge 1994, p. 157).

The formation of local women's committees and the appointment of women's officers after the local elections of 1981 had a profound effect. A wide range of women's issues was put onto the agenda, bringing women and the liberation movement into direct contact with the state apparatus, and providing a training ground in equality politics. The two most notable outcomes were mainstreaming and diversification. Equality policy began not just to be inserted into other policy areas, but to cast its net wide, beyond the formal remit of law (especially in relation to employment and education), into health issues and into the private domain – violence against women, for example.

Despite her views, and her fall from office in 1991, Thatcher remained a potent force in British politics, and may well be one of the reasons for the continuing gender gap in voting in the 1992 election. This gap in favour of the Conservatives effectively ensured that they stayed in power, despite the tremendous disparity between the dearth of Conservative policies on women and the much more developed and comprehensive approaches of both the Labour and Liberal Democratic parties. However, it became increasingly clear that the Conservative Party was only superficially 'modern'. With Thatcher gone, and without her populist contact with the country, it increasingly looked like a moribund and out-of-touch political organization.

John Major's first Cabinet was the first all-male one since 1964. It was indicative of a political party that was not aware of some basic political realities of both value and presentation. Major soon made an adjustment, but his last Cabinet still contained only two women. In 1991, Major announced a significant initiative – Opportunity 2000 – on the steps of Downing Street. Closer inspection revealed that this was not a new policy, but publicity for the launch of a private sector campaign originally designed to get women into the upper levels of management (Forbes 1996). Major did instigate a reasonably assertive set of internal bureaucratic measures to ensure that women would begin to be represented at the higher levels of the Civil Service. However, there was to be no new legislation, despite repeated calls from the EOC, until the Conservatives were forced from office in May 1997.

While the Conservative Party basked successfully in the glow of the reflected glory of a woman leader, the Labour Party was going through the long and painful process of adjusting to the emerging political culture in order to present itself successfully as a real challenger to the Conservatives. In terms of equality policy, it was much more introspective and productive. Labour local authorities – particularly the Greater London Council (GLC) until its disbandment in 1986 – had led the way in the development of equality policy. It also served as a training ground for a succession of politicians who would progressively have an impact on the development of Labour's sex equality policies at the annual conferences, and eventually fill key positions in government.

An Unusual Climate: Continuity and Rupture 1992–1997

Major's mandate

The surprise victory for the Conservatives in the 1992 election gave Major a second chance to implement his view of an appropriate equality policy in the governance of Britain. His characterization of Conservative policy emphasized opportunity for all, underpinned by a reportedly sincere awareness of and concern for the kinds of discrimination experienced by women and minority ethnic groups. He accepted that there was some role for government, and reorganized the responsibility for his 'opportunity' policy implementation among Whitehall departments. The Department for Education and Employment (DfEE), under Gillian Shepherd, took over lead responsibility, ending the long-standing Home Office involvement with the EOC. The first specifically designated minister of women was Ann Widdecombe, associated with the right wing of the party on social issues. It was not too long before David Hunt replaced her, thereby becoming the first but by no means the last male minister responsible for women (the current Scottish minister for women, in 1998, is male).

These changes were not so much party policy as developments taken forward by a combination of Major's decisions and the momentum of government. All the small changes introduced over time – the focus on Civil Service recruitment and promotion, appointments to government bodies – continued, and were increasingly having their impact as reports were being produced and changes taking place. Equal opportunities rubrics were by this time appearing in all manner of legislation, including the obvious areas like employment and education, but also in local government, children's and family law, and crime bills.

The government's general approach to equality policy was on international display at the Fourth UN World Conference on Women at Beijing in 1995. The Conservative Party has a distinctive view of women. They are regarded as different in special ways, but not a distinct and needy group in society. This view is revealed in the focus upon a 'partnership' of women and men 'based on equality of opportunity and mutual respect', and in the emphasized point that reducing poverty and powerlessness 'is *not* just a "women's issue"' (Chalker 1995, pp. 1, 5). Four commitments were made:

- mainstreaming a gender perspective into all policies
- ensuring that *all* women . . . have equal opportunities, choices and rights
- supporting women's promotion to the top of public and working life, and
- working in partnership with NGOs and others with an interest to take forward the objectives of the Platform. (Chalker 1995, p. 2)

Inevitably, the one area in which the party had a role to play in equality policy concerned the European Union (EU). Throughout the 1980s and 1990s the European Commission developed its equality policies, moving from a strict equal-treatment position to more radical and interventionist policies (Hoskyns 1996). At the same time, specific British legislation and policies were under scrutiny for failing to meet the terms of the Treaty of Rome. With the support of the EOC, the government's unequal treatment of women and men in respect of retirement age was successfully challenged in the European Court of Justice. For the Conservative Party at large, this was an unacceptable intrusion into the affairs of Britain. Even worse were the post-Maastricht discussions about parental leave. The consideration of maternal and paternal leave touched upon family policy, wherein the sanctity of the nuclear unit sustained by stereotypical gender roles has never come under serious challenge in the party.

One result was the unedifying spectacle of Gillian Shepherd, minister for employment, insisting on the European stage that pregnancy be regarded as an illness. This was something of a betrayal of feminist principles, not to mention of the campaign to develop awareness about pregnancy, but was done in order to restrict the direct effect of any decision on British domestic policy and to minimize the changes that would have to be made under the treaty. This is the clearest example of the internal politics of the Conservative Party affecting a specific aspect of sex equality policy (apart from the controversial Clause 28 of the Education Reform Act, outlawing education on gay and lesbian lifestyles in the classroom).

On a broader level, Major maintained a policy based on a series of distinctions concerning the public and the private sector. Central government had a responsibility to conduct its affairs within existing law and even best practice, and should ultimately be accountable to the prime minister for its performance. Here equal treatment was backed up by monitoring. Other reaches of government – agencies, for example – were constrained to behave similarly (depending on the content of their contract) and health trusts ought to do so, while the armed forces continued to enjoy legal immunity until the courts overturned it. In other words, every step away from Major and the Whitehall machine legitimated a lower level of expectation and significant reductions in compliance and accountability. Within the private sector, the government restricted itself entirely to exhortation and continued support for Opportunity 2000. At this level, responsibility for action had shifted dramatically, in two senses. First, action beyond the legal minimum was a voluntary matter, and second, the onus for change increasingly settled onto the wronged individual.

At the level of party organization, little was done effectively to address the shortfall of women representatives of the Conservative Party in Parliament. There was encouragement to women to come forward, whereupon some training was provided, but the party had no means of dealing with the persistent bias against women in the selection system. The most high profile activity had been championed by the erstwhile Conservative MP Emma Nicholson. Nicholson used the Conservative Women's Organization conferences as a platform for the launch of a series of younger women's rallies and 'highflyers' conferences', designed to attract 'non-left feminist[s]' to the party and hence onto candidate lists (Kelly 1994, p. 255). It is impossible to describe the Conservative approach as a success, as tables 6.2 and 6.3 below show. Nicholson's high-profile defection to the Liberal Democratic Party at Christmas 1996 underscores the point.

The Conservative policy on sex equality was by the time of the 1997 election well developed and consistent with the overall philosophy of the party. At the practical level, Major's government felt that it could comfortably claim credit for its approach and outcomes. Individual effort within a meritocratic order could earn rewards; the employment of women had increased dramatically; vouchers for nursery education had been introduced and provision would be extended further. These things represented a pragmatic and effective approach without the damage that had been done by radical methods such as positive discrimination in the United States. The contrast with the Labour Party was held to be clear. The Conservatives offered real change that related to the everyday lives of ordinary women rather than the ideological, divisive and impractical measures being promoted by the Labour Party.

Labour's leap forward

Labour's defeat at the 1992 election made possible a key victory for women, and further opportunities to develop party policy with regard to sex equality. The election defeat provided two sets of data on different aspects of the representation of women, supporting claims that the Labour Party had to be much more proactive. First, the Labour Party suffered a significant gender gap in voting behaviour. The party had once more failed to represent the interests of women, and so failed to attract the same level of support it enjoyed from men. Second, the number of Labour women elected to Parliament once again increased only marginally, bringing into question once more the issue of representation of women in government and the methods the party employed to select women as candidates that stood a chance of being elected. Until 1992, the Labour Party had in practice been wedded to the same approach as the Conservatives –

encouragement, fine words and commitments, but no effective procedures to produce a substantive change in outcomes.

Activists pushed for the implementation of quotas which would address both issues simultaneously, and which would have had a powerful symbolic effect. Quotas had been on the Labour Party agenda since 1989, and conference had agreed in 1990 to apply a 40 per cent quota to the National Executive Committee. Norris and Lovenduski (1995) argue that Labour Party members characteristically see themselves as representing groups in society, in contradistinction to the Conservative and Liberal Democratic parties, where the individual is sovereign, and representation is in terms of public service and universalistic principles. Under John Smith's leadership of the party, women found an ally. The quota policy in relation to winnable seats was passed as part of a deal to win a one-member-one-vote (OMOV) decision at the 1993 annual conference. A traditional Labour Party and trade union 'stitch-up' had this time delivered something for women. This was fortunate, since it was clear that the full quotas policy was attracting some powerful opposition from both men and women.

The policy meant that women-only shortlists of candidates became mandatory in half of all constituencies where the seat would be vacant at the next general election. Since these seats were held by the Labour Party, they were, by definition, almost guaranteed to return the Labour candidate. The quota policy would therefore produce a predictable increase in the number of women MPs. Women-only shortlists would also be required in half of the most marginal (i.e. technically winnable) seats being contested. Any electoral advance by the Labour Party would produce a proportional increase in the representation of women.

Both the other major parties expressed their total opposition to the policy. The Conservatives dismissed it as gesture politics, and warned of the likely negative consequences of positive discrimination. The Liberal Democrats opposed it in principle, since it deviated so sharply from the idea of equal treatment and equality of opportunity in favour of an imposed equality of outcome (Squires 1996, p. 75).

The policy met with both success and failure. Predictably, it did run into some opposition in the party, as local constituency parties sought to have a mixed shortlist or retain the previous challenger for the seat. As Kelly notes, the shortlist policy was seen by many Party members 'as a misguided exercise and a colossal waste of time', while others argued that it was 'a valuable consciousness-raising exercise' that had successfully created 'a new culture' vital for a more open competition for seats in the future (Kelly 1996, p. 39). Almost all of the disputed cases were resolved, sometimes with the intervention of Labour's NEC. However, two disgruntled men took the exclusion from a shortlist to industrial tribunal, which found against the policy. No challenge was made to the tribunal decision, and the quota policy was officially dropped. Tony Blair's personal preference that the policy should not continue beyond the 1997 general election thus became policy (Kelly 1996, p. 39). However, by this time most of the selections had been made. There were no appeals against the women already selected, and the practice appears to have carried on informally in any event (Kelly 1996).

The 1997 General Election: Campaign and Aftermath

What women say they want – at election time

The voting pattern of women at general elections reveals an historic advantage, a gender gap, in favour of the Conservative Party. Norris has pointed out that the extension of the franchise to women and the resultant emergence of a gender gap stood in the way of 'an unbroken period of Labour governments from 1945 to 1979' (Norris 1996, p. 334). Table 6.1 shows the support for the Conservative and Labour parties over the last five elections. The gender gap is calculated by subtracting the difference between Conservative and Labour percentage votes for men from the difference between the percentage votes for women. Although the gender gap is not always large, the distribution of votes in marginal seats can mean that it is crucial to the outcome of the general election. A gender gap greater than zero signifies that the Conservative Party potentially reaps the electoral benefit.

The gender gap and the heavy targeting of marginal seats gave both women's organizations and the parties an interest in finding what would affect women's votes. In March 1977, the Women's Communication Centre published the results of an extensive survey, based on the views of some 10,000 women. 'What women want *on politics*' compared the concerns of women with the commitments of the parties (Adcock and Tibballs 1997). Three overall conclusions demonstrated that the political parties had yet to move beyond a largely rhetorical and instrumental engagement with sex equality. Women's issues and measures to address inequality might 'figure prominently in the parties' separate strategy documents on women', but they did 'not figure strongly in mainstream policy agendas' (Adcock and Tibballs 1997, p. vii). Moreover, within the traditional policy areas, such as employment, Europe, economic policy and education, 'women's priorities and concerns [were] different from those issues highlighted by the parties' (Adcock and Tibballs 1997, p. vii). Finally, personal security was much more salient for women than national security. These general

Table 6.1   *Support for Conservative and Labour parties at general elections 1979–1997 by gender (per cent)*

General election	Conservative		Labour		Gender gap
	Men	Women	Men	Women	
1979	45	49	38	38	3
1983	46	45	30	28	2
1987	44	44	31	31	1
1992	46	48	37	34	6
1997	31	32	45	45	1

Gender-gap figures are based on voting figures that have not been rounded up or down; 1997 data is based on a BBC/NOP Exit Poll (Kellner 1997, p. 617)
Source: Norris 1996, p. 335

findings underpinned the specific details of what women said they wanted from the political system. Eight expectations stood out:

- equal rights and status in society;
- equal pay and work conditions;
- equal representation in politics, power structures and decision making;
- action on ageism;
- equal lesbian and gay rights, and an end to prejudice;
- freedom to develop beyond gender stereotypes and social restrictions;
- open access to information;
- equal access to public space.

What the parties offered

Although all three parties had policy documents that related specifically to women, the manifestos are largely free of an explicitly gender dimension. The Conservative document actually promised little, but claimed that 'women are succeeding in Britain'. They promised to 'ensure women have equal opportunities in education and the workplace', but the mechanism for so doing is 'keeping our economy buoyant and our labour markets flexible' (Conservative Party 1997, p. 341). As far as education is concerned, this is bizarre; for the workplace, it indicates that persuasion not enforcement, and private rather than public action, remain the preferred implementation options. The Liberal Democrats promised to promote equality in the workplace 'with tougher obligations on employers to establish equal opportunities procedures and pursue the principle of equal pay for work of equal value' (Liberal Democratic Party 1997, p. 377). Of particular note was the promise of an Equal Treatment Act that would introduce collective remedies and put the onus of proof on the employer (Adcock and Tibballs 1997, p. 6). In general, this reveals a commitment to strengthen formal or legal equality and a faith in a procedural approach to implementation. The Liberal Democrat policy paper 'Equal citizens: proposals to promote the equal treatment of women' makes this clear. They want 'not special treatment for women but equal treatment' (Adcock and Tibbals 1997, p. 5). In terminology and sentiment that was to be repeated by Gordon Brown (*Guardian*, 12 August 1997) when he become the new chancellor, the Liberal Democrats claim that 'Our aim is not equality of outcome, but equality of opportunity' (Adcock and Tibballs 1997, p. 5).

References to women in the Labour manifesto may be scarce, and there is no acknowledgement of the gendered nature of poverty and inequality, but it is possible to claim that some of the policies are gender sensitive, such as the nursery education policy, lone-parent provisions, pensions and family policy. Labour's 'Strategy for women' document presented equality policy as a matter of extending individual rights and ending unjustifiable discrimination. The rights language is reminiscent of both the Conservative and Liberal Democrat approaches. As in the latter, sex equality and equal pay legislation would be simplified so that redress would be easier to seek and obtain. The Labour Party was already committed to the appointment of a minister for women with

Cabinet rank. To provide 'lean but powerful machinery' necessary to secure 'real equality for women', it proposed moving the Conservatives' Sex Equality Branch out of the DfEE into the Cabinet Office. Also, a parliamentary select committee on women's affairs would be considered, while the commitment to an annual debate on women's issues in the House of Commons would remain (Adcock and Tibballs 1997, pp. 70–1). The idea of a minister for women with full Cabinet rank was opposed by both the Conservatives and the Liberal Democrats.

Women in the election

The year 1997 was a watershed in British electoral politics. The Conservative government was swept from office and replaced by a resurgent Labour Party intent on presenting itself as modernized, politically attuned to contemporary concerns and values, and determined to implement a thoroughly trailed policy manifesto. Overnight, the representation of women in the House of Commons leapt from 58 to 121. Of these, 101 were Labour MPs, many in Parliament as a direct result of the Labour Party's policy of having women-only shortlists. The principal aim – to make a significant breakthrough towards the target of 50 per cent women MPs in the Parliamentary Labour Party (PLP) after ten years or three general elections – was achieved. Table 6.2 compares the experience for selected women candidates in the last two elections. It shows that the chances of a woman being elected a Labour MP increased nearly two and a half times, resulting in just short of a threefold increase in their number and doubling the representation of women in Parliament. At the same time, the total number of women candidates for a slightly larger number of seats in the country went up by a mere 12 per cent.

Table 6.3 compares the performance of the parties, underpinned as they are by different views on sex equality and quotas as a method to ensure that the opportunity provided is a real rather than formal one. It shows that the

Table 6.2 *Labour women candidates at general elections 1992–1997*

General election	Women candidates	Women elected	Success rate	Women in PLP	Labour women in Commons	All women in Commons
1992	138	37	27%	14%	6%	9%
1997	155	101	65%	24%	15%	18%

Table 6.3 *Women candidates and elected MPs from three main parties 1997*

Women	Conservative	Labour	Liberal Democrat
Candidates	66 10%	155 24%	147 23%
Elected	13 8%	101 24%	3 6.5%

Conservatives failed to provide a substantial number of opportunities for women even to stand for Parliament. The Liberal Democrats, meanwhile, provided nearly as many opportunities as Labour, but with minimal success. The opportunities in both Conservative and Liberal Democratic parties secured outcomes, on this evidence, that greatly favoured men. Only the Labour Party can claim that women and men, once selected, had an equal chance of success at the election. For Labour women, the opportunity was enhanced, and it was matched by the outcome.

New brooms

When Blair entered 10 Downing Street as prime minister on 2 May 1997, he completed the long march of the Labour Party from a mass party of the industrial heartland of mid-twentieth-century Britain to a social democratic party in the European tradition. Perhaps the defining moment had already come, with his appeal to conference in 1994 to amend Clause IV. The following January, Blair explained his brand of socialist values. Equality, he felt, should be conceived 'not in the sense of uniform equality of outcome, but pursued rather as the goals both of equality of respect and status and of fairer distribution of rewards and opportunities' (in Jones 1996, p. 141). In government, Blair has revealed that his approach to sex equality reflects this rather bland account. His initiatives are not far along the continuum from the low level of activity of Major's government. Blair did not fulfil the party policy in relation to a Ministry for Women.

Nevertheless, the newly formed government had five women frontbench ministers instead of just two, and there were twenty-one women in the government as a whole, compared to ten before 1 May. The Sex Equality Branch was shifted to the Cabinet Office, and the first Cabinet subcommittee on women's issues was set up. By contrast, the new Conservative shadow team was composed of thirty-eight men and just three women (only one of whom was in the Shadow Cabinet). Harriet Harman and her ministerial colleagues moved quickly to implement some of the changes for which women inside and outside the Labour Party had been campaigning for some time.

These changes in the elected government indicate welcome but somewhat belated and halting steps toward political maturity for Britain. A Council of Europe comparison of forty countries places the Blair government tenth in a league table for representation in government posts (22.73 per cent), with the UK ranked twelfth in terms of women parliamentarians (*Guardian*, 24 October 1997, p. 11). In both cases, the election of a Labour government had a significant impact on the rankings. The impact on the political opportunity structure for women takes place on a number of levels. First, the increased presence of women in key posts will have a direct effect on the kinds of policy that are brought forward. Second, these women represent links to other women and to women's interests and activities that had remained relatively marginalized under the Conservative government. Third, the effect on the symbolic order is significant if unquantifiable. Sex equality policy is just one of the areas where the effect of the presence of women will be considerable. There is now the opportunity for the most sustained set of changes for women since the liberal reforms of the 1970s, when the basic legal and institutional framework for dealing with sex discrimination was first established.

The impact on the policies of the political parties will also be quite profound, if for different reasons. The Labour Party's wilderness years were not wasted by women activists and those committed to equality of opportunity. Policies were tried and tested at local authority level, and steadily transferred through the policy machinery and party conferences into a wide-ranging and thorough set of prescriptions for the incoming government. The questions now are threefold: first, how much of that agenda will the government accept and implement; second, how will the party react; and third, what will the party, now so full of confidence and energy, propose, if not demand?

The Conservatives have an entirely different problem. Although their electoral support did not fall to a catastrophic level, their parliamentary representation has dropped dramatically. Ironically, the Conservative Party has always been able to claim good support from women, but the bulk of these are older women, from whom the party draws its greatest strength in the local associations. The most radical option to get more Conservative women is the idea (endorsed at the 1997 Tory conference) that woman should comprise 25 per cent of candidates interviewed in the first round. Despite the evidence from Labour and Liberal Democratic experience that this will have little effect on the eventual number of women selected as candidates, other policy options are seen as too radical because they breach the freedoms of constituency associations and individuals.

The essential problem for the Liberal Democratic Party is the two-party system. There is evidence to show that women preferred the overall political approach of the Liberal Democrats in the election, even though this did not translate into votes. At their conference, a majority voted to introduce quotas for shortlists, but the vote fell short of the two-thirds majority needed to approve a measure of such constitutional significance. The same policy was accepted in relation to the list system for election to the European Parliament.

Conclusion: The Impact of Party Policy

On the evidence, it is reasonable to conclude that women's access to the political opportunity structure has improved, and that the new government has begun to introduce some of the changes that women want. However, the government is, by its party character, more accessible to a number of groups in society that were previously excluded from the policy debates and the exercise of influence. Therefore, a comparative perspective is needed. It is necessary to ask whether women now enjoy 'equal availability of political influence' (Brighouse 1996). Here the evidence is less encouraging for women. In practical terms, the performance of the government in relation to its manifesto and policy-paper commitment gives mixed messages. Instead of a women's minister with full Cabinet rank and the status and strategic location of a place in the Cabinet Office, the post has been doubly downgraded. Harriet Harman, ironically, has to do a double day; she is minister of state for social security *and* minister for women. She has an *unpaid* junior, Joan Ruddock, with a new Women's Unit in the Department of Social Security. The unit will 'equality proof' policy papers from other departments, but with reduced resources compared to arrangements set up by the Conservatives when in office. Whatever their merits, policies not backed up by proper resources are just as vulnerable as ideas without powerful sponsors.

Harman clearly takes her task seriously, and has been quick to establish connections with women in and out of government and Parliament. A women's Cabinet subcommittee has been set up, and randomly selected 'juries' of women to study and evaluate government proposals have been mooted. Nevertheless, there is no woman employed at senior policy level, despite Labour setting up twenty policy reviews and ten task forces in its first one hundred days of government.

It is reasonable to conclude, then, that the new government has increased the availability of political influence for women, but that equal availability has not been achieved, and appears not to be recognized as a problem. Whether that will change does not entirely depend upon the success or otherwise of the measures adopted, and new measures that may be adopted. Howe and Johnson have shown that the party, ideology and the approach to the use of state power are likely influences on these outcomes. The offsetting variable is the way that incumbency radically alters the policy-making process. For government, the key actors are 'government leaders and their senior policy advisers, not individual citizens, rights groups *or even rank-and-file members of parties*' (Howe and Johnson 1995, p. 260). Signs that agreed party policy will once more play a minor role in government decisions over equality policy are already abundant. Indeed, the 1997 Labour conference was devoid, for the first time for many years, of a high-profile debate on equality for women and did not produce any new commitments. The other key influence is Europe. In November 1997, the European Court of Justice decided to support a more permissive interpretation of positive action measures to increase the representation of women. This decision will have a wide and deep impact on sex equality politics in the next five years. Specifically, positive action to choose a woman over an equally qualified man until women compose 50 per cent of the relevant workforce is for the first time deemed legitimate. This change is tantamount to a change in British law from the current rather restrictive provision to a freedom to act that is more interventionist and outcome-oriented.

Conventional analysis suggests that the power and influence of party activists on Conservative sex equality policy will increase while the party is in opposition, and that the reverse will be true for the Labour Party. Changes to the organization and control of policy-making at the Labour conference in 1997 may well exacerbate this tendency. It is entirely feasible, however, that an offsetting political pattern will emerge. The public feminism (however mild its form) of the new women ministers, networked with backbenchers, the women's movement and unaffiliated women in the community, may amount to a source of innovation and energy that is creative and powerful enough to overcome some of the structural, institutional, behavioural and attitudinal impediments to any political programme to promote sex equality. Given the recent political history of sex equality politics, one of the most appropriate benchmarks for evaluation of the Labour government is the practical performance of local authority politicians and workers from 1979 to 1997.

Chronology of Significant Developments: April 1992 to October 1997

May 1992	Conservatives win general election
February 1993	Emily's List launched to promote women MPs in Labour Party
April 1994	Conservative government blocks EC parental leave directive
September 1994	Labour conference approves quotas for women
June 1994	DfEE launches 'Fair Play for Women' initiative
May 1995	Employment secretary and minister for women's affairs Michael Portillo blocks EC part-time workers directive
June 1995	Fourth UN World Conference on Women, Beijing, addressed by Baroness Chalker; EOC publishes report showing that compulsory competitive tendering exacerbates sex discrimination
February 1996	Labour Party's quota policy ruled discriminatory
May 1997	Labour wins general election – record number of women enter Parliament, mostly Labour
June 1997	Hague elected leader of Conservative Party – appoints one woman to Shadow Cabinet
July 1997	First Cabinet subcommittee on women's issues meets
September 1997	Liberal Democratic Party conference agrees quotas for European elections, but not for British contests
October 1997	Conservative conference recommends 25 per cent rule for first stage of candidate selection
November 1997	Government opens World Wide Web page for women; European Court of Justice allows positive action to produce gender parity

References

Adcock, C. and Tibballs, S. 1997 'What women want *on Politics*', London: Women's Communication Centre.

Brighouse, H. 1996 'Egalitarianism and equal availability of political influence', *Journal of Political Philosophy*, 4/2, June, pp. 118–41.

Chalker, Baroness 1995 *Annex 2: Baroness Chalker's statement at the Fourth Conference on Women, 5 September 1995*, London: Department for Employment and Education.

Charmley, J. 1996 *A History of Conservative Politics, 1900–1996*, Basingstoke: Macmillan.

Conservative Party 1975 'Widening horizons: women and the Conservative Party', London: Conservative Party.

Conservative Party 1997 'Conservative Party Manifesto', in T. Austin (ed.) *The Times Guide to the House of Commons May 1997*, London: Times Books.

Forbes, I. 1996 'The privatisation of sex equality policy', in J. Lovenduski and P. Norris (eds) *Women in Politics*, Oxford: Oxford University Press/Hansard Society for Parliamentary Government.

Gladwin, M. 1996 'Movements for equality: the nature of equality politics in Britain', PhD thesis, University of Southampton.

Hodge, M. 1994 'Working within local government: lessons learned', in J. Shaw and D. Perrons (eds) *Making Gender Work*, Buckingham: Open University Press.

Hoskyns, C. 1996 *Integrating Gender: Women, Law and Politics in the European Union*, London: Verso.

Howe, B. and Johnson, D. 1995 'Variations in enforcing equality: a study of Canadian provincial human rights funding', *Canadian Public Administration Journal*, 38/2, pp. 242–62.

Jones, T. 1996 *Remaking the Labour Party* London: Routledge.

Kellner, P. 1997 'Why the Tories were trounced', *Parliamentary Affairs*, 50/4, pp. 616–30.

Kelly, R. 1994 'The Party Conference', in A. Seldon and S. Ball (eds) *Conservative Century*, Oxford: Oxford University Press.

Kelly, R. 1996 'Selecting parliamentary candidates', *Talking Politics*, 9/1, pp. 36–43.

Lewis, J. 1992 *Women in Britain since 1945*, London: Institute of Contemporary British History.

Liberal Democratic Party 1997 'Liberal Democratic Party Manifesto', in T. Austin (ed.) *The Times Guide to the House of Commons May 1997*, London: Times Books.

Lovenduski, J. and Randall, V. 1993 *Contemporary Feminist Politics*, Oxford: Oxford University Press.

Meehan, E. 1985 *Women's Rights at Work: Campaigns and Policy in Britain and the United States*, London: Macmillan.

Norris, P. 1996 'Mobilising the "Women's vote": the gender-generation gap in voting behaviour', *Parliamentary Affairs*, 49/2, pp. 333–42.

Norris, P. and Lovenduski, J. 1995 *Political Recruitment*, London: Routledge.

Squires, J. 1996 'Quotas for women: fair representation?', in J. Lovenduski and P. Norris (eds) *Women in Politics*, Oxford: Oxford University Press/Hansard Society for Parliamentary Government.

Wainwright, H. 1997 *Guardian*, 4 August, G2, p. 4.

Wilkinson, H. 1994 *No Turning Back: Generations and the Genderquake*, London: Demos.

Wilson, E. 1980 *Only Halfway to Paradise*, London: Tavistock Publications.

Guide to Further Reading

Jane Lewis's *Women in Britain since 1945* (London: Institute of Contemporary British History, 1992) focuses on the increase in the percentage of married women in paid employment, the divorce rate and illegitimacy to document the nature and extent of changes for women, and argues for the continuing existence of a gender order. *Women in Politics* (Oxford: Oxford University Press/Hansard Society for Parliamentary Government, 1996), edited by Joni Lovenduski and Pippa Norris, is a volume of commissioned chapters that explores positional, organizational and policy gender biases against women across a wide range of subjects and areas. It provides information and analysis of the slow improvement for women in terms of presence and the persistent resistance to change in policy and organization terms. *Making Gender Work* (Buckingham: Open University Press, 1994), edited by Jane Shaw and Diana Perrons, brings together academics and politicians, and details the many attempts to promote and advance equality policy in a variety of institutional settings. It is a good source for different approaches, and for an historical sense of strategic and political action.

Cathryn Hoskyns's *Integrating Gender: Women, Law and Politics in the European Union* (London: Verso, 1996) is a thorough and contextual account of the European dimension of women's rights. It catalogues the increasingly interventionist role of the European Union, the Commission and the European Court of Justice. It gives plenty of examples where the UK's role is criticized.

Joni Lovenduski and Vicky Randall have produced the definitive account of the women's movement, the changing political opportunity structure, and developments in women's ideas, actions and the political system from the late 1970s to the early 1990s, in *Contemporary Feminist Politics* (Oxford: Oxford University Press, 1993). It is an excellent source of the historical contributions of women in a host of organizations, detailed within a robust analytical framework. Elizabeth Meehan, in *Women's Rights at Work: Campaigns and Policy in Britain and the United States* (London: Macmillan, 1985), provides a classic comparative account of campaigns under two very different political structures. It explains why Britain has the laws it does have, as well as providing a critique of their effectiveness.

Helen Wilkinson's pamphlet *No Turning Back: Generations and the Gender-quake* (London: Demos, 1994) is based on the view that the increasing engagement of women in the public domain has resulted in changing relations between women and men and the emergence of a more feminized set of social and cultural values. Elizabeth Wilson's *Only Halfway to Paradise* (London: Tavistock Publications, 1980) is an authoritative account of the period 1945–1968, in relation to the impact on women of post-war policy and the political and campaigning activities of women.

7 | Northern Ireland

Michael Cunningham

Synopsis

The following chapter traces the evolution of British government policy in Northern Ireland and, in particular, focuses upon the development of an 'intergovernmental' approach to managing the problem, the extent of cross-party agreement, and tensions within the Labour and Conservative parties.

The Historical Context: Party Policy 1945–1992

It is important at the outset to note that British party policy towards Northern Ireland is, if not unique, different in fundamental ways from that pertaining to virtually all other areas under consideration in this book. First, until the late 1960s Westminster had little day-to-day involvement in Northern Ireland affairs, owing to the existence in Northern Ireland since 1920 of a devolved administration. Second, the Labour and Conservative parties have not contested seats within the province. This has arguably meant that there has been less incentive for them to develop policy which could be offered to the electorate as being substantially different from each other's; and, relatedly, the third point is that many commentators have argued that a practical bipartisanship has operated in the construction of party policy. Bipartisanship may be defined as a 'general agreement between the two main British political parties on the principles of their *constitutional* approach towards the conflict in Northern Ireland' (Dixon 1995a, p. 148). However, this should not obscure the fact that there have been very important changes in Northern Ireland policy over the period in question. Therefore, a bipartisan policy does not equate with a static one. Also, inter- and intra-party tensions over policy have frequently occurred. These factors will be a common thread running through the subsequent sections.

From the devolution settlement to direct British reinvolvement

The Government of Ireland Act of 1920 established the constitutional relationship between Westminster, the imperial Parliament, and the devolved administration, commonly known as Stormont, which had responsibility for the six counties of Northern Ireland following partition. This relationship is of great significance because it both emphasized the ultimate sovereignty and therefore responsibility of the Westminster Parliament for Northern Ireland and also granted to Stormont control of many important policy areas. Thus, when this settlement began to unravel in the late 1960s, partly because the nationalist community accused the unionist administration of discrimination in areas of public policy, the British government had the ultimate responsibility. This caused much friction with Stormont, which had become accustomed to a *laissez-faire* approach from Westminster that encouraged the belief in a *de facto* sovereignty.

The division of responsibility between the two governments was as follows. 'Excepted' areas were those outside Stormont's remit, which were to be retained by the sovereign Parliament; principal among these were control of the armed forces, regulation and control of external trade, issuing of coinage, and control of all major sources of revenue including income tax, surtax and custom and excise duties. The second and intermediate category was 'reserved' matters. These were not the responsibility of Stormont but could be granted to an all-Ireland Assembly which the two Irish parliaments could establish under the terms of the 1920 Act. This assembly was never established so these powers, including control of the banking system, the postal system and the Supreme Court of Northern Ireland, were retained by Westminster. The third category was 'transferred' matters, which included electoral arrangements and responsibility for law, order and security, and these were within the legislative and administrative competence of the Stormont parliament. These were areas of much political sensitivity and, along with the provision of services by local authorities and the location of inward investment, would form the basis of complaints of discrimination by the nationalist community. (For an assessment of this topic see Whyte 1983.)

Having sketched the constitutional position as formulated in the 1920 Act, both the reason for the settlement and the legacy of it need to be examined. There are two principal interpretations of Britain's role in this period. The first, and more widely accepted, is that partition was a somewhat messy compromise by which the British government recognized the political divisions within Ireland and also, unsurprisingly, tried to engineer a settlement which suited its own agenda. This included trying to remove, or at least isolate, Ireland from the political 'mainstream'; home rule in the south and devolution in the north were desirable so that Ireland would become a residual matter at Westminster. This 'quarantining', as Paul Arthur (1983) has termed it, was influenced by the fact that between the mid-1880s and 1920 Ireland had been arguably the most contentious and bitter issue in British parliamentary politics, and it thus suited all British parties at this juncture to remove it at far as possible. The second view, held traditionally by nationalists and much of the British left, is that partition was a more malign policy which underpinned unionist domination in part of Ireland and ensured a continued colonial presence for the British state, by which it could safeguard both strategic and economic interests. In essence, the first view sees Britain as trying to deal with the 'realities' of a sectarian division while the second emphasizes more its role in creating, or at least bolstering, such divisions.

However one interprets the above, after 1920 the British Parliament seemed largely content to operate a policy (if one can dignify it as such) of what it probably conceived to be benign neglect towards Northern Ireland. As well as ultimate responsibility over Stormont, the more practical resource of financial subvention was a possible method by which Westminster could monitor and intervene in the actions of Stormont. As was revealed by Richard Crossman in the late 1960s, British Parliament and government had little detailed knowledge of this relationship (Crossman 1977, p. 187). Additionally, in the early 1920s, a convention was established at Westminster whereby questions relating to 'transferred' matters were considered *ultra vires* since they were the responsibility of Stormont.

This is not to say that there was no interest at all shown by sections of either government or the political parties towards Northern Ireland events or the actions of the unionist-controlled Stormont government. For example, both the Cabinet and the Colonial Office expressed reservations over the funding by the British government of the security forces developed by Stormont, and in 1937 Stafford Cripps visited Northern Ireland to canvass for a united Ireland and to support working-class mobilization against the unionist government, though to little effect (Canning 1985, p. 232). The point is that, particularly in the post-war period, it is doubtful whether one can talk of a 'policy' towards Northern Ireland from either of the two main British parties. Rather there was a general disposition of support for unionism – and the Unionist party – from the Conservatives, while the Labour party had inherited the old Liberal position of a diffuse sympathy for nationalism based on a belief that Ireland should be one political unit. However, the Free State's neutrality in World War II, which was contrasted to the sacrifices of the North, and the establishment of the Irish Republic in 1949 led to the development of a more pro-unionist sympathy among the Labour Party leadership. In essence, neither party had the desire or a strategy to recast what had come to be seen as a permanent settlement constructed in the 1920s. This helps to explain why the recurrence of the troubles in the late 1960s came as such a shock to the British political establishment.

British reintervention 1969–1972

This section will briefly review the principal constitutional initiatives of the period 1969–1972 and bring out the principles and assumptions that underlay them. These will then be examined in the light of differences between, and similarities in, party policy to test further the thesis of 'bipartisanship' mentioned above.

The period 1969–1972, while one of massive upheaval and significant change in the party system in Northern Ireland, can be simply summarized. The Labour government up to 1970 attempted to deal with the problem of renewed violence by a strategy of directing and supervising reforms which would be implemented by the unionist government of Stormont; for example, in the area of security, better redress for citizens through the creation of ombudsmen, and ongoing reform of housing allocation. Essentially, it was hoped that the grievances of the civil rights movement could be addressed without undermining the authority of the Stormont government, thus avoiding direct rule of the province. This policy was pursued through informal and formal consultations between Northern Ireland and British officials and politicians. The reason for this strategy was outlined in the section above – the desire for the 'quarantining', as far as possible, of Northern Ireland.

This policy was widely endorsed by the Conservative opposition. Both the Labour home secretary of the period, James Callaghan, who had responsibility for the policy, and the Conservative 'shadow', Quintin Hogg, have stressed the importance of a bipartisan approach, fearing that disputes could inflame the situation and give succour to extremists (Dixon 1995a, pp. 154–5). This was largely accepted by the parliamentary parties, but tensions arose as the limitations of the policy became evident. To succeed, it had to placate the civil rights movement and a re-emerging and militant nationalism, while at the same time carrying with it sufficient of the unionist population to prevent those accepting reform from being outflanked by more 'hardline' loyalists. Whether this could have been achieved is hypothetical, but the increasing violence resulted in severely strained relations between Labour and the Conservatives. Labour felt that Reginald Maudling, the Conservative home secretary after 1970, was allowing Stormont excessive latitude in the dictation of security policy and that he was not being active enough in building on the reform programme of 1969–1970. The tensions over security are revealed in the introduction of internment in August 1971. In the Commons debate of September, Labour did not oppose the government on the grounds that division might encourage extremism in Northern Ireland, but sixty-eight Labour MPs, mostly from the left of the party, were among those who forced a division. Two months later, for the first time since the recurrence of the 'troubles', the opposition voted against the government; the occasion being a major debate over security policy.

The significance of this division should not be overemphasized. It was in part a tactic to placate backbench concerns by the Labour leadership, and in part a way to express concern over the extent of Stormont's role in policy-making, rather than a wholesale condemnation of Conservative strategy. There are two notable developments in the period before the introduction of direct rule in 1972. The first is that, albeit tentatively and as a long-term aspiration, Harold Wilson, leader of the opposition, advocated a unified Ireland, thus laying a marker for later developments in the Labour party. In the past Wilson had made sufficient pro-nationalist gestures for the civil rights movement to hope for a more interventionist approach following Labour's electoral success in 1964; however, little concrete had materialized. Wilson's position may have been influenced by the importance of the Irish electorate in Britain. The second is that intra-party tensions were manifest in this period; many Conservative MPs increasingly saw the issue as a 'law and order' one requiring a tougher security policy against terrorism, while, conversely, a vocal minority of Labour backbenchers were concerned about emergency legislation and the perceived 'slowing down' of a strategy of constructive reform. These divisions thus represented a wider ideological difference between the parties.

From direct rule to the Anglo-Irish Agreement

The suspension of Stormont in 1972, the immediate impetus being the unionist government's refusal to relinquish control of security policy, and the introduction of a new devolved administration, with guaranteed minority representation at executive level, at the end of 1973 helped to strengthen bipartisanship (for more details of this initiative and later ones see Cunningham 1991). The adoption of this policy under William Whitelaw, the first secretary of state for Northern Ireland, marked a significant shift in government policy. It was a recognition that a government in Northern Ireland composed of representatives of only one of the two main communities was unlikely to provide stability. Provisions for a Council of Ireland (which never materialized) in which matters of mutual interest, north and south, could be discussed with representatives of the Irish Parliament indicated that the government believed that Northern Ireland was not a solely 'internal' question; that is, one in which only the UK had a legitimate interest. This marked the introduction of what may be termed the 'Irish dimension'. Although later developments would supersede these structures, the principles of 'power sharing' and a bilateral approach to the management of the problem would reappear in various forms.

There was a very high degree of consensus over the ending of Stormont and the attempt to introduce 'power sharing'. The Labour Party was largely supportive, and among the Conservatives only nine opposed the second reading of the bill to suspend Stormont, and only two opposed the motion to approve the White Paper which set out the proposals for a 'power-sharing' administration.

Following a loyalist strike, the 'power-sharing' executive collapsed in May 1974. The subsequent years to 1979 are marked by a series of abortive initiatives to resurrect some form of 'partnership' system of devolved government with a downgraded 'Irish dimension'. It is not only hindsight which makes these attempts look likely failures and British policy seem lacking in ways forward. Towards the end of this period two currents can be seen to be emerging. First, a Conservative lobby, particularly influenced by Airey Neave, shadow spokesman for Northern Ireland 1975–1979 and a confidant of Margaret Thatcher, emerged, which advocated an 'integrationist' approach. It believed that devolution should be abandoned or scaled down, given the failures of the preceding period, and that Northern Ireland should be governed, as far as possible, like the rest of the UK (for details see Cunningham 1995). Second, there was growing discontent within the Labour Party about the emphasis placed on security by Roy Mason, secretary of state from 1976 to 1979. This was later to be reflected in two developments, in part related to the gains made by the left at constituency level and in the National Executive Commitee (NEC): Labour's formal adoption of 'unity by consent' in 1981 and its opposition in 1983 to the renewal of the Prevention of Terrorism Act (PTA – emergency legislation which had been introduced by a Labour government in 1974). These issues will be returned to later.

The advent of Thatcher to the premiership fuelled integrationist expectations, yet the initiatives of both Humphrey Atkins and James Prior, the successive secretaries of state, followed the broadly devolutionist track. Additionally, the Anglo-Irish Agreement (AIA) of November 1985, by formally recognizing the right of the Irish Republic to be consulted over Northern Ireland policy, both extended and institutionalized the 'Irish dimension' for discussions of AIA (see O'Leary 1987; Connolly and Loughlin 1986). There is something of a paradox here: why did Thatcher, a self-proclaimed unionist and one personally close to Neave, adopt policies so objectionable to integrationists and many unionists? These points will be considered further in the conclusion when the parameters of policy are discussed, but various explanations have been offered. First, if, as Robert Blake maintains, 'the Conservative Party could be regarded as the party of English nationalism' (cited in Aughey 1996, p. 225), it could be that Thatcher's instinctive unionism did not extend to a full appreciation of Irish unionist sensibilities, although many unionists themselves felt she had been corrupted by officials, particularly those in the Foreign Office, who favoured a bilateral approach to the problem partly to appease American interests. Secondly, *realpolitik* and the chance to leave her imprint on history may have persuaded her that the integration of the Irish Republic into the process of managing Northern Ireland was necessary. Whatever the case, 1979 did not witness the advent of a more pro-unionist policy.

The years between 1985 and 1989 are largely dominated by the British government's fidelity to the AIA, a position strongly supported by the opposition despite occasional tensions over the operation of bilateral relations and widespread, if unsuccessful, opposition from unionists (for more on which see Aughey 1989). Cox has identified the appointment of Peter Brooke as secretary of state in July 1989 as marking the beginning of a new phase in policy leading to the Downing Street Declaration (DSD) of December 1993 (Cox 1996, p. 187). To provide continuity, this will mark the starting-point for the following section.

An Unusual Climate: Continuity and Rupture 1992–1997

This section details the principal events leading up to the Framework Documents of 1995 and responses to them and then assesses the extent of agreement and division both between and within the two major British parties in the 1990s.

From the Brooke/Mayhew talks to the Downing Street Declaration

As with previous attempts in the 1970s and 1980s, prospects for all-party (i.e. Northern Ireland party) agreement appeared poor in the late 1980s, so it perhaps needs to be explained why Brooke instigated a new round of talks. As with previous initiatives the British government was sensitive to accusations of passivism or quietism, so a policy of 'doing something' had intrinsic worth. Also, as the AIA had alienated unionists, an attempt at creating conditions whereby it could be transcended had the, albeit faint, prospect of reintegrating them into the political process. Lastly, government contacts with Sinn Fein led the government to believe that elements of the party were looking for a way into constitutional politics, which Brooke hoped to encourage.

The detail of the tortuous process need not detain us; suffice to say that negotiations with the parties lasted from January 1990 to March 1991 before an agenda was announced for talks. These collapsed in July 1991 following procedural wranglings and unionist demands that articles 2 and 3 of the Irish Constitution, which lay claim to Northern Ireland, should be repealed as a sign of good faith rather than be used as a bargaining tool by the Irish government. What is more significant here is the British government's conceptualization of the problem. It is in this period that the 'three-strand' approach became formalized. This marked a recognition by the British government that three relationships had to be addressed in any attempted settlement which would transcend the AIA. Strand 1 consisted of relations between the communities in Northern Ireland; strand 2 relations between the North and the Republic; and strand 3 relations between Great Britain and Ireland and, relatedly, the institutional expression of these. It is clear that this marked a continuity with the AIA in that the 'Irish dimension' was maintained, but also developed it in that it opened the possibility that strand 2 could result in cross-border structures. This endorsed a broadly nationalist perspective and reflected the thinking of John Hume, leader of the Social Democratic and Labour Party (SDLP), the largest nationalist party in Northern Ireland. As Cox states, 'what was notable about this episode was the clear evidence that the British government valued its relationship with Dublin, and specifically the Agreement's legacy of the Inter-Governmental Conference, more highly than the sensibilities of their own citizens of the British tradition in Ireland' (1996, pp. 189–90). A renewed attempt at talks took place under the new secretary of state, Patrick Mayhew, after the general election of April 1992. In July he announced the formal launch of strands 2 and 3, although strand 1 had not been completed. The process ground to a halt in November of that year.

Perhaps more significant than the abortive talks were the attempts made by both Brooke and Mayhew to stress that the British government had no interest in promoting or facilitating a particular settlement in Northern Ireland, beyond the criterion that it would require the consent of the two traditions in Northern Ireland. From late 1990 links had been made between Sinn Fein and the British government (though long denied by the latter), and hints at Britain's neutral or arbiter role were clearly designed as an incentive for the Irish Republican Army (IRA) to renounce violence and for Sinn Fein to enter into negotiations with other constitutional parties.

Hence, in November 1990, Brooke affirmed British 'neutrality' and emphasized the legitimacy of the nationalist tradition, concluding that 'the British Government has no selfish strategic or economic interest in Northern Ireland: our role is to help, enable and encourage' (cited in Cox 1996, p. 198). This formulation was to be repeated over the following years in much the same language and, in a speech in Coleraine in December 1992, Mayhew again emphasized both the legitimacy of nationalism and advocacy of a united Ireland

and that Britain had no interest in promoting a particular settlement but was to act as a facilitator.

How significant were these statements of Brooke and Mayhew? Arguably they said nothing new, in that policy since at least the early 1970s illustrated that successive governments were quite prepared to enact policies which affronted much of the unionist community and that, since increasing intergovernmental links with the Irish Republic following summits in the early 1980s, they accepted a bilateral approach in excess of that which was acceptable to important elements of that community. What had changed was the candour with which this was expressed. The logic of government thinking ran as follows. Hume had been trying to convince Sinn Fein of Britain's neutrality, which meant the main task for nationalists was to forge accommodation with unionism within the structures of an 'agreed' Ireland (Hume's somewhat vague shorthand for possible all-Ireland linkages). Therefore, these statements would bolster Hume's position and elements in Sinn Fein who were amenable to it. (For Sinn Fein and IRA thinking, see O'Brien 1993; Dillon 1993; Smith 1995.) With respect to other actors, the explicit acceptance by the Republic's government of the necessity of northern majority consent to any new structures would, it was hoped, reassure unionists (a belief later bolstered by the Official Unionist Party's sanguine response to the DSD) and the bilateral approach to managing Northern Ireland would be further strengthened.

The Downing Street Declaration and the Framework Documents

The Downing Street Declaration of 15 December 1993 was a joint statement by John Major, the British prime minister, and Albert Reynolds, the Irish taoiseach. Two features of the declaration should be noted. First, it was a masterpiece of diplomacy in that it was addressing and trying to reassure various and contending political actors; this explains the 'tortuous syntax' which Paul Arthur identifies (1994, p. 219). Second, rather than being a detailed blueprint for specific reforms it was a statement of basic positions and intentions which the two governments believed must underpin any future negotiations. If one cuts through the 'tortuous syntax', the main points were as follows. First, the British government reiterated support for the 'three-stranded' approach and its lack of selfish strategic or economic interest in Northern Ireland; second, the Irish government stated that self-determination for the Irish people must 'be achieved and exercised with and subject to the agreement and consent of a majority of the people of Northern Ireland' (HMSO 1995, para. 5). Third, most commentators argue that, despite the formal 'balancing act', the declaration was underpinned by nationalist assumptions, with much more emphasis being placed on the possibility of Irish unity than on the current status of Northern Ireland as part of the UK. This is because one of the principal aims of the declaration was to convince Sinn Fein that enough of its agenda was being addressed, thus encouraging an IRA ceasefire and so allowing Sinn Fein to enter into all-party negotiations.

The two governments published the Joint Framework Documents in February 1995, in a period of optimism following the IRA and loyalist paramilitary ceasefires of August and October 1994 respectively. Principally the documents 'fleshed out' the bones of the DSD, based on the consent principle, north and south, and the possible institutional structures to embody the 'three strands'. Those envisaged were a new assembly for Northern Ireland with substantial 'transferred' legislative and executive responsibilities as in 1973; a system of committees, broadly proportional to party strengths, to oversee departmental activities; and 'a system of detailed checks and balances intended to sustain confidence in the institutions' (para. 5). With respect to strand 2, new institutions were envisaged which could have consultative and harmonizing powers over a wide range of policy areas, including for example, in the latter case, energy, trade, health, economic and education policy. If inter-party agreement were reached executive responsibilities could be extended to cross-border agencies. Proposals for strand 3 read as follows: 'both Governments envisage a new and more broadly-based Agreement, developing and extending their co-operation, reflecting the totality of relationships between the two islands, and dedicated to fostering co-operation, reconciliation and agreement in Ireland at all levels' (para. 39).

The term 'framework' is crucial. As in 1993, this was a working document, the stated aim of which was to assist party discussion and negotiation, and as such had to attempt to appeal to a diverse audience. It was not clear how certain tensions could be resolved. For example, would unionist representatives be prepared to take part in the operation of cross-border structures, or at least those with sufficient powers to recommend them to the SDLP? Could unionists withhold their consent from such operations even though a duty was to be placed on members of an assembly to participate in them (para. 25)?

Party positions and divisions

The above section has outlined government policy and the major developments within Northern Ireland; the following one will highlight the extent of inter-party disagreement and also tensions and differences of emphasis within the parties. It should be noted that the period since the late 1980s has marked a shift from an attempt to marginalize Sinn Fein via the AIA to a strategy of attempted incorporation, and there may therefore be a *prima facie* reason for thinking such a marked shift would have repercussions for both Conservative and Labour parties.

Conservative intra-party divisions

Within the Conservative parliamentary party, dissent from and opposition to the initiatives after the Brooke/Mayhew talks were limited to a handful of MPs. The 'pro-integrationist' lobby of the 1980s never mobilized above about thirty MPs; a total of twenty-one opposed the AIA. This grouping had lost key members by the 1990s through death and retirement, and by the time of the DSD and the Framework Documents there was widespread support for the government in the parliamentary party. For example, during the prime minister's Commons statement on the DSD of 15 December 1993 (HC vol. 234, cols. 1071–93), only three

MPs voiced concerns: Tony Marlow and Nicholas Winterton exhorted Major to endorse the union more strongly, and Nicholas Budgen pointedly enquired whether the government had any 'strategic or economic interest' in Wolverhampton (his constituency). Among other MPs, including Andrew Hunter and David Wilshire, Norman Lamont is perhaps the most prominent of those who expressed concern over what they felt to be an insufficient commitment to the union by the Conservative government of 1992–1997.

The reasons for widespread backbench endorsement are threefold. First, Major was eager to reassure MPs that the government would not act as 'persuaders' for a united Ireland, was opposed to joint authority, by which the UK and the Republic would share administration of Northern Ireland, and had no timetable for constitutional change. As long as northern majority consent was respected, virtually all Conservative MPs could support government initiatives within this parameter. Second, though this is difficult to quantify precisely, the majority of MPs have no profound interest in Northern Ireland and therefore it is not an issue on which they are disposed to dissent. Third, although party loyalty is not perhaps as pervasive as before the 1970s (see Norton 1978), it is still an important tradition within the party and reinforces the previous point. Similarly in the Commons statement on the Framework Documents on 22 February 1995 (HC vol. 255, cols. 355–70), Major emphasized the safeguards for unionists in Northern Ireland, including a referendum to be held before any constitutional changes and the government's repeated commitment to consent.

By contrast, Conservative activists articulated their concerns about shortcomings in government policy. A well-organized campaign in the late 1980s culminated in a conference vote in 1989 to recognize Conservative associations in Northern Ireland, against the wishes of the party hierarchy, which argued that this would risk splitting the pro-union vote and that Northern Ireland Conservatives had opposed the AIA. Aughey interprets this as a 'peasants' revolt', and the argument for recognizing Northern Ireland associations, based on principle and justice, struck a chord with the rank and file (Aughey 1994, pp. 144–7; see also Cunningham 1995).

Access to the opinions of Conservative activists and members, as canvassed by the party, is difficult for non-members and published work (e.g. Whiteley et al. 1994) does not consider attitudes concerning Northern Ireland. However, Aughey provides a guide to early 1990s feeling, based on the party's Contact Discussion Programme: 'there remains within the party a fundamental willingness to support the leadership position, whatever its prospects for success, but no sympathy for the prospect of British withdrawal' (Aughey 1994, p. 147). Respondents were supportive of Northern Ireland associations and the possibility of integration if devolution failed; thus setting them apart from the leadership.

These tensions are also apparent in the mid-1990s. At the 1994 conference forty-six motions called for a more explicit backing of the union, revealing discontent with the government's 'agnostic' position. Mayhew made it clear that he would not act as a 'persuader' for the union. Matthew D'Ancona, a *Times* journalist, whose opinion should be treated with caution owing to his pro-union sympathies, claimed that most of the discontent was stage-managed out of sight, that Major's Northern Ireland policy was 'profoundly distrusted by many of his own party activists' (*The Times*, 13 October 1994), and that backbenchers did not question the leadership sufficiently. The leader in the following day's edition of *The Times* claimed that many activists still felt strongly about the union, in contrast to most British people's indifference. A further review of the relative influence of different sections of the party will be undertaken in the concluding section.

Labour Party policy and internal divisions

Bipartisanship was briefly considered in the introduction, and Labour has been broadly supportive of Conservative policy in the 1990s despite a formal commitment to 'unity by consent' adopted in 1981. This is still official policy but fails to reveal the evolution of Labour's position and internal disagreements. Two strands of thinking to be found in the Parliamentary Labour Party (PLP) in the 1980s have receded in importance. The first, which the journalist Ruth Dudley Edwards has termed 'republican chic' (see e.g. *Sunday Times*, 9 October 1994), is associated with those either supporting 'Troops Out' and/or sympathizers with Sinn Fein. This decline is closely associated with that of the left of the party, since there is a relation, though not exact coincidence, between the positions. Representatives of this group include Tony Benn, Jeremy Corbyn and Ken Livingstone. The second grouping, which Edwards calls the 'Emerald Islers', is closer to the SDLP and advocates unification on the basis of what Edwards sees as a somewhat old-fashioned, romantic view of Irish nationalism. This strand is influenced by Labour's inheritance of the older Liberal/radical interpretation of Irish history, which believes Ireland should be one political unit. An exemplar of this position is Kevin McNamara, who was party spokesman on Northern Ireland between 1987 and late 1994.

The formulation 'unity by consent' is intended to signal that unity is a long-term aspiration while recognizing that unionists cannot be coerced. However, in earlier versions, such as in the 1987 manifesto, it was phrased 'no group or party will be allowed to exercise a veto on political development, or any policies designed to win consent'. This obviously begs the question of how meaningful consent was if Labour was unwilling to accept unionist lack of consent and sought to undermine it. The contradictions in this policy and the lack of a clear strategy to promote it have been examined elsewhere (see Bew and Dixon 1994; Dixon 1992); suffice to say that by the early 1990s McNamara was becoming increasingly vague about how consent might be measured and Neil Kinnock was emphasizing how the process of unification might take many decades.

A vague and diffuse preference for, and disposition towards, nationalism over unionism – closely related to the second strand identified above – still suffused the Labour party at grass-roots level, but appeared to be of declining significance in policy-making. The relative lack of importance of the issue was illustrated by its omission from the policy reviews of the late 1980s and early 1990s. Subsequently, external events and changes within the party have helped to blur inter-party divisions. First, both the DSD and the Framework Documents, as argued above, explicitly embrace a 'green' agenda; that is, one that emphasizes the all-Ireland context of the problem and the legitimacy of the nationalist identity and aspiration. Therefore, the Labour leadership has embraced the initiatives, albeit criticizing the detail of Conservative government activity at certain junctures.

An indication of this direction was the replacement of McNamara by Marjorie (Mo) Mowlam as chief spokesperson in October 1994, widely seen as symbolizing a move away from a pro-nationalist position. In an interview in 1995 she stated: 'I accept that a Labour government, when in office, would not act as a persuader to a united Ireland...we would instead act as a persuader to a balanced political settlement' (*New Statesman and Society*, 17 March 1995). The author of the article interpreted this period as the rebirth of bipartisanship, as Mowlam stated that Labour would not bring down the government on a vote of confidence if it were called on the basis of opposition to the Framework Documents. The July 1995 debate on the renewal of the 1974 Act under which direct rule is exercised also illustrates the closeness of Mowlam to the government. This built upon earlier indications of change; in September 1994 Tony Blair stated that the DSD and the IRA ceasefire had altered the entire context of Northern Ireland politics and that the DSD in particular 'overtook all the historical positions of all parties' (*Daily Telegraph*, 30 September 1994). Therefore, no specific settlement was being advocated by Labour.

The attempt to balance what can be seen as Blair's 'modernizing' position with the party's residual 'green' sympathies was manifest at the 1994 conference, when an NEC statement was approved as follows: 'Labour...seeks to encourage a balanced constitutional settlement leading to an agreement in Ireland which will have the support of both traditions in Ireland.' However, to placate the 'greener' wing the historic commitment to unification by consent was also upheld. Edwards considered Labour policy to be as agnostic as Major's and felt the debate to be 'platitudinous' and full of meaningless, 'feel-good' phrases (*Sunday Times*, 9 October 1994). The leadership's desire to avoid overt dissension was revealed in the next conference, which the *Guardian* described as stage-managed and a *de facto* suppression of debate, as Northern Ireland was jointly considered with nine other subjects (7 October 1995).

The tide may be turning against them but the 'green' tendency is not yet exhausted, and at a fringe meeting of the 1995 conference a new nationalist pressure group, the Agreed Ireland Forum, was established, with McNamara, Livingstone and Clive Soley among its membership. However, in recent years the opposite tendency has been more evident, as represented by Democracy Now, founded in July 1992. This is a group within the PLP which advocates Labour Party organization within Northern Ireland and which its opponents at least see as being pro-unionist, as do some Labour groupings in Northern Ireland, though the former does not necessarily imply the latter. Principal figures include Kate Hoey, Harry Barnes, Nick Raynsford and Calum MacDonald. By 1994 one estimate of membership was fifty-three Labour MPs, though claims for such ginger groups are notoriously unreliable (*Sunday Times*, 9 October 1994). The tensions between this group and 'green' pressure groups were apparent in a polemical pamphlet written in 1993 by McNamara and two other Labour MPs, Roger Stott and Bill O'Brien, attacking the demand for Labour representation in Northern Ireland (McNamara et al. 1993). The leadership itself is keen to distance itself from the campaign; Blair calling it 'at best, a diversion and, at worst, possibly an obstacle' to the political process (cited in Barnes 1995, p. 89).

The establishment of a select committee for Northern Ireland is a useful case study through which these tensions are revealed. Labour had traditionally been opposed to a select committee, as such a body was seen as having 'integrationist' overtones, and many members particularly objected to its introduction as a 'pay-off' for Unionist support for the Conservatives in the Commons. In the debate in March 1994, Jim Marshall and McNamara vehemently criticized the government on these grounds, while Hoey, Barnes and Frank Field were much more supportive of the idea and did not vote against the motion to establish the select committee.

To conclude, throughout the 1990s Labour supported the Conservative governments' constitutional policy while attacking aspects of Major's relationship with the Unionists and emphasizing differences around economic policy and the protection of civil rights (see, for example, Mowlam 1995). As in other policy areas, Blair and his close advisers have tried to ensure the muting of dissent, and neither the party integrationists nor the 'green' advocates discussed above are likely to have a significant impact on policy; of the latter tendency, McNamara demonstrated his dissatisfaction with policy in general and support for the Conservative government over decommissioning in particular by resigning as a Civil Service spokesman in September 1995.

The 1997 General Election: Campaign and Aftermath

The issue of Northern Ireland was, as usual in general elections, not of great salience in the campaign of 1997 and one that did not rank high on the list of the British electorate's concerns. In the campaign period tensions did emerge between the parties. In March Michael Howard, the home secretary, accused Labour of being 'soft' on terrorism at the time of IRA activity in Britain, and Labour's John Prescott attacked the Conservatives' reliance on the parliamentary support of the Ulster Unionists for survival (*Fortnight* 361, May 1997). However these were spats of relatively little significance and two possibilities being mooted by commentators were potentially of greater importance. One was that, after the election, the Conservatives in Parliament might have a more right-wing profile and adopt a more unionist position; the other was that Labour, if elected, might adopt less stringent conditions for Sinn Fein's entry into talks (e.g. a shorter period between a renewed ceasefire and its admission to talks). Either of these could have strained bipartisanship, and the extent to which this happened will be reviewed below.

The Labour Party manifesto for the 1997 election emphasized its bipartisan role in opposition and expected the Conservatives to reciprocate when Labour won. Two other points should be highlighted from the brief section devoted to Northern Ireland. First, Labour committed itself to the 'three-strand' approach enshrined in the Framework Documents, and second, it attempted to adopt a neutral position endorsing neither the claims or aspirations of unionism nor those of nationalism:

Labour recognises that the option of a united Ireland does not command the consent of the Unionist tradition, nor does the existing status of Northern Ireland command the consent of the Nationalist tradition. We are therefore committed to reconciliation between the two traditions and to a new political settlement which can command the support of both. (Labour Party 1997, p. 35; see also O'Leary and Evans 1997, p. 679)

For its part, the Conservative Party manifesto spoke of cherishing the Union and Northern Ireland's place within it; yet this did not seem to override the earlier positions of secretaries of state that the leadership, at least, would not act as 'persuaders' for the union.

The remainder of this section will deal with three topics: the elections of 1997 and their implications, the policy of the new Labour government, and the extent to which bipartisanship has been maintained.

The elections of 1997

Between the beginning of May and late June there were four elections which could have affected policy towards Northern Ireland. These were the general election of 1 May, the Northern Ireland local elections of 22 May, the Irish general election of 6 June and the subsequent appointment of Bertie Ahern as taoiseach in late June, and the elections for the leadership of the Conservative party which culminated with William Hague's victory on 19 June. Ostensibly, the results of the first three elections appeared to favour a shift towards a nationalist agenda and, therefore, away from a unionist one. The massive Labour victory in May 1997 with a large overall majority removed the influence the Ulster Unionist party had had under the Major administration. Also, despite Blair's claim that traditional party positions had been overtaken by recent events (see above), a Labour victory gave rise to unionist concerns for three reasons. First, there persisted the belief among unionists that the Labour party generally, if not the leadership, had 'greener' sympathies than the Conservatives. Second, David Trimble, leader of the Ulster Unionist Party, believed that Mowlam, appointed secretary of state by Blair, was more favourable to the early admission to talks by Sinn Fein than was her leader (*New Statesman*, 25 April 1997, p. 16). Third, whether or not there was a difference between Mowlam and Blair (which she denied), it was feared that Labour would more forcefully pursue Sinn Fein's inclusion in the talks process.

Within Northern Ireland the overall trend in voting patterns gave little succour to unionists, despite their winning thirteen of the eighteen Westminster seats. For the first time the combined nationalist vote (Sinn Fein and the SDLP) had exceeded 40 per cent of votes cast; Sinn Fein won 16.1 per cent, compared with 10 per cent in 1992 (for more details of trends see O'Leary and Evans 1997). The results indicated that Sinn Fein had not suffered from the ending of the IRA ceasefire in February 1996, either because many nationalists blamed British intransigence and 'stalling' for its collapse or because they differentiated between Sinn Fein and the IRA.

The local elections of May saw Sinn Fein improve marginally on its general election performance to gain 16.9 per cent of the votes cast, in its best ever performance. The two elections indicated the solid basis of its support and, while there was no chance of its inclusion in talks due to start on 3 June without an IRA ceasefire, the results allowed Sinn Fein representatives to emphasize the party's mandate and to argue that any strategy aimed at marginalizing it would not work.

The detail of politics in the Republic is beyond the scope of this chapter. However, it should be recorded that nationalists were heartened by the establishment of a Fianna Fáil-led coalition and the defeat of the Fine Gael/Labour/ Progressive Left coalition in June 1997. This was because historically Fianna Fáil has been the most nationalist of the major parties in the Republic and also because John Bruton, the outgoing taoiseach and leader of Fine Gael, was more sensitive to the concerns of unionists and more critical of Sinn Fein than the previous Fianna Fáil leader and Ahern's predecessor, Albert Reynolds (*Independent*, 10 June 1997; *New Statesman*, 13 June 1997). It was hoped by northern nationalists that the new administration would exert more pressure on the British government to allow Sinn Fein into talks and shift the focus from reassuring unionists. Ahern also stated that if Blair were to adopt the role of spokesman for unionists in Northern Ireland, he himself would play the same role for the nationalist community.

The last of the elections under consideration in this section resulted in Hague's accession to leadership of the Conservative Party. Early indications suggest that the Conservative disaster at the general election, Hague's victory and the appointment of Andrew Mackay as shadow Northern Ireland spokesman have not borne out the predictions of a shift on Irish policy alluded to above. Noting his low profile earlier in his parliamentary career, cynics have argued that it is difficult to locate Hague's ideological position with any degree of certainty, and there is no evidence that he had a particular interest in Ireland or was likely to advocate a change in policy. A 1990 typology of the Conservative parliamentary party located Mackay as being a member of the 'Tory right' and more specifically associated with the 'law and order' lobby (Norton 1990, p. 53). However, he does not appear to be associated with the small group of Conservative MPs discussed above who have lobbied for a more explicit defence of the union and for the government to act as 'persuaders'. Among that group, two prominent members, Lamont and Budgen, lost their seats in the general election. Four others were no longer in parliament after the election; Bill Walker lost his seat, Michael McNair-Wilson and Terry Dicks retired, and Barry Porter had died in November 1996. It therefore seems likely that this group's influence is in decline.

Labour policy

Blair had promised to give Northern Ireland and the revival of the 'peace process' a high priority after the election. On 16 May he made an important speech while visiting the province. In it the emphasis was on reassuring the unionist community that he was not pushing a 'green' agenda. The following extracts give the flavour:

My agenda is not a united Ireland – and I wonder just how many see it as a realistic possibility in the foreseeable future...Let me make one thing absolutely clear. Northern Ireland is part of the United Kingdom because that is the wish of the majority of the people who live here. It will remain part of the UK for as long as that remains the case...Unionists have nothing to fear from a new Labour government. A political settlement is not a slippery slope to a united Ireland. The Government will not be persuaders for unity. (*Guardian*, 17 May 1997)

An earlier indication of Blair's eagerness to reassure unionists was illustrated by his meeting with Trimble before his meeting with Bruton, the Irish taoiseach, to discuss the revival of the 'peace process'.

The logic of policy runs along the following lines. It appeared, and later events of September 1997 were to bear this out, that some unionists would join the talks process scheduled for that month if the government could convince them of its commitment to the principle of consent; that is, that the majority of people in Northern Ireland would have to approve any change in the status of Northern Ireland. The other side of the equation was to offer some concessions to the nationalists and in particular to encourage another IRA ceasefire. This was done in part by appearing more flexible over the questions of decommissioning, the time scale of a renewed IRA ceasefire, and linkages with Sinn Fein. These issues will now be addressed in turn.

The issue of decommissioning was a complex and shifting one. Sinn Fein's position was that arms would only be handed over at the successful conclusion of talks, and the party argued that Major had 'moved the goalposts' in laying such emphasis on decommissioning instead of building on the fact that 'military action' had ended in August 1994. One can state the equation thus: most unionists argued that if the IRA ceasefire were permanent it had no need of weapons; on the other side were those, including many nationalists, who believed that if the ceasefire were permanent it did not matter if weapons were retained and that, even if they were surrendered, new supplies could be secured if the military campaign were to be revived. Symbolism is also an important factor here in that Sinn Fein did not want the ceasefire, or any renewal as occurred in July 1997, to be viewed as a defeat or as surrender.

Blair's tactical response to this seeming impasse was twofold. First, he tried to de-emphasize the issue and reduce the centrality accorded to it by the government in 1995–1996. Second, in late June it was revealed that the government was endorsing the 'middle way', favoured by the commission led by former US Senator George Mitchell, of 'parallel decommissioning'. Under this, some weaponry would be given up concurrently with the talks process rather than before Sinn Fein's admission (as unionists wanted) or at their conclusion (*Guardian*, 26 June 1997). Some unionists, including the Ulster Unionist Party, seemed reassured by Blair's emphasis on consent (see above) and were thus prepared to meet with Sinn Fein, if not to negotiate, without prior decommissioning.

Blair and Mowlam were also keen to maintain the momentum of the process. To this end, in agreement with the Irish government and US President Clinton, it was announced in late June that Sinn Fein could be included in talks within six weeks of a renewed ceasefire. Talks were due to resume in September and Blair had earlier given a May 1998 deadline for their conclusion; on 20 July a renewed ceasefire was called. The third element to the strategy of 'keeping Sinn Fein on board' was the maintenance of contact via government officials despite Blair's claim that all links had been severed. The denial of communication with Sinn Fein and the IRA by British governments was, of course, not new. Taken together, the three points outlined above indicate a change not of policy but rather of style and presentation. Between May and September 1997, Labour tried to ensure that the parties to the conflict could accuse it of neither procrastination nor of not making its position clear through the maintenance of channels of communication, especially as the former accusation had been levelled at the last Conservative administration.

In addition, three specific reforms aimed at conciliating the nationalist community were to be introduced. Two of these had been developed in opposition and were included in the Queen's Speech at the opening of Parliament in mid-May. One was to establish a commission to consider the contentious question of marches in Northern Ireland and thus remove responsibility concerning possible bans or rerouting from the police. The second was the reform of the structure and system of accountability of the police, the Royal Ulster Constabulary (RUC). Police personnel are disproportionately drawn from the unionist community and many nationalists believe that the RUC is not even-handed in its treatment of the two communities. The third reform, announced at the Labour Party conference in September, was the intention to remove the power of internment (detention without trial) from the statute book. Internment had not been used since 1975 but its introduction in 1971 is still marked by annual Republican rallies, and this reform was described as a 'hugely symbolic concession to the nationalist community' and was criticized by unionists (*Guardian*, 1 October 1997).

Other examples could be given of Labour's attempt at a balancing act in this period; the attempt to reassure unionists on the issue of consent while engaging in specific reforms to conciliate nationalism and to ensure Sinn Fein stayed within the 'peace process'. This policy paid dividends, as Sinn Fein entered talks with three of the five unionist parties (the Ulster Unionist Party and the two small parties with paramilitary links, the Ulster Democratic Party and the Progressive Unionist Party) in attendance.

Bipartisanship

The question of bipartisanship can be briefly summarized. There has been little evidence in the post-election period of a decline in bipartisanship. Blair's policy, as indicated above, may have embraced a more forceful style but there was no rupture with the broad parameters. In the Commons Hague assured Blair that 'Conservative members are anxious to maintain the previously successful bipartisan approach ... provided that the government's actions continue to be in the interests of the people of Northern Ireland' (HC vol. 296, col. 851, 25 June 1997). The party conferences of autumn 1997 revealed no significant dissent, either within parties criticizing the leadership or between government and opposition, and the Labour Party conference was marked by a mood of reconciliation (with the attendance of one of the smaller loyalist parties) rather than by the 'green' tinge of recent years (*Guardian*, 1 October 1997).

Conclusion: The Impact of Party Policy

The consistency of policy

Some commentators have argued that British government policy towards Northern Ireland has been either neglectful and/or inconsistent (for the latter point see e.g. O'Malley 1983). However, a review of the 1990s would suggest that these positions are not tenable. This period has seen consistent ministerial and diplomatic effort, and this has been enacted within broadly consistent parameters. In 1987 O'Leary argued that a 'twin-track' bureaucratic strategy had been developed by the Northern Ireland Office (NIO). This was composed of an 'internal track', which aimed to secure the broadest possible agreement within Northern Ireland, and an 'external track', which was intended to promote good relations with the Republic of Ireland and the USA to avoid international embarrassment (O'Leary 1987). Interviews with NIO and Foreign Office officials in the late 1980s confirmed this view, and O'Leary and McGarry endorsed the claim by Paul Arthur made in 1983 that British policy-making procedures were characterized by quarantining Northern Ireland from 'mainstream' British politics and maintaining international respectability (O'Leary and McGarry 1996, pp. 235–6). These three authors thus reject the claim that British policy is one of 'crisis management' or simply reactive or *ad hoc*. In a recent review O'Leary highlights the contradictions and inconsistencies of policy in the period of Conservative rule, but also makes the point that they 'mask a deeper reality, the slow development of a more consistent and sensitive approach to the management of Northern Ireland' (O'Leary 1997, p. 663).

How do these analyses fare in a consideration of the 1990s? Generally, a strategic continuity has marked British policy, which is not to say that tactical adjustments and inconsistencies are absent. British policy in the 1990s is different from that of the 1980s; the most important development is the contrast between the AIA and the initiatives of 1993 and 1995. The former, like the preceding devolutionary attempts, was constructed with the aim (though not necessarily the sole one) of marginalizing Sinn Fein, while the latter were premised on the possibility of incorporating that party on the basis of a cessation of violence. This fits with Paul Arthur's claim that 'inclusivity' and 'process' have marked more recent developments in Anglo-Irish relations, which include the principle that all parties possessing a veto must be part of the solution (Arthur 1996, p. 120). However, this change in policy should not mask continuities with the previous decade. The bilateral strategy, although greater in scope, can be traced back to at least the Thatcher–Charles Haughey summits of 1980, which laid the foundation of the AIA of 1985. Also, the 'quarantining' strategy has been maintained, as has the attempt at establishing a local assembly, operating on the basis of some form of 'partnership' between representatives of the two principal communities.

In brief, therefore, the argument is that British policy has not witnessed significant changes or ruptures in the 1990s; rather it has developed within pre-existing parameters. The most significant development outlined above was largely determined by perceived changes in the politics of Sinn Fein.

Actors in the policy process: external

Having argued that a large degree of consistency in policy exists, an attempt will be made to identify some of the actors that mould it. It is difficult with precision to attribute the relative influence of all the interested parties, but some points can be made. First, the role of 'external' actors (i.e. non-UK agencies) is important. Northern Ireland is anomalous in policy-making in that it is neither solely a domestic nor solely a foreign policy issue (see Ruane and Todd 1996, ch. 8, for a consideration of Ireland's relation to the concept of 'Britishness'). As already discussed, in an attempt to manage a regional conflict in which local unionist elites had failed, British governments have accepted the right of the Republic of Ireland to be involved, and its input has increased in the 1990s. This involvement has been facilitated and encouraged by the perception of the 'problem' by two important international actors: the European Union (EU) and the USA.

The EU, and its predecessors, have generally been careful not to appear to be interfering in the domestic matters of a member state; this is particularly true of the Commission and the Council of Ministers (Hainsworth 1996, p. 132). However, the importance of the European 'dimension' is that the EU broadly supports an inter-state approach to managing the conflict. This was endorsed in the Haagerup report, the first European Community report on the political situation in Northern Ireland, which appeared in 1984. Since that time the European Parliament has consistently supported the AIA, power sharing and British–Irish cooperation (Ruane and Todd 1996, p. 283). As Ruane and Todd point out, the significance of this is not that the European Parliament takes an explicitly pro-nationalist position, but rather that conceptions of majority rule and notions of indivisible sovereignty which have traditionally underpinned the unionist case are not widely held on the European stage. Therefore, European perceptions are generally more likely to give succour to a broadly nationalist view of the Irish question, including the belief that Northern Ireland is not an integral part of the UK, than a unionist one. (This fear is heightened for many unionists by Hume's record of assiduous lobbying in the European Parliament.) The joint Anglo-Irish approach suits both governments, albeit for different reasons, and could probably be maintained irrespective of European endorsement. However, in line with the 'external track' discussed above, EU support is no doubt welcomed by the British government, although criticism of aspects of security and human rights policy has often proved an irritant.

A subsidiary benefit has been that membership of the EU has provided another platform for bilateral meetings of the two governments, though this has perhaps become less important as contacts have been formalized through the Intergovernmental Conference following the AIA. Although disagreements obviously occur, Moxon-Browne has stated that 'none the less, the regular meetings between the two governments under the aegis of the Community have provided opportunities for "megaphone diplomacy" to be softened and for discreet dialogue to take its place' (1992, pp. 49–50).

The second principal 'external' actor is the USA. Two significant points should be made here. First, direct US governmental involvement has been greater in the 1990s than in earlier periods of the troubles, with Clinton, in both his administrations, having more interest in and knowledge of Ireland than his predecessors. This reflects both electoral arithmetic and the search for foreign policy success. Second, the influence of US involvement has largely acted in favour of a broadly nationalist perspective. This is because of the influence of the Irish-American lobby, which both the SDLP and the Irish government have cultivated since 1977 to counter the influence of those groups implicitly or explicitly sympathetic to the IRA. Also, the political language and rhetoric used by nationalists to support reform aimed at benefiting the minority community in Northern Ireland have proved amenable to the American public (see Ruane and Todd 1996, pp. 273–9).

American involvement, both official and unofficial, was both high-profile and significant in the mid-1990s. For example, three prominent Irish-Americans were influential in convincing Sinn Fein in August 1994 that Republican concerns would be kept on the agenda in the event of a ceasefire. Clinton's visit in late 1995 was to demonstrate his personal commitment to the process, and the thorny question of the decommissioning of weapons was handed to a panel chaired by Mitchell. Anglo-American relations were not always smooth in this period, particularly with respect to what the British government saw as the indulging of Sinn Fein at certain times. However, the fact that the US government was 'tied into' the principles of the Anglo-Irish process, including the acceptance of the need for northern majority consent to change and the ending of violence, as well as the possible inward American investment and other financial support in the event of a settlement were bonuses for the British government and helped to insulate it from international embarrassment.

Actors in the policy process: internal

Two broad models of explaining state activity and policy-making – the pluralist and Marxist – both seem inadequate in identifying key players within Britain in the fashioning of Northern Ireland policy. The absence of pressure groups within the British polity with significant interest in Northern Ireland renders the former insufficient. As for the latter, the contemporary strategic and economic marginality of the province, allied to the decline in links, both political and personal, between the elites of Britain and unionism, means there is a lack of an obvious 'ruling-class' interest in the direction of Northern Ireland policy. A 'state-centred' approach, which focuses more on governmental and official initiative in policy than on social groups' influence, is a more useful approach (see Skocpol 1985). It is difficult to isolate the relative influence of different state agencies over time, although the model discussed at the start of this section implies that the permanent administration, through the NIO and the Foreign Office, is important in defining the parameters of policy. However, this does not mean that individual politicians are mere cyphers. For example, O'Leary and McGarry argue that the process leading to the initiatives of 1993 and 1995 may have been aided by the accession as prime minister and taoiseach of Major and Reynolds respectively in 1990–1991 (O'Leary and McGarry 1996, p. 332). However, it does not seem that Major's succession to Thatcher or Bruton's replacement of Reynolds as taoiseach led to major changes in policy, which demonstrates a continuity that outlives particular individuals.

Influence within the parties

The second section above outlined intra-party divisions concerning Northern Ireland policy, so this will not be repeated here. Generally, the leaders of the two main parties in Britain in the 1990s have not been much constrained in the construction of policy. The extent of backbench disquiet has not forced reappraisal on either Blair or Major, although the latter's tough stance on decommissioning has been attributed to reliance on right-wingers' support at a time of a diminishing parliamentary majority (O'Leary and McGarry 1996, p. 351). The influence of activists within the two parties is likewise relatively small. The leadership's defeat over recognition of Northern Ireland Conservatives (see above) was offset by the party's lukewarm or arm's-length relationship with associations in the province, and the failure of Conservatives to win a single seat in the forum elections of May 1996 demonstrates their marginality, which helps the leadership's policy of neglect. Although hard evidence is difficult to find, it is likely that activists of the Labour and Conservative parties would favour, respectively, a more pro-nationalist and pro-unionist stance by the leaderships. However, the issue is of too little electoral salience for them to risk party disunity over the issue. There is some debate over interpretation of opinion poll data (see e.g. Cochrane 1994, 1995; Dixon, 1995b), yet it seems clear that the British electorate is largely unconcerned with the issue of Northern Ireland. This increases the autonomy of the party leaderships.

Do parties make a difference?

The electorate's general indifference is another factor reinforcing the bipartisan approach introduced above; the opposition has little incentive to contrast itself with the government and, in May 1996, Mowlam argued that diverging from government policy would run the risk of slowing down the peace process by encouraging the Northern Ireland parties to 'hold out' for a better deal after the election. In 1996 O'Leary and McGarry summed up Labour policy thus: 'What was trumpeted as a policy of supporting the Government when it was right on the peace process in practice became a policy of supporting the Government whatever it did on the peace process' (1996, p. 369). However, Mowlam was keen to distinguish Labour policy by criticizing the government over economic policy and its failure to introduce a Bill of Rights, to reform the RUC, and to introduce a statutory body to adjudicate over routes in the marching season following the North report and to speed up the release of paramilitary prisoners (*Fortnight* 336, February 1995; *Independent*, 17 February 1997). On balance, though, this does not mark a breach with bipartisanship, since on other, more crucial areas, such as decommissioning and the forum elections, Labour has supported the government. (For a critique of Labour policy from a pro-Republican perspective, see Bennett 1996.)

Security policy has also witnessed a convergence. In March 1996, for the first time since 1983, Labour did not oppose the renewal of the PTA but abstained, as the Conservative government had committed itself to a wide-ranging review of anti-terrorist legislation. This shift provoked twenty-five Labour MPs to protest by voting against renewal and failed to prevent Howard, then home secretary, from accusing Labour of being 'soft' on terrorism in March 1997. This provoked outrage from his Labour shadow, who claimed that the government had breached a bipartisan agreement not to exploit terrorism for party advantage in the election campaign.

Could parties make a difference?

Those who have argued that the major British parties should contest elections in Northern Ireland have done so for a variety of reasons (see Roberts 1987). There is the principled reason that the people of Northern Ireland should be able to vote for the parties likely to compose the government that rules them. There are also the arguments that rely on beneficial outcomes: that party policy would be better informed because of the input of the Northern Ireland membership and electorate, and the possibility that the dominant confessional cleavage would be replaced by socio-economic patterns of voting. With respect to the last point, recent research argues that the results may not be so positive, since the British parties may take support from the 'middle ground' in Northern Ireland, and that the electorate may identify a specific British party with their ethnic group rather than vote on class or socio-economic grounds (Duffy and Evans 1996). As meaningful party organization in Northern Ireland remains highly unlikely, the question of whether it would result in the parties more clearly differentiating their policies in order to gain support remains hypothetical. A broad bipartisanship, though not without tensions, will continue.

Chronology of Significant Developments: April 1992 to October 1997

November 1992	Collapse of Northern Ireland inter-party talks
April 1993	Start of series of discussions between John Hume and Gerry Adams
December 1993	Downing Street Declaration issued by British and Irish governments
August 1994	First IRA ceasefire begins
October 1994	Loyalist paramilitaries' ceasefire begins
February 1995	Joint Framework Documents published by British and Irish governments
February 1996	IRA ceasefire collapses

May 1996	Elections to Northern Ireland Forum (to provide party representatives for talks)
May 1997	Labour wins British general election; Sinn Fein gain two seats; Mowlam appointed secretary of state for Northern Ireland
July 1997	IRA renew ceasefire
September 1997	Resumption of inter-party talks. Democratic Unionist Party (DUP) and United Kingdom Unionists (UKU) boycott them

Refrences

Arthur, P. 1983 'Anglo-Irish relations since 1968' *Government and Opposition* 18(2), 157–74.

Arthur, P. 1994 'The Anglo-Irish Joint Declaration: towards a lasting peace?' *Government and Opposition* 29(2), 218–30.

Arthur, P. 1996 'Anglo-Irish Relations' in Aughey, A. and Morrow, D. (eds) *Northern Ireland Politics*. Harlow: Longman.

Aughey, A. 1989 *Under Siege: Ulster Unionism and the Anglo-Irish Agreement*. London: Hurst.

Aughey, A. 1994 'Conservative party policy and Northern Ireland' in Barton, B. and Roche, P. (eds) *The Northern Ireland Question: Perspectives and Policies*. Aldershot: Avebury.

Aughey, A. 1996 'The party and the Union' in Norton, P. (ed.) *The Conservative Party*. Hemel Hempstead: Harvester Wheatsheaf.

Barnes, H. 1995 'New Labour in a new Northern Ireland' *Parliamentary Brief*, May, p. 89.

Bennett, R. 1996 'New Labour and Northern Ireland' *New Left Review* 220, 153–9.

Bew, P. and Dixon, P. 1994 'Labour party policy and Northern Ireland' in Barton, B. and Roche, P. (eds) *The Northern Ireland Question: Perspectives and Politics*. Aldershot: Avebury.

Canning, P. 1985 *British Policy towards Ireland 1921–1941*. Oxford: Oxford University Press.

Cochrane, F. 1994 'Any takers? The isolation of Northern Ireland' *Political Studies* 42(3), 378–95.

Cochrane, F. 1995 'The isolation of Northern Ireland' *Political Studies* 43(3), 506–8.

Connolly, M. and Loughlin, J. 1986 'Reflections on the Anglo-Irish Agreement' *Government and Opposition* 21(2), 146–60.

Cox, W. H. 1996 'From Hillsborough to Downing Street – and after' in Catterall, P. and McDougall, S. (eds) *The Northern Ireland Question in British Politics*. Basingstoke: Macmillan.

Crossman, R. 1977 *The Diaries of a Cabinet Minister. Vol. 3: 1968–70*. London: Hamish Hamilton.

Cunningham, M. 1991 *British Government Policy in Northern Ireland 1969–89: Its Nature and Execution*. Manchester: Manchester University Press.

Cunningham, M. 1995 'Conservative dissidents and the Irish question: The "pro-integrationist" lobby 1973–94' *Irish Political Studies* 10, 26–42.

Dillon, M. 1993 *The Enemy Within*. London: Doubleday.

Dixon, P. 1992 'Labouring under an illusion?' *Fortnight* 303 and 304, February/March.

Dixon, P. 1995a '"A House divided cannot stand": Britain, bipartisanship and Northern Ireland' *Contemporary Record* 9(1), 147–87.

Dixon, P. 1995b 'Internationalization and Unionist isolation: a response to Feargal Cochrane' *Political Studies* 43(3), 497–505.

Duffy, M. and Evans, G. 1996 'Building bridges? The political implications of electoral integration for Northern Ireland' *British Journal of Political Science* 26(1), 123–42.

Hainsworth, p. 1996 'Northern Ireland and the European Union' in Aughey, A. and Morrow, D. (eds) *Northern Ireland Politics*. Harlow: Longman.

HMSO 1995 *A New Framework for Agreement*. London: HMSO.

Labour Party 1997 *New Labour: Because Britain Deserves Better*. Labour Party general election manifesto. London: Labour Party.

McNamara, K., Stutt, R. and O'Brien, B. 1993 'Oranges and Lemons'. London.

Mowlam, M. 1995 'A rosier future?' *Fortnight* 336, February.

Moxon-Browne, E. 1992 'The impact of the European Community' in Hadfield, B. (ed.) *Northern Ireland: Politics and the Constitution*. Buckingham: Open University Press.

Norton, P. 1978 *Conservative Dissidents: Dissent within the Parliamentary Conservative Party 1970–74*. London: Temple Smith.

Norton, P. 1990 '"The lady's not for turning" but what about the rest? Margaret Thatcher and the Conservative Party 1979–89' *Parliamentary Affairs* 43(1), 41–58.

O'Brien, B. 1993 *The Long War*. Dublin: O'Brien Press.

O'Leary, B. 1987 'The Anglo-Irish Agreement: folly or statecraft?' *West European Politics* 10(1), 5–32.

O'Leary, B. 1997 'The Conservative stewardship of Northern Ireland, 1979–97: sound-bottomed contradictions or slow learning?' *Political Studies* 45(4), 663–76.

O'Leary, B. and Evans, G. 1997 'Northern Ireland: la fin de siècle, the twilight of the second Protestant ascendancy and Sinn Fein's second coming' *Parliamentary Affairs* 50(4), 672–80.

O'Leary, B. and McGarry, J. 1996 (2nd edn) *The Politics of Antagonism: Understanding Northern Ireland*. London: Athlone.

O'Malley, P. 1983 *The Uncivil Wars: Ireland Today*. Belfast: Blackstaff.

Roberts, H. 1987 'Sound stupidity: The British party system and the Northern Ireland question' *Government and Opposition* 22(3), 315–35.

Ruane, J. and Todd, J. 1996 *The Dynamics of Conflict in Northern Ireland: Power, Conflict and Emancipation*. Cambridge: Cambridge University Press.

Skocpol, T. 1985 'Bringing the state back in: strategies of analysis in current research' in Evans, P., Rueschemeyer, D. and Skocpol, T. (eds) *Bringing the State Back In*. Cambridge: Cambridge University Press.

Smith, M. L. R. 1995 *Fighting for Ireland?: The Military Strategy of the Irish Republican Movement*. London: Routledge.

Whiteley, P., Seyd, P. and Richardson, J. 1994 *True Blues: The Politics of Conservative Party Membership*. Oxford: Clarendon Press.

Whyte, J. 1983 'How much discrimination was there under the Unionist regime 1921–68?' in Gallagher, T. and O'Connell, J. (eds) *Contemporary Irish Studies*. Manchester: Manchester University Press.

Guide to Further Reading

For more details of the complex evolution of the 'peace process' the following are useful guides: P. Bew and G. Gillespie, *The Northern Ireland Peace Process 1993–1996: A Chronology* (London: Serif, 1996); D. McKittrick, *The Nervous Peace* (Belfast: Blackstaff, 1996); and E. Mallie and D. McKittrick, *The Fight for Peace: The Secret Story behind the Irish Peace Process* (London: Heinemann, 1996). There is no single text dedicated to British party policy in recent years; however ch. 9 in B. O'Leary and J. McGarry, *The Politics of Antagonism: Understanding Northern Ireland* (London: Athlone, 2nd edn, 1996), and ch. 8 in J. Ruane and J. Todd, *The Dynamics of Conflict in Northern Ireland: Power, Conflict and Emancipation* (Cambridge: Cambridge University Press, 1996), are useful. For more detail the chapters and articles cited in the references above should be consulted.

8 | Local Government and Devolution

Howard Elcock

Synopsis

Local governments existed before the centre became the dominant arbiter of public policies. They developed party systems which enabled local electors to determine coherent policies locally as well as nationally. However, tension between central and local government increased from the 1970s. During the Conservative hegemony local authorities' powers were steadily and drastically reduced, to such a degree that there seemed little point in maintaining the system at all.

Also during the 1970s, nationalist party successes led to an attempt to grant devolution to Scotland and Wales, which took up two years of parliamentary time. Its failure led directly to the defeat of the Labour government and the election to office of Margaret Thatcher. By the 1990s, however, increasing discontent in Scotland, Wales and the north of England produced renewed demands for devolution.

By 1997, all parties except the Conservatives were firmly committed to devolution. With the election of Tony Blair and New Labour to office in May of that year, extensive constitutional reform, including devolution and renewed powers for local government, seemed certain to produce a radical new constitutional order by the dawn of the millennium.

The Historical Context: Party Policy 1945–1992

Party politics in local government

Local government is unique among the issues discussed in this book, not only because it poses major policy issues for the parties nationally but because councils are the only domestic arenas for the party struggle apart from Parliament. Local councillors are the British public's sole elected representatives other than MPs. Hence we must discuss local government both as part of British constitutional arrangements, which are likely to be significantly affected by the Labour government's devolution and other proposals, and as a set of political institutions with their own democratic structures and processes. The roles of the parties in local government must be considered in terms both of the politics of local authorities themselves and of the impact of the policies of successive governments on the powers, structures and management of these authorities.

Since the reorganizations of 1973 in England and Wales and 1974 in Scotland, most local authorities have been dominated by party politics, although there is a lingering reluctance by the few remaining independent or minor party councillors to accept the hegemony which the major parties have now established in most authorities. The development of party politics in local authorities was initiated by the Labour Party, which from early in its history established disciplined party groups. From its beginnings Labour was a party with a socialist programme, which required the united efforts of its elected representatives to ensure the passage of its measures through Parliament (Pelling 1963). A sizeable number of Labour councillors won election in the 1920s, and the need to establish a disciplinary regime similar to that adopted by the Parliamentary Labour Party (PLP) was recognized by the party locally and nationally. Hence it adopted model standing orders for Labour groups on local authorities at its 1929 conference. These were slightly modified the following year, but they then remained in force until being modified again in the early 1970s. Most Labour groups throughout the country have adopted these standing orders with minor variations to reflect local practices. Their fundamental principle was and still is that Labour councillors must support the majority decisions taken by the Labour group of all councillors taking the Labour whip, and must not speak or vote against them. The group may permit individual abstentions for reasons of conscience but not public opposition to group decisions.

This was a new and threatening method of proceeding as far as many non-Labour councillors were concerned: as one observer put it, 'Liberal democracy, a political system designed for the bourgeois, may not absorb large scale working class involvement unchanged but one may find that the rules of the liberal democratic game are changed considerably by the new participants' (Baxter 1972). The discipline of Labour groups was born of the solidarity of the trade union movement; hence it was in a real sense an innovation resulting from the increasing involvement of working-class people in local politics.

The appearance on many urban councils of coherent, disciplined Labour groups compelled their opponents to respond by organizing themselves, in order to mount effective opposition and defeat Labour proposals when that party had a substantial number of councillors but could not on its own secure a majority (Bulpitt 1967). Sometimes such groups were organized by the Conservative and Liberal parties, but in other places purely local groupings came into existence, some of which survived until the early 1970s.

In rural areas where Labour was weak, the tradition of independent councillors who voted as individuals on the issues coming before the council survived until the 1970s (Lee 1963). In any case, many non-Labour councillors argued that party politics should have no place in local government because the role of councillors was to ensure that services were provided by the council as cheaply and efficiently as possible, therefore all those of goodwill should be able to work together to ensure this, and attempts to drive radical policies through the council were inappropriate (see Birch 1958). However, in 1974 many of these rural areas were combined in new local authorities with urban areas which possessed highly developed party machines whose activities were extended to the whole of the new council's area (Elcock 1975; Stanyer 1976). In 1986 the Widdicombe Committee argued that party politics was on balance beneficial in local government because it produces consistent decision making from the council and its committees (Widdicombe Committee 1986).

Patterns of leadership and decision making

In some cities, the tight discipline imposed by Labour Party rules gave rise to the development of centralized styles of leadership in which a 'city boss' dominated the affairs of the council, supported by a small number of henchmen in the council, the party organization and the local trade union movement (Jones and Norton 1979; Elcock 1981). The key to such leaders' power was the holding of multiple offices by themselves and their friends. Thus the leader of the council was usually the chairman of the Finance and General Purposes Committee, with overall control of the city's budget. This was the nearest most councils had to a coordinating committee before corporate management, when each council was a loose federation of departments and committees which were not subject to policy or managerial coordination except through the control exercised through Labour Party groups, some of which were themselves dominated by the city bosses.

In other cities a more collective, democratic but still centralized decision process existed. In the early 1960s, Victor Wiseman wrote a detailed account of Leeds City Council's decision-making process, which made it clear that its Labour group members watched warily for signs that any of their number were accruing to themselves excessive power: 'when a chairman starts to talk of "my committee" he should be watched with suspicion' (Wiseman 1963, p. 137). The Labour group usually met twice during each cycle of committee meetings, once to determine the line to be taken on the items coming before the next council meeting and once for general policy discussions. Its advisory committee met frequently and seems to have been relatively open in its decision making (Wiseman 1963). It was the only body where the policies of the council's departments and committees could be coordinated.

Dominant leadership became less common in Labour-controlled councils after the reorganization of 1974 because 'Members have recently become less willing to contract out their power to the strong leader' (Norton 1979, p. 221). Three reasons can be adduced for this. First, the new local authorities created by the Local Government Act of 1972 often included among their members the political leaderships of more than one former council, with the effect that council and party offices were vigorously contested (Elcock 1975). Second, Labour Party rules were changed to reduce the possibility of the Labour group and the city party organization being dominated by the same people. Lastly, the establishment of two-tier local government in the former county borough areas enabled many teachers and lecturers to stand for election to a local authority for the first time, because they had previously been employees of the only council in their areas and legally barred from seeking election to the council which employed them (Elcock 1981). In consequence, 'a more intellectual and policy oriented membership required a more democratic approach' (Norton 1979, p. 219).

In the Conservative Party the tradition of strong leadership in local government seems to be even more robust and durable, because of the tradition in that party that the leader is the embodiment of Conservative policies for the time being. R. T. McKenzie recorded that 'When appointed, the Leader leads and the party follows except when the party decides not to follow; then the Leader ceases to be Leader' (1963, p. 145). Equally, a former leader of Leeds City Council, when asked what would happen if Conservative councillors disagreed with council policy, immediately responded, 'Well, I suppose they would have to get rid of me' (author's information). Again, Conservatives in Croydon acknowledged that a 'political elite of seven people: "The Tory caucus with the Town Clerk there"', ran Croydon London Borough Council (Saunders 1976, p. 219).

The development of corporate management in the 1970s (Elcock 1994, ch. 9) has been a further spur to collective decision making, because most local authorities then established policy and resources committees to review the committees' decisions before their approval by the full council meeting. Hence a device for collective policy coordination was built into the formal structures and procedures of most local authorities. Although real decision making still usually takes place in the ruling party group's executive committee, the Policy Committee provides a collective forum for coordination (Elcock 1994, ch. 10). There are increasing indications, however, that this device has resulted in a widening difference developing between leading and backbench councillors. The former coordinate council policy and sit on the Policy and Resources Committee. They also become extensively involved in the management of the council's resources, while the backbenchers are largely preoccupied with dealing with the concerns of the residents of the wards they represent. The majority of councillors prefer the latter role anyway (Elcock 1994, ch. 3).

Where no one party has overall control, different structures and processes may exist. Such councils have always existed, but they have become more common in recent years as the Liberal Democrat Party has eroded the electoral power bases of both the other major parties through its 'community politics' strategy. In the classic 'hung' council, decisions are uncertain until the final vote in the council chamber, which creates much uncertainty because officers will hesitate to implement committee decisions in case they are reversed by the full council. Andrew Blowers's (1977, p. 309) view, as a member of Bedfordshire County Council, was that decisions could only be reached through 'a long series of negotiations among the parties'. He saw this as a recipe for increasing the power of the officers; he wrote of the members' 'frustration . . . at the inability to exercise any effective control over the bureaucracy' (Blowers 1977, pp. 311–12). Again, Stuart Haywood (1977) argued that establishing a Policy and Resources

Committee in Beverley Borough Council was futile because it had no majority which was able to coordinate the policies of the service committees. In consequence, the committee was abolished after two years and replaced with an old-style Finance Committee. However, such uncertainty is seen by leading Liberals in the successor council, the East Riding of Yorkshire, as an opportunity for enterprising decision making and responsiveness to the councillors' electors (author's information).

More consistent policy control in a hung council can be achieved if one party is supported in office by the votes of another. Most frequently the Labour group holds office with Liberal Democrat support (see Barlow 1987; Clements 1987). However, this arrangement may collapse if there is a major policy disagreement between the two parties, as occurred over Avon County Council's budget in 1987 (Clements 1987). Steve Leach and John Stewart (1988) found four types of regime in hung councils:

- non-partisan councils, where the extent of local controversy was limited and the level of local political consensus was high, and where little inter-party conflict occurred;
- joint administrations or minority administrations, where two parties agreed to maintain a stable administration by keeping one or both of them in office;
- authorities which were governed by the mayor or chair's casting vote because the number of councillors from each of two parties was exactly equal, as was the case in Bradford City Council in the late 1980s;
- councils with no settled administration, where chairs are elected for each meeting and decisions cannot be finalized until the whole council meets.

Where a council becomes hung after a period of party control, the chief executive officer may have to negotiate a series of conventions with the party leaders on the basis of which business can proceed through the council and its committees and decisions can be made, rather than an atmosphere of continual uncertainty pervading all the authority's business (Widdicombe Committee, 1986, appendix G; Barlow 1987).

The view from the centre: parties, governments and local councils

Local politics is therefore varied and lively, at least for its active participants, although interest in it among the general public is notoriously weak. Until 1979 it also attracted relatively little interest from the centre. Two views about the proper place of local government in the British constitution generally prevailed. One, which we may call the 'agent' or more controversially the 'Whitehall' view, is that local authorities exist to implement the government's policies by the provision of services at the local level (Jones and Travers 1994). This view is reflected in the legal principle of *ultra vires*, under which a local authority may do only those things which it is specifically empowered to do under the legislation passed by Parliament. Unlike their Continental counterparts, British local authorities have no power of general competence, although since 1972 councils have been permitted to spend a small proportion of their budgets on almost anything which councillors perceive as being in the interests of some or all of the inhabitants of their authority's area. Also, the central government expected that the national totals of local government spending would be close to the totals prescribed by the Treasury, and indeed, these totals have almost always been within plus or minus 2 per cent of the Treasury's total (Jones and Stewart 1983).

The alternative view of the proper function of local authorities is the one originally promulgated by J. S. Mill (1978, first published 1862) and reiterated many times since: that local authorities are community governments which have the right and duty to govern in accordance with the expressed wishes of the voters in each council's area. Thus Mill argued that local authorities exist for three purposes:

- to protect citizens' freedom by preventing the concentration of power in the hands of the national government;
- to encourage participation and political education among the people of the area by enabling citizens to participate in decision making, as well as training politicians to assume national office later in their careers;
- to increase national efficiency by accommodating service provision to local circumstances and holding professional service providers to account to the people's representatives.

On this view, local authorities have the right to pursue policies contrary to those adopted by the national parties, and the growing domination of local politics by programmatic political parties has made it increasingly likely that they would do so.

Before 1980 most local authorities most of the time carried out their own policies and ran their services relatively free from political interference from Whitehall, as long as they stayed within the law. However, they were subject to varying degrees of supervision by central government departments (Griffith 1966). There were occasional clashes which ended up being resolved in the courts. Notable conflicts included the Poplar case in 1928, when Labour councillors were prosecuted for paying their workers wages in excess of nationally agreed rates, and the Clay Cross case in the early 1970s, when a Labour-controlled urban district council in Derbyshire refused to increase its council house rents in line with the Housing Finance Act of 1972. In both these cases the councillors concerned were eventually surcharged for illegal expenditure and the government's policies prevailed. Again, in 1985 a battle royal developed between the Thatcher government and Liverpool City Council over the latter's reluctance to set a budget within the time limit and the expenditure guidelines imposed by the government, which resulted in the eventual surcharge and disqualification of most of that city's Labour councillors.

However, local government has had its successes in the courts too. In 1976 a local authority successfully defended its action space against ministers in the field of education. The Conservatives won control of Tameside Borough Council and reversed a scheme adopted by their Labour predecessors to abolish the area's three grammar schools and establish comprehensive secondary education there, in fulfilment of the main plank of their election campaign. The Labour minister attempted to prevent them doing so, but in the subsequent case before the Court of Appeal, the judges upheld the council's right to determine its own education policy (Griffith 1977). A few years later, though, the judges showed less respect for election manifestos when they struck down the Greater London Council's (GLC's) 'Fares fair' policy of heavily subsidizing bus and Underground fares, despite the evident popularity of the measure and its prominence in the manifesto on which Labour won control of the GLC in 1981.

The Tameside case was evidence of the rising party temperature in the world of central and local government relations. The post-war consensus on education had come under increasing strain in the 1960s and 1970s because Labour governments were trying to secure non-selective secondary education throughout the country (Jennings 1977). Relations between central and local government became more fraught during and after the 1976 financial crisis, when local authorities were attacked by ministers for overspending and extravagant staffing. As a result, the government appointed a committee chaired by Sir Frank Layfield QC to review local government finance. When it reported in 1976 the committee warned that the vitality of local democracy was in danger of being destroyed by local authorities' excessive dependence on central government grants. The government took no action to restore local authorities' financial autonomy, however.

This was partly because almost all the available parliamentary time was being devoted to passing legislation in the government's ultimately unsuccessful attempt to grant devolution to Scotland and Wales, which had been stimulated by nationalist successes in Scottish and Welsh by-elections. The Scottish and Welsh nationalist parties were campaigning for the independence of those nations from the United Kingdom; the Scottish National Party's (SNP's) cause had been strengthened by the discovery of large oil deposits off that country's shores, which led the SNP to campaign vigorously on the slogan 'It's Scotland's oil.' The nationalist by-election victories were the result more of the unpopularity of a Labour government, with a narrow parliamentary majority struggling with harsh economic times, than of any upsurge of support for independence; but they forced the government to attempt to grant devolution to Scotland and Wales, especially because it needed to retain nationalist support in the House of Commons to survive. The government's failure to gain sufficient support from the Scottish and Welsh people for its devolution proposals (in referenda held, ironically, on St David's Day 1979) led directly to the government's defeat in a Commons motion of confidence and consequently to the calling of the May 1979 general election, at which a Conservative government was elected – led by a singularly determined prime minister, Margaret Thatcher, with a radical 'New Right' programme to reduce the role of the state in British society.

In consequence, the stage was set for a sustained and unrelenting attack on local government, for reasons which were a mixture of ideological commitment and personal animosity. The new government was determined to reduce taxation and 'get the state off the backs of the people'. Ministers believed that some local authorities were spending excessively on socialist policies. Thatcher herself seems to have borne a grudge against local government. Devolution was summarily removed from the political agenda for the duration of what was to be an eighteen-year Conservative hegemony.

The 1980s: three fronts of attack

Change in the constitutional position of local government began early in the Thatcher era and developed on three fronts (Elcock 1994, 1997a). Until then, councils had been largely left to their own devices so long as the national expenditure sums added up more or less to the Treasury's approved totals. Now, under the Local Government, Planning and Land Act of 1980, steps were taken for the first time to control the spending decisions of individual councils by establishing a system for assessing centrally what each council needed to spend in order to provide services at a 'standard' level – the Grant Related Expenditure Assessment (GREA, now the Standard Spending Assessment, SSA). The council's main government grant would be based on this assessment and additional expenditure would have to be met by the local taxpayers unaided by government grant. Penalties were introduced to render the impact of extra spending on local taxpayers still more severe. In 1984 legislation was passed which enabled the secretary of state to restrict or 'cap' a council's expenditure, so in effect setting a legal limit on how much income councillors could raise from local taxation for the first time since the reign of Elizabeth I (Travers 1987). This was followed by the most radical (and unsuccessful) change of all: the introduction of the community charge or poll tax. This was a flat-rate charge per person levied on almost all adults living in each council's area. It was first collected in 1989 in Scotland and 1990 in England and Wales, but it was widely regarded as an unfair imposition, largely because it resulted in sudden and erratic variations in the amount of local tax households were required to pay. After the poll tax had been defeated by popular resistance (Tonge 1994; Butler et al. 1994) it was replaced by the less hated council tax. The episode demonstrated Thatcher's increasing tendency to succumb to 'groupthink' and her consequent refusal to listen to views other than her own (Dunleavy 1995). The impact of the poll tax and subsequent events on local government itself was further to reduce the already limited financial autonomy of local authorities, because the introduction of the community charge was coupled with the introduction of the uniform business rate, which reduced the proportion of their income over which local authorities had control to between 15 and 20 per cent.

Second, the Thatcher government made it abundantly clear that if local authorities resisted their policies, they could and would be swept away. In 1980 and 1981 the Labour Party was outstandingly successful in the local elections. In the latter year it gained control of the GLC and four metropolitan county councils from the Conservatives, giving it control of all the seven councils which governed England's major conurbations. The GLC became a leading centre of opposition to Thatcher's policies. In consequence, Thatcher's Cabinet inserted a last-minute pledge in their manifesto for the 1983 election to abolish the GLC and with it the metropolitan county councils. Despite massive opposition, including a highly effective publicity campaign mounted by the GLC against its own abolition, the legislation was driven through Parliament and the seven councils ceased to exist on the stroke of midnight on 31 March 1986 (Lansley et al. 1989)

The third area of central–local government conflict concerned the provision of services by local authorities. Councils had traditionally provided services through their own departments and workforces, which were often inefficient, particularly as a result of cosy restrictive practice agreements between local government trade unions and councils, particularly Labour-controlled ones. Local government services were widely perceived to be inefficient, unsympathetic and unresponsive, because the provision of many services was highly rule-bound and they were administered from central offices in the town or county hall. This phenomenon, which Hoggett and Hambleton (1987) call 'bureaucratic paternalism', resulted in extensive public dissatisfaction with local authority services, exacerbated during the winter of 1978–1979 by a series of strikes among local authority and other workers which became known as the 'Winter of Discontent'. In consequence, the legitimacy accorded by the public to local authorities and the services they provided was weakened, and public disillusion with public services in the wake of these events undoubtedly contributed to Thatcher's election victory in May 1979.

During the 1980s, two trends developed in the provision of services by local government. The first, inspired by the Thatcher government, was a concerted effort to promote more commercial behaviour by local authorities in order to increase the efficiency of their services and secure the transfer of local government functions to private firms wherever possible. The government's policy response to public disenchantment with public services was hence inspired by its New Right ideology. It imposed compulsory competitive tendering (CCT) on a narrow range of services, mainly in the field of highway and house construction and repairs in the 1980 Local Government, Planning and Land Act. It also empowered local authorities to put other services out to competitive tender, and although most local authorities were lukewarm about this new discretion, some Conservative-controlled authorities, like Southend and Wandsworth, responded with enthusiasm. The result was that some of their services, like Southend's refuse collection, were transferred to private companies. Another Act gave all council tenants the right to buy their council houses at discounts related to the lengths of their tenancies.

This policy reached its peak in the late 1980s and early 1990s, when CCT was progressively extended first to the manual or blue-collar functions of local authorities and then to their white-collar activities. Simultaneously, under the National Health Service and Community Care Act of 1990, local authorities were charged with assessing elderly and disabled clients for community care, but they were required to provide 85 per cent of the services required through contracts with private companies or voluntary agencies. In consequence, many local authority residential homes and day care centres were sold to private firms or voluntary organizations.

Local authorities' response to CCT has in the main been to improve the efficiency of their own departments in order to win contracts for their service provision against private sector competition. In this they have been highly successful. In the first round of CCT, 75 per cent of contracts were won by the in-house tender from the Direct Service Organizations, established by local authorities to bid for the services put out to tender (Painter 1990). In the north of England the percentage was still higher, at 93 per cent (Shaw et al. 1994, 1995). Ministers have sought to tighten the rules to make it more difficult for in-house tenders to succeed, but so far without much success, partly because the private sector has not always been able or keen to tender effectively for local authority contracts. Hence, the principal impact of the government's policies was to provoke local authorities to improve their management and eliminate restrictive practices within their own organizations, in order to defeat private sector competitors.

The final manifestation of the government's determination to increase the efficiency of local government has been an increasing tendency to remove functions from local councils and transfer them to organizations governed by boards appointed by ministers, who can take decisions more quickly than is permitted by the democratic procedures of local councils. This has given rise to increasing concern about the lack of accountability of the governors of such bodies, popularly dubbed 'quangos' (quasi-non-governmental organizations) or the 'New Magistracy', which are now responsible for the spending of more public funds locally than local authorities themselves. In turn, concern about the lack of accountability of the 'quangocracy' has been used to justify proposals for elected assemblies in Scotland, Wales and the English regions to which these bodies could be made accountable.

The New Urban Left

The second trend in local government management resulted from the Labour successes in the local government elections of the early 1980s, which produced many new councillors who brought new ideas and enthusiasms to local government – the 'New Urban Left' (Gyford 1983). They recognized the need to improve the relationship between local authority service providers and their users. They therefore developed a wide range of initiatives to improve those relationships. These ranged from redesigned offices, telephone help lines and improved access for members of the public to senior officers, to more or less ambitious schemes of decentralization to ensure that services are provided from local bases where service users can easily go to request services or complain (Fenwick 1995; Hoggett and Hambleton 1987). The more ambitious of these decentralization schemes also involved the establishment of neighbourhood committees or fora in order to encourage community participation in local authority decision making (Islington Borough Council 1987). This development of community participation was also encouraged by Liberal Democrat councillors, notably in the London Borough of Tower Hamlets (Burns et al. 1994). Such initiatives were part of equal opportunities strategies devised in order to increase participation by women, ethnic minorities and other groups, particularly those with alternative lifestyles, who do not readily participate in conventional local politics and government.

The third plank of the New Urban Left's approach was the development of alternative economic strategies and the establishment of local enterprise boards

(Cochrane and Clarke 1990). Such strategies were intended to be test beds for the Labour Party's Alternative Economic Strategy (AES), but the local enterprise boards were also concerned with securing new investment in declining industrial areas. Notable among them were the Greater London Enterprise Board (GLEB), created by the GLC, and the West Midlands Enterprise Board, established by the West Midlands Metropolitan County Council. Another was Lancashire Enterprise, established by Lancashire County Council. Although two of these three councils have now ceased to be, the enterprise boards still exist, although their ties with local government have been weakened.

The initiatives of the New Urban Left were submerged by the policies of the Conservative government. They have also been frustrated by financial constraints, but many of the decentralization schemes and other initiatives still exist, and may be revived if local authorities recover some of the discretion and financial freedom of manoeuvre of which they have been deprived in recent years. Many of the leaders of the New Urban Left have now been elected to the House of Commons. Indeed some have become ministers in the Labour government elected in May 1997, so local government has been deprived of the enthusiasm and inspiration of such leading figures as Ken Livingstone, Margaret Hodge and David Blunkett. It remains to be seen how far distinctive New Urban Left councils and policies will re-emerge under the Labour government.

An Unusual Climate: Continuity and Rupture 1992–1997

The 1990s: the nadir for local government

The combined effects of financial pressure, the changes to the local taxation system, the introduction of CCT and the market system for community care, together with the ever growing number of quangos, meant that the powers of local authorities had been greatly reduced by the time John Major became prime minister in November 1990. So much had local government declined that the Cabinet seriously considered abolishing it altogether during the summer of 1991 (Jenkins 1995). It survived but has been further weakened, in part by the continuation of the previous government's policies but also by new developments under Major. Anthony Barker has argued that the New Right ideological tempo increased rather than diminished after Major succeeded Thatcher (Barker 1995).

In particular, Major's 'Big Idea', the Citizen's Charter (Cabinet Office 1991), was intended to change the relationship between public services and their users by making them more like those between a customer and his or her private sector supplier (see Chandler 1997). Public service organizations are now expected to publish their standards of services and set targets for achieving higher standards of service provision. They must also publicize the means by which members of the public who are dissatisfied with the service can complain and obtain appropriate redress. The effect of this was that, at the local level, political democracy and participation would be increasingly replaced by a form of economic democracy, under which local decisions would be made by local customers purchasing services and choosing the supplier from whom they made those purchases

(Waldegrave 1993). In consequence, the role of local authorities would further diminish as more services were provided by private companies or voluntary agencies. This process was reinforced by the extension of CCT to an increasingly wide range of white-collar local government functions and the developing market in community care.

Major's government also had to resolve the problems resulting from the failure of the poll tax to win public acceptance. Michael Heseltine was appointed secretary of state for the environment for the second time, with a remit in particular to replace the hated community charge with a council tax as promised in the 1992 Conservative general election manifesto. The council tax was a reversion to property taxation, but one element of the poll tax was retained in that single persons living alone receive a 25 per cent discount on their council tax bills.

Furthermore, local government was now subjected to a further bout of structural reorganization, which was intended primarily to increase local authorities' efficiency, although ministers claimed that they were redesigning the system to take account of community sentiments. Heseltine published two consultative papers, one proposing innovations in the internal management of local authorities, including possible experiments with directly elected mayors (DoE 1991a). The second proposed a reorganization of the structure through a Local Government Commission for England, which was charged to review local authority boundaries, taking account of community sentiments (DoE 1991b). This was a response in particular to the critics of the new counties created in the 1970s, notably Avon, Cleveland and Humberside, who had ceaselessly argued for a reversion to traditional boundaries. It was also a recognition of community dissatisfaction with the merger of Rutland into Leicestershire and a number of other similar issues (Leach 1996).

In Scotland and Wales, local government was reorganized by the respective secretaries of state to create unitary structures. Both ministers claimed to have consulted community opinions, but there was a widespread impression that the new structures had been imposed to reduce the number of local authorities, create unitary local government and, where possible, give electoral advantage to the Conservative Party. In the last, however, ministers were unsuccessful: the Conservatives won few seats in the first elections to the new Scottish and Welsh local authorities, a harbinger of their elimination from parliamentary representation there in the 1997 general election. In both countries, too, the nationalist parties were once more gaining in strength, as was indicated in the elections to the new local authorities. The SNP in particular launched a new campaign for independence within Europe, arguing that the development of the 'Europe of the Regions' would make it easier for an independent Scotland to survive and prosper as a member state of the European Union (EU) or as a highly autonomous region within a loose UK structure.

In England, the Local Government Commission was appointed under the chairmanship of Sir John Banham. It divided the counties into four *tranches* and began work on those areas where agreement was easily obtained, notably the Isle of Wight, where the first unitary council was established in 1994. The abolition of Avon, Cleveland and Humberside and their replacement by unitary authorities was also achieved fairly quickly, but in many areas local opinion supported the existing two-tier structures. The secretary of state, on the other hand, had a strong preference for unitary local government, which resulted in acrimonious disputes with Sir John Banham and led to the latter's resignation in March 1994. By the time of the 1997 general election, the commission's work was almost complete, although some of the new local authorities were only to come into existence in the late 1990s.

The 1997 General Election: Campaign and Aftermath

By 1997, then, local government was a helpless patient being operated upon by an unsympathetic surgical team. It had survived the threat of total abolition in 1991 only to face radical restructuring and reduction in its powers by a government which was seeking to replace public services with real or surrogate markets. Local government is not a subject which normally features at all largely in election campaigns. However, in the period leading up to the 1997 election, constitutional reform was being thrust onto party political agendas by several forces. One was an increasing number of lobby groups pressing for change in the light of the Thatcher and Major administrations' alterations to the constitutional balance, including Charter 88, the Constitution Unit, the Freedom of Information Campaign and Liberty. Although none of these organizations commanded mass public support, they were backed by many eminent professional and business people, and by their campaigning they attracted many thousands (if not millions) of adherents. The urgency of constitutional reform was increased by accusations of improper practice by ministers and others, notably the arms for Iraq affair, which was the subject of the Scott Inquiry, and the cash-for-questions scandal, which brought disgrace to several Conservative backbenchers. In consequence, leading figures in the Labour Party took an increasing interest in constitutional reform as a major plank of that party's manifesto for the coming general election.

A second source of pressure for constitutional reform was the revived and increasingly insistent demands for devolution for Scotland and Wales, especially the former. The introduction of the poll tax in Scotland a year earlier than in England and Wales had particularly infuriated Scottish opinion, especially among political activists. A Constitutional Convention met in Edinburgh in 1989 to prepare a devolution blueprint, and support for it was widespread. The Labour and Liberal Democrat parties, as well as the SNP, collaborated in the deliberations of the convention, while the Conservatives maintained their outright hostility to devolution. Furthermore, the SNP campaign for independence within Europe seemed more credible than its earlier campaigns for complete sovereignty. The demand for devolution in Wales is less insistent, but it was reflected in Plaid Cymru gains in local elections there. These demands were reinforced by the increasingly weak performance of the Conservative Party in Scotland and Wales, which demonstrated that the people of those countries were being subjected to the policies of a government whose support was largely based in southeast England and whose policies the Scots and Welsh increasingly rejected.

In some English regions too there were increasing demands for regional government. A Campaign for a Northern Assembly was established in 1993 to press for the establishment of a regional assembly in the north of England. It won considerable support from local authorities, professional people, academics and political activists. The business community is not supportive of regional government but it is not adamantly opposed to it and wishes to see greater decentralization of administrative functions to the regions (Lanigan 1996). The region's local authorities have renamed their regional association the North of England Assembly of Local Authorities, and they intend that this organization could constitute the basis for an indirectly elected regional chamber as an interim stage towards the possible creation of an elected assembly (Elcock 1997b).

In the two years leading up to the 1997 general election, the Labour Party made extensive plans for devolution and regionalism. The party's manifesto for the 1997 election promised devolution for Scotland and Wales, provided that the people there confirmed that they wanted it in referenda to be held in the autumn of 1997. It also forms part of an agenda for constitutional reform which was agreed between the Labour and Liberal Democrat parties early in 1997 and is now being developed by a Cabinet committee composed of members of both parties. The Labour Party prepared proposals too for the gradual creation of regional governments in some or all the English regions, by first creating indirectly elected chambers to oversee regional administration, which could later lead to the establishment of regional assemblies provided that there is evidence of real popular demand for them (Labour Party 1995). Labour also proposed to establish a new, strategic, elected council for London, to be led by a directly elected mayor.

Further impetus for constitutional change is coming from the EU, in part because of the need for regional structures with which the European Commission, especially its Regional Affairs Directorate (DG XVI), can relate in developing its regional policies and distributing its regional development funds (Elcock 1997c). The consequent need for a regional focus for government policy and administration was recognized by the Major administration in 1994 through the establishment of ten integrated government offices, which combine the regional responsibilities of three government departments. They control single regeneration budgets made up of funds allocated to the former regional offices of the Department of the Environment, the Department of Employment and the Department of Trade and Industry.

In addition, the government's repeated defeats at the hands of the European Court of Human Rights (nearly forty in all) and the European Court of Justice have indicated that, in order to bring British constitutional arrangements into line with those of the other member states of the EU, major constitutional changes are necessary. Lastly, the EU has extensively promoted the principle of subsidiarity. In 1985 the Council of Europe adopted its European Charter of Local Self-Government, the incorporation of which into domestic law would for the first time give British local authorities a guaranteed place in the constitutional firmament (see Commission for Local Democracy 1995).

Only the Conservatives firmly resisted this tide of constitutional reform. All the other parties promised more or less extensive reform, in particular devolution for Scotland and Wales. Specific pledges on local government were fewer in number but Labour indicated a number of particular intentions for reform (Travers 1997). These included:

- permitting councils to spend funds accrued from the sale of council houses, which they had been forced by the Conservative government either to hold in their balances or to use to reduce their debts, with the result that the building of council houses had virtually ceased and many are in poor states of repair;
- the eventual abolition of local tax capping, but the retention of a reserve capping power;
- return of the business rate to councils' control, so increasing the proportion of a council's revenue which can be determined by councillors rather than ministers from 20 to 45 per cent;
- the abolition of the compulsory element in CCT, but stronger means to check on councils' efficiency in providing their services. In extreme circumstances the Audit Commission would be able to send in commissioners to take over from a council which was judged to have failed.

On the wider local government front, the Labour Party indicated that it would permit greater experimentation with local authorities' electoral systems and management structures, including the introduction in some authorities of directly elected mayors. Specifically, a new strategic authority for London led by an elected mayor was promised in the manifesto, together with commitments to Scottish and Welsh devolution and, less firmly, regional government in England.

The Labour Party therefore proposed to reverse many of the restrictions imposed on local authorities during the Thatcher and Major eras and to restore at least some of council's lost powers, functions and discretion, as well as increasing the accountability of the quangos. However, strong central controls were likely to be retained, not least because, with Blair in Downing Street, 'it is virtually certain the Tories will pour back into county and town halls throughout the land' (Travers 1997). Accepting the right of local communities to elect councillors who will confront a Labour government and refuse to do its bidding is a hard psychological step for ministers to take. On the other hand, it will permit the revival of the lively local party politics which has characterized most local authorities at least since the 1973–1974 reorganizations.

Conclusion: The Impact of Party Policy

Labour won the 1997 general election with a massive majority and there can be no excuse, in terms of parliamentary arithmetic at least, for the new government not carrying through its manifesto commitments on local government and constitutional reform. The government has made a promising start on this agenda. The devolution referenda were held in September 1997. The Scottish vote produced a three-to-one majority for establishing a Scottish Parliament and two-to-one support for giving it tax-raising powers. All local government areas in Scotland supported the Parliament and all but two (Orkney and Dumfries and Galloway) voted for it to have tax-varying powers. A week later the Welsh voted for their own assembly by a very narrow margin of less than 7,000 votes on a turnout of 50 per cent. The Welsh-speaking and heavily Labour areas backed devolution strongly, but English-speaking and more Conservative areas voted almost equally heavily against it. The legislation to establish the new assemblies was promised for the winter of 1997–1998. Given the government's huge majority, the assemblies and their associated administrative arrangements will be in place by the year 2000. The first elections to the Scottish Parliament and the Welsh Sennedd will take place in 1999. At the 1997 Conservative conference, Viscount Cranborne, Conservative leader in the House of Lords, indicated that a future Conservative government would not reverse Scottish devolution now that it seemed to be 'the settled will' of the Scots (*Guardian*, 11 October 1997), but Michael Ancram, opposition spokesman on constitutional reform, argued that a second referendum should be held in Wales in view of the close result and low turnout there (*The Times*, 8 October 1997).

The future for the English regions looks less certain. The deputy prime minister, John Prescott, is proceeding with the creation of regional development agencies, but ministers are divided on the merits of proceeding with the party's proposal for regional chambers and the possible creation of regional assemblies. They may be still more hesitant after the weak support for devolution in the Welsh referendum. However, support is building in some English regions for the establishment of indirectly elected chambers, based on existing regional local government associations, to control the work of the regional development agencies.

The new government is also tackling the problem of unelected local and regional agencies and their governing members: the quangocracy. A number of Conservative appointees have been removed and replaced by Labour nominees, but there is no sign yet of a wholesale return of these bodies to accountability to elected representatives at either the local or the regional level.

In local government itself, the legislation to establish the elected strategic authority for London with its elected mayor is proceeding. A promise has been given to abolish CCT in early 1998. It is to be replaced by a 'best value' scheme designed to ensure high levels of efficiency and responsiveness to service users. Chancellor Gordon Brown announced in his first budget that the local expenditure capping regime is to be retained for the coming year, but Hillary Armstrong, the minister for local government, promised the 1997 Labour Party conference that 'crude general rate-capping' will be abolished. However, in July 1997, the government confirmed that Oxfordshire and Avon and Somerset's budgets would be capped in 1997–1998 despite local and national protests from within the Labour Party. Local government hopes for the total abolition of capping may therefore be premature, but ministers are discussing increasing the proportion of local authorities' expenditure which councillors can determine and reducing the extent to which local government spending must be controlled within the national public expenditure totals (Chisholm et al. 1997). Sir Norman Fowler, opposition spokesman on the environment, told the 1997 Conservative Party conference that his party would abolish capping if it were re-elected, a move to boost morale among Conservative councillors (*The Times*, 10 October 1997).

Prescott is chairing a new Local Government Partnership committee made up of representatives of local authorities and Whitehall departments. In September 1997, substantial sums of capital receipts from council house sales, which had been frozen by the former Conservative government, were released to councils to spend on new housing programmes. This decision indicates that the Labour government is in earnest about restoring at least some of local authorities' lost discretion over their finances.

Greater experimentation with leadership and management structures will soon be allowed, including elected mayors and experiments with new forms of participation. The local government minister told the Labour Party conference in 1997 that the objective would be 'less meetings of the council and more involvement with the local community'. Within local government itself a series of possible reforms is being discussed, especially in terms of increasing public participation in council decision making, which would radically alter the relationship between councils and the public (Corrigan 1997; Filkin 1997).

Potentially the most radical step of all is the government's signing the European Charter of Local Self-Government. In consequence, local authorities will no longer be purely the playthings of a sovereign Parliament. Their existence and status are instead guaranteed by a piece of European law, which will form part of what will increasingly look like a written British constitution when it is combined with the incorporation of the European Convention of Human Rights and the devolution settlement. The days of the unwritten constitution now seem to be numbered.

On the other hand, it remains to be seen what will happen if and when the electorate reacts against the Blair government and expresses its disenchantment by electing Conservative or Liberal Democrat majorities to councils and perhaps regional assemblies up and down the land. Such a trend is not inevitable but on past experience it has to be regarded as likely. One possibility is that Conservative New Right councils will reduce services to levels below those which ministers regard as acceptable. It would seem, however, that the government will retain sufficient control to compel them to increase service levels and expenditure to at least a minimal acceptable level: indeed, ministers have always had powers to do this through regulation and central inspectorates (Griffith 1966). The acid test of the Labour government's commitment to local democracy will come if and when a Conservative council wishes to pursue policies which are radically different from those of the Blair government.

The last question has to be whether the new government will be able to restore local democracy in the face of significant opposition from the Civil Service. Local government has done its best to improve its ability to address Whitehall effectively by creating a single Local Government Association, which can speak to ministers and their officials on behalf of local authorities with a single voice. It is now involved in the Central–Local Government Partnership being chaired by the deputy prime minister. At present this association is under Labour control, but its relationship with Labour ministers could deteriorate if the Conservative Party gains control of the association as a result of extensive Labour defeats in local elections in the coming years. Beyond this lies the hostility of many civil servants to local government and all its works (Jones and Travers 1994). Hence, the new Labour ministers will need to overcome a good deal of Whitehall resistance if local democracy is once again to become a significant force in the land. None the less, the omens now seem set fair for a local government renaissance after it came to the brink of extinction in the early 1990s.

Chronology of Significant Developments: April 1992 to October 1997

March 1992	Welsh Secretary of State (David Hunt) announced proposals for 23 new Welsh unitary authorities.
April 1992	Council tax replaced community charge
May 1992	Re-election of Conservative government under John Major
July 1992	Local Government Commission for England (LGCE) begins work
July 1993	Scottish secretary (Ian Lang) announced proposals for 28 new Scottish unitary authorities
March 1994	Dismissal of Sir John Banham as chairman of the LGCE; announcement of 21 new unitary authorities for Wales
March 1995	Final report of LGCE submitted to the secretary of state for the environment
April 1995	First elections held for new Scottish and Welsh local authorities and for the English unitary authorities including the replacement unitary authorities in former Avon, Cleveland and Humberside counties
May 1995	Vesting Day for Isle of Wight council – the first English unitary authority
April 1996	New Scottish and Welsh local authorities took office, also Vesting Day for the successor authorities in Avon, Cleveland and Humberside
May 1997	Election of Labour government under Tony Blair with a majority of 179 over all other parties
September 1997	Referenda held in Scotland and Wales to approve the government's devolution proposals – majorities achieved in both countries, but Welsh majority very small
April 1998	Referendum vote on proposal for an elected mayor and Greater London Authority. Proposals approved by a 3–1 majority but on a turnout of only 30 per cent

References

Barker, A., 1995: 'Light and shade in Lady Thatcher's ideological bequest: the ideological aggressiveness of the Major government', paper read to the Annual meeting of the American Political Science Association, Chicago, September.

Barlow, John, 1987: 'Lancashire County Council', in Elcock, H. and Jordan, A. G. (eds), *Learning from Local Authority Budgeting*, Avebury: Avebury Press, pp. 37–49.

Baxter, R., 1972: 'The working class and Labour politics', *Political Studies* 20, pp. 97–107.

Birch, A. H., 1958: *Small Town Politics*, Oxford: Oxford University Press.

Blowers, A., 1977: 'Checks and balances: the politics of minority government', *Public Administration* 55, pp. 305–16.

Bulpitt, J., 1967: *Party Politics in English Local Government*, Harlow: Longman.

Burns, D., Hoggett, P. and Hambleton, R., 1994: *The Politics of Decentralisation: Revitalising Local Democracy*, London: Macmillan.

Butler, D. E., Adonis, A. and Travers, T., 1994: *Failure in British Government: The Politics of the Poll Tax*, Oxford: Oxford University Press.

Cabinet Office, 1991: *The Citizen's Charter*, Cm 1599, London: HMSO.

Chandler, J. (ed.), 1997: *The Citizen's Charter*, Dartmouth: Dartmouth Press.

Chisholm, M., Hale, R. and Thomas, Derek (eds), 1997: *A Fresh Start for Local Government*, London: CIPFA.

Clements, R., 1987: 'Avon County Council', in Elcock, H. and Jordan, A. G. (eds), *Learning from Local Authority Budgeting*, Avebury: Avebury Press, pp. 25–36.

Cochrane, A. and Clarke, A. 1990: 'Local enterprise boards: the short history of a radical initiative', *Public Administration* 68, pp. 315–35.

Commission for Local Democracy, 1995: *Final Report. Taking Charge: The Re-Birth of Local Democracy*, London: Commission for Local Democracy/Municipal Journal.

Corrigan, P., 1997: 'New government for old', *Local Government Management* 1 (21, Summer), pp. 18–19.

DOE (Department of the Environment), 1991a: *Local Government Review: The Internal Management of Local Authorities in England: A Consultation Paper*, London: HMSO.

DOE (Department of the Environment) 1991b: *The Structure of Local Government in England: A Consultation Paper*, London: HMSO.

Dunleavy, P., 1995: 'Policy disasters: explaining the UK's record', *Public Policy and Administration* 10(2), pp. 52–70.

Elcock, H., 1975: 'English local government reformed: the politics of Humberside', *Public Administration* 53, pp. 159–66.

Elcock, H., 1981: 'Tradition and change in Labour politics: the decline of the city boss', *Political Studies* 29, pp. 439–47.

Elcock, H., 1994: *Local Government: Policy and Management in Local Authorities*, 3rd edn, London: Routledge.

Elcock, H., 1997a: 'Local government: becoming a backwater or heading for renewal?', *Talking Politics* 10(1), pp. 35–43.

Elcock, H., 1997b: 'Territorial debates about local government: or don't reorganise! don't! don't! don't!', paper read to the ECPR Standing Group on Regionalism conference on devolution, University of Northumbria, February.

Elcock, H., 1997c: *A Choice for the North*, Public Policy Research Unit Research Paper no. 1, University of Northumbria.

Fenwick, J., 1995: *Managing Local Government*, London: Chapman and Hall.

Filkin, G., 1997: 'Breakthrough to change', *Managing Local Government* 1 (21, Summer), pp. 20–1.

Griffith, J. A. G., 1966: *Central Departments and Local Authorities*, London: G. Allen and Unwin.

Griffith, J. A. G., 1977: *The Politics of the Judiciary*, London: Fontana/Collins.

Gyford, J., 1983: *The Politics of Local Socialism*, G. Allen and Unwin.

Haywood, S. C., 1977: 'Decision-making in local government: the case of an independent council', *Local Government Studies* NS 3, pp. 41–55.

Hoggett, P. and Hambleton, R., 1987: *Decentralisation and Democracy*, Bristol: School of Advanced Urban Studies.

Islington Borough Council, 1987: *Going Local: Decentralisation in Practice*, London: Islington Borough Council.

Jenkins, S., 1995: *Accountable to None*, London: Penguin.

Jennings, R. E., 1977: *Education and Politics: Decision-Making in Local Education Authorities*, London: Batsford.

Jones, G. W. and Norton, A., 1979: *Political Leadership in Local Authorities*, Birmingham: INLOGOV.

Jones, G. W. and Stewart, J. D., 1983: *The Case for Local Government*, London: G. Allen and Unwin.

Jones, G. W. and Travers, T., 1994: *Attitudes to Local Government in Westminster and Whitehall*, Commission for Local Democracy Research Report no. 5.

Labour Party, 1995: 'A choice for England', consultation paper.

Lanigan, C., 1996: 'Supporters and opponents of regional government in the north-east', *Public Policy and Administration* 11(2), pp. 66–78.

Lansley, S., Goss, S. and Wolmar, C., 1989: *Councils in Conflict: The Rise and Fall of the Municipal Left in Britain*, London: Macmillan.

Leach, S., 1996: 'Local government reorganisation: a test case', in Leach, S, Davis, H. and associates, *Enabling or Disabling Local Government*, Milton Keynes: Open University Press, pp. 41–58.

Leach, S. and Stewart, J., 1988: 'The politics of "hung" councils', *Public Administration* 66, pp. 35–56.

Lee, J. M., 1963: *Social Leaders and Public Persons*, Oxford: Oxford University Press.

McKenzie, R. T., 1963: *British Political Parties*, London: Heinemann.

Mill, J. S., 1978: *Representative Government*, London: Collins/Fontana.

Norton, A., 1979: 'The evidence considered', in Jones, G. W. and Norton, A. (eds), *Political Leadership in Local Authorities*, Birmingham: NLOGOV, pp. 206–31.

Painter, J., 1990: 'Compulsory competitive tendering: the first round', *Public Administration* 69, pp. 191–210.

Pelling, H. M., 1963: *A Short History of the Labour Party*, London: Macmillan.

Saunders, P., 1976: *Urban Politics*, London: Penguin.

Shaw, K., Fenwick, J. and Foreman, A., 1994: 'CCT for local government services: the experience of local authorities in the north-east of England', *Public Administration*, 72(2), pp. 201–17.

Shaw, K., Fenwick, J. and Foreman, A., 1995: 'Compulsory competition for local government services in the United Kingdom: a case of market rhetoric and camouflaged centralism', *Public Policy and Administration* 10(1), pp. 63–75.

Stanyer, J., 1976: *Understanding Local Government*, London: Fontana.

Tonge, J., 1994: 'The anti-poll tax movement', *Politics* 14(3), pp. 93–9.

Travers, T., 1987: *The Politics of Local Government Finance*, London: Unwin Hyman.

Travers, T., 1997: 'Hollowed out halls', *Guardian*, 5 March.

Waldegrave, W. 1993: *The Reality of Reform and Accountability in Today's Public Services*, London: Public Finance Foundation.

Wiseman, H. V., 1963: 'The working of local government in Leeds', *Public Administration* 41, pp. 51–69, 137–55.

Widdicombe Committee, 1986: *The Conduct of Local Authority Business*, Cmnd 9797, London: HMSO.

Guide to Further Reading

There are now numerous textbooks on local government but they go out of date quickly. Howard Elcock's *Local Government: Policy and Management in Local Authorities* (London: Routledge, 3rd edn, 1994), has the benefit of practical experience. David Wilson, Chris Game, S. Leach and G. Stoker, *Local Government in the United Kingdom* (London: Macmillan, 1994), is thorough and has lots of excellent artwork. John Gyford, *Citizens, Consumers and Councils* (London: Macmillan, 1991), is stimulating on customer relations and similar initiatives. A recent discussion of consumer relations and other management issues is John Fenwick's *Managing Local Government* (London: Chapman and Hall, 1995). Gerry Stoker, *The Politics of Local Government* (London: Macmillan, 2nd edn, 1991), is directly relevant to the subject matter of this chapter. Steve Leach, Howard Davis and associates, *Enabling or Disabling Local Government* (Milton Keynes: Open University Press, 1996), is an outstanding recent contribution to the literature, and is especially strong on reorganization. John Stewart is the doyen of local government scholars. His *New Management of Local Government* (London: Unwin Hyman, 1986), has had considerable influence on the development of local government management since it appeared.

There are also a number of specialist journals which students wishing to specialize in this subject should review. Prominent academic journals are *Local Government Studies* and *Local Government Policy-Making*, both produced by the Institute of Local Government Studies at the University of Birmingham. Other academic journals which cover local government issues are *Public Administration, Public Policy and Administration* and *Teaching Public Administration*. Other journals produced primarily for the practitioner but which contain much useful material for the student include *Local Government Management*, published by the Local Government Management Board, the *Municipal Review* and the journal of the new Local Government Association when it appears. A journal which has many stimulating articles aimed at both practitioners and students is *Public Money and Management*, published by the Public Finance Foundation (the research arm of CIPFA – Chartered Institute of Public Finance and Accountancy). On devolution matters, *Federal and Regional Studies* is a stimulating international journal. Its spring 1998 edition discussed British devolution in the light of the new government's policies.

9 | Parliament and the Civil Service

Robert Pyper

Synopsis

During most of the period since 1945, Parliament and the Civil Service have been relative backwaters as far as party policy is concerned. The political parties have generally tended to operate on the assumption that the machinery of governance will be fit for the purpose of activating their major policy priorities. Parties tend to be concerned with ends rather than means, and in this sense, the creation and fine-tuning of policy towards Parliament and the Civil Service has not been a constant concern for any of the parties, although there have been periods of special significance. Policy-making in these spheres has largely been the preserve of party leaderships.

The Historical Context: Party Policy 1945–1992

In order to impose some kind of structure upon our examination of the development of party policy over this extended period, it makes sense to offer distinct accounts of policy towards Parliament and the Civil Service.

Parliament

Superficially, at least, it is a relatively simple task to ascribe broad policy approaches to the Conservatives, and to the Liberals, in respect of Parliament. In opposition for all but a decade of the twentieth century, the Liberal Party and its successor the Liberal Democrats adopted a stance of root-and-branch reform. In part, this was a logical development of the party's traditional propensity for reform (evinced by, *inter alia*, the 1911 Parliament Act), and partly the product of disenchantment with the constitutional status quo, which seemed to consign the party to perpetual opposition. Within the Conservative Party, however, the case for constitutional reform was always harder to accept, and Parliament's place as a venerable institution of the realm determined the adoption of a generally defensive, protectionist policy stance in the face of proposed changes of radical hue. Notwithstanding this, the Conservative Party's willingness to embrace moderate constitutional change yielded two judicious reforms of the House of Lords during the period 1958–1963, a preparedness on the part of the party's leadership to countenance more fundamental reform of the Lords in the late 1960s, and the advent of a new system of select committees in the House of Commons in 1979.

It is much more difficult to put forward a thumbnail sketch of Labour's attitude to Parliament. Ostensibly radical and reformist, from its earliest days Labour rhetoric favoured wide-ranging parliamentary restructuring, with a particular focus on the House of Lords. During the period from 1945, this rhetoric of parliamentary reform rarely found its way into formal party policy documents, however, and once in power, the Labour Party's attitude to Parliament as an institution was distinctly pragmatic.

Labour's historical antipathy towards the House of Lords was allayed to some extent by the behaviour of the upper house in the early phase of the Attlee government. Led by Lord Salisbury, the Conservative peers adhered to the convention that it would be wrong for their house to vote down government measures which had clearly been endorsed by the electorate (K. O. Morgan 1985, pp. 83–4; Shell 1992, p. 13). With an election looming, however, and fearful of the Lords' potential to become more obstructive through utilization of its delaying powers, in the autumn of 1947 the Labour government introduced a Parliament bill which limited the period of delay to one year. The bill became law in 1949. Interestingly, during the period leading up to the passage of the 1949 Parliament Act, all-party discussions took place on the issue of the composition of the House of Lords. The Labour, Conservative and Liberal leaders reached an agreement on some points of principle, including a preference for reform rather than abolition, more equitable party representation, and an end to heredity as the sole criteria for membership (Shell 1992, p. 14). No agreement was reached on the powers of the Lords, and with a lack of motivation to pursue the matter on the part of the Labour leadership (K. O. Morgan 1985, p. 85), the opportunity passed.

If Labour's policy towards the House of Lords was distinctly pragmatic rather than ideological between 1945 and 1951, much the same could be said for the Conservative approach in government until 1964. Faced with a potentially intractable dilemma, the Conservatives opted for a policy compromise. The dilemma arose due to Labour's long-term commitment to comprehensive reform of the Lords, and that party's concomitant ambivalence regarding the creation of new Labour peers. With the proportion of Labour peers falling in the 1950s, and Conservative prime ministers in any case reluctant to confer hereditary titles on their political opponents, the Macmillan government took action to enhance the standing of the House of Lords, and incidentally to give effect to one element of the 1948 cross-party agreement (Shell 1992, p. 16). The 1958 Life Peerages Act facilitated the 'legitimate' reinforcement of Labour's strength in the upper house, while serving the ultimate Conservative purpose of bolstering the Lords. A further rationalization of the Lords' affairs came with the passage of the 1963 Peerage Act, under which renunciation of peerages was permitted. This was less a matter of party policy than a consequence of the Benn affair (Benn 1988, pp. 1–60) and the resultant report of a joint Commons/Lords select committee (see Shell 1992, pp. 18–19).

Labour returned to power in 1964 possessed by a zeal for internal, structural reform of Parliament. This enthusiasm fed off a growing concern with the Commons' apparently atrophying powers of scrutiny and the inherent weaknesses of the traditional methods of parliamentary accountability, which had been laid bare by the Crichel Down affair of 1954 and its extended aftermath (Griffith 1987; Justice 1961; Nicolson 1986). The class of 1964 Labour backbenchers contained a core of MPs who were tuned into the current debates about the efficacy of Britain's institutions, and, from 1966, they had an ally in Cabinet in the form of Richard Crossman, lord president of the Council and leader of the House of Commons. Before moving on from this post in 1968, Crossman had introduced an experimental range of new Commons select committees (based, in part, upon the recommendations of the cross-party Procedure Committee), overseen the introduction of the Parliamentary Commissioner for Administration, and initiated plans for reform of the House of Lords (Crossman 1976; Howard 1990, pp. 279–89; Gregory and Hutchesson 1975).

The Wilson government's abortive attempt to reform the Lords provides us with an example of a policy formulated by party leaders in Parliament coming unstuck in the face of a backbench revolt. Although the 1968 White Paper *House of Lords Reform*, and the resultant 1969 Parliament (No. 2) Bill, were broadly (if somewhat unenthusiastically) supported by both the government and opposition front benches, and a substantial majority of the active peers, the proposals became bogged down in committee, and the bill was dropped. The scheme envisaged phasing out hereditary membership of the Lords and, in the meantime, drawing a distinction between voting and non-voting peers. Many Labour backbenchers, led by Michael Foot, believed the proposed reform did not go far enough, and they joined Conservative supporters of the status quo, led by Enoch Powell, to stymie the bill (J. Morgan 1975; Shell 1992, pp. 20–3). For the remainder of this period, indeed, until the election of the Blair government in 1997, Lords reform was not a serious proposition. No mention was made of the House of Lords in Labour's 1974 election manifestos, although conflict between the Labour government and the peers between 1974 and 1979 saw the party conference renew Labour's pledge to abolish the upper house. Without an overall majority in the Commons, however, the party leadership lacked the means (and, it should be added, the will) to implement this policy.

Conservative policy had settled on the creation of a partially elected upper house, but despite pressure from the party conference in the early 1980s (Shell 1992, p. 26) Margaret Thatcher refused to pursue the issue. This can be ascribed to lack of interest rather than any innate respect for the Lords, since throughout her years in power she suffered occasional embarrassing reverses at the hands of the peers and she did not hide her contempt for them. This undoubtedly helped soften Labour's attitude towards the House of Lords, and begin the process whereby Labour would return to a policy of reform rather than abolition.

Perhaps the paucity of parliamentary reform during most of the Thatcher years stemmed from an early misjudgement. In 1979 the new leader of the

House of Commons, Norman St John Stevas, secured Cabinet backing for the creation of a new system of select committees, modelled in part on the recommendations of the 1977–1978 Procedure Committee (Baines 1985). The prime minister was initially hostile to this reform, but was eventually persuaded by the idea that these committees might embarrass Whitehall departments, towards which she had a much greater antipathy. However, the willingness of the committees to criticize government policy and embarrass ministers over the years arguably played a part in ensuring that this marked the end rather than a beginning to Thatcher's career as a parliamentary reformer.

John Major's assumption of the premiership in November 1990 heralded no 'policy' change in relation to Parliament, in the sense that there were no immediate plans for structural reform in the drawer of the new occupant of No. 10. However, if the hallmark of parliamentary Thatcherism was a thinly disguised contempt for this institution, this first phase of the Major premiership, culminating in the 1992 general election, was characterized by a more open and friendly style, perhaps reflecting his power base in the Conservative Party: 'he was the ordinary backbenchers' choice' (Riddell 1994, p. 48).

Labour's attitude to Parliament was not transformed by the fall of Thatcher. One implication of the extended Thatcherite hegemony was the growth of an electoral reform faction within the Labour Party. Labour's weakened parliamentary position encouraged some party figures to lobby for policy change. The argument that a more proportional party balance at Westminster would have limited the period of Conservative power became sufficiently attractive (even if somewhat embarrassing to most of the party's leaders) to lead Neil Kinnock to set up a working party on electoral reform under Professor Raymond Plant, while committing a future Labour government merely to consider Plant's report. Kinnock became rather entangled in the electoral reform issue late in the 1992 election campaign, when his personal doubts about proportional representation (PR) (shared by most of the leadership, with the exception of Robin Cook and Jack Cunningham) came into conflict with his desire to reach out to the Liberal Democrats as potential coalition partners. Beyond a short section on the Plant working party, the party's 1992 election manifesto mentioned Parliament only briefly, but contained pledges to 'improve the procedures and facilities' of the Commons, strengthen scrutiny of European legislation, introduce fixed parliamentary terms, and replace the House of Lords with an elected second chamber (Labour Party 1992, pp. 24–5).

The Civil Service

Analysing the post-war development of the Civil Service, Peter Hennessy was struck by the anomaly of 'Why the most radical administration between David Lloyd George and Margaret Thatcher failed to reform the Civil Service, as an integral part of its programme and as a necessary condition of its success' (Hennessy 1989, p. 127). Harold Laski and others on the left on the Labour Party, the Fabians, and even Clement Attlee himself in the early 1930s had argued for Civil Service reform as a precursor of social and economic change (Attlee had changed his view on this by 1945), but there was a paucity of detailed policy, and Labour's 1945 election manifesto offered only a vague commitment to 'better organisation' of Whitehall (Theakston 1995, pp. 63–4). Encountering commitment and cooperation rather than resistance or sabotage from their senior officials, Labour ministers were largely content to leave Edward Bridges, head of the Civil Service and permanent secretary of the Treasury, to fend off the occasional reformist foray from Labour MPs or the Fabian Society, while managing some relatively low-key changes to the administrative structure (K. O. Morgan 1985, pp. 85–93; Theakston 1995, pp. 66–73).

Labour's attitude to the Civil Service for much of this period tended to show the strains between the party's commitment to *dirigisme*, which implied the need for good working relations with senior officials, and its suspicion of the mandarins' class background and alleged establishment sympathies. The precise nature of the working relationships between particular Labour ministers and their senior civil servants provided a further complicating factor. Some of these relationships were excellent, as with Roy Jenkins and his Home Office and Treasury officials; some were poor, as with Crossman and his Department of Education officials. Tony Benn's experience as a minister in the years 1964–1970 and 1974–1979 confirmed his belief that many senior civil servants would do all in their power to thwart a radical minister, but he was never able to secure changes in party policy in order to deal with this perceived problem, largely because any attempt to allow ministers to remove senior officials at will raised the spectre of politicization.

With the Conservatives, similar tensions were in evidence, this time between the party's traditional antipathy towards 'big government' and all who sail in her (with officials often viewed by the party's right wing as closet socialists), and a sometimes rather grudging respect on the part of Conservative ministers for the general level of competence displayed by a genuinely impartial, non-partisan officialdom.

These tensions were less apparent in the 1950s than thereafter. Indeed, the broad policy similarities between the 1945–1951 Labour administrations and the Conservative governments of 1951–1964 made it difficult for the Conservatives even to fulfil their 1951 manifesto commitment to 'simplify' the Whitehall machine and cut 'waste and extravagance'. As Kevin Theakston notes, 'It was never going to be easy for the Conservatives to cut the size of the Whitehall bureaucracy when, rather than adopting an economic liberal platform, they were basically presenting themselves in the 1950s as better at running the Keynesian welfare state than the Labour Party' (Theakston 1995, p. 80). In fact, the Conservatives secured only incremental cuts in the numbers of non-industrial civil servants during the 1950s, while the reluctance to pursue fundamental issues relating to the functioning and purpose of Whitehall was demonstrated in the restricted terms of reference of the 1953–1955 Royal Commission on the Civil Service. The Priestley Commission was narrowly focused on pay and conditions of service, and produced a low-key report (Theakston 1995, pp. 74–5). Despite the discussions which had taken place within the Conservative Party in the late 1940s on the subject of Civil Service reform (Theakston and Fry 1994, p. 392) there was no commitment to this on the part of ministers or senior officials, and the occasional structural changes which took place in Whitehall during the 1950s were driven by practical concerns rather than party policy or philosophy (Seldon 1987, pp. 77–8). By the end of this extended period of power in 1964, the Conservatives had accepted the recommendations of the 1961 Plowden report and introduced a new approach to public expenditure planning and control along with a reorganization of the Treasury. Some Whitehall departmental amalgamations began (most notably with the creation of the Ministry of Defence in 1964), but more fundamental arguments for the modernization of the Civil Service (from the Conservative Political Centre, for example) and for the advent of official accountability foundered on the rock of the Macmillan government's indifference and intransigence (Theakston and Fry 1994, p. 392; Fry 1981, p. 37).

Propelled by growing concerns about the alleged failure of the Civil Service to adapt and modernize to face the challenges of the late twentieth century, together with gnawing anxieties centred on the part played by apparently outmoded institutions in Britain's relative economic decline, waves of reform began to hit Whitehall from the late 1960s onwards (presaged by the Wilson government's ultimately abortive attempt to counterbalance Treasury power through the creation of the Department of Economic Affairs). The extent to which the Civil Service reforms of these years were fundamentally and directly influenced by party policy is difficult to assess. The ideas of groups and individuals within the parties undoubtedly played a part in shaping these reforms, but it seems likely that they were mainly generated as practical solutions to the ongoing challenges of governance, albeit subject to external influences ranging from party policy to current managerial theory. The work of the Fulton Committee, culminating in its 1968 report, became the focus of attention for those seeking to reform the Civil Service.

Reforms stemming more or less directly from Fulton's recommendations included the creation of a new grading and pay structure, changes to the recruitment system, experiments with accountable management techniques, the 'hiving off' of certain executive operations from mainstream Whitehall departments, and the establishment of a Civil Service Department and a Civil Service College (Hennessy 1989, pp. 190–5; Theakston 1995, pp. 91–106). Fulton embodied the spirit of the 1964–1970 Wilson governments in the sense that the committee's chairman had been an associate of Harold Wilson in the wartime Civil Service, and the report's tone reflected many of the criticisms of the Civil Service which had become common currency within Wilson's circle of close colleagues (Thomas Balogh's critique of Whitehall 'amateurism' found an echo in the report). None the less, the Fulton report's main recommendations were accepted by the opposition leader Edward Heath, despite the fact that the Conservatives, alone of the major parties, did not submit formal evidence to the committee (although it should be noted that Fulton did not accept some important elements of the party submissions, including Labour's suggestion that ministers should be supported by Continental-style *cabinets*). The Conservative leadership had been formulating its approach to the Civil Service with the help of a group of businessmen, some of whom were seconded to Whitehall following the 1970 election (Campbell 1993, p. 316; Hennessy 1989, p. 212).

It fell to Heath's government, from June 1970, to implement key elements of Fulton. The incomplete implementation of the report, by both Labour and

Conservative governments, is a tale which need not be related here. However, it is important to note that, although it was not perceived as such by many senior civil servants at the time, the Fulton report was fundamentally sympathetic towards the concept of the Whitehall bureaucracy, albeit in modernized form (Theakston 1995, p. 90). Margaret Thatcher observed the mixed results of Fulton, abandoned some of the innovations which had stemmed from the report (including the Civil Service Department, and the moribund system of strategic management, PAR), and embarked upon a much more radical and antipathetic programme of Civil Service reform in the 1980s. The policy of Civil Service reform under Wilson, Heath and Thatcher was driven by the party leaders and their senior colleagues, often (in the case of the Conservatives) drawing on the advice of friendly businessmen.

Aspects of Heath's 'quiet revolution' were driven by the fashions and fads of the time, including the mania for 'giant' organizational structures, which spawned Whitehall amalgamations. However, some of his initiatives were to be more lasting, particularly the initial implementation of Fulton's hiving-off schemes and the attempts to embed modern business practices in parts of the Whitehall machine. One of the businessmen charged with this task, Derek Rayner, returned to government as Thatcher's efficiency adviser in 1979. The Rayner scrutinies sparked off a series of managerial changes which culminated in a major study of the structure and management of the Civil Service by Rayner's successor, Sir Robin Ibbs, in 1987 (Drewry and Butcher 1991, chs 10 and 12; Pyper 1995, ch. 3). The Ibbs 'Next Steps' report concluded that the Civil Service was too large and its activities too diverse to be managed as a single unit (Efficiency Unit 1988). The Thatcher government's acceptance of the report launched the most significant structural and managerial reform of the Civil Service in more than a century, and led directly to the creation of the executive agencies which now form the basis for most Civil Service work. The agencies, headed by chief executives with significant managerial freedoms but ultimately accountable to ministers, are judged against a set of key output, financial and service quality targets.

To a very great extent, the 'Civil Service policy' of the Thatcher governments was the personal policy of the premier. Influenced by her own experience in the Department of Education and Science between 1970 and 1974, together with her reading of Leslie Chapman's insider accounts of Whitehall 'waste' (L. Chapman 1979), she located responsibility for Civil Service affairs with relatively junior and compliant ministers, while giving roving roles to Rayner, Ibbs and their successors in her Downing Street Efficiency Unit.

The Labour Party's attitude to Thatcher's reforms moved gradually from scepticism tinged with hostility to almost complete acceptance. Although critical of the job losses which became associated with aspects of 'Raynerism', and initially fearful that Next Steps presaged the break-up of the Civil Service, Labour fought the post-Next Steps general elections committed to continuing the programme. Giles Radice, Labour's chairman of the subcommittee of the Treasury and Civil Service Select Committee, and some of the output from the centre-left think-tank the Institute for Public Policy Research (IPPR), played an important role in persuading Neil Kinnock and his colleagues that the Civil Service reforms were, on the whole, rather sensible and appropriate (Davies and Willman 1991). None the less, there was an occasional disparity between the Radice perspective and that of John Marek, Labour's official spokeman on Civil Service matters, and Gerald Kaufman, the former minister, who was persistently critical of Next Steps.

Labour's acceptance of the managerial changes which had taken place in the Civil Service, including the direct recruitment of senior managers (often from the private sector), the advent of pay and promotion 'flexibilities', devolved budgets, performance indicators and the general drive to achieve 'value for money', was indicative of the party's slow embrace of what had previously been derided as elements of naked Thatcherism but had come to be viewed as manifestations of the new public management. To a large extent, this happened by default, or at least in the background, since Kinnock's policy review exercise of the late 1980s virtually ignored Civil Service issues.

The fall of Thatcher in 1990 brought no significant change in policy towards the Civil Service, beyond a slight alteration of tone, signalled by the advent of the Citizen's Charter (Citizen's Charter 1991; Drewry 1993; Falconer 1996). Where his predecessor's attempt to modernize, scale down and make the bureaucracy more efficient seemed to be driven by an innate antipathy towards the public service ethos, Major professed his faith in the value of good-quality public services, and proffered the Citizen's Charter as a means of achieving this. The drive to reduce the size of the service continued under Major, although a lack of immediate success on this front brought criticism from within the Conservative Party and the subsequent announcement of new targets.

While Labour found fault with Major's development of the market testing initiative within the Civil Service, the lack of prominence accorded to this and other matters of Civil Service policy was shown by the fact that Labour's 1992 general election manifesto made no substantive mention of the Civil Service, beyond the commitment to create a new government department, the Ministry for Women (Labour Party 1992, p. 24).

An Unusual Climate: Continuity and Rupture 1992–1997

In the wake of its rather surprising victory in the 1992 general election, the Conservative government's policy towards the Civil Service was founded on consolidation coupled with elements of change, while its policy towards Parliament was largely amorphous before being pushed into some shape under the pressure of the 'sleaze' crises. In both categories, policy was formulated and driven by the party leadership, although there is some reason to suspect that the response to the issue of parliamentary ethics was partly influenced by opinion within the Conservative grass roots (Kelly 1995). For Labour, these were years of internal turbulence and soul-searching, due to the successive shocks of a largely unexpected election defeat and the death of John Smith. As Tony Blair and the 'modernizers' set about the party's structures, processes and ideology, some areas of policy were fundamentally overhauled and taken beyond the Kinnock/Smith prescriptions (Mandelson and Liddle 1996; Rentoul 1996; Shaw 1994). The Civil Service and Parliament escaped close attention during the Blair policy revolution, although the party's approach to the latter was subject to an element of revision. Once again, the key policy-making role was played by the party leaders, perhaps to an even greater extent than in the past, due to the overt centralization of authority within Blair's New Labour.

As was the case for most if not all of the post-war period, during the years 1992–1997 it was easier to measure the policy difference between the two main parties with reference to Parliament rather than to the Civil Service. Despite the occasional rhetorical flourish from opposition spokespeople, Conservative and Labour policy towards the Civil Service moved along broadly similar lines between the 1992 and 1997 general elections.

The Civil Service

John Willman has argued that the Major government 'intensified the pace of change in the civil service' and, 'far from stilling the revolution, Mr Major has spurred it on and backed more radical measures' (Willman 1994, p. 64). This seems to overstate the case for Major's 'radicalism' by playing down the essential continuity between the Civil Service policy of the Thatcher and Major administrations. Fresh initiatives and new approaches were apparent in the Major years, but the policy compass was set by Thatcher and Major rarely wandered off the route. Historians are likely to identify the mid- to late 1980s as the point when the Civil Service began to be transformed (albeit pointing to the origins of the key reforms in earlier periods), while seeing the Major years as noteworthy but not especially distinctive.

Following the 1992 election victory, Major restructured the central management of Civil Service affairs by bringing three key units (Next Steps, Efficiency and Citizen's Charter) together in the new Office of Public Service and Science (later the Office of Public Service). A casualty of this process was Sir Peter Kemp, the permanent secretary charged with managing the Next Steps project, who was dismissed by his new minister, William Waldegrave, on the grounds that a new approach was needed in the new department. Unusually, an alternative post was not found for Kemp, and he was obliged to resign. His strong belief in the need for cultural diversity within the executive agencies clashed with the Major government's plans to impose new efficiency targets on the chief executives, and his *enfant terrible* image left him without support within the group of senior mandarins led by Sir Robin Butler. There is some evidence to suggest that the departure of Kemp marked a turning point in the development of Next Steps: while the pace of agency-creation was not affected, there was a certain loss of momentum in the drive to give chief executives increased operational freedoms (Theakston 1995, p. 136). Major's instinct for consolidation was timely, as there had been growing fears about the 'Balkanization' of the Civil Service and the concomitant erosion of its fundamental principles (R. A. Chapman 1992). None the less, his government's continued adherence to the principles of delegated management was signalled by the passage of the 1993 Civil Service Management of Functions Act, which allowed the component parts of the increasingly federal Civil Service to determine a wider range of terms and conditions of service without reference to the centre.

As we have seen, the most significant (and successful) modern attempt to transform the shape and management of the Civil Service, the Next Steps programme, was initiated by the Thatcher government in 1988, and had developed its own momentum by the time Major became prime minister. The new premier pushed on with Next Steps, and by the end of his term in office over 75 per cent of the Civil Service was located within executive agencies, of which 138 were Next Steps agencies (Next Steps Team 1997). Individual agencies were subjected to quinquennial reviews, during which all future options, including privatization, were considered. As a result of this process, eleven agencies (including Her Majesty's Stationery Office – HMSO – and the Recruitment and Assessment Services Agency) had been privatized by 1997 (Next Steps Team 1997, p. 61).

Labour's attitude towards Next Steps remained broadly supportive. Criticisms, when they came, tended to focus on the *causes célèbres* associated with the Prison Service Agency and the Child Support Agency, during which the opposition parties would attack on the issues of ministerial conduct or lack of accountability, while lauding the general principles and impact of Next Steps. Blair's senior policy advisers on the Civil Service admitted that executive agencies 'have improved the delivery of government services through better management and delegation' (Mandelson and Liddle 1996, p. 251).

The broad structural and managerial changes brought about through Next Steps were coupled with a development of the efficiency strategy in the form of the market testing initiative. This had been announced in November 1991, in the *Competing for Quality* White Paper, which set out the government's plans to expand competitive tendering (now styled 'market testing') within the public sector, and the Civil Service in particular (White Paper 1991). The full programme of departmental and executive agency activities to be subject to market testing was published after the 1992 general election, in the context of the first report on the Citizen's Charter, thus emphasizing the link between the charter and the search for efficient public services (Citizen's Charter 1992, pp. 58–64). Market testing was centrally managed by Waldegrave, Richard Mottram (Kemp's successor and permanent secretary of the Office of Public Service and Science) and the prime minister's efficiency adviser Peter Levene. As it developed, the programme became embroiled in controversies surrounding its failure to meet its initial targets, job losses, the imposition of targets on unwilling agency chief executives, and the attempted privatization of mainstream (as opposed to peripheral) Civil Service activities (First Division Association 1992; Hencke 1993; Labour Research 1993; Pyper 1995, pp. 64–70). Within an adjunct to market testing, the Private Finance Initiative, attempts were made to involve the private sector in public capital spending programmes. The perceived excesses of the market testing programme became the focus for Labour's opposition to the government's Civil Service policy, with questions being asked about the true value of the 'efficiency savings', the sums spent on management consultants, and the extent to which private companies were complying with their government contracts (Mandelson and Liddle 1996, pp. 252–3). In a 1993 discussion paper Labour's Mo Mowlam called for a moratorium on market testing (Theakston 1997, p. 17). However, it was not clear whether the principles behind market testing were being seriously questioned.

Partly designed to differentiate Major's civil and public service policy from that of his predecessor, and partly to counter the opposition parties' interest in citizens' rights and constitutional change, the Citizen's Charter encompassed a range of linked initiatives. The charter had been launched by Major in 1991 and continued to occupy the 'flagship' position in the context of the government's Civil Service policy. In fact, the charter extended beyond the Civil Service *per se*, into the public service at large, but its attempts to secure qualitative improvements in the management and delivery of services, while enhancing the means for redressing consumers' grievances, had a particular resonance in many of the executive agencies. The government's quinquennial review in 1996 lauded the charter's achievements (Prime Minister 1996), but some observers saw charterism as a triumph of style over substance, pointing to the initiative's impoverished definition of citizenship, its failure to create genuinely new mechanisms of accountability and redress, and its elements of farce (such as the abortive telephone help line, Charterline, and the Cones Hotline). The opposition parties supported the idea of enhanced answerability and better service delivery (Labour even argued that Major had 'stolen' the charter concept from the customer contract initiatives within some Labour-controlled local authorities), but questioned the extent to which this could be achieved without extra funding.

The 1993 White Paper on open government (White Paper 1993) provided further evidence of Major's desire to distinguish his general approach from that of his predecessor. However, although the resultant policy saw the government committed to publish more background papers, facts and analysis, it offered no challenge to the extant official secrets provisions (Pyper 1995, pp. 159–61). Another White Paper was published the following year, offering an overview of recent civil service changes and some clues about future developments (Prime Minister 1994). This document's theme was 'continuity and change', and its publication represented something of a compromise between the forces within the government and the Conservative Party pushing for further radical reforms, and those (including the prime minister and the head of the Civil Service, Butler) who perceived low morale within the service and favoured more incremental change coupled with the preservation of core values and principles (Massey 1994). Token criticism of *Continuity and Change* by Labour's spokesman (Norton-Taylor 1994) could not disguise the essential similarity between the parties on key Civil Service issues. Labour's acceptance of the new public management's central tenets was a reflection of political reality in the UK, and also indicative of the common ground occupied by the 'modernizers' here, the Labour administrations in Australia and New Zealand, and the Clinton presidency's proponents of 'reinventing government'.

By that stage, however, the Civil Service policy of the Conservative government had been opened up to attack from a new direction. The Scott Inquiry and subsequent report into the 'arms for Iraq' affair (Adams and Pyper 1997; Bogdanor 1996; Norton-Taylor et al. 1996) raised serious questions about the apparent cynicism shown by senior officials in their dealings with Parliament, and the extent to which they had colluded with ministers to mislead MPs. The opposition parties focused attention on the negative impact of an extended period of Conservative government upon the Civil Service. Overt politicization was seen to have been less of a problem than the creation of a particular, unquestioning mind-set, which foreclosed options and proffered advice to ministers on the basis of what they wanted to hear rather than needed to know.

Parliament

Parliamentary policy became a particular problem for the Major government during its final phase. Policy was distinctly reactive, driven by the need to respond to developing crises. Serious allegations concerning the links between Conservative MPs (some of them ministers), parliamentary lobbyists and commercial interests forced the government to react by setting up the Nolan Committee on Standards in Public Life in October 1994. The committee recommended tighter rules on the acceptance of jobs by former ministers, and the establishment of a Parliamentary Commissioner for Standards to oversee new rules on members' interests. The commissioner, Sir Gordon Downey, embarked upon an investigation of the 'cash-for-questions' and 'cash-for-amendments' affairs, which engulfed a group of MPs (including the former ministers Neil Hamilton and Tim Smith) and dogged the government until and beyond the calling of the 1997 general election (Leigh and Vulliamy 1997).

In the meantime, Labour's parliamentary policy was being subjected to subtle alteration. In truth, much of the policy was rather opaque, consisting of generalized comments from shadow ministers about 'modernizing' Parliament, but offering little in the way of detailed exposition. The promise of change, however vague, was none the less enough to differentiate the opposition parties from the Conservatives, who demonstrated no interest in parliamentary reform. The area of Labour's parliamentary policy which changed following Blair's assumption of the leadership related to the House of Lords. The 1992 manifesto commitment to an elected second chamber was adhered to by Smith, but this policy was quietly dropped by Blair in favour of a vaguer commitment to reform. The key figures in the creation of the revised policy were Blair, Lord Richard (Labour leader in the Lords), and Blair's mentor Derry Irvine, the future lord chancellor (Rentoul 1996, pp. 465–7). Now the priority was merely ending the voting rights of heriditary peers, with a promise to examine other options, and 'perhaps' introduce a directly elected 'element' (Mandelson and Liddle 1996, p. 205).

The 1997 General Election: Campaign and Aftermath

Party policy towards Parliament and the Civil Service did not figure prominently in the course of the long 1997 general election campaign, with the notable exception of the 'sleaze' issues, which served to focus attention on the attitudes of the parties towards parliamentary ethics and standards of conduct.

Manifestos

The party manifestos contained only a few clues about these aspects of policy. The Conservatives cited a record of 'breaking up cumbersome bureaucratic structures' and enhancing accountability via the Citizen's Charter (Conservative Party 1997, p. 29). Beyond a plan to require all government agencies to apply for Chartermarks (awards for full and effective compliance with the charter), and a pledge to legislate on the basis of the 1993 open government White Paper, future policy towards the Civil Service remained vague. Parliament fared no better, with the relevant section presenting a resumé of the limited, technical changes introduced in the period since 1979 (only the advent of the new select committees amounted to a substantial reform), a statement of opposition to the other parties' proposals, and a commitment to give select committees a role in legislative scrutiny (Conservative Party 1997, pp. 49–50).

The Civil Service did not feature directly in the manifestos of Labour or the Liberal Democrats, although the functioning of departments and agencies would be affected by these parties' commitment to a Freedom of Information Act. The opposition parties devoted some, limited, space to Parliament in their manifestos. The Liberal Democrats were committed to 'modernization' of the Commons (a fixed four-year term, PR, reducing the numbers of MPs, introducing tougher rules on conduct and outside interests, improving legislative scrutiny), transforming the Lords into a 'predominantly elected' house (over two Parliaments), and reforming party funding (Liberal Democrats 1997, p. 43). Labour also utilized the buzz-word 'modernization', although, as we have seen, the proposed reform of the Lords was to be limited to ending the rights (voting and sitting) of hereditary peers, with further reform dependent upon the proposals of a committee of both houses. A select committee would review the procedures of the Commons, Prime Minister's Questions would be made 'more effective', and the process for scrutinizing European legislation would be overhauled. Additionally, Labour was pledged to reform party funding and put future options for the Commons electoral system to a referendum (Labour Party 1997, pp. 49–50).

New government policy: the first six months

During the first six months of the new government, at least some flesh began to appear on the bones of Labour's policies towards the Civil Service and Parliament. Interestingly, the broad similarity between Labour and Liberal Democrat policies on constitutional matters was reflected in the decision to give Paddy Ashdown and his senior colleagues seats on a consultative Cabinet committee. This fuelled some resentment amongst Labour MPs and activists who were already concerned about the centralist tendencies of New Labour policy-making, and now saw political opponents apparently being given a say in policy (Draper 1997, pp. 116–17; White 1997a). The real significance of this committee remains to be seen.

The new government launched its parliamentary policy with a reform of the routine for Prime Minister's Questions. A single, thirty-minute session on Wednesdays was introduced to replace the old system of two fifteen-minute sessions on Tuesdays and Thursdays. A special select committee on modernization, chaired by Ann Taylor, the leader of the House of Commons, embarked upon a review of Commons' procedure with the aim of improving legislative scrutiny and enhancing executive accountability. Even in these early stages, some doubts emerged regarding the real motivation behind modernization: to strengthen Parliament or make life easier for the executive? Taylor's statements about the need to enhance the ability of MPs to hold the government accountable sat uneasily with Blair's reminder to the Parliamentary Labour Party (PLP) on 7 May that it was not elected to obstruct the government. Many of the new MPs were 'shocked by the brutality of the message' (Draper 1997, p. 32).

During the second week of the new administration it became clear that there would be no time in the first session of Parliament to implement the limited Lords reform pledged by the manifesto. At the party conference in October 1997 Blair succeeded in defusing criticism of this delay, and rallying his party, by warning the Lords not to 'try to wreck' the government's devolution proposals. Indeed, it had become clear by that stage that the creation of a Scottish Parliament and a Welsh Assembly would, potentially, have a more significant long-term impact on the Westminster Parliament than any other element of the Blair government's policy towards Parliament.

As expected, there were significant elements of continuity in the Blair government's Civil Service policy. David Clark, the chancellor of the Duchy of Lancaster and public service minister, announced that the Citizen's Charter would continue, albeit subject to 'relaunching' and 'refocusing'; the proposed moratorium on market testing was dropped in favour of a slightly more selective use of the policy; the Private Finance Initiative continued; and the new government announced its first privatization (the sale of 60 per cent of the Commonwealth Development Corporation) in October 1997 (Theakston 1997, pp. 17–18; White 1997b). Some steps were taken to address the accountability problems associated with the two most controversial executive agencies (Home Secretary Jack Straw announced that Home Office ministers would once again answer directly to Parliament for the Prison Service, while the Child Support Agency was to be subjected to an overhaul) but Next Steps rolled on, as expected.

An important policy shift was introduced by Chancellor Gordon Brown when, only five days into the new administration, he announced that the first stage of a Treasury reorganization would involve giving the Bank of England operational control over interest rates. The genesis of this policy lay in a Fabian pamphlet, written by Ed Balls in 1992. The idea was further developed when Balls became Brown's policy adviser, and ultimately agreed with Blair (Draper 1997, pp. 25–8; Thomas 1997). The election manifesto made only oblique mention of decision making on monetary policy, and the timing of the announcement was decided upon after the election.

Labour's long-standing commitment to produce a Freedom of Information Act (based on extensive work already done in opposition) seemed to come under question when dates for publication of a White Paper were repeatedly postponed and stories emerged regarding Clark's failure to have the policy prioritized within a Cabinet committee chaired by Lord Irvine (Draper 1997, pp. 51, 167–8).

However, the main focus of attention during this first phase of the new government's Civil Service policy was the issue of appointments. The merger of Environment and Transport in Deputy Prime Minister John Prescott's new 'super-department' saw the departure of Sir Patrick Brown, permanent secretary at Transport and a leading implementer of the Conservatives' privatization policies, although it was by no means clear that this was a causal factor (Theakston 1997, p. 4). In any case, the appointment (from January 1998) of Richard Wilson as Butler's successor as cabinet secretary and head of the Civil Service was welcomed within Whitehall (Butler 1997, p. 15; Theakston 1997, p. 4). The real problems with appointments arose at lower levels of the hierarchy. In particular, the influx of fifty-three political advisers created immediate tensions and strains between the new government and certain elements of the Civil Service (Draper 1997, pp. 118–19, 158; Theakston 1997, pp. 5–6). Many of the newcomers took up media liaison roles (the so-called 'spin-doctors') which seemed to overlap with the functions of the Civil Service information officers. As a result, seven information officers left their posts and the Civil Service first commissioner urged the prime minister to curtail political appointments (Draper 1997, p. 118; Hencke 1997; Pierce 1997).

It should be noted that debates concerning the alleged 'politicization' of parts of the Civil Service are not new, and the initial problems within the Whitehall information service should be seen in the context of a generally smooth transition, for which the new prime minister personally thanked the head of the Civil Service (Draper 1997, p. 119). In the longer term, the ethical issues surrounding the relations between ministers, civil servants and Parliament may be addressed in a Civil Service Act, which would develop and entrench the extant Civil Service Code (Theakston 1997, pp. 11–12).

Conclusion: The Impact of Party Policy

Party policy towards Parliament and the Civil Service has developed at quite different rates in the period since 1945.

Parliamentary policy has, on the whole, changed only marginally, and the changes have tended to be reactive rather than proactive. Thus, the select committee reforms of the 1960s and late 1970s, and the new approach to ethics and standards of conduct in the 1990s, stemmed in large measure from influences external to the parties themselves (academic, media and public debates about the efficacy of parliamentary scrutiny and widespread concern about 'sleaze'). Where change has taken place, it has stemmed from the party leadership rather than other potential sources of policy within parties. For example, Labour's approach to the House of Lords, which was the subject of an incremental but significant adjustment during the period between 1992 and 1997, clearly changed at the behest of the leader and his senior colleagues.

Civil Service policy changed more significantly over the period from 1945. Once again, the changes were managed and controlled by the party leaders, primarily when in government. During the most significant period of policy change, that which encompassed the Thatcher government's Civil Service reforms, it could be argued that the policy of one party was distinctly proactive, took the policies of the other parties along in its wake, and played a central role in shifting state policy, public opinion and the parameters of political debate. However, even in that context, it would be wrong to claim that party policy developed autonomously. Theakston and Fry (1994, p. 401) point out that

'Conservative ideas about Whitehall reform have not necessarily been original or distinctly "conservative".' The Conservative Party's Civil Service policy represented the fusion of various ideas and approaches, including the traditional Tory 'efficiency' agenda (Theakston and Fry 1994, p. 401), New Right theories of the state (Smith 1996) and contemporary management science. We should also reiterate the point that, while being carried along by the Thatcher reforms, Labour's policy towards the Civil Service was being influenced to some extent by the new approaches of the Labour parties in Australia and New Zealand and the 'reinventing government' agenda of the American Democrats, as well as by more traditional, Fabian attitudes towards Whitehall.

Chronology of Significant Developments April 1992 to October 1997

July 1992	Dismissal of Sir Peter Kemp
November 1992	First Report on the Citizen's Charter
July 1993	White Paper, *Open Government*
July 1994	Civil Service White Paper, *The Civil Service: Continuity and Change*
October 1994	Establishment of Committee on Standards in Public Life (Nolan Committee)
May 1995	First Report from Nolan Committee; establishment of Parliamentary Commissioner for Standards
February 1996	Scott report (*Report of the Enquiry into the Export of Defence Equipment and Dual-Use Goods to Iraq and Related Prosecutions*)
September 1996	Five-year review of Citizen's Charter
May 1997	Bank of England given operational control over interest rates; Prime Minister's Question Time reformed
June 1997	First meeting of select committee on modernization of the Commons
July 1997	Liberal Democrats allocated seats on Cabinet committee
August 1997	Richard Wilson confirmed as successor to Sir Robin Butler (from January 1998)

References

Adams, J. and Pyper, R. 1997 'Whatever Happened to the Scott Report?', *Talking Politics*, 7 (2).

Baines, P. 1985 'History and Rationale of the 1979 Reforms' in Drewry, G. (ed.) *The New Select Committees. A Study of the 1979 Reforms*. Oxford: Clarendon Press.

Benn, T. 1988 *Out of the Wilderness. Diaries 1963–67*. London: Arrow.

Bogdanor, V. 1996 'The Scott Report', *Public Administration*, 74 (4).

Butler, R. 1997 'The Changing Civil Service', unpublished paper, Future Whitehall Conference, Church House, London, 24 September.

Campbell, J. 1993 *Edward Heath. A Biography*. London: Pimlico.

Chapman, L. 1979 *Your Disobedient Servant*. Harmondsworth: Penguin.

Chapman, R. A. 1992 'The End of the Civil Service?', *Teaching Public Administration*, 12 (2).

Citizen's Charter 1991 Command Paper 1599 Session 1990–91.

Citizen's Charter 1992 First Report. Command Paper 2101 Session 1992–93.

Conservative Party 1997 *You Can Only Be Sure with the Conservatives*. London: Conservative Central Office.

Crossman, R. H. S. 1976 *The Diaries of a Cabinet Minister. Vol. 2*. London: Hamish Hamilton/Jonathan Cape.

Davies, A. and Willman, J. 1991 *What Next? Agencies, Departments and the Civil Service*. London: Institute for Public Policy Research.

Draper, D. 1997 *Blair's Hundred Days*. London: Faber and Faber.

Drewry, G. 1993 'Mr Major's Charter: Empowering the Customer', *Public Law*, Summer.

Drewry, G. and Butcher, T. 1991 *The Civil Service Today*. 2nd edn. Oxford: Blackwell.

Efficiency Unit 1988 *Improving Management in Government: The Next Steps*. London: HMSO.

Falconer, P. 1996 'Charterism and Consumerism' in Pyper, R. (ed.) *Aspects of Accountability in the British System of Government*. Eastham: Tudor.

First Division Association 1992 'Market Testing', *FDA News*, 12 (10).

Fry, G. K. 1981 *The Administrative 'Revolution' in Whitehall*. London: Croom Helm.

Gregory, R. and Hutchesson, P. 1975 *The Parliamentary Ombudsman*. London: Allen and Unwin.

Griffith, J. A. G. 1987 'Crichel Down: The Most Famous Farm in British Constitutional History', *Contemporary Record*, 1 (1).

Hencke, D. 1993 'Job Tenders Rile Whitehall', *Guardian*, 26 January.

Hencke, D. 1997 'Whitehall Press Officers Sound Off', *Guardian*, 17 October.

Hennessy, P. 1989 *Whitehall*. London: Secker and Warburg.

Howard, A. 1990 *Crossman. The Pursuit of Power*. London: Pimlico.

Justice 1961 *The Citizen and the Administration. The Redress of Grievances*. London: Stevens.

Kelly, R. 1995 'The Left, the Right and the Whipless: Conservative Divisions since 1992', *Talking Politics*, 8 (Autumn).

Labour Party 1992 *It's Time to Get Britain Working Again*. London: Labour Party.

Labour Party 1997 *New Labour: Because Britain Deserves Better*. London: Labour Party.

Labour Research 1993 *Privatising the Government*. London: Labour Research.

Leigh, D. and Vulliamy, E. 1997 *Sleaze: The Corruption of Parliament*. London: Fourth Estate.

Liberal Democrats 1997 *Make the Difference*. London: Liberal Democrats.

Mandelson, P. and Liddle, R. 1996 *The Blair Revolution. Can New Labour Deliver?*. London: Faber and Faber.

Massey, A. 1994 'Old Wine in New Bottles', *Parliamentary Brief*, 2 (10).

Morgan, J. 1975 *The House of Lords and the Labour Government*. Oxford: Oxford University Press.

Morgan, K. O. 1985 *Labour in Power 1945–51*. Oxford: Oxford University Press.

Next Steps Team 1997 *Next Steps Briefing Note October 1997*. London: Office of Public Service.

Nicolson, I. F. 1986 *The Mystery of Crichel Down*. Oxford: Clarendon.

Norton-Taylor, R. 1994 'Civil Service Principles "Under Threat"', *Guardian*, 14 July.

Norton-Taylor, R., Lloyd, M. and Cook, S. 1996 *Knee Deep in Dishonour. The Scott Report and its Aftermath*. London: Victor Gollancz.

Pierce, A. 1997 'Writing on Wall for Whitehall Press Machine', *The Times*, 17 October 1997.

Prime Minister 1994 *The Civil Service: Continuity and Charge*. Command Paper 2627 Session 1993–94.

Prime Minister 1996 *The Citizen's Charter – Five Years On*. Command Paper 3370 Session 1995–96.

Pyper, R. 1995 *The British Civil Service*. Hemel Hempstead: Prentice Hall/Harvester Wheatsheaf.

Rentoul, J. 1996 *Tony Blair*. London: Warner.

Riddell, P. 1994 'Major and Parliament' in Kavanagh, D. and Seldon, A. (eds) *The Major Effect*. London: Macmillan.

Seldon, A. 1987 'The Churchill Administration 1951–1955' in Hennessy, P. and Seldon, A. (eds) *Ruling Performance. British Governments from Attlee to Thatcher*. Oxford: Blackwell.

Shaw, E. 1994 *The Labour Party since 1979. Crisis and Transformation*. London: Routledge.

Shell, D. 1992 *The House of Lords*. 2nd edn. Hemel Hempstead: Harvester Wheatsheaf.

Smith, M. J. 1996 'Reforming the State' in Ludlum, S. and Smith, M. J. (eds) *Contemporary British Conservatism*. Houndmills: Macmillan.

Theakston, K. 1995 *The Civil Service since 1945*. Oxford: Blackwell.

Theakston, K. 1997 'New Labour, New Whitehall?', unpublished paper, Annual Conference of the JUC Public Administration Committee, Civil Service College, Sunningdale, 1–3 September.

Theakston, K. and Fry, G. 1994 'The Party and the Civil Service' in Seldon, A. and Ball, S. (eds) *Conservative Century. The Conservative Party since 1900*. Oxford: Oxford University Press.

Thomas, R. 1997 'Mr Balls Beams at Dream Come True', *Guardian*, 7 May.

White, M. 1997a 'Blair's New Lab–Lib Pact', *Guardian*, 23 July.

White, M. 1997b 'Blair to Unveil First Sell-Off', *Guardian*, 22 October.

White Paper 1991 *Competing for Quality: Buying Better Public Services*, Command Paper 1730 Session 1990–91.

White Paper 1993 *Open Government*, Command Paper 2290 Session 1992–93.

Willman, J. 1994 'The Civil Service' in Kavanagh, D. and Seldon, A. (eds) *The Major Effect*. London: Macmillan.

Guide to Further Reading

There is no shortage of texts covering Parliament and the Civil Service, although few address the issue of party policy in any detail. Philip Norton's *Does Parliament Matter?* (Hemel Hempstead: Harvester Wheatsheaf, 1993) and Donald Shell's *The House of Lords* (Hemel Hempstead: Harvester Wheatsheaf, 1992) are sound accounts. The modern history of the Civil Service is analysed succinctly in Kevin Theakston's indispensable *The Civil Service since 1945* (Oxford: Blackwell, 1995), while the author's *The British Civil Service* (Hemel Hempstead: Prentice Hall/Harvester Wheatsheaf, 1995) and Peter Hennessy's *Whitehall* (London: Secker and Warburg, 1989) provide commentary and analysis on this evolving institution.

10 | Environmental Policy

Robert Garner

Synopsis

In the last decade or so, the environment has become an important political issue. By themselves, however, the major British political parties have had relatively little impact on the development of environmental policy. Instead, the parties have merely responded, inadequately in most cases, to compelling scientific and technological evidence, and to public concern promoted by the environmental movement. Moreover, British parties are constrained by the supra-national nature of environmental policy-making, which severely limits their room for manoeuvre.

The Historical Context: Party Policy 1945–1992

Policies relating to the natural environment in Britain date back to the nineteenth century but it is only since the 1960s that the 'environment' has emerged as a distinct policy area, and only in the past decade or so that political parties have attempted to develop a comprehensive policy for the environment. To make sense of British environmental policy, it is useful to distinguish between the two main systems through which environmental policy is implemented (Blowers 1987, p. 279). There are overlaps between these two systems, not least because – since its formation in 1970 – the Department of the Environment has figured heavily in both, but the two systems do contain distinct networks of agencies created by separate legislative initiatives. In the first place, the land-use planning system has emerged as a result of a variety of development and conservation measures introduced since 1945. Second, the pollution control system, which has its origins in the nineteenth century but which has been transformed since the 1970s, is concerned with regulating emissions into the air, water and soil.

Environmental policy and politics before the 1980s

For much of the post-war period, much of the controversy, such as it was, surrounding the environment in Britain centred on development and conservation issues. Their high profile was caused by the visible damage being done to the countryside, coupled with the opportunities for interested parties to participate in the land-use planning system. This system was largely created by a series of measures (in particular, the 1947 Town and Country Planning Act and the 1949 National Parks and Access to the Countryside Act) introduced by the 1945–1950 Labour government and was very much part of the post-war ideological consensus, accepted by succeeding Conservative governments, emphasizing the desirability of state planning and direction (Rydin 1993).

By contrast, the regulation of industrial emissions has typically been conducted in secret, with inspectors given a great deal of latitude to negotiate with the managers or owners of industrial plants in order to reach a consensus on the volume and nature of the pollution permitted (O'Riordan and Weale 1989, pp. 278–9). The British pollution inspectorate emerged in a haphazard, fragmented and piecemeal fashion (Vogel 1986). Since the 1860s, more and more industrial processes have been regulated and different inspectors appointed to control particular substances (radioactive or toxic waste) or media (air, water, soil).

Public perceptions of an environmental crisis were heightened by various well-publicized disasters and by academic research which indicated that disaster loomed if the world continued to produce and consume at an ever-growing rate (Meadows et al. 1972). Despite these warnings, and the limited international responses to them, and despite the existence of domestic environmental legislation, environmental issues were rarely politically salient in Britain up to the end of the 1970s, not least because the parties showed little interest in, and certainly were not divided on, them. Within all three major parties environmental ginger groups were formed (the Socialist Environment and Resources Association 1973, the Liberal Ecology Group 1977 and the Conservative Ecology Group 1977), but all three lacked any official status within their respective parties and had little discernible influence (Flynn and Lowe 1992, pp. 10–11).

The 1980s: the decade of the environment

From the standpoint of the early 1980s, it could not have been predicted that by the end of the decade the environment would be established as a mainstream political issue. The 1979 and 1983 elections were dominated by the traditional ideological battles between left and right centring on economic issues. As Robinson (1992, pp. 24–5) points out, whilst the environment was 'now firmly established within party agendas' it 'was nothing more than a "token" declaration, there to look good, but achieving little'.

The Thatcher government's uninterest in environmental issues was obvious, and not at all surprising given neo-liberal hostility towards the regulatory structures most environmentalists regard as essential to achieve environmental objectives. A Cabinet leak in the early 1980s revealed, for example, that the intention of the government was to 'reduce over-sensitivity to environmental considerations' (Flynn and Lowe 1992, p. 12). The only substantial environmental measure introduced by the first Thatcher government was the 1981 Wildlife and Countryside Act, and the process by which the legislation was drafted and its eventual content reveal a great deal about the government's lack of commitment to conservation objectives. Not only were conservation groups largely excluded from participating in the drafting of the bill, but the final proposals were seriously flawed, not least because, by failing to bring farmers under the control of the planning system and by failing to give adequate powers to the state conservation agencies, little was done to impede the environmental damage caused by intensive agriculture (Lowe et al. 1986, ch. 6).

Amongst the major parties, it was the Liberals who showed the most concern for environmental issues in the 1970s and who have been the 'greenest' of the mainstream parties since (Robinson 1992, pp. 20–1). In the 1970s, this greater environmental interest was partly a product of a radical faction in the party, whose influence on policy-making at the annual conference was marked, and partly a product of the party's emphasis on local community politics, where the quality of the environment was often an issue. It is undoubtedly the case, too, that the 'green' credentials of the Liberals owe a great deal to their distance from power and the consequent need to avoid making difficult political choices. In this context, it is interesting to note that one of the key problems in the alliance between the Liberal Party and the Social Democratic Party (SDP) in the first half of the 1980s was that the SDP's David Owen regarded Liberal radicalism on environmentalism in general, and on nuclear issues in particular, as electoral handicaps, and succeeded in diluting the Alliance's environmental commitments in the 1983 and 1987 elections (Garner and Kelly 1993, pp. 214–17).

It was only in the latter part of the 1980s that the environment began to move up the political agenda. Central to the party political response was the apparent 'conversion' of Thatcher to green issues, announced publicly in speeches made in 1988 (McCormick 1991, pp. 58–60). These speeches were coupled with action. In the international sphere, the Thatcher government accepted Britain's responsibility for acid rain, and facilitated an agreement on the reduction of chlorofluorocarbons (CFCs), the major cause of ozone depletion. Furthermore, Nicholas Ridley was replaced as environment secretary by the much more environmentally friendly Chris Patten. In domestic legislative terms, new pollution control agencies were created. Her Majesty's Inspectorate of Pollution (HMIP) was designed to integrate the existing fragmented inspectorates and became operational after the passage of the 1990 Environmental Protection Act, and the National Rivers Authority (NRA) was set up in 1989 to regulate emissions into Britain's waterways. In addition, the government's initially extensive nuclear power programme had been all but scrapped by the end of the 1980s (Saward 1992). In conservation policy, the Thatcher government tackled, with some success, the farming subsidies in the Common Agricultural Policy (CAP), which encouraged intensive agriculture, and sought to compensate farmers who chose to operate in less environmentally damaging ways. Finally, Patten was responsible for liaising with a variety of government departments to produce a White Paper, *This Common Inheritance* (Department of the Environment 1990).

Published in September 1990, this document was the first attempt by any British government to produce a comprehensive and integrated set of environmental proposals. As a consequence, the other major parties were forced to respond with their own policy statements, the Liberal Democrats publishing 'What Price our Planet?' and Labour 'An Earthly Chance' (Carter 1992a, pp. 126–30).

The 'greening' of the Conservatives can be largely explained in terms of external factors to which the party was forced to respond. Electoral expediency undoubtedly played a role, as opinion polls in the mid to late 1980s indicated rising public concern about the state of the environment. Apparently symbolizing this sea-change in political attitudes, the Green Party, originally formed in 1973, came from nowhere to win 15 per cent of the vote in the 1989 European Parliament elections. In these circumstances, it is not surprising that the major parties sought to manoeuvre themselves into a position where they could reap the greatest political advantage (Flynn and Lowe 1992, pp. 25–9).

Other external factors were of equal, if not greater, importance in explaining the Conservative government's about-turn on the environment. The move towards integrating environmental decision making across government departments – seen most noticeably in *This Common Inheritance* – and the rationalizing of pollution control inspectorates within one agency – at least partly achieved by the creation of HMIP – was the product of a consensus amongst environmental experts that this was the most effective means of achieving environmental objectives (Weale 1992, pp. 102–8). The downgrading of nuclear power was also the product of external factors. The anti-nuclear movement played its part in raising public awareness of the potential dangers of generating nuclear power and disposing of spent nuclear material, and their case was given an enormous fillip by the Chernobyl disaster in 1986. Arguably even more important, however, was the true cost of nuclear power, which was revealed as unattractively high as a result of the auditing made necessary by the government's electricity privatization proposals (Greenaway et al. 1992, pp. 116–38).

Above all, supra-national commitments were increasingly constraining the ability of British parties to act, or choose not to act, unilaterally. In particular, after the 1986 Single European Act, the European Union's (EU) involvement in environmental policy-making was enhanced, not least because the treaty revisions included the establishment of the EU's legal competence to tackle environmental issues, and both the substance of British policy and the nature of the policy machinery designed to implement it were increasingly determined in the Council of Ministers and the European Commission (Hildebrand 1992; Haigh 1990; Judge 1992). To give one example, the unprecedented debate about the quality of British drinking and bathing water and the eventual creation of the NRA came about entirely as an unintended consequence of the government's privatization of the regional water authorities (McCormick 1991, pp. 96–8). Initially, the intention was to transfer environmental responsibility to the privatized water companies, but since this was illegal under EU law, the government was forced to create a new public agency to perform the task.

The 'greening' of the Conservative Party can also, in part, be explained by 'internal factors relating to the actions and positions of key personalities, and to ideological developments' within the party (Robinson 1992, p. 4). In the first place, it might be argued that, as a science graduate, Thatcher was more likely than most to be persuaded that severe global environmental problems did exist and that action was required to deal with them. A less charitable view is that she saw the promotion of global environmental issues as a means of strengthening 'her position as an international statesperson' (McCormick 1991, p. 65). Whatever Thatcher's motives, her appointment of Patten, by far the 'greenest' member of the Cabinet, as environment secretary in 1989 is an example of an internal party appointment having a significant effect on the direction of a policy area.

Patten was on the 'wet' or paternalistic wing of the party and environmental protection was often ideologically justified from within this tradition of Conservatism. Indeed, the internal debate about the environment was inextricably linked with the wider debate about the ideological direction of the Conservative Party, and the policy shift towards greater concern for environmental protection in the latter part of the 1980s might be regarded as a symbol of the declining influence of the free market rational individualism associated with Thatcher. Thus, while Ridley's ideological guide had been Adam Smith, Patten invoked Edmund Burke in his first conference speech as environment secretary. Burke, Patten argued, reminds 'us of our duties as trustees for the nation, as good stewards of its traditions, its values and its riches' (Flynn and Lowe 1992, p. 31).

The conflict between these two wings of the Conservative Party was most evident in conservation and land-use policy. After the 1983 election, in particular, a number of Tory backbenchers representing rural constituencies in the south-east of England joined forces with conservation groups to express their unease about the government's stated intention of relaxing development controls in the countryside. To some degree, this was prompted by the electoral consequences of such a move and the government, well aware of the threat posed by the Alliance in many southern constituencies, did take steps to ensure that the countryside was not subject to the haphazard development that deregulation had permitted in many urban areas.

There was also, though, an ideological dimension to the conservation issue. Traditional 'one nation' Conservatism was invoked by those interested in protecting Britain's national heritage from the ravages of urban expansion. The Bow Group, for instance, a 'wet' faction within the party, sided very much with the conservationists. 'Green voters and Conservative voters', one of its publications stated, 'share an instinct for preserving what is good and fine and traditional around us. The nature conservationist is a natural Conservative' (quoted in Flynn and Lowe 1992, p. 20; see also Johnson 1981; Carlisle 1984). The deregulation versus conservation issue was also invoked by Michael Heseltine, a significant landowner himself, as part of a broader attack on Thatcherism which ultimately led him to challenge for the leadership of the party in 1990 (Flynn and Lowe 1992, pp. 24–5).

A false dawn

In retrospect, what became known as the decade of the environment proved to be a false dawn. There was no discernible shift in environmental policy as a result of John Major's arrival in Downing Street. Rather, with the onset of recession, the environment, whilst now established as a major issue, began to slip down the political agenda once again.

In the 1992 general election, environmental policy hardly figured at all, the issue constituting a peripheral part of the two major party's manifestos (Carter 1992b, p. 444). The only domestic commitment made by the Conservatives was the setting up of an Environmental Protection Agency (EPA) to incorporate the work of HMIP and the NRA, a pledge which 'reflected a remarkable near-consensus across government, opposition parties and the network of pressure groups with an interest in the issue of environmental regulation' (Carter and Lowe 1995, p. 38). Labour differed from the Conservatives only in promising more ambitious targets for the reduction of carbon dioxide (CO_2) and tougher pollution standards.

The Liberal Democrats did attempt to turn the environment into an election issue. Nine pages were devoted to the subject in their manifesto and the party planned to promote environmentalism as one of its major concerns (Carter 1992b, p. 444). In the event, the environment was 'scarcely mentioned by the major parties at any point during the campaign' (Rootes 1995, p. 75). Even the Liberal Democrats reasoned as the campaign progressed that there was little political capital to be made in focusing on environmental issues, turning their attention instead, as the two main parties had done, to economic issues and later, as a hung Parliament became a distinct possibility, to constitutional reform.

An Unusual Climate: Continuity and Rupture 1992–1997

During Major's second term as prime minister, environmental politics and policy did not regain the saliency they had achieved in the latter part of the 1980s. This was partly because the political parties had, to some degree, responded to environmental concern, thereby depoliticizing the issue and reducing the need for high-profile public pressure. Equally important was the longevity of the recession, which, as before, turned attention away from environmental issues to more traditional economic themes. Coupling this with the government's perilous parliamentary position, and the constant internal conflict in the Conservative Party over Britain's role in Europe, it is hardly surprising that environmental issues failed to become a major preoccupation of the government. It was common for environmentalists to praise Environmental Secretary John Selwyn Gummer's genuine commitment to environmental issues but to see him as an isolated figure, 'a prisoner', as the executive director of Greenpeace put it, 'in a disinterested [*sic*] government' (*Guardian*, 12 March 1997). Finally, as the internationalization of environmentalism, exemplified by the Earth Summit of June 1992, became more pronounced, it was increasingly recognized that Britain's room for manoeuvre was significantly reduced and, even more pertinently, that British governments could, in any case, make only a limited contribution to the health of the planet.

The Environmental Protection Agency

The bill to create the EPA was eventually introduced during the 1994–1995 parliamentary session and the new institution began its work in April 1996. The initiative was first announced by Major in 1991 during his first environment speech as prime minister (Carter and Lowe 1995, pp. 38–9), and had already been suggested in *This Common Inheritance* a year earlier (Department of the Environment 1990, p. 43).

Neither the existence of the agency nor its particular character, however, owes much to the party system. Rather, it was a culmination of the integrationist approach recommended by environmental experts and set in train by the Conservatives in the 1980s. The creation of HMIP had left water-quality regulation and waste disposal in the hands of other agencies (the NRA and local authorities respectively) and the EPA was designed to subsume these functions, together with the regulation of air pollution, under the control of one body (Carter and Lowe 1995, pp. 40–2). The exact character of the EPA came about as a result of a massive consultation exercise with interested parties begun in 1991. Furthermore, amendments made to the original draft proposals came about primarily as a result of criticisms from environmentalists rather than from Conservative backbenchers or the opposition parties (Garner 1996, pp. 102–3).

The growing impact of the European Union

Since 1987, the impact of the EU on British environmental policy has grown, not least because of the effects of the Single European Act and the Maastricht Treaty. Conflict between the European Commission and the British government on environmental policy was endemic between 1989 and 1992, but it came to a head in the run-up to the signing of the Maastricht Treaty. As with Major's general relationship with the EU, both before and after the 1992 election, conflict over environmental policy had more to do with his own party's divisions over Europe than with the objective merits of the case. The catalyst was the appointment of the Italian socialist Carlo Ripa di Meana as the environment commissioner in 1989. Unlike most previous incumbents, he was determined to be inflexible in the interpretation of directives and to pursue miscreants in the European Court (Haigh and Lanigan 1995, p. 25).

Britain had been threatened with court action on a number of occasions, including that of its failure to comply with directives dealing with the quality of bathing water. The key decision, however, occurred in 1991, when Ripa di Meana called a halt to seven British construction projects on the grounds that they had failed to comply with a 1985 EU directive which insisted upon an environmental assessment preceding any major development. These included, most importantly, the M3 extension at Twyford Down and the Channel Tunnel rail link. Major allegedly responded by threatening to obstruct the signing of the Maastricht Treaty and, according to Haigh and Lanigan (1995, p. 27), since the commission was well aware that the actions of DGXI (the part of the EU bureaucracy responsible for environmental policy) could increase the influence of the Eurosceptics in the Conservative Party, 'DGXI was ordered to tone down its actions.' Whether or not this is correct, it is true that, in July 1992, legal action was dropped against most of the construction projects and delayed in the case of the alleged infringement of the bathing water directive (McCormick 1993, p. 275).

Rio and after

Environmental issues have become increasingly global in scope, and effective action requires international cooperation. The international community has long recognized the necessity of linking together environmental issues with other pressing concerns – such as poverty and debt – in the developing world if progress is to be made and, to this end, a conference organized by the United Nations Environment Programme (UNEP) in 1987 sought to operationalize the principle of 'sustainable development' (World Commission on Environment and Development 1987). The summit held in Rio de Janeiro in June 1992 aimed to take this process further.

Given the hype surrounding it, the Rio Summit (otherwise known as the Earth Summit or, to give its full title, the United Nations Conference on Environment and Development) was always going to be a disappointment. For his part, Major, anxious to be seen on the international stage and to show his commitment to environmental issues, was the first political leader to announce he would attend, and the British government did sign the five official agreements made. Of these, only two – on biological diversity and climate change – are legally binding and both contain few specific commitments and, even more crucially, provide no new sources of finance, thereby failing to address the issue of the North/South divide (Thomas 1993). Over 150 countries eventually signed the convention on climate change, which seeks a reduction in three greenhouse gases – including, most importantly, CO_2 – to their 1990 levels by the end of the twentieth century. In addition, all signatories, under the so-called Agenda 21 agreement, were asked to report to a newly created United Nations Commission on Sustainable Development to indicate the progress made.

The environmental record of Major's Conservative government after 1992 should be seen largely in the context of the agreements entered into at Rio. This record was mixed. Two new administrative initiatives (an advisory panel of experts on sustainable development and a 'round table' of thirty members drawn from all sections of the community) were announced in January 1994 (Dodds and Bigg 1995, pp. 13–15), but there is little evidence that they were particularly effective in setting the agenda for the government's environment policy. In addition, the government published four documents outlining its post-Rio strategy, but these were heavily criticized by environmentalists for, as Andrew Lees of Friends of the Earth pointed out, being 'old commitments repackaged' and for lacking 'any meaningful targets and timetables' (*Guardian*, 26 January 1994). Even some of the limited number of commitments made were derailed by the political constraints that would effect any government seeking to make hard choices.

The land-use planning system is the chief instrument for ensuring biodiversity in Britain, and this remained largely unchanged between 1992 and 1997. Gummer did introduce tougher planning guidelines in 1994, mainly to deter the building of out-of-town shopping centres, and these were strengthened even further early in 1997. While this led to a steep decline in planning applications, the failure to produce a concurrent strategy to deter the use of cars resulted in existing shopping centres reporting a huge increase in trade (*Guardian*, 15 February 1997). The long-standing weaknesses, from an environmental perspective, remain. In particular, intensive agriculture is still vigorously pursued and, as has been seen most notably in the road-building programme (see below), the conservation agencies have no formal power to prevent the destruction of land which they have designated as species-rich Sites of Special Scientific Interest (SSSIs) or Areas of Outstanding Natural Beauty.

The main planks of the government's strategy to achieve the goals of the Rio climate convention consisted of a plan to introduce value added tax (VAT) on domestic fuel in two stages, to 8 per cent in 1994 and 17.5 per cent a year later, to increase road fuel duty, and to introduce various schemes to encourage energy efficiency (Maddison and Pearce 1995, pp. 131–5). Imposing new taxes, whether for environmental or other reasons, is politically sensitive and the full increase in VAT was blocked by Conservative backbenchers, well aware of its potential electoral consequences (*Independent*, 15 December 1994). The political sensitivity of introducing environmental taxes was encountered again in 1996 when the government introduced a landfill tax. Although a useful scheme which encouraged local authorities to recycle as much waste as possible, it was still attacked by Labour during the 1997 election campaign as one of the government's twenty-two tax rises (*Independent*, 30 September 1996; *Guardian*, 25 April 1997).

In the event, the British government easily achieved the target set by the Rio Summit. Indeed, with a reduction in (1990) CO_2 levels of 4–8 per cent, Britain's record was better than that of almost every other industrialized country (*Guardian*, 19 February 1997). The target, however, was not particularly exacting, and was made to seem more impressive because of some 'wildly inaccurate' predictions which had suggested that CO_2 emissions in Britain were likely to rise substantially by the end of the century. The rise failed to happen, not as the result of the government's direct concern for the environment, but largely as the unintended by-product of a big reduction in the coal industry and the greater use of gas for energy generation. Finally, in this section, it is instructive to note that Britain's CO_2 emissions now constitute only about 2 per cent of the global total (Maddison and Pearce 1995, p. 129).

Transport policy

The increasing number of motor vehicles on the roads of Britain is, in many ways, a symbol of the modern environmental crisis (Button 1995, pp. 174–81). The issue shot to prominence in Britain with the emergence of self-styled road protesters who, from the early 1990s, began to take direct action against the use of cars in general (through the so-called 'Reclaim the Streets' movement) and in an attempt to stop particular construction projects. From a party political standpoint, the significance of the road protesters is that they have operated outside of the party system. Even the Greens, a party in steep decline since the high point of their 1989 electoral performance, have been strangely irrelevant to the activities of the protesters. Clearly, the main parties have failed to appeal to a section of society which has no confidence in conventional politics in general and the mechanisms for determining land use in particular.

The effect of the road protests has been to highlight the issue of unsustainable transport policies and to make minor celebrities of some of the protesters themselves. Their influence on government policy, however, has been minimal and they certainly were not responsible for the substantial cut in the road-building programme announced in the mid-1990s. Rather, the government's desire to cut public spending was undoubtedly a key factor. Moreover, in as far as environmental concerns were a cause, a Royal Commission on Environmental Pollution (1994) report, in which the growth in road traffic was described as 'unsustainable' and the government was urged to introduce measures to reduce the demand for traffic, had a considerable impact. Perhaps of greater importance still was an emerging consensus, accepted in part by the road lobby, that far from being an answer to road congestion, building new roads positively encourages additional traffic (O'Riordan and Jordan 1995, p. 243; *Guardian*, 26 October 1994). This new orthodoxy was enshrined in the government's green paper on transport policy published in April 1996 (*Financial Times*, 26 April 1996).

Humans and animals

The issue of humans' relationship with animals was also prominent during Major's second term as prime minister. The protests against the export of live farm animals, which reached a peak early in 1995, were another indication of the inability of the party system to reflect public concerns. The scale of the opposition to the common practice of sending calves abroad, to be raised for veal in husbandry systems which had been outlawed in Britain, took the government by surprise and, whilst William Waldegrave, secretary of state in the Ministry of Agriculture, never suggested he would like to see the end of the trade, he did emphasize the need to secure reforms. On the other hand, the Labour front bench, mainly due to the efforts of the party's animal welfare spokesman Elliot Morley, sided with the protesters and supported calls for a ban on live exports.

As with many of the issues discussed in this chapter, the real significance of the live exports controversy was not the inter-party differences that emerged but the inability of *any* party to implement its policy goal in the face of the growing supra-national authority of the EU. Thus, as the government regularly, and perhaps conveniently, explained, it is illegal under European law for Britain to ban the live export of animals to other member states, just as it would be to prohibit the import of veal meat produced by the crate system which is banned in Britain. Despite Labour's claim that it would ban live exports, it has, since being elected in 1997, conformed to the reality of policy-making by merely calling for a European-wide ban, an objective which will be very difficult to achieve.

The influence of the EU was equally apparent in the outbreak of bovine spongiform encephalopathy (BSE) in cattle. Fears that the disease was related to the growing incidence of Creutzfeldt-Jakob Disease (CJD) in humans led to an EU ban on the export of British beef products in the spring of 1996, thereby forcing the government to take tougher measures to tackle it than they might otherwise have done (Baggott 1996). The European dimension of the issue is clearly crucial, but such a focus has helped to divert attention away from the environmental issues central to the BSE crisis. The use of recycled sheep protein in cattle feed is widely thought to be the most likely cause of BSE, and this practice is but one small characteristic of an intensive agricultural system which puts cost and convenience above everything else. Ironically, the EU, within which agribusiness interests are extremely influential, has traditionally been the leading promoter of intensive methods.

Labour in opposition

Despite the precariousness of Major's hold on power for much of the period between 1992 and 1997, the Labour Party had little opportunity to influence environmental policy. At the 1994 conference, the party did adopt a policy document, 'In Trust for Tomorrow', which one commentator retrospectively described as 'the strongest environment policy statement ever produced by a mainstream party' (Willmore 1997). Of particular importance were the commitments to introduce an integrated transport policy and to make substantially greater cuts in greenhouse gas emissions than the government had proposed. Moreover, the revised Clause IV of Labour's constitution contained an enduring commitment to environmental protection (*Sunday Times*, 30 April 1995).

In the run-up to the 1997 election, however, the environment was all but forgotten. Blair said little about Labour's plans, and of the 10,000 words in the party's pre-election document 'Road to the Manifesto' 'perhaps 200 of them touch on environmental questions' (Young 1996). A better guide, perhaps, to Labour's priorities were the two occasions when the parliamentary party eschewed the opportunity to support the government on measures which would have had a positive impact, although a largely unintended one, on the environment. A combination of political opportunism and the desire to protect the party's traditional constituencies led Labour to oppose the government's plans to close coal mines and to increase VAT on energy to 17.5 per cent. One would not have expected Labour to behave otherwise in these cases, but it does provide some indication of the party's reluctance to take the difficult choices necessary for environmental protection.

The 1997 General Election: Campaign and Aftermath

As before, the environment failed to become a major election issue in 1997. Once again, the Liberal Democrats produced the most radical set of environmental proposals. The manifesto committed the party to the introduction of a range of taxation measures designed, among other things, to produce extensive cuts in greenhouse gas emissions (30 per cent by 2010). These included reducing (by over 90 per cent) the price of a tax disk for cars with engines below 1600 cc, increases in fuel duty and a carbon tax on fossil fuels (*Independent*, 2 April). In addition, the Liberal Democrats advocated sweeping changes to agricultural policy, including a reduction in the use of pesticides and greater financial assistance to encourage farmers to switch to less intensive methods (*Guardian*, 16 April 1997).

The Conservatives launched a thirty-page manifesto dedicated to environmental policies, but the commitments offered were disappointingly thin. The major promises were a new pollution tax for business, the details of which were not forthcoming, an environmental audit commission to coordinate information for shareholders and customers about the 'green' record of companies, more grants for energy saving, and an overall cut in CO_2 emissions of 10 per cent by 2010 (*Guardian*, 28 March 1997). Particularly disappointing was the absence of a coherent transport policy. While continuing 'to encourage public transport', the manifesto stated, 'we recognise the needs of road users, and will continue to work with the private sector to sustain our road building and maintenance programme' (Conservative Party 1997, p. 31).

Labour's environmental commitments were, superficially at least, much more promising. Of particular importance was the recognition of the interconnected nature of environmental problems and the consequent necessity of ensuring that environmental policy 'is not an add-on extra, but informs the whole of government, from housing and energy policy through to global warming and international agreements' (Labour Party 1997, p. 4). The central aim of the specific environmental commitments in the manifesto was to cut CO_2 emissions by 20 per cent of their 1990 level by 2010, a much more ambitious target than the one set by the Conservatives. This was to be achieved, in particular, by a shift to renewable energy sources, the creation of an environmental task force from the unemployed and, most importantly of all, the introduction of an integrated transport system. Labour said little about countryside policy, the one exception being a commitment to allow a free vote on hunting.

Despite the fairly extensive coverage in the party manifestos, environmental policy was, perhaps predictably, virtually ignored in the campaign. One set-piece debate, organized by Friends of the Earth at the end of March, brought together the environmental spokesmen of the three main parties (*Independent*, 26 March 1997), but this failed to raise the profile of the issue. In so far as a dialogue between the two parties did emerge, Labour condemned the Conservatives for lack of ambition and the Conservatives responded by claiming that Labour's policies would not achieve the party's 'unrealistic' target for reducing CO_2 emissions, a charge with some validity, particularly given Labour's intention to reduce VAT on domestic energy supplies to 5 per cent (*Guardian*, 16 April 1997, 25 April 1997). In the meantime, the Green Party, which had even debated in the autumn of 1996 whether or not to contest the election, before eventually deciding to field about seventy candidates, disappeared without trace.

Labour in power

As with the Conservative Party, internal factors have helped to shape the character of Labour's environmental policy in the past, and will continue to do so now the party is in government. In particular, Labour's roots in the organized labour movement and its reliance on support from the urban working class have traditionally provided powerful constraints against the adoption of rigorous environmental policies. Of special significance, as an internal factor constraining Labour's environmental efforts, is the trade union movement. Still the most important financial source for the Labour Party, trade unions continue to be generally suspicious of environmental measures which might threaten the jobs of their members. As late as 1994, for instance, the Transport and General Workers Union and the Amalgamated Engineering and Electrical Union voted against Labour's environmental programme at the party conference (*Guardian*, 5 October 1994).

One of the major purposes of Labour's modernization in the past decade or so has been to change the party's image as a representative of the working-class producer, and the greater emphasis on environmental issues may be a reflection of the diminished influence of the trade unions within the party. The voters' desire for economic growth and low levels of taxation, however, is still a powerful motivating factor and will reduce Labour's ability to achieve its rather limited environmental goals. As an indication of the low priority given to the environment, it is instructive to note that Prime Minister Tony Blair's hour-long speech at the Labour conference in 1997 contained only one brief sentence on the issue.

So far, however, there are some promising signs that the Labour government will pay more than lip service to environmental issues. The merger of the environment and transport departments is useful from an environmental perspective and is a necessary condition for the effective delivery of an integrated transport policy, a commitment which Labour was intent upon honouring with the publication of a White Paper in the spring of 1998 (*Guardian*, 23 July 1997). The government has also committed itself to a significant increase in the use of renewable energy sources (*Observer*, 25 May 1997). Equally encouraging was the announcement that Britain is to give up its opt-out from an EU ban on dumping radioactive waste at sea, phase out chemical discharges, and halt the dumping of oil and gas installations in the sea (*Guardian*, 3 September 1997).

At the international level, the commitment of Blair – along with Cabinet members John Prescott, Robin Cook, Michael Meacher and Clare Short – to achieving progress in the reduction of greenhouse gas emissions has been evident. In Blair's address to the New York Earth II Summit in June 1997, he attacked the United States for not tackling the issue and urged greater aid for developing countries (*Guardian*, 24 June 1997). Moreover, the British government played a leading role in the negotiations conducted at the summit held in Kyoto, Japan, in early December 1997. Not only did the British delegation honour Labour's manifesto commitment by agreeing to a 20 per cent cut in

CO_2 emissions by 2010, as part of an overall EU reduction of 8 per cent, it also played its part in persuading the United States to agree a 7 per cent cut in its own CO_2 emissions. Whether or not Labour can deliver such a large reduction, however, is an open question, particularly given the government's economic priorities. The attitude of Chancellor Gordon Brown is a crucial factor and, according to a former policy adviser to Meacher, the Chancellor is, at best, lukewarm to the commitment (Willmore 1997).

Conclusion: The Impact of Party Policy

This chapter has revealed that political parties in Britain have played a minor role in the shaping of environmental policy. On occasions, party has played an autonomous role in the furthering of environmental objectives, and the support of key individuals within parties has sometimes proved to be important. Internal limitations on the 'greening' of the parties have also been evident. Both major parties articulate ideologies, defended from within by powerful vested interests, which extol the virtues of economic growth, despite the environmental costs which may result. This helps to explain why the Liberals, unencumbered by such vested interests, are the greenest of the mainstream parties.

These internal factors apart, party policy on the environment has been primarily shaped by a wide variety of external forces. Public pressure, articulated and aggregated by the environmental movement, has played an important, albeit unquantifiable, role. In addition, some environmental objectives – such as the creation of the NRA and the policy shift away from nuclear power – have come about as unintended by-products of government policy. In the environmental field, moreover, the role of experts is particularly influential. On a global scale, for instance, scientific evidence for ozone depletion and global warming has been a prerequisite for political action, while the characteristics of national reform have been shaped by a knowledge that integrating environmental policy objectives across a range of government activities is essential.

Above all, British parties are being increasingly constrained by the decisions made in supra-national decision-making arenas. As the only international organization 'with the power to agree environmental policies binding on its members' (McCormick 1991, p. 128), the EU has a profound influence on British environmental policy, with this influence intensifying as a result of the Single European Act and the Maastricht Treaty. Furthermore, British environmental policy is now structured by decisions taken on the global stage, a development which reflects the salutary fact that Britain's contribution to the protection of the environment is but a leaf in the wind unless other, more powerful, states also act decisively.

As Gray (1995) points out, the environmental record of British governments since the late 1980s tends to be regarded either as a fundamental departure from the past or as a mere rhetorical exercise designed to placate public concern. One can agree with Gray that the reality lies somewhere in the middle, so that while 'we have not witnessed a fundamental sea-change . . . the government has exhibited more than merely rhetorical concern for the environment' (Gray 1995, pp.

1–2, 10). The key constraint remains the influence of economic interests both within the two major parties and within the policy networks surrounding development-oriented government departments. We noted earlier how the Liberals have traditionally been the greenest of the three main parties, yet they remain a relatively peripheral force in British electoral politics, partly at least because they do not represent key interests within British society. Since the prevailing ethos of business and labour has traditionally emphasized the objective of economic growth, any government will be faced with enormous hostility to the pursuit of a radical environmental agenda.

Chronology of Significant Developments: April 1992 to October 1997

June 1992	UN Conference on Environment and Development (the Earth Summit) held in Rio de Janeiro
January 1994	Government publishes four documents on sustainable development as part of the commitments made at the Rio Summit
October 1994	Royal Commission on Environmental Pollution report on transport policy published; Labour conference adopts environment policy document, '*In Trust for Tomorrow*'
December 1994	Government plans to increase VAT on domestic fuel from 8 per cent to 17.5 per cent abandoned following opposition from some Conservative backbenchers
March 1996	EU votes for ban on British beef exports as a result of new evidence which supports the view that humans are at risk; campaigners against the Newbury by-pass removed by police
April 1996	EPA becomes operational; government publishes green paper on transport policy, the first comprehensive review for twenty years
September 1996	Government introduces landfill tax scheme to encourage recycling; Green Party conference defeats a motion calling for the party not to contest the forthcoming election
March 1997	Liberal Democrats publish election manifesto; Conservatives publish a thirty-page 'green manifesto'
June 1997	Earth II Summit held in New York

References

Baggott, R. (1996) 'Where is the Beef? The BSE Crisis and the British Policy Process', *Talking Politics*, 1 (9), pp. 2–8.

Blowers, A. (1987) 'Transition or Transformation? Environmental Policy Under Thatcher', *Public Administration*, 65, pp. 227–94.

Button, K. (1995) 'UK Environmental Policy and Transport', in Gray, T. (ed.) *UK Environmental Policy in the 1990s*, Basingstoke: Macmillan, pp. 173–88.

Carlisle, K. (1984) *Conserving the Countryside*, London: Conservative Political Centre.

Carter, N. (1992a) 'The "Greening" of Labour', in Smith, M. J. and Spear, J. (eds) *The Changing Labour Party*, London: Routledge, pp. 118–32.

Carter, N. (1992b) 'Whatever Happened to the Environment? The British General Election of 1992', *Environmental Politics*, 1, pp. 442–8.

Carter, N. and Lowe, P. (1995) 'The Establishment of a Cross-Sector Environment Agency', in Gray, T. (ed.) *UK Environmental Policy in the 1990s*, Basingstoke: Macmillan, pp. 38–56.

Conservative Party (1997) *You Can Only Be Sure with the Conservatives*, London: Conservative Party.

Department of the Environment (1990) *This Common Inheritance: Britain's Environmental Strategy*, Cmnd 1200, London: HMSO.

Dodds, F. and Bigg, T. (1995) *The United Nations Commission on Sustainable Development: Three Years since the Rio Summit*, London: UNED-UK.

Flynn, A. and Lowe, P. (1992) 'The Greening of the Tories: The Conservative Party and the Environment', in Rudig, W. (ed.) *Green Politics Two*, Edinburgh: Edinburgh University Press, pp. 9–36.

Garner, R. (1996) *Environmental Politics*, Hemel Hempstead: Harvester Wheatsheaf.

Garner, R. and Kelly, R. (1993) *British Political Parties Today*, Manchester: Manchester University Press.

Gray, T. (1995) 'Introduction', in Gray, T. (ed.) *UK Environmental Policy in the 1990s*, Basingstoke: Macmillan, pp. 1–10.

Greenaway, J., Smith, S. and Street, J. (1992) *Deciding Factors in British Politics: A Case Study Approach*, London: Routledge.

Haigh, N. (1990) *EEC Environmental Policy and Britain*, 2nd edn, London: Longman.

Haigh, N. and Lanigan, C. (1995) 'Impact of the European Union on UK Environmental Policy Making', in Gray, T. (ed.) *UK Environmental Policy in the 1990s*, Basingstoke: Macmillan, pp. 11–17.

Hildebrand, P. M. (1992) 'The European Community's Environmental Policy', 1957 to 1992: From Incidental Measures to an International Regime?', *Environmental Politics*, 1 (4), pp. 13–44.

Johnson, S. (1981) *Caring for the Environment: A Policy for Conservatives*, London: Conservative Political Centre.

Judge, D. (1992) '"Predestined to Save the Earth": The Environment Committee of the European Parliament', *Environmental Politics*, 1 (4), pp. 186–212.

Labour Party (1997) *New Labour: Because Britain Deserves Better*, London: Labour Party.

Lowe, P., Cox, G., MacEwen, M., O'Riordan, T. and Winter, M. (1986) *Countryside Conflicts: The Politics of Farming, Forestry and Conservation*, Aldershot: Gower.

Maddison, D. and Pearce, D. (1995) 'The UK and Global Warming Policy', in Gray, T. (ed.) *UK Environmental Policy in the 1990s*, Basingstoke: Macmillan, pp. 123–43.

McCormick, J. (1991) *British Politics and the Environment*, London: Earthscan.

McCormick, J. (1993) 'Environmental Politics', in Dunleavy, P., Gamble, A. and Peele, G. (eds) *Developments in British Politics 4*, Basingstoke: Macmillan, pp. 267–84.

Meadows, D. H., Meadows, D. L., Randers, J. and Behrens III, W. (1972) *The Limits to Growth: A Report for the Club of Rome's Project on the Predicament of Mankind*, New York: Universe.

O'Riordan, T. and Jordan, A. (1995) 'British Environmental Politics in the 1990s', *Environmental Politics*, 4 (4), pp. 237–46.

O'Riordan, T. and Weale, A. (1989) 'Administrative Reorganisation and Policy Change: The Case of Her Majesty's Inspectorate of Pollution', *Public Administration*, 67, pp. 277–95.

Robinson, M. (1992) *The Greening of British Party Politics*, Manchester: Manchester University Press.

Rootes, C. (1995) 'Britain: Greens in a Cold Climate', in Richardson, D. and Rootes, C. (eds) *The Green Challenge: The Development of Green Parties in Europe*, London: Routledge, pp. 66–90.

Royal Commission on Environmental Pollution (1994) *Eighteenth Report: Transport and the Environment*, London: HMSO.

Rydin, Y. (1993) *The British Planning System: An Introduction*, Basingstoke: Macmillan.

Saward, M. (1992) 'The Civil Nuclear Network in Britain', in Marsh, D. and Rhodes, R. (eds) *Policy Networks in British Politics*, Oxford: Oxford University Press, pp. 75–99.

Thomas, C. (1993) 'Beyond UNCED: An Introduction', *Environmental Politics*, 2 (4), pp. 1–27.

Vogel, D. (1986) *National Styles of Regulation: Environmental Policing in Great Britain and the United States*, Ithaca NY: Cornell University Press.

Weale, A. (1992) *The New Politics of Pollution*, Manchester: Manchester University Press.

Willmore, I. (1997) 'Sun Sets on a Greener Future', *Guardian*, 23 July.

World Commission on Environment and Development (1987) *Our Common Future*, Oxford: Oxford University Press.

Young, H. (1996) 'Black Hole in Blair's Green Agenda', *Guardian*, 30 July.

Guide to Further Reading

There is one book-length study focusing specifically on the environmental policy of the major parties and, although it was published some time ago, M. Robinson's *The Greening of British Party Politics* (Manchester: Manchester University Press, 1992) is still a worthwhile introduction to the subject. Substantial articles on Labour, such as N. Carter, 'The "Greening" of Labour', in Smith, M. J. and Spear, J. (eds) *The Changing Labour Party* (London: Routledge, 1992), and the Conservatives, such as A. Flynn and P. Lowe, 'The Greening of the Tories: The Conservative Party and the Environment', in Rudig, W. (ed.) *Green Politics Two* (Edinburgh: Edinburgh University Press, 1992), exist, but they are equally dated. More recent is chapter 7 of R. Garner, *Environmental Politics* (Hemel Hempstead: Harvester Wheatsheaf, 1996), which draws upon the three previously mentioned works and also serves as a general introduction to environmental politics and policy-making. The journal *Environmental Politics* is a useful source and there is much of value in the volume edited by T. Gray, *UK Environmental Policy in the 1990s* (Basingstoke: Macmillan, 1995). The British Green Party's development has not yet been the subject of a book-length study, but a number of articles in *Environmental Politics* have dealt with it and D. Richardson and C. Rootes (eds) *The Green Challenge: The Development of Green Parties in Europe* (London: Routledge, 1995) provides a comparative account of Green parties in Europe.

Conclusion
Does Party Policy Matter?

Richard Kelly

It will be recalled from the introduction that the defining feature of political parties is their quest for governmental power, either immediately or in a more long-term fashion. It will also be recalled that parties do this by condensing and articulating various public interests so that the electorate has a clear, packaged choice of policies at a general election.

The view that parties allow such a choice, however, rests heavily on two conditions. First, there must be a clear and substantial contrast between the main parties' policies. Secondly, there must be general confidence that a party elected through public support for specific policies will then implement those policies in government. If it is evident that parties in office cannot translate their policies into reality, then the notion that they offer voters a chance to change society becomes meaningless.

Party membership, and the parties' reputation for allowing popular involvement in politics, are also likely to crumble if parties in government are unable (or unwilling) to effect changes that would not simply have occurred anyhow; it is true that party membership was relatively high in the 'consensual' 1950s, but this was to a great extent a product of class alignment – a phenomenon which has since largely disappeared. Research indicates that the 'social' attractions of political parties are diminishing and that the new generation of members is not just smaller but also more motivated by specific policy concerns (Seyd and Whiteley 1992). Modern party members, in other words, expect not just more of an influence in policy formation, but clear and effective policy action from their party when it reaches government. Likewise, the parties' capacity to make parliamentary government more 'efficient' is much less impressive – to activists and voters alike – if it is felt that parties with a Commons majority seldom use it to effect significant policy changes.

In short, the credibility of British political parties owes much to a perception that their policies can 'make a difference' in office. But does that perception really exist and, if so, is it misplaced?

The Thatcher Legacy

The 1980s did much to strengthen the idea that the policies of governing parties could engineer major socio-economic change. This belief is borne out by a string of academic works which appeared during the latter part of the decade – the very titles of which are suggestive: *Mrs Thatcher's Revolution* by Peter Jenkins (1987), *The Thatcher Years: A Decade of Revolution in British Politics* by John Cole (1987), *Thatcherism and British Politics: The End of Consensus?* by Dennis Kavanagh (1987), and *The Thatcher Phenomenon* by Hugo Young and Ann Sloman (1986).

Many of the chapters in this study (particularly chs 3, 4 and 8) point to the far from inevitable changes wrought by the Thatcher governments. In this respect they offer strong support to the study by Kavanagh mentioned above, one which argued that the Thatcher governments proved what a sufficiently determined and programmatic government could achieve. Kavanagh recalled an essay, written in 1978 by Tory MP Rhodes Boyson, which pointed to six vital policies that would need to be effected if Britain were to be transformed in the way most Tories wanted. These were: the reduction of income tax and a top rate of 60 per cent, a substantial increase in police numbers and pay, the ending of exchange controls and the statutory monopoly of nationalized industries, a 5 per cent cut in annual government spending, and the replacement of state welfare with a voucher scheme. Kavanagh argued that all but the last two policies had been fulfilled by 1985 – an extraordinary achievement given their ambitious nature. He argued further that there had been 'significant discontinuities' of policy in many other areas, such as trade union reform, the rejection of incomes policies and 'tripartite' decision making, the toleration of rising unemployment and the reversal of long-standing arrangements in local government (Kavanagh 1987, p. 283). Andrew Gamble agreed that Thatcherite policies had changed the terrain of British politics and society, claiming that 'the traditional post-war argument about different kinds of state intervention' had been replaced by a much broader debate (Gamble 1988, p. 315). Riddell's survey of *The Thatcher Decade* (another revealing title) offered further support, noting that the 'political agenda has changed. The policy focus has shifted from the problems of producers and trade union obstruction to the freeing of markets and the extension of consumer choice' (Riddell 1989, p. 208). Thatcher's willingness to defy the pressures for 'consensus' from both internal and external sources was saluted not just by the radical right; left-wingers like Tony Benn contested that Thatcherism showed what could be achieved by a Labour government that was 'prepared to pursue doggedly its own brand of class policies' (*Campaign for Labour Party Democracy* 1982).

For many on the left, the Thatcher years also had echoes of a particularly effective period of Labour government – that of Clement Attlee (1945–1951) – which, through its nationalization and welfare policies, established the parameters of political debate in Britain for the next quarter of a century (Higgins 1984). In relation to Labour, the Thatcher years offered a further, albeit oblique reason for arguing that party policy mattered. For most of the Attlee years, there was already in place a new, social democratic consensus – the Tories having moved quickly to adopt the popular aspects of Labour's 1945 policy agenda. Yet Labour reacted to Thatcher's victory in 1979 by adopting its own alternative brand of radicalism, providing voters with not just affirmation that a governing party's policies were having a big effect, but the chance of heading off in a dramatically different direction. At the time of the 1983 general election, the claim that party policies could make little difference, and that there was little difference between them, was not easily borne out.

Thatcherism's Impact: A Cynical View

Although the 1983, and to a lesser extent 1987, general elections showed a clear divergence between the main parties' policies, it is not clear that voters were therefore offered a plausible choice. The fact that Labour's popular vote plunged to 28 per cent and 31 per cent in those elections suggests that Labour's own policies were implausible to the bulk of voters and that Labour did not offer the more 'sensible' (and therefore less radical) alternative they actually wanted.

This analysis, which argues that for Labour to have won in 1983 or 1987 it needed to be closer to the policies of the government (a view implicitly accepted by Labour's last three leaders), ties in with the main 'revisionist' charge concerning the Thatcher governments: that many of the policy changes which occurred in the 1980s, upon which our authors reflect, would have occurred regardless of her three election victories. That Labour failed to understand these changes is, allegedly, the main reason for its electoral failure; yet even if, by fluke, Labour had won with its 1983 and 1987 policies, the argument runs that it could still not have reversed most of the changes which pass – erroneously – for 'Thatcherism'.

Ben Pimlott observed in 1989 that 'Britain is very different now from what it was in 1979; but it was also very different in 1959 from what it was in 1949 after a decade of consensus politics' (p. 43), his point being that any ten-year period is bound to witness huge policy changes. Pimlott asserts that Thatcherite policies only sailed with tides which were already altering politics and society. Thatcher's task of revoking the social democratic consensus was made much easier by the fact that that was already discredited by events in the 1970s; this was arguably why she won the 1979 election. As Vincent (1987, p. 285) stated, 'Many of the decisions that shaped government in the 1980s had already been made under Labour' – the introduction of monetary discipline after 1976, and a recognition that nationalized industry was not working (see NEDC Report 1976, quoted in Veljanovski 1988, pp. 59–60), being prime examples.

It is undeniable that the growth of a white-collar society in the 1980s was as influenced by the long-term decline of heavy industry (and the corresponding shift towards a service-based economy) as by the policies of the Conservatives, which were after all merely a response to such changes. Fielding and Tonge, in their survey of trade unions in chapter 1, also suggest that, though the Acts of 1980, 1982, 1984 and 1988 did weaken union power, there were much more pressing factors behind the unions' decline as a political force – without which the Tories' own legal reforms might not have been possible. Chief among these was the relentless rise in blue-collar unemployment and the inevitable demise of those industries upon which union strength was based. The Fielding–Tonge analysis therefore casts doubt upon whether union power (in so far as it ever existed) could have survived the 1980s, irrespective of party policy.

Our authors also accept that the anti-Keynesian posture of the Thatcher governments was scarcely unique in democratic western states. During the 1980s there was a shift towards such policies in West Germany, the USA, Canada, Netherlands, Belgium, Japan, Sweden, Denmark and Norway. Even more significant was the adoption of a monetarist programme in France, after the socialist government swept to power promising the opposite (Kavanagh 1987, pp. 304–9).

Rose Reassessed

This line of argument appears to lend weight to a thesis first expounded in 1980 by Professor Richard Rose in his book *Do Parties Make a Difference?*. Rose made three central points which have particular relevance to this chapter: first, that party policy is largely reactive rather than proactive *vis-à-vis* public opinion; second, that rival party policies have more in common than their advocates care to admit; third, that policy developed by the parties via their own machinery has surprisingly little influence upon the actions of a government.

In their surveys of the 1945–1992 period, our authors generally accept that, for most of that period, there was a strong consensus between the two parties. As Cook and McKie wrote of the 1964 election, the contest was 'less between competing philosophies, much more about which set of managers was likely to get the better set of results' (1972, p. 34). Given that much the same could be said of the 1992 and 1997 general elections, British politics seems to have come full circle in this respect, with the deep divisions of the 1980s being very much an aberration.

For Rose (echoing the analysis of Anthony Downs over twenty years earlier: see Downs 1957), this tendency towards consensus was a product of how party policy really worked in a modern democracy. Parties, as pointed out in the introduction, are primarily interested in attaining office which, for Rose, meant reflecting (and not, as some radicals recommend, changing) the views of non-aligned voters. Rose implied that these non-aligned voters are, by definition, 'middle-of-the-road', which tends to draw the policy of major parties to the same centre ground. If there are substantial differences between the parties' policies, as there were in 1983 and 1987, this normally means that one party (Labour in this case) has either ignored or hopelessly misread floating voter opinion, thus securing an emphatic victory for its rival. Rose believed it to be no coincidence that during the 1945–1970 period, when each party governed for roughly seventeen years, the policy differences between those parties were marginal, whereas a period of prolonged government by one party (as after 1979) often points to a polarization of policy. Put simply, if there is to be more than one party of government, then the parameters of policy debate cannot be too wide.

Rose did not dispute the existence of adversary politics. But he did insist that, in a period of 'normality' (unlike the 1980s), the bulk of manifesto pledges would have a bipartisan flavour – like 'we attach importance to the maintenance of law and order', 'we shall improve the quality of life for the elderly', 'we are concerned about opportunities for school leavers' and so on. Many of the differences between party manifestos stemmed from what Rose called 'talking past' each other; one party promising to build more council houses than the other (as in 1951) being an illustration. In other words, Rose claims that manifesto clashes are deliberately exaggerated by their proponents, with policy differences concerning details and points of emphasis rather than grand principles (Rose 1980, p. 203).

In developing this argument, Rose was not drifting into uncharted waters. Robert McKenzie had argued that the 'oligarchic' structure of both main parties was necessary to ensure that their policies did not stray as far from the middle ground as activists might wish (McKenzie 1955, pp. 635–50). If a party does seem to have 'gone radical', this is often because it has sensed a similar change of mood among the electorate; parties thus respond to change rather than instigate it. As Peter Hennessy wrote, the 'radicalism' of the Attlee government needs to be put in historical context:

> A huge advantage (for the government) was the highly disciplined condition of the British people. Almost six years of total war had left almost no citizen untouched by its rigours, whether in the form of a siege economy on the home front or by military service abroad. The population was used to receiving orders and to strict regulation [which] helped create an atmosphere in which centrally directed schemes of national improvement became a norm and not a pipedream. (Hennessy and Seldon, 1987, pp. 32–3)

Sarlvik and Crewe (1983) have also contested that Thatcherite policies after 1975 were assisted by a change of public attitudes during the 1970s, when there was a growing hostility to trade unions and nationalized industries and a growing interest in lower taxation, greater individual choice and a sterner approach to law and order. Likewise, the Conservative failure to reduce public spending in the bold way it initially suggested (as a share of gross domestic product it never fell much below 1979 levels) owed much to a lack of political courage which, as Brian Lund points out (ch. 3), stemmed from its failure to alter public thinking on welfare policy. The Thatcher governments had hoped to promote a 'cultural revolution' in which the 'dependency culture would be replaced by the enterprise culture' (Kavanagh 1997, p. 133), yet surveys conducted by the end of the 1980s indicated that this 'crusade' had failed. The public was seen to favour the extension of public services rather than further tax cuts, more public ownership rather than further privatization, and a country 'which emphasised the social and collective provision of welfare' rather than one in which 'individuals are encouraged to look after themselves' (Kavanagh 1997, p. 133).

Such data seems to confirm Rose's thesis that the party policy has a limited ability to fashion public opinion. What he could not foresee, however, was that governments consistently at odds with public opinion over many key policies (as were the Thatcher governments) could still get re-elected given a certain and highly peculiar combination of circumstances – such as a weak and divided opposition, qualified economic optimism and perverse good luck (as provided, for example, by the Falklands War). It is also quite likely that the Thatcher governments' electoral success, in defiance of much popular opinion, may encourage future governing parties to be less sensitive to public mood than Rose ever imagined possible.

Parties in Power?

The Thatcher governments, however, could not detract from what is arguably the central fact about post-war British politics, one which is still overlooked by many textbooks. That fact is the interdependence of the British economy and the limited control exercised by British politicians over Britain's economic destiny. As many of our contributors acknowledge, so much control over various aspects of public policy flows from economic security – in which case it may be argued that British political parties, and the British political process in general, are much less decisive than we care to imagine. As one observer of the post-war scene commented:

> The major source of Britain's difficulties is to be located among the non-state actors...Politicians in power prate and posture, taking the credit and the blame for the interplay of international market forces, without usually being responsible for either the good or bad results. (Hayward, quoted in Ingle 1987, p. 191)

This analysis complements Rose's research, which established that the implementation of manifesto promises normally accounts for less than a fifth of what governments get up to – most of their work being *ad hoc* responses to unforeseen events. Our authors generally agree that many landmarks in post-war British history would have occurred whichever party was in power and would have elicited a broadly similar response: the sterling crises of 1947 and 1949, the Suez crisis of 1956, the oil crisis of 1973, the International Monetary Fund's intervention in 1976, and the devaluations of 1967 and 1992 being conspicuous examples. The Labour governments of the 1960s and 1970s are always invoked to support this sort of argument, simply because it was felt by many of those involved that there was a marked gap between policy promise and policy performance.

There is a vast literature concerning these Labour governments, and many of the book titles – *Labour in Power?* (Coates 1980), *Office Without Power* (Benn 1989), *Breach of Promise* (Ponting 1989) – are themselves revealing about the feeling the governments created. A favourite test case in such studies is the record of the Department of Economic Affairs (DEA), set up in 1964 with the intention of bringing about a 25 per cent increase in gross domestic product (GDP) by 1970; the actual increase was only 14 per cent and the DEA was effectively shut down after two years. The next Labour government came to power in 1974 promising a 'fundamental and irreversible shift of power and wealth', yet ended up pursuing an early form of monetarism and severe wage restraint. The claim that these governments failed on their own terms is therefore not without justification, and to put the blame on individuals seems inadequate; after all, with Harold Wilson, Denis Healey, Roy Jenkins, Barbara Castle, Tony Crosland, Richard Crossman, Peter Shore, Shirley Williams et al., these governments were blessed with the intelligentsia of British social democracy. A more compelling explanation is provided by another such luminary, Harold Lever:

> These governments overestimated their ability to shape and manage the complex drives of a mature economy. They wrongly assumed that governments could produce remedies for all its problems...The real world obstinately refused to conform to the principles of a party manifesto. (*Listener*, 22 November 1984)

Tony Benn has offered a broader analysis of why radical party policy is often not brought to fruition, one which embraces not just the restraints of international finance-capitalism, but institutional restraints in Britain – notably Whitehall, the City, the security forces, the military chiefs and the mass media, all of which conspire against fundamental change (Hennessy and Seldon 1987, p. 307). Benn, however, is no fatalist, and argued after 1979 that Labour policy could make a radical difference once Labour was in office, provided the party were sufficiently prepared and determined; this would require above all a parliamentary leadership more accountable to the party rank and file (see introduction).

Yet it is not only Labour governments which show the difference between a party's policy promises and its policy record in government. The government of Edward Heath came to power in 1970 promising policies which heralded a 'quiet revolution', overturning Keynesian social democracy in favour of a more bracing, market-led society. There was to be less state intervention in industry, a rejection of the prices and incomes policies practised in the 1960s, less public spending, and a reform of the trade unions. The Conservatives were not ill-prepared for office, having devoted an extraordinary amount of time in opposition to policy research (Campbell 1993). Indeed, central to the 1970 Tory campaign was a pledge to 'close the gap' between the rhetoric and actual policy of party politicians – a barbed reference to the contemporary view of Wilson's government.

Heath's government did not foresee the problems that would engulf it within two years of office, and its policy 'U-turn' of 1971–1972 was a fevered response to rising unemployment, public hostility and the threat of electoral disaster. Nevertheless, the record of Heath's government after 1972 was a startling contradiction of its original policy aims. The economy was reflated, public expenditure was increased, and there were much sterner prices and incomes policies than anything witnessed in the 1960s. Indeed, Heath's government – having promised *laissez-faire* in industry – turned out to be one of the most *etatiste* since the war, vainly seeking re-election in defence of policies it had explicitly repudiated three and a half years earlier.

Thatcher's regime too is not immune to the charge that governments are hidebound by internal and external restraints, and therefore ill-equipped to fulfil their initial policies. Of particular interest here is the Thatcher government's early stress upon monetary discipline. Yet between 1981 and 1984, the money supply (control of which was supposedly essential to the government's anti-inflationary strategy) rose by 50 per cent against a target of 16–30 per cent, and continued to rise at around 20 per cent a year. By early 1986, the government was considered guilty by many of its ideological advisers of a 'potentially reckless monetary binge' and 'a reflationary feast of backdoor Keynesianism' (Sherman 1988). As Fielding and Tonge's chapter reveals, the Tory claim that economic policy in the 1980s embodied 'the resolute approach' from a 'lady who was not for turning' merits stern qualification, as does any claim that there was an 'economic miracle'; although economic growth rose significantly after 1979, by 1989 it had reverted to the rates of 1969, when Britain was already derided as 'the sick man of Europe'.

On another plane, no account of Thatcherite policies could overlook the fate of the poll tax, which Thatcher billed 'the flagship' of her third administration. After virtually unprecedented levels of public opposition, it was watered down to almost a travesty of the original policy before finally being scrapped – representing what Butler et al. (1994) consider 'a supreme example' of 'failure in British government'. It is telling that this blatant policy failure should be associated with the most dogmatic and determined of post-war ministries.

After Thatcher

For students of party policy, the Thatcher era may come to represent a sort of Indian summer, in which the governing parties' reputation for effective action was revived. The fall of Thatcher in 1990 marked not only a more sober style of government, but also a more sober assessment of what party policy could hope to achieve.

For much of this century, the perceived importance of party policy has stemmed from a belief that it could be effected as a result of winning national general elections. As indicated earlier, this belief had been questioned long before the 1990s. But scepticism seemed to become more focused following Thatcher's departure from office in 1990. Two related factors contributed to this development.

First, there is what Andrew Marr (1995) calls 'the big story of our times', which is that 'power has blown away from the traditional nation state to the international markets and the big companies which ride them'. Marxists have always argued that those who have economic power dictate the agenda of national governments. But the internationalization of capital has made that power all the more dynamic and politically unaccountable. The global market, Marr observes, has 'the power to impose economic pain in order to limit national policies to the market's own views of financial orthodoxy' – a view largely corroborated by the first chapter of this study.

Politicians are not by nature fatalistic, and political science is seldom diagnostic without also being prescriptive. Marxists used to argue that the impotence of politics *vis-à-vis* economics could be ended by revolution and a new 'mode of production'. During the 1990s, it became more common to argue that the solution now involved matching the internationalization of capital with the internationalization of government. This leads to the second drain upon the potency of party policy *qua* national government – the movement towards an integrated European state (Pilkington 1995).

Again, an awareness that British politicians are constrained by membership of the European Union (EU, *née* European Community) predates the 1990s. It existed in the years leading to Britain's entry in 1973 and during the referendum on continued membership in 1975, and led to a rupture inside the Labour Party in 1981. As Fergus Carr's chapter reminds us, following the European Communities Act 1972, British governments accepted that laws emanating from (what is now) the EU's institutions take precedence over those passed at Westminster and that, in the event of conflict between the British Parliament and the EU, the final verdict rests with the European Court of Justice. The British government, through the European Council of Ministers, naturally contributes to the formulation of EU policy and has the power of veto in many cases. Yet this veto is not easy to exercise in practice, owing to the effect of increased majority voting in the council and related pressure to concede and compromise in the interests of pursuing national agendas.

The limitation placed upon governing party policy at Westminster increased from the mid-1980s, when there was a steady increase in Europe's policy responsibilities and the extent of majority voting in the Council of Ministers (the Single European Act 1986 and Maastricht Treaty of 1991 being crucial landmarks). This was shown vividly during the bovine spongiform encephalopathy (BSE) crisis of 1996, when the policy of the Conservative government had to be recast following a ban on the export of British cattle in the Council of Ministers (Tory ministers being outvoted in the council).

After the 1997 election, the British government retained its ambivalence towards further European monetary integration. Yet many on the centrist wings of the two main parties (as well as the centre party itself, plus the Scottish and Welsh nationalist parties) believe that Britain cannot for long resist such integration while remaining an effective member state (Gaffney 1996). For Eurosceptics in the Tory Party, the implication of that belief is devastatingly clear: the end of independent, sovereign states, with Tory governments in London 'reduced to the status of a charge-capped borough council' (Congdon 1990). And such fears are not confined to the right. Bryan Gould's decision to quit British politics in 1994 arose from his belief that European monetary union would preclude any Keynesian dash for full employment by a future Labour government (Gould 1995).

Party-Free Policy?

If the growing irrelevance of party policy is sensed by voters, this offers an obvious reason for their loss of interest in party activity. Those on the left, for example, are in no doubt that 'parties lose members as soon as they seem unable to change anything' (*New Statesman and Society*, editorial, 29 September 1995). Throughout the western world, in fact, there is evidence of diminished interest among voters. The 1993 International Social Attitudes survey found that, among advanced industrial societies, only Australia had a majority who were 'very' or 'fairly' interested in politics. In Britain the figure was 41 per cent, with 34 per cent 'not very' or 'not at all' interested, while a Gallup poll in the same year found that most British voters thought their politicians were liars (*New Statesman and Society*, 3 December 1993). This disenchantment seems particularly marked among the young. According to a Demos report in 1995, only 43 per cent of first-time voters actually used their vote in the 1992 general election (*Daily Telegraph*, 29 September 1995), and by the mid-1990s the average age of Labour and Tory members was 48 and 62 respectively (Seyd and Whiteley 1992, p. 32; Whiteley et al. 1994, p. 43). Despite the prospect of a wholesale change of party government, the 1997 general election 'excited less interest than any other in living memory', with the turnout (71.4 per cent) being the lowest since the war (Curtice and Steed 1997).

Yet this lack of interest should not be confused with attitudes towards public policy generally. The explosion of organized protest against the poll tax (1989–1990), the Child Support Agency (1993–1994), the export of veal (1994–1995), the Brent Spar oil platform (1995), the second runway at Manchester Airport (1996–1997), and Labour's 'countryside offensive' (1997–1998) all point to a vital development: the politically aware are turning from a traditional, party-based model of activity, based upon a generality of policy, to a new policy-specific approach – one which lends itself to group rather than party activity. The above examples indicate that these trends are not confined to those with leftish tendencies – the Countryside Alliance, for example, attracting 'impeccably dressed farm owners alongside marchers from *Living Marxism*' (*Daily Telegraph*, 2 March 1998).

Even within the parties themselves, there appears to have been a loss of confidence in their own policies and a curious flirtation with unelected 'experts'. Between 1992 and 1997, for instance, it may have seemed strange to hear leftish politicians argue that the policy interpretations of bankers (at the proposed European Central Bank) and judges (at the European Court of Human Rights) should prevail over those of elective governments; indeed, one of the new government's first acts in 1997 was to free the Bank of England from the operational control of ministers.

This anti-party culture was again demonstrated by the willingness of British judges to challenge openly the political judgement of ministers – as when the lord chief justice rebuffed Home Secretary Michael Howard's call for more custodial sentencing in 1995. Encouraged by the 'sleaze' which engulfed John Major's government in 1994, it became quite fashionable to argue, by the late 1990s, that we now required a more 'objective' approach to politics than that allowed by party policy. This argument (closely linked to support for constitutional reform) asserted that various 'binding principles' should be defined for politicians by those who were somehow 'above' party policy – be they bankers in Bonn, bureaucrats in Brussels or judges in the Hague.

At the same time, there seemed to be growing support for a more 'direct' form of democratic policy-making, one which by-passed party politicians through extensive use of referenda – it being argued that voters were now mature enough to make policy decisions themselves, rather than passing this power to party-based MPs they anyhow distrusted (Pilkington 1997). This trend was again reflected in Labour's 1997 manifesto, which promised referenda on a range of constitutional reforms.

Rescuing Party Policy

The notion of 'direct', as opposed to traditional, representative democracy has clear theoretical attractions for anyone who believes that power in society should rest with the bulk of its citizens. However, the case for this dynamic, Athenian form of government is weakened by one central reality: there seems little public support for it. Voters may be unimpressed with those elected to make decisions for them, but they still seem a long way from wishing to take those decisions themselves; the turnouts for the Scottish and Welsh devolution referenda in September 1997 (60 per cent and 50 per cent) were even lower than that of the preceding general election. Even on the crucial issue of Europe, evidence of public enthusiasm for a referendum is sketchy, as the most hardened of Eurosceptic MPs were forced to acknowledge (Batchelor 1994).

A propos constitutional reform, Robert Pyper's chapter reminds us of a central reality, namely, that it can give important political powers to the unelected. If there is to be a movement towards a more 'codified' constitution, with more attendant powers for courts and judges, then an important point needs to be considered: that government by elective party politicians, no matter how imperfect, has the merit of accountability. Party policy may well be formed with an eye to vote-getting, but this is not always a bad thing if it means being sensitive to public opinion. This is a problem still to be solved by devotees of European integration, aware that the present structure has an inherent 'democratic deficit' (Geddes 1993). Both Maastricht and the Amsterdam Treaty of 1997 gave new powers of 'co-decision' to the European Parliament, whose elections British parties already contest vigorously; yet its control over the EU executive in Brussels is at present even less than that exercised by Westminster over Whitehall. If a fully integrated European state is not to be dominated by unaccountable officials, then the European Parliament will have to be strengthened again – in which case party policy *vis-à-vis* the EU will assume greater urgency. With the two main parties forging closer links recently with the European Socialist Party and European People's Party, there are already signs that they are poised to refocus their policies in a way that (they hope) will give them more influence over the supra-national forces already affecting this country.

In this sense, some might argue that the Europeanization of government is in fact the saviour of party policy in Britain. As the *New Statesman and Society* pointed out (22 June 1990), it has already proved impossible for any 'progressive' governing party to ignore the internationalization of markets and the omnipresence of multinational corporations – both of which have the power to blow such governments off course. A supra-national political system was needed precisely because the policies of national governing parties were no longer autonomous (or, to be more precise, even less autonomous than they had been), and therefore needed the assistance of like-minded parties elsewhere, particularly in Europe.

If the Euro-federalist dream is realized, party policy may have to refocus itself – not just at Continental but also at a more local level. Euro-federalists tend to argue that their scheme would involve national governments losing power not just to a federal government in Brussels, but to regional governments within their own national boundaries. According to this analysis, economic, environmental and foreign policy matters would be among those which passed 'upwards', while most other policies would pass 'downwards' to regional assemblies in Brittany, Tuscany, Bavaria, Humberside, East Anglia and so on – hence the vision of a 'Europe of the Regions' so eagerly embraced by Plaid Cymru, the Scottish National Party (SNP) and to a lesser extent parties in Northern Ireland (see chs 2 and 7). In short, far from being redundant in a federal Europe, party policy could be rejuvenated.

Caution Required

During the 1990s, such 'big' ideas have occupied many a seminar or tutorial in higher education. But, as is often the case with seminar discussion, it all has a rather surreal flavour. A 'Europe of the Regions' or a 'United States of Europe' is a neat theory but one which tends to ignore huge practical difficulties. By 1998, the time scale for a single currency, for example, still looked fraught with problems, with the task of 'convergence' proving trickier than originally thought. There was throughout the EU growing scepticism about the political and economic consequences of greater union, its enlargement only exposing the problem of central direction.

In many ways, the credibility of federalism never fully recovered from the financial crisis of September 1992. In one respect, Britain's free-fall from the exchange rate mechanism (ERM) was another blistering example of governing party policy being powerless in the face of modern economic conditions; membership of the ERM had been crucial to the Tories' election manifesto just five months earlier. Yet, in another sense, it showed that European integration was not after all the solution to this problem and certainly no guarantee of economic security in government. This raises questions about 'throwing the baby out with the bathwater': is it wise to allow Europe to usurp further areas of non-economic policy if it cannot guarantee in return a more manageable and predictable economy for member states?

It is easy to forget that British governments still have immense discretionary powers which affect enormously the way we live. As a result, it is crazy to argue that it now matters not which party wins a British general election. As chapters 3, 4, 5, 6, 8, 9 and 10 (in particular) reveal, there was nothing inevitable about many of the policy changes which have occurred in British government since 1945 – changes which had a profound effect upon millions of people. As Howard Elcock shows (ch. 8), even in local elections, changing party policy can still make a huge impact upon ordinary voters – witness the retention of state grammar schools in some areas but not others.

One would also need a relentlessly jaundiced view of party politicians to argue that they seek office purely for personal glory. If politicians are unusually vain, their vanity often springs from a conviction that, through success at a British election, their parties' policies can make a lasting impression upon the way we live. European union and a globalized economy have undeniably eroded the effect national party policy can have; but there is a huge difference between erosion and elimination.

Across the capitalist world, economic power has become more diffuse. This, in turn, has made people question the conventional sources of political authority. For this reason alone, the early twenty-first century is likely to see a continuing debate about which governmental structures are best suited to the vicissitudes of a modern economy. Yet it can be stated with a fair degree of confidence that, wherever representative government is seen to lie, party policy will closely follow. Parties may no longer be the sole or even main agency of political participation. But, through their policies, they remain exclusively capable of aggregating interests and ideas, while giving voters the chance to elect or dismiss governments – particularly important given that the bulk of voters still want only occasional involvement in the political system. At the close of the 1990s, the focal point of party policy may be shifting; yet it remains vital to anyone interested in the role of government and the dynamics of public administration.

References

Batchelor A. (1994) 'The Referendum We Never Had', *Talking Politics*, 6, 3.

Benn T. (1989) *Office Without Power*, London, Arrow.

Butler D., Adonis A. and Travers T. (1994), *Failure in British Government: The Politics of the Poll Tax*, Oxford, Oxford University Press.

Campaign for Labour Party Democracy (1982) Labour Party conference pamphlet.

Campbell J. (1993) *Edward Heath*, London, Cape.

Coates D. (1980) *Labour in Power?*, London, Longman.

Cole J. (1987) *The Thatcher Years: A Decade of Revolution in British Politics*, London, BBC Publications.

Congdon T. (1990) 'The Last of England', *Spectator*, 23 June.

Cook C. and McKie D. (eds) (1972) *The Decade of Disillusion*, London, Macmillan.

Curtice J. and Steed M. (1997) 'The Results Analysed' in Butler D. and Kavanagh D. *The British General Election of 1997*, Basingstoke, Macmillan.

Downs A. (1957) *An Economic Theory of Democracy*, New York, Harper.

Gaffney J. (ed.) (1996) *Political Parties and the European Union*, London, Routledge.

Gamble A. (1988), *The Free Economy and the Strong State*, London, Macmillan.

Geddes A. (1993) *Britain in the European Community*, Manchester, Baseline.

Gould B. (1995) *Goodbye to All That*, London, Macmillan.

Hennessy P. and Seldon A. (eds) (1987) *Ruling Performance*, Oxford, Blackwell.

Higgins S. (1984) *The Benn Inheritance*, London, Weidenfeld and Nicolson.

Ingle S. (1987) *The British Party System*, Oxford, Blackwell.

Jenkins P. (1987) *Mrs Thatcher's Revolution*, London, Cape.

Kavanagh D. (1987) *Thatcherism and British Politics: The End of Consensus?*, Oxford, Oxford University Press.

Kavanagh D. (1997) *The Reordering of British Politics*, Oxford, Oxford University Press.

Marr A. (1995) 'The Real Enemy is the Money Market', *Spectator*, 9 September.

McKenzie R. T. (1955) *British Political Parties*, London, Heinemann.

Pilkington C. (1995) *Britain in the European Union Today*, Manchester, Manchester University Press.

Pilkington C. (1997) *Representative Democracy in Britain Today*, Manchester, Manchester University Press.

Pimlott B. (1989) 'The Audit of Thatcherism', *Contemporary Record*, 3, 1.

Ponting C. (1989) *Breach of Promise*, London, Hamish Hamilton.

Riddell P. (1989) *The Thatcher Decade*, Oxford, Blackwell.

Rose R. (1980) *Do Parties Make a Difference?*, London, Macmillan.

Sarlvik B. and Crewe I. (1983) *Decade of Dealignment*, Cambridge, Cambridge University Press.

Seyd P. and Whiteley P. (1992) *Labour's Grass Roots*, Oxford, Clarendon Press.

Sherman A. (1988) 'Time to Bring Back Sir Keith Joseph', *Sunday Telegraph*, 28 August.

Veljanovski C. (1988) *Setting the State*, London, Weidenfeld and Nicolson.

Vincent J. (1987) 'The Thatcher Governments 1979–1987' in Hennessy P. and Seldon A. (eds) *Ruling Performance*, Oxford, Blackwell.

Whiteley P., Seyd P. and Richardson J. (1994) *True Blues*, Oxford, Oxford University Press.

Young H. and Sloman A. (1986) *The Thatcher Phenomenon*, London, BBC Publications.

Appendix I
British General Election Results 1945–1997

Bracketed figures show percentage share of UK vote.

	Con	Lab	Lib[a]	Others[b]
1945	213 (39.8)	393 (47.8)	12 (9.0)	22 (3.4)
1950	298 (43.5)	315 (46.0)	9 (9.1)	3 (1.4)
1951	321 (48.0)	295 (48.8)	6 (2.5)	3 (0.7)
1955	344 (49.7)	277 (46.4)	6 (2.7)	3 (1.2)
1959	365 (49.4)	258 (43.8)	9 (5.9)	1 (0.9)
1964	304 (43.4)	317 (44.1)	9 (11.2)	0 (1.3)
1966	253 (41.9)	363 (48.0)	12 (8.5)	2 (2.6)
1970	330 (46.4)	287 (43.0)	6 (7.5)	7 (3.1)
1974 Feb.	297 (37.9)	301 (37.1)	14 (19.3)	23 (5.7)
1974 Oct.	277 (35.9)	319 (39.2)	12 (18.5)	26 (6.4)
1979	339 (43.9)	268 (36.9)	11 (13.8)	17 (5.4)
1983	397 (42.4)	209 (27.6)	23 (25.4)	21 (4.6)
1987	375 (42.3)	229 (30.8)	22 (22.6)	24 (4.3)
1992	336 (41.9)	271 (34.4)	20 (17.8)	24 (5.9)
1997	165 (30.7)	418 (43.2)	46 (16.8)	30 (9.3)

[a] The 'Lib' total denotes that of the Liberal Party until 1979. In 1983 and 1987, it denotes that of the Alliance between the Liberal and Social Democratic Parties. In 1992 and 1997, it denotes that of the Liberal Democratic Party.
[b] Since 1974, 'Other' parties include the main Ulster Unionist parties, which until then had been included in the Conservative total.

Appendix II
Leaders of Conservative, Labour and Centre Parties 1945–1997

The Conservative Party

1940–1955: Winston Churchill
1955–1957: Anthony Eden
1957–1963: Harold Macmillan
1963–1965: Alec Douglas-Home
1965–1975: Edward Heath
1975–1990: Margaret Thatcher
1990–1997: John Major
1997–: William Hague

The Labour Party

1935–1955: Clement Attlee
1955–1963: Hugh Gaitskell
1963–1976: Harold Wilson
1976–1980: James Callaghan
1980–1983: Michael Foot
1983–1992: Neil Kinnock
1992–1994: John Smith
1994–: Tony Blair

The Centre Parties

For most of the post-war period, the 'centre' of British party politics was represented principally by the Liberal Party. In 1981, another 'centre' party –

the Social Democratic Party (SDP) – was founded by disgruntled members of the Labour Party. Between 1981 and 1987, the Liberals and SDP were bound by an Alliance involving joint leadership, joint campaigns and joint election manifestos. There was, however, no single Alliance leader or organization. In the wake of the 1987 general election, this was considered by the bulk of Liberal and SDP members to be a handicap and, between the summer of 1987 and the spring of 1988, a merger of the two parties was negotiated. A new party duly emerged, under the leadership of Paddy Ashdown, in March 1988. Following the merger, a minority of Social Democrats disowned the new party and rallied around a Continuing SDP led by David Owen: poor election results and fading interest led to this being disbanded in 1990. An independent Liberal Party continued to function at local government level in certain parts of England and Wales.

The Liberal Party

1945–1956:   Clement Davies
1956–1967:   Jo Grimond
1967–1976:   Jeremy Thorpe
1976–1988:   David Steel

The Social Democratic Party

1982–1983:   Roy Jenkins
1983–1987:   David Owen
1987–1988:   Robert Maclennan

NB: Though the SDP was founded in 1981, it was not until 1982 that a single SDP leader was elected.

The Liberal Democrats

1988–:   Paddy Ashdown

NB: Following its launch in 1988, the party was initially called the Social and Liberal Democrats, later abbreviated to the Democrats. In the autumn of 1989, the title of Liberal Democrats was finally agreed.

Index